History
and
Systems
of
Modern
Psychology

History
and
Systems
of
Modern
Psychology
A CONCEPTUAL APPROACH

Kenneth P. Hillner

GARDNER PRESS, INC.
New York

GARDNER PRESS, INC.
19 Union Square West
New York 10003

Library of Congress Cataloging in Publication Data
Hillner, Kenneth P.
   History and systems of modern psychology.

   Bibliography: p.
   Includes index.
   1. Psychology—History. 2. Psychology—Philosophy—
History. I. Title. [DNLM: 1 Psychology—History.
2. Systems theory. BF 81 H654h]
BF95.H54   1984   150'.9   83-5596
ISBN 0-89876-030-5

Book Design by Raymond Solomon

*This book is dedicated to my wife, Sally,
and our two sons, Paul and Andrew.*

Overview
Contents

Analytical

Contents

Acknowledgments

Many people contributed to the composition and production of this book. The understanding and patience of my wife Sally (nee Sarah) made writing this book possible. The Psychology Department of South Dakota State University and its chairman, Al Branum, provided an environment in which long-term projects, such as book writing, are actively encouraged. Dean Allen Barnes of the Arts and Science College (Division) allowed the labor on this project to contribute to my total faculty workload. Necessary duplication was performed by the South Dakota State printing department. Hundreds of students over the past decade stimulated me to become actively interested in the area of history and systems of psychology.

I wish to acknowledge my long-standing intellectual debt to Frank Restle, my Ph.D. mentor, who recently passed away.

I wrote this book because writing is fun and is also a form of therapy for me. My parents always provided me with an atmosphere in which scholarly endeavors were appreciated; and my two sons, Paul and Andrew, love school and ideas and believe their father is something special when he is writing.

Kenneth P. Hillner

Preface

The diverse activities and concerns of the professional psychologist often obscure the fact that psychological research and practice occur in the context of some underlying conceptual framework. Every psychologist must make certain assumptions, usually philosophical in nature, about such things as reality, truth, man, object of study, and methodology. The content of these assumptions collectively defines a given psychologist's conceptual approach to psychology. A given conceptual approach to psychology existentially can be referred to as a system.

The emergence of various systems of psychology in the 1870s and 1880s in both Europe and America formally marked the beginning of psychology as an independent intellectual/academic discipline. For instance, certain events occurred in the Germanic university system under the influence of Wilhelm Wundt (the founding of structuralism); and the psychogenic approach to abnormal behavior was formalized by Sigmund Freud in Vienna (the founding of psychoanalysis). Structuralism, which amounts to a science of the mind or conscious experience, is recognized as the first system of experimental psychology. Psychoanalysis constitutes the first of many such comprehensive conceptual approaches to the psychological nature of man to originate in the medical or psychiatric environment.

The postulation of various systematic approaches to psychology became so pervasive that the history of psychology over the past century can be viewed as a progression of a basic set of dominant or highly influential systems. If we regard the beginning of modern psychology as contemporaneous with the inception of the seventeenth century British school of epistemological philosophy known as British empiricism, then the appearance of structuralism and psychoanalysis in the 1870s and 1880s can be thought of as demarking the history of modern psychology into two phases: presystemic and systemic.

The systemic phase of psychology can be divided into two distinct subperiods: a classical school era and the contemporary system phase. The psychological systems that appeared prior to 1930 now are referred to as classical schools of psychology. A representative, but not exhaustive, listing of such schools would include structuralism, functionalism, Gestalt psychology, behaviorism, and psychoanalysis. The post-1930 conceptual approaches to psychology that evolved from the classical schools are referred to semantically as contemporary systems. Four more or less mutually exclusive systems currently are competing for the right to be called "the psychology." They are (1) neobehaviorism, (2) humanism, (3) latter-day depth psychology, and (4) dialectical psychology.

The distinction between a classical school and a contemporary system represents more than a simple temporal demarcation. There are numerous substantive differences between these two classes of systems, a representative sampling of which is discussed in Chapter 1.

It is the purpose of this book to focus on the systemic phase of modern psychological history by analyzing the major classical schools and contemporary systems of psychology along a common set of interpretive dimensions. These dimensions, which include object of study and permissible methodology, are delimited and previewed in Chapter 1. The presystemic phase of modern psychology also is characterized briefly in the context of discussing the origin and historical antecedents of structuralism, the first experimental system.

The various schools/systems are covered in loose historical order—with the exception of psychoanalysis. Freud's approach is distinctive on at least two points: (1) It is both a classical school and a contemporary system. (2) It is the only conceptual approach to be considered that did not originate in the academic environment. The psychoanalytic discussion appears after presentation of the major experimental psychological systems and before consideration of the humanistic and dialectical systems.

A single chapter is devoted to each school/system, with the exception of the behavioristic approach. The many subvariants of this approach transcend the classical school/contemporary system dichotomy. Separate chapters are allotted to classical Watsonian behaviorism, contemporary Skinnerian radical behaviorism, and contemporary cognitive behaviorism. Because the behavioristic orientation has provided the conceptual framework for American experimental psychology for much of the twentieth century and has often served as the object of philosophical analysis, a special introductory chapter on behaviorism is included. The chapters on the subvariants of behaviorism are pivotal: They are located in the middle of the text, so that the discussion in the prior and succeeding chapters (with the exception of the chapter on psychoanalysis) leads up to and reacts to them.

The book opens with an introductory chapter that presents necessary analytical distinctions and preview comments and closes with a short summary chapter that traces the historical and intellectual relationships among the individual schools/systems. The intervening chapters on the individual systems can be perused in any order desired. Each of the content chapters is largely self-contained, although some cross-referencing to other chapters/systems does occur.

The exposition assumes some prior familiarity with the basic content areas of psychology, such as sensation, perception, learning, motivation, behavioral pathology, development, and personality—knowledge of which is usually obtained in the standard introductory psychology course. Since the presystemic roots of psychology include philosophy, and since each school or system of psychology possesses a specific philosophical milieu, some rudimentary knowledge of philosophy also will be helpful in reading the text.

History
and
Systems
of
Modern
Psychology

1

Introduction

Preview

This introductory chapter has five interrelated purposes:

1. To characterize formally the notion of a psychological system and its relationship to psychological theory.
2. To classify and preview the nine systems to be analyzed.
3. To present the differential properties of a classical school and contemporary system.
4. To evaluate the possible relevance of Thomas Kuhn's model of science for interpreting the systemic phase of modern psychological history.
5. To delineate and preview the six interpretive dimensions to be used for analyzing the systems.

1

System Versus Theory

The Notion of a System

At an informal level, a system is any conceptual approach to psychology. A system entails the specific set of beliefs that underlie a given psychologist's brand of psychology. At a more formal level, a system is a set of philosophical assumptions relative to what constitutes (1) the proper object of study of psychology and (2) the acceptable methodology of psychology. As such, a psychological system is a specific philosophical approach to organismic (human) experience, behavior, or both. The two most important philosophical assumptions associated with any psychological system concern the mind–body problem and the nature of man. Aspects of these two philosophical issues are discussed later.

There should be no problems, at this juncture, associated with interpreting the notions of (1) object of study and (2) methodology. Object of study refers to such entities as the content or functioning of consciousness, phenomenal experience, overt behavior, molar acts, unconscious processes, structural personality traits, neurotic or psychotic symptoms, and sensory receptor or neuronal activity. The basic point is that each system of psychology has its own distinctive orientation with respect to the object of psychological description. Methodology covers such entities as laboratory experimentation, naturalistic observation, introspection, phenomenological analysis, psychometric testing, free association, and survey techniques. Each system of psychology postulates its own characteristic, or standard, procedural route to the accumulation of psychological truth.

The critical aspect of a system, at this point, relates to its *permissibility* component. The philosophical assumptions implicit in a system determine the *permissible* objects of study and *permissible* methodological techniques. It is in this sense that a system is said to define the basic subject matter of psychology and the specific methodological techniques by which it is investigated.

The implications of a specific system extend far beyond basic subject matter and methodology, the two definitional attributes. The framework of a particular psychological system has extensive ramifications for every aspect and level of the content psychology subsumed by the system. For example, the philosophical assumptions inherent in a system in large part determine both the preferred type of explanatory entities and the preferred form of explanation subsumed by the system; they aid in defining the most relevant or crucial research problems; they determine the nature and format of the rudimentary data generated by the system; and they affect the possible practical application or social utility value of the system.

The notion of a system is really a class or generic concept. It is possible for a given system of psychology to be composed of or reducible to many different subsystems or subvariants. There are, for example, many different brands of behavioristic psychology to which the general label of behaviorism is applicable. Each of the nine conceptual approaches to psychology analyzed in the text is treated as an independent system, irrespective of its possible status as a subvariant of a more generalized, comprehensive system.

The Notion of a Theory

In a broad interpretation of the notion of a theory, it is certainly possible to argue that a system is a theory, although not every theory is a system. But system and theory usually are assigned distinctive, nonoverlapping properties by most psychologists. A theory can be defined as a set of higher order interpretive statements that is used (1) to explain already verified empirical relationships or (2) to generate hypotheses subject to experimental test. A theory is a hypothetical device that resolves the nature of a given psychological fact or helps explain the particular behavior or experience generated in a given psychological experiment.

Any psychological system contains theory, but the theory is an entity distinct from the system itself. A psychological system implicitly constrains the forms and types of theory an adherent of the system can use. Rarely does a system specify or dictate a particular theory; it merely sets limits to the range of acceptable variation of theory. For example, behaviorism postulates that man is like a machine, and a given behaviorist could construct a machine-based mathematical model to explain and/or predict the behavior of a subject in a given experimental situation, whereas a humanistic psychologist stresses the uniqueness of each individual human being and would refuse to reduce behavior to a mathematical equation.

By definition, a system is all-pervasive, universal, or totalistic. A system establishes the intellectual or conceptual relevance of an academic discipline in the first place in the sense that it entails an object of study and methodology not subsumed by any other (academic) discipline. No psychology exists independent of, or outside the confines of, a specific system. A theory is focused around a specific psychological process or a specific content subarea of psychology: there are theories of learning, motivation, perception, personality, development, social behavior, behavior pathology, and the self or self-fulfillment, to name a few. Rarely does a theory explain or predict more than one psychological process or substantive area of psychology.

Classification and Preview of the Nine Psychological Systems

Table 1-1 displays a descriptive classification system for the nine psychological schools/systems to be analyzed by the text.

Each of the first five columns of the table denotes an input dimension, that is, an analytical, classificatory dimension on which any school or system of psychology must have a value and on which the various schools/systems can be compared. The classificatory input dimensions are (1) generic type, (2) substantive content, (3) orientation, (4) purpose, and (5) practical application/social utility. Note that an object-of-study specification, one of the definitional attributes of a system, does not appear as an explicit input dimension. Such a specification is implicit in the generic type column.

The last two columns of the table denote derivative, output dimensions, which specify the particular classical school and/or contemporary system that is associated with a given combination of input values.

The approximate historical span of each school/system is denoted immediately below its entry in the table. A contemporary system has no termination year specified because, by definition, it still exists. Note that depth psychology, or psychoanalysis, is listed in both the classical school and contemporary system columns.

The nine psychological systems can be previewed by describing the nature and possible values of the five input dimensions.

Generic Type

A particular system can be assigned to one of three broad categorical types: (1) epistemological, (2) action, or (3) combined epistemological/action. An epistemological system focuses on mind, mental events or processes, or conscious experience. The label "epistemological" derives from the branch of philosophy that is concerned with the nature and source of truth—epistemology. Structuralism and cognitive behaviorism are epistemological systems. An action system

Table 1-1

A Classification System for the Nine Major Classical Schools and Contemporary Systems of Psychology

Generic Type	Substantive Content	Orientation	Purpose	Practical Application/Social Utility	Specific Classical School	Specific Contemporary System
Epistemological (mind, mental events and processes, conscious experience)	Cognitive	Objective	Analysis of the structure of conscious experience into its elements	None	Structuralism 1880–1920	
	Cognitive	Objective	Analysis of mental processes and information-processing mechanisms	Possible, but not indigenous		Cognitive behaviorism 1960–
Action (overt behavior)	Learning	Objective	Resolution of organismic adaptation in terms of mental capacities	Indigenous	Functionalism 1880–1930	
	Learning	Objective	Prediction and control of overt behavior	Indigenous	Watsonian behaviorism 1913–1930	Skinnerian behaviorism 1938–
	Perceptual	Subjective	Resolution of conscious experience and behavior in terms of psychophysical fields	Possible, but not indigenous	Gestalt psychology 1912–1950	
Epistemological/action (both mental events and overt behavior)	Personality	Objective	Understanding/rectification of the psychodynamics of the organism	Indigenous	Depth psychology: psychoanalysis 1885–	Depth psychology: psychoanalysis 1885–
	Adjustment	Subjective	Understanding the phenomenal world/status of the organism	Indigenous		Humanistic psychology 1960–
	Developmental	Subjective–objective	Analysis of the organism as a point in dialectical/developmental space: unalienated man	Indigenous		Dialectical psychology 1970–

focuses on overt behavior, and also is concerned with the adaptation of the organism to the environment. Functionalism, Watsonian behaviorism, and Skinnerian behaviorism are action systems. A combined epistemological/action system deals with both mental events and overt behavior. This class of systems is very heterogeneous with respect to composition, because there are many levels at which, or perspectives from which, a dual interest in mental events and overt behavior can be integrated. Gestalt psychology, psychoanalysis, humanism, and dialectical psychology are combined systems.

Some flexibility exists with respect to the assignment of a system to a particular generic type. For instance, functionalism is interested in mental capacities, but always in relation to the adaptation of the organism to the environment, which connotes an implicit focus on overt behavior. Cognitive behaviorism quantifies overt behavior, but uses such activity to make inferences about cognitive events. Humanistic psychology focuses on the subjective feeling state or conscious awareness of the organism, but in an overall adjustment context. One of the purposes of the subsequent chapters is to justify the particular generic assignations used in Table 1-1.

Substantive Content

A psychological system also functions as a specific kind of content psychology, primarily because it tends to emphasize one particular psychological process over others. Both the epistemological and action systems are quite monolithic with respect to substantive content; the heterogeneous nature of the combined systems allows a more variable set of content psychology identifications.

Any epistemological system is a cognitive psychology. Structuralism, in effect, brought British empiricism, with its stress on mental elements and association, into the laboratory. Cognitive behaviorism amounts to an information-processing psychology in which traditional psychological processes such as perception, learning, memory, problem solving, and thinking are conceptualized as information transduction, transmission, organization, and retrieval activities.

Any action system is a learning and/or conditioning psychology. An action system makes learning, in general, and conditioning, in particular, the fundamental psychological process responsible for behavioral change. Functionalism had its own characteristic approach to learning and memory research, and the Watsonian and Skinnerian forms of behaviorism amount to virtual conditioning psychologies. Since the action systems encompass the dominant twentieth century

American experimental systems, learning has constituted the primary content area of American experimental psychology. Many behavioristic systems are known more as learning psychologies than as forms of behaviorism (see Chapter 5).

The combined-system class is not inherently associated with any particular content area or psychological process. Gestalt psychology basically is a perceptual psychology, with learning, motivational, and problem-solving overtones. Psychoanalysis can be construed as a personality psychology, with developmental and motivational overtones. Humanistic psychology is not concerned with any of the traditional psychological processes, but focuses instead on the self or self-fulfillment in an adjustment or therapeutic context. Dialectical psychology primarily is a developmental psychology, with implications for social interaction processes and cognition.

Orientation

A psychological system can be either objective or subjective with respect to orientation. It is also possible for the claim to be made that a system integrates objectivity and subjectivity in a meaningful way. Whether a system is objective or subjective depends on the particular stand that it takes with respect to (1) the existence of a reality independent of the cognitions of the psychological subject and (2) the status of the psychological subject. The term "psychological subject" covers, for example, the participant in a laboratory experiment, the patient in a therapy session, and the respondent in a survey.

OBJECTIVE SYSTEMS

A psychological system is objective if it assumes the existence of a reality independent of the cognitions of the psychological subject and uses the output of the psychological subject merely as a means of inferring the nature of this reality. An objective system is not interested in the psychological subject *per se*, but rather in the abstract psychological processes or events acting on or manifested by the subject. The objective orientation requires a rather impersonal approach to the generation of data, in which attention is focused on a standard, average, typical, or statistical subject that absorbs all sorts of individual difference parameters. The psychological subject often is called an *object* in the context of the objective orientation. An objective system must be concerned with the reliability and validity of its empirical data because they are supposed to mirror an external reality.

Objective systems include (1) any epistemological system, (2) any action system, and (3) Freudian psychoanalysis.

The cognitive psychology subsumed by an epistemological system postulates the existence of a uniform set of mental events or processes characteristic of each psychological subject and attempts to study them. The basic focus is on the abstract cognitive processes themselves, not on the organism exhibiting them.

The learning psychology subsumed by an action system postulates the existence of a set of basic associational laws or conditioning mechanisms characteristic of each psychological subject and attempts to study them. The primary focus is on the associational/conditioning processes themselves, not on the organism exhibiting them. Watsonian and Skinnerian behaviorism constitute the exemplars of an objective system: they attempt to predict and control *overt* behavior in an explicit *environmental* situation by means of *operationally specifiable* experimental techniques.

Freud presumed the existence of an elaborate psychodynamic system, characteristic of each organism, and attempted to induce it through free association, dream analysis, and other techniques. One of the critical differences between psychoanalysis, as a form of therapy, and other kinds of therapy is that psychoanalysis presumes the existence of an objective, external reality.

SUBJECTIVE SYSTEMS

A psychological system is subjective if it does not presume the existence of a reality independent of the cognitions of the psychological subject and treats the output of the psychological subject as an end in itself. It is merely used to infer the belief system, feeling state, self-image, and the like, of the psychological subject. A subjective system focuses on the individual organism and the nature of his/her psychological reality. The subjective orientation essentially is a *phenomenological* approach to reality. *Phenomenology* is concerned only with the subjective psychological world of the organism and how it can be externalized. Any subjective psychological system is necessarily a phenomenological system. The subjective orientation requires a more informal approach to the generation of data, in which two-way interaction, or give and take, between the experimenter and subject is required. A subjective system need not be concerned with the reliability or validity of its data because they need not mirror an objective reality.

A subjective system is a combined system because it always resolves overt behavior in terms of the organism's own view of the world. Both Gestalt psychology and humanism constitute subjective systems. Gestalt psychology studies the phenomenal experience of the organism, particularly its phenomenal perceptual experience, in relation to various psychophysical fields, and also explains overt behavior in terms of an underlying psychological, not physical, environment. Humanistic psychology attempts to resolve any significant psychological aspect of an organism in terms of constructs that have ecological validity for the organism. Numerous versions of contemporary humanistic psychology are actually forms of phenomenological psychology, the prototypical case being Carl Rogers' self-theory or person-oriented approach. Many psychologists use the terms "humanism" and "phenomenology" equivalently.

OBJECTIVITY VERSUS SUBJECTIVITY

Objective and subjective are relative notions (as will become apparent in the discussion of the methodology of structuralism in Chapter 2). Both the objectively oriented and the subjectively oriented psychologist deal with response output from a psychological subject. The objective psychologist prefers to obtain such output under rigidly experimenter-controlled input conditions, which ordinarily dictate the form and categorization of the output. The subjective psychologist usually prefers to obtain response output in a basically unconstrained situation that puts no limitations on the form of the output itself. The objective psychologist is willing to sift through the response output of many subjects to discover some common base, such as a postulated underlying psychological process. The subjective psychologist is unwilling to do this and merely constructs the psychological universe of the individual subject.

SUBJECTIVE–OBJECTIVE SYSTEMS

Table 1-1 contains only one psychological system that claims to combine objectivity and subjectivity: the dialectical approach. This system integrates the two orientations presumably by refusing to deal with the psychological subject independently of the experimenter (or the environment) and by refusing to deal with the environment (or the experimenter) independently of the psychological subject. Dialectical psychology assumes that a transactional relationship exists between the subject and experimenter in any psychological investigation, such that the subject and experimenter together constitute an irreducible, emergent unit of analysis. Psychological truth, or reality, must be stated in terms of the experiences of both parties to the transaction. Thus, while an objective system entails the psychology of a standard, statistical subject and a subjective system entails the psychology of an individual, unique organism, the combined subjective–objective orientation of dialectical psychology entails the psychology of both the subject and experimenter in an emergent relationship.

Purpose

A brief purpose statement is presented for each of the systems in column 4 of Table 1-1. Implicit reference already has been made to these statements while interpreting the first three input dimensions of the classification scheme. Only two systems, Watsonian behaviorism and Skinnerian behaviorism, are describable in terms of the same basic goal: the prediction and control of overt behavior. Note the wide variety of purposes associated with the combined epistemological/action systems, reflecting the heterogeneity of this generic category. The succeeding chapters analyze in depth the purpose of each system and describe how it is accomplished.

Practical Application or Social Utility Possibilities

Each of the nine systems, with the exception of psychoanalysis, originated in the academic environment; thus they constitute academic systems. The eight academic systems, except for humanism, constitute systems of experimental psychology: They focus on or are willing to admit the relevance of one or more of the traditional psychological processes, such as cognition, learning, perception, and development.

A nonacademic system, such as psychoanalysis, or a nonexperimental system, such as humanism, is usually called an applied system. This implies that the practical application or social utility value of the system is indigenous to the nature and structure of the system. This does not mean that an academic/experimental system possesses no practical application or social utility value. To demonstrate this, column 5 of the classification scheme specifies the possible applied relevance of each system.

Only one experimental system—structuralism—has no applied value. The structuralists actively eschewed any practical application relevance for their discipline. The other epistemological system, cognitive behaviorism, and the perceptually oriented Gestalt psychology do possess possible practical application/social utility value, although it is not indigenous. Any action system possesses indigenous applied value because such a system focuses on overt behavior. The fundamental psychological propositions of the system are stated in terms of or relate directly to behavior. The functionalist system is credited with starting applied psychology in America, and the Watsonian and Skinnerian brands of behaviorism constitute virtual behavioral technologies. Dialectical psychology is also indigenously applied in orientation, primarily because it refuses to divorce human beings from the cultural and social milieu in which they exist.

The Differential Properties of a Classical School and Contemporary System

At least three significant conceptual differences characterize the distinction between a classical school and contemporary system: (1) status of the object-of-study specification, (2) nature of theory, and (3) interpretive status in Kuhn's model of science.

Status of the Object-of-Study Specification

CLASSICAL SCHOOLS

With the exception of the nonacademic psychoanalytic system, the various classical schools can be meaningfully distinguished in terms of their basic subject matter:

1. Structuralism explicitly focused on conscious experience and possessed no formal concept of behavior.
2. Functionalism explicitly focused on consciousness, but also implicitly focused on behavior.
3. Gestalt psychology explicitly focused on both conscious experience and behavior.
4. Watsonian behaviorism explicitly focused on behavior and either denied the existence of consciousness or found it irrelevant.

The exact denotative meaning of the terms "conscious experience," or "consciousness," and "behavior," as well as the perspective from which they were studied, differed among the schools. But the notions of conscious experience and behavior functioned as actual metaphysical concepts or categories; and the basic purpose of a classical school could be meaningfully stated in terms of its specified object of study. As a corollary of the metaphysical status of the object-of-study specification, the dimension of permissible methodology served as a critical metaphysical battleground for the various schools.

CONTEMPORARY SYSTEMS

Contemporary systems either do not formally distinguish between conscious experience and behavior or, if they do, informal provision via conversion statements is made for the kinds of phenomena subsumed by the other labeling. Contemporary systems cannot be meaningfully distinguished in terms of their basic subject matter:

1. Skinnerian behaviorism focuses on overt behavior, but extends the concept to include the content of perceptual and introspective awareness or conscious experience.
2. Cognitive behaviorism deals with various symbolic or mental processes interpreted as physical events.
3. The object of study of humanism can be conceptualized as holistic adaptation, which is a behavioral construct, or as subjective feeling/awareness, which is an aspect of conscious experience.
4. Freud's version of depth psychology postulates a psychic determinism that makes internal mental processes and overt behavior inseparable components of a closed system.
5. Dialectical psychology studies nonalienated, nonabstracted man, in which context the distinction between conscious experience and behavior is vacuous.

The notions of conscious experience and behavior function merely as semantic categories in the contemporary system context. The basic purpose of a contemporary system cannot be meaningfully stated in terms of an object-of-study specification. Since the terms conscious experience and behavior possess only linguistic reality for the contemporary psychologist, the dimension of permissible methodology is more meaningfully resolved and evaluated in terms of the ultimate purposes of the various systems.

SUMMARY

A classical school of psychology can be meaningfully characterized in terms of its basic subject matter and methodology. A contemporary system of psychology only can be meaningfully described in terms of its ultimate purpose, with methodology being of secondary consideration. This distinction probably is related to the fact that the initial systems of psychology, the classical schools, sought to justify a new professional discipline, whereas the later, contemporary systems sought expansion and application of an already established one.

Nature of Theory

Theorization during the era of the classical schools was quite primitive according to contemporary standards and consisted of general philosophical or orienting principles, such as association, creative synthesis, emergent wholes, motivational sequences, and habit formation by conditioning.

Contemporary theories are virtual blueprints of how a specific behavior or empirical phenomenon is produced. In one form of contemporary behavioristic psychology, the vogue is to construct very explicit mathematical models for behavior in specific, strictly delimited, experimental tasks (see Chapter 5).

This difference between a classical school and a contemporary system is not merely a product of increased knowledge and analytical skill on the part of the psychologist, but also represents a refocusing of the creative efforts of the discipline. Creative efforts are no longer focused on system construction; they now are directed primarily to theory construction. In the numerous psychology texts entitled *Systems and Theories*, or variants thereof, *systems* refer to the classical schools and *theories* to the numerous higher order explanatory and predictive interpretive statements constructed by psychologists operating in the context of a contemporary system.

Interpretive Status in Kuhn's Model of Science

In the context of Kuhn's model of science, a classical school definitely is preparadigmatic in nature, though it is still an open question as to whether any contemporary system can be legitimately regarded as a paradigm. The following section discusses the meaning and significance of this difference between a classical school and a contemporary system.

Kuhn's Model of Science and the Systemic Phase of Modern Psychological History: The Paradigm Issue

The academic systems, with the exception of humanistic psychology, constitute experimental systems in the traditional sense of the term. Psychology is viewed as a science in the context of each of these academic/experimental systems. The nature of science ultimately is a philosophical question, and the philosophy of science is a legitimate subarea of philosophy. The traditional philosophical view regards science fundamentally as a rational or logical endeavor. Thomas Kuhn questioned this classic view of science by promulgating a model of scientific practice/activity that basically is psychological/sociological in orientation.

Kuhn's Model of Science

According to Kuhn, normal science is conducted in the context of a paradigm. A paradigm refers to the sum total of the metaphysical assumptions, basic theory, experimental methodology, and already well-documented empirical findings that underlies ongoing research activity in the science. Through the conduction of normal science, a discovery eventually is made that is anomalous, that is, is not in accord with the dictates or content of the paradigm. If the paradigm cannot be adjusted to incorporate the anomaly, a crisis occurs, the paradigm breaks down, a so-called scientific revolution results, and a new paradigm is created. Two other aspects of Kuhn's model should be pointed out.

First, the notion of a paradigm covers only one stage in the practice of science. A given science goes through a long preparadigmatic phase before the paradigmatic phase is entered. During the preparadigmatic phase, a given science is fragmented at both the conceptual and the procedural level. During the paradigmatic phase, by definition, there is only one paradigm; there are no competing paradigms, as long as the science that is conducted is normal.

Second, Kuhn only intended his model to describe meaningfully the conduction of physical science, including physics, chemistry, and perhaps astronomy. He did not intend his basic formulation to be necessarily applicable to the so-called social sciences, including psychology, sociology, and economics. Nor did he empirically evaluate his notions in the social science context.

Application to the Systemic Phase of Modern Psychological History

The classical schools of experimental psychology are preparadigmatic in nature. They actively competed with each other with respect to object of study, methodology, orienting principles, and the like. The critical aspect of Kuhn's view of science relative to the systemic phase of modern psychological history is whether psychology has advanced beyond the preparadigmatic phase: Can any contemporary experimental system be regarded as a paradigm? There is no simple or clear-cut answer. A good case could be made for either a positive or negative resolution of the paradigm issue. A positive resolution would require the notion of a paradigm in psychology to be only an approximation of its rather idealized representation in a physical science context. A negative resolution would highlight some of the fundamental differences between a social science and a physical science in an adverse way to the detriment of psychology.

Preview of the Six Interpretive Dimensions

The nine systems ideally should be analyzed in terms of a common set of interpretive dimensions. This guarantees uniformity in presentation and encourages comparison among the systems. The following six dimensions will be used.

1. Origin and specific historical antecedents. This dimension includes the specific events leading to the appearance of the system, and the general intellectual, philosophical, and cultural trends or forces that had an effect on the system.
2. Chief historical figures associated with the system. This dimension entails a brief professional or personal biography of the founder(s) of each system.
3. Object of study and basic subject matter. This dimension involves that aspect of the psychological subject that serves as the unique object of analysis for the system. Recall that the object-of-study specification is one of the definitional attributes of a system.
4. Method of study and permissible methodology. This dimension specifies the prescribed procedural route to psychological truth associated with the system. It also constitutes one of the definitional attributes of a system.

5. Illustrative or characteristic experimentation and primary research areas or problems associated with the system. This dimension highlights the specific research focus of the system and those psychological processes emphasized by the system.

6. Historical legacy of a classical school and current relevance or significance of a contemporary system. This dimension puts each system into historical perspective by describing the contributions of the system to the overall discipline of psychology.

The significance of each dimension and the emphasis placed on a given dimension will vary for the different psychological systems. This is one way in which any special or unique characteristics of a system can be incorporated in the analysis. Other possible interpretive dimensions, such as basic philosophical assumptions relating to the nature of man and the mind–body issue, any special theoretical predilections subsumed by the system, and the basic goal(s) of the system, are covered informally in the analysis.

Bibliography

Briskman, L.B. Is a Kuhnian analysis applicable to psychology? *Science Studies,* 1972, 2, 87–97.

Coan, R.W. Dimensions of psychological theory. *American Psychologist,* 1968, 23, 715–722.

Kuhn, T.S. *The Structure of Scientific Revolutions.* Chicago: University of Chicago Press, 1962.

Lichtenstein, P.E. Psychological systems: Their nature and function. *Psychological Record,* 1967, 17, 221–240.

Masterman, M. The nature of a paradigm. In I. Lakatos and A. Musgrave (Eds.), *Criticism and the Growth of Knowledge.* London: Cambridge University Press, 1970.

McGeoch, J.A. The formal criteria of a systemic psychology. *Psychological Review,* 1933, 40, 1–12.

Spence, K.W. The nature of theory construction in contemporary psychology. *Psychological Review,* 1944, 51, 47–68.

2

Structuralism

Introduction

In many respects, structuralism constitutes the ideal physical realization of the abstract notion of a classical school. The two primary historical figures associated with the school, Wilhelm Wundt in Germany and Edward Titchener in America, served as bona fide authority figures who commanded the admiration and respect of their adherents. Both the basic subject matter of the system and the methodology permissible within it were quite delimited and were delineated clearly. Structuralism was such a tightly knit and prefocused system that many historians regard this as the primary reason for its eventual demise. Structuralism was like a giant, lumbering dinosaur that could not adapt to a changing environment.

The dominant historical interpretation of structuralism is that the system lacks any significant contemporary residues. Its historical significance derives solely from the fact that it was the first academic/experimental psychology and demarked the formal separation of psychology from physics, philosophy, and physiology. In the context of this view, the significant historical question associated with structuralism is its origin: Why did structuralism arise in the first place? Accordingly, I shall treat the origin and specific historical antecedents of structuralism as the key analytical dimension of the chapter and postpone consideration of structuralism's presystemic (or intellectual) and pragmatic (or sociological) roots until the end of the chapter.

As an illustration of the arbitrariness of historical judgment, structuralism, especially Wundt's contributions, are beginning to be viewed in a new, more sympathetic light by many contemporary psychologists. The current focus on the cognitive/mental apparatus, entailing a concern for perceptual and memorial imagery and for the cognitive correlates of psycholinguistics and language behavior, constitutes a symbolic, if not logical, extension of the original structuralist program. The somewhat arbitrary designation of 1979 as the centennial anniversary year of Wundt's establishment of a psychological laboratory also has contributed much to the mellowing of the dominant historical interpretation of structuralism. In the context of this more sympathetic contemporary view, the historical legacy of structuralism is just as significant an analytical dimension as is its origin.

To a person who has been exposed only to contemporary behavioristically oriented psychology, the content of structuralism is strange and even downright unnatural. We must demonstrate that the school was a perfectly legitimate or predictable component of nineteenth century science. We shall be critical of structuralism—it is fashionable to be critical of structuralism. Most of its critics, however, do not realize that the same basic set of criticisms also applies to behavioristic and functionalistic psychology. There are no criticisms that are unique to structuralism, and it is unfair to regard the structuralist school as a mere historical or intellectual oddity.

Wundt did not use the term structuralism to denote his system of psychology. He preferred "voluntarism," and his system generally was known in Germany as existentialism (not to be confused with the contemporary denotation of the term). William James first formally distinguished between structural and functional psychology, and it was Titchener who applied the term structuralism to both his own and Wundt's brand of psychology. Although Wundtian voluntaristic psychology was more general and comprehensive than Titchenerian structuralist psychology and included a *Völkerpsychologie* (folk psychology) component dealing with human beings as social and linguistic creatures, the two systems were continuous with each other, and we are not going to be concerned with the few, relatively minor differences existing between them. If anything, Titchener can be credited with transporting the spirit and focus of Wundtian psychology to America more or less intact.

Object of Study; Basic Subject Matter

Initial Overview

Structuralism focused on the mind—not its dynamics or functioning, but its content or structure. The object of study for structuralism was the content of conscious experience, and the goal of the structuralist program amounted to an analysis of conscious experience into its elementary units. These elementary units were definitively and existentially mental in nature and were supposed to be revealed by the systematic use of direct, critical introspection.

The basic structuralist program consisted of three interrelated questions concerning the nature of conscious experience—Titchener's famous *what*, *how*, and *why*?

1. The *what* question entails the aforementioned analysis of mental phenomena into fundamental elements by systematic introspection. How many elementary types of mental events exist?

2. The *how* question poses the problem of synthesis. How are the elementary units combined to form the content of the never-ending stream of consciousness?

3. The *why* question relates to the explanation of mind or conscious experience. Why does conscious experience occur or whence does it originate?

Before these questions can be answered, it is necessary to consider the exact denotative meaning the structuralists assigned to the concept of conscious experience.

The Nature of Conscious Experience

What the structuralists meant by conscious experience is not necessarily congruent with the common, everyday use of the term. The structuralist distinguished between *immediate* conscious experience and *mediate* conscious experience. Only the former served as the unique and proper object of concern for psychology; the latter could be the focus of any other science, such as physics or chemistry.

Although the difference between immediate and mediate conscious experience was clear-cut for the structuralist, the distinction is metaphysical in nature and thus difficult to characterize. An example should help. Suppose a structuralist places a bright red apple in someone's line of sight and requests the person to report on the content of his/her current perceptual awareness. The person, as observer, can do one of two things: (1) report on the perceived presence of the apple itself, or (2) report on the sensory experience of red or bright, as presumably set up by the apple. The first kind of report uses verbal categories that refer to meaningful stimulus objects known to be external to the self. The second kind of report does not use meaningful thing or object language, but merely characterizes the rudimentary sensations of which the observer is aware. The first kind of report entails mediate experience; the second is what is meant by immediate experience.

As a crude analogy, the content of mediate conscious experience is a matter of perception, whereas the content of immediate conscious experience is a matter of sensation. The structuralist assumed that an observer is only directly aware of, or directly experiences, the various sensory attributes of an external object, not the external object itself. The existence of the external object, as a component of mediate experience, is an inference based on the content of immediate experience. (It should be noted that in the context of contemporary psychology, perception is not necessarily based on sensation; sensation also can be based on perception. For example, the color or brightness of an object often is resolved according to a prior determination of what the object is.)

The structuralists chose to focus on immediate experience, instead of mediate experience, more or less by default. Mediate experience refers to the ultimate source of immediate experience—that is, external objects or physical stimuli. Mediate experience and/or external objects had been the object of analysis for other sciences, such as chemistry and physics, for centuries. Immediate experience was a unique aspect of a living organism that had not yet been a subject of empirical analysis by any other science. The structuralists never seriously entertained overt behavior as a proper object of study because it is a component of mediate experience. The overt behavior of an organism Y exists in the mediate experience of an observer X.

The Elementary Units of Conscious Experience

Structuralists analyzed the content of immediate conscious experience in terms of three different kinds of elementary units or mental elements: (1) sensations, (2) images, and (3) affections or feelings. Elementary means "incapable of further reduction." These three classes of irreducible mental elements presumably were empirically based, in the sense that they were supposedly the product of the systematic use of direct, critical introspection. As is the case with the fundamental units of analysis of any discipline, they really were metaphysical in nature, as evidenced by the fact that the later structuralists reduced feeling or affection to sensation, and that Wundt and Titchener did not agree on the number of dimensions or attributes that were associated with each kind of mental element.

SENSATIONS

Sensations are the elementary units of conscious experience (the content of consciousness) that arise in the context of an external object–observer relationship. They are the rudimentary mental events that an observer directly or immediately experiences while being stimulated by some external, physical stimulus. (Note that the preceding discussion of immediate experience was solely in terms of visual sensations.) By definition, sensations are associated with physical stimuli: They are stimulus-specific and occur only when a physical stimulus is present. The content of conscious experience in the absence of physical stimulation does not consist of sensations. This might not seem like a restrictive aspect of the denotation of a sensation until it is remembered that the physical stimulus is a component of mediate experience. The observer is not supposed to report on mediate experience; and, technically, only the experimenter and not the observer knows whether a sensation or some other kind of mental element is the current focus of interest in an introspective session. In other words, the differentiation between a sensation and some other kind of mental element, such as an image, *cannot* be made on the basis of the content of the immediate experience itself.

Structuralists postulated the existence of seven kinds of sensations, which corresponded to the seven different sensory modalities known at the time: visual, auditory, olfactory, gustatory, cutaneous, kinesthetic, and organic. For instance, the experience of a certain color is a visual sensation; the experience of a certain pitch is an auditory sensation; the experience of a certain smell is an olfactory sensation.

The assignment of a given sensory experience to a specific sensory modality is equivalent to naming that sensation. As we shall see shortly, the name of a sensation is one of the attributes of a sensation, and is one of the dimensions on which a given sensory experience can vary. A given sensory experience can be assigned to a particular sensory modality on the basis of any one of three criteria: (1) introspective similarity, (2) knowledge of the sense organ involved, or (3) knowledge of the type of physical stimulus used. The first criterion is the preferred one in the context of the structuralist system, but it begs the question of the identification of the first sensation ever experienced in a particular modality. The last criterion is inconsistent with the overall structuralist methodology because it requires appeal to mediate experience.

A given sensory experience was assumed to possess certain attributes. An attribute is simply a specific descriptive dimension on which a sensation can vary. Titchener distinguished among five such attributes: (1) quality, (2) intensity, (3) duration, (4) vividness, and (5) extension. Wundt admitted only to quality and intensity. Quality refers to the aforementioned nominal dimension: the name or typology of the sensation, such as visual or auditory. Intensity relates to the strength, magnitude, or degree of the sensation: a bright color, or a loud sound, for example. Duration is simply the temporal aspect of a sensory experience: how long it persists over time. Vividness refers to the clearness of the sensory experience, where clearness is defined as a function of the observer's attentive state, not as a function of any characteristic of the external stimulus. Extension refers to the location of the sensation and the amount of space it occupies. Only visual and cutaneous (tactile) sensations possess the attribute of extension.

IMAGES

Images are the elementary units of conscious experience (the content of consciousness) that occur in the absence of an external object–observer relationship. They are the rudimentary mental events that an observer experiences after the external, physical stimulus has been withdrawn. As such, images are residues of sensation and do not occur in an existential vacuum. Although an image is not relatable to an external, physical stimulus event currently present, some past environmental event must serve as the ultimate reference point for the image. Since the observer cannot report on mediate experience, technically only the experimenter, and not the observer, knows whether the content of current consciousness is a sensation or an image—that is, only the experimenter knows when the original external stimulus event was withdrawn.

Structuralists postulated the existence of seven kinds of images, corresponding to the seven recognized sensory modalities. Each modality possessed its own characteristic imagery, in addition to its own characteristic sensation, although Titchener was not sure that the kinesthetic sense gave rise to residues of sensation, or images. Each of the seven kinds of images possessed the same set of attributes that the corresponding sensation did: five attributes for Titchener; two for Wundt. An attempt was made to distinguish between a sensation and an image in terms of these attributes. It was believed that, in general, an image possessed less quality, intensity, and vividness than its corresponding sensation, although it was also recognized that under certain conditions an image could be more intense, more vivid, and qualitatively stronger than the corresponding sensation.

The notion of imagery is merely a logical or conceptual extension of that of sensation, with respect both to the basic classificatory typology and the descriptive dimensions or attributes of variation. Structuralists, however, also used the term imagery to characterize certain mental events that ultimately were empirically (as opposed to nativistically) based, but were not as directly or immediately tied down to specific prior environmental stimulus events. These included recurrent images, hallucinatory images, dream images, and memory images.

FEELINGS OR AFFECTIONS

Feelings or affections, as elementary units of consciousness, also were associated with the presentation of an external, physical stimulus event. A sensation, or sensory experience, was presumed to be accompanied by an affective component. Stimulation of any of the seven sensory modalities gave rise to a subjective feeling state, but the specific qualitative content of the state was independent of the modality that was stimulated. Titchener assumed that the qualitative attribute of feeling existed either at a pleasant or an unpleasant value with no mixture. He also assumed that a feeling varied in intensity and in duration. For Titchener, feelings, unlike sensations, possessed only three attributes: quality, intensity, and duration.

Titchener's conception of feelings or affections sometimes is referred to as a one-dimensional theory, because of the unitary qualitative aspect (pleasant or unpleasant) of a feeling state. By comparison, Wundt had a three-dimensional conception of feelings. He presumed that feelings varied on three independent qualitative dimensions concurrently: (1) pleasure–displeasure, (2) tension–relaxation, and (3) excitement–depression.

Although all three structuralist mental elements—sensations, images, and feelings—are completely subjective entities from the strict behaviorist's viewpoint, feelings constitute the most subjective component of them all. Titchener reduced the second and third Wundtian qualitative dimensions to sensation. Later structuralists, such as Nafe, reduced the one remaining Titchenerian attribute to sensation.

The Problem of Synthesis

The structuralists did not approach the problem of synthesis as actively and systematically as they did the question of the fundamental elements—probably because the logically prior problem of analysis was never resolved to every structuralist's satisfaction. The British empiricist doctrine of associationism served as a general principle of synthesis for Wundt and Titchener. This doctrine has both operational and conceptual aspects.

OPERATIONAL ASPECTS

The operational aspects relate to the actual, or working, laws of association that determine which specific mental elements get connected. A representative sampling from the set of operational laws would include (1) contiguity, (2) similarity, (3) frequency or repetition, (4) intensity, and (5) inseparability. (Today we would call these operational laws "empirical laws"; variants of them are used in the subarea of the psychology of learning known as verbal learning.) Contiguity served as the primary associative law for the structuralist, as it did for practically every kind of non-Gestalt psychologist. This law states that mental elements that are temporally co-occurring have a high probability of forming an associative connection, so that the later appearance of one of the elements elicits the recall of the other(s).

CONCEPTUAL ASPECTS

The conceptual aspects relate to the nature of association at a philosophical or theoretical level. Two logically distinct interpretations of an association were postulated by the British empiricists: mechanical compounding and creative synthesis. In mechanical compounding, the content of the resulting association was regarded as the mere linear sum of its constituent elements, that is, the resultant whole is equal to the sum of its parts. This can be classified as a rational interpretation, in which the output is predictable from knowledge of the input. In creative synthesis, the input elements combine to generate a resulting product, but the latter need not bear any resemblance to the input elements. This interpretation amounts to a kind of mental chemistry in which the compound possesses properties not characteristic of its constituent elements. Creative synthesis can be classified as an empirical interpretation, in which the output is not predictable from knowledge of the input. The creative synthesis interpretation originally arose because mechanical compounding could not account for some of the known laws of color mixture, and also could not represent the complex notion of "everything" in a realistic way.

The structuralists assumed the creative synthesis interpretation of the nature of an association. In the context of Wundtian structuralism, it was called the doctrine of apperception. In the context of Titchenerian structuralism, it served as the basis of a theory of meaning. The meaning of a given core mental element was provided by the associational milieu, or context, in which it appeared. Remnants of this core–context theory of meaning still exist.

CREATIVE SYNTHESIS AND THE CONTENT OF CONSCIOUSNESS

Structuralists accounted for the content of ongoing conscious experience in terms of a synthesis of the three fundamental kinds of mental elements. They construed the elementary sensations, images, and affections as combining associatively in a creative synthesis context to form the content of current awareness. Consciousness at any moment in time consisted of a combination of (1) current perceptions, (2) complex ideas or memorial constructions, and (3) various complex subjective feeling states. Current perception amounted to an associative combination of elementary sensations. Complex ideas primarily amounted to an associative combination of elementary images. Complex feeling states amounted to a synthesis of elementary feeling states from various sources.

The Origin of Conscious Experience: The Explanation of Mind

The question of the source of conscious experience, or the mind, is related to the structuralist's position on the mind–body issue. The structuralists advocated a form of dualism known as psychophysical parallelism, in which both mind (mental events) and body (physical, physiological events) exist, but constitute independent, noninteracting entities that merely covary. Mental events and physical events were conceived as merely parallel processes. For the structuralist, any component or aspect of conscious experience was correlated with some underlying physiological, neuronal, or brain event, although not every such event necessarily had a representation in conscious experience. By the time Wundt had established experimental psychology as an independent academic discipline in the late 1870s, knowledge of physiology and the nervous system had become quite sophisticated. No structuralist seriously entertained the notion that the mind, or consciousness, constituted an independent, causative entity, completely divorced from physiological or physical processes.

To underscore the physical correlates of conscious experience, Wundt referred to his psychology as a physiological psychology, although it is not such in the contemporary sense of the term. Since Wundt and the structuralists did not work out the laws governing the structure of conscious experience at a physiological level, a more realistic reason for considering the structuralist system a physiological one is the methodology employed by the structuralist. Introspection had been used by experimental physiologists who investigated the various sensory systems and receptors.

It also should be pointed out that the mind is an aspect of immediate experience, whereas the body in general is a component of mediate experience. Immediate experience is the experience of an *experiencing* body or organism; immediate experience is contingent on an *experiencing* organism. At a philosophical level, dualistic parallelism is a convenient way of representing this relationship between immediate experience and mediate experience.

Method of Study; Permissible Methodology

Initial Overview

Structuralists analyzed the content of current consciousness by means of direct, critical introspection. Any attempt at formally defining the notion of introspection would amount to an exercise in circularity because the definition would be merely a redescription of Titchener's basic "what question" as the primary goal of the structuralist program. For instance, "introspection is the systematic and controlled self-observation of the contents of one's immediate experience" and "introspection is the process of externalizing the content of one's consciousness under controlled and systematic conditions" are circular statements when juxtaposed to the basic goal of structuralism.

The term introspection cannot be applied to one specific monolithic self-observational procedure; it is merely generic, covering a broad class of self-observational procedures. The physical realization of introspection in terms of a given procedure varied from laboratory to laboratory: Wundt's in Leipzig, Külpe's in Würzburg, Titchener's at Cornell. What the different variants of introspection had in common was a stress on systemization and control. Every structuralist emphasized that introspection, as legitimate scientific methodology, should not be confused with the everyday connotations of the term. The specific brand of introspection that has filtered down into contemporary consciousness is Titchener's, and we shall focus on his interpretation.

Titchenerian Introspection

Titchener's approach to introspection can be characterized in terms of (1) his rather elaborate specification of the properties that an acceptable introspective trial and/or session must possess, and (2) his insistence on the use of a trained or practiced subject as the introspective observer.

THE CHARACTERISTICS OF AN INTROSPECTIVE TRIAL/SESSION

Titchener abstracted the technical requirements of a legitimate introspective experience in terms of four basic characteristics:

1. The observer must be able to determine when the stimulus or critical experimental event (operation) is introduced on each trial.
2. The observer must be in a state of readiness or strained attention on each trial.
3. Observations, the content of the verbal report, must be repeatable over trials.
4. The experimental conditions must be capable of variation along different dimensions across trials with attendant systematic changes in the experience of the observer.

Note the striking similarity between these four requirements and the characteristics of a nonintrospective experiment performed by a contemporary behaviorist. An analogous set of characteristics would be applicable to the latter, even though the phenomenon of interest changes from an observer's private experience to a subject's overt behavior:

1. The subject must be able to determine when a trial begins.
2. The subject must be alert and act in good faith on each trial.
3. Behavioral observations must be repeatable over trials.
4. The experimental conditions must be capable of variation

along different dimensions across trials with attendant systematic changes in the behavior of the subject.

The fourth condition encompasses the essence of an experiment, or the scientific method. Thus, if introspection is to be criticized as being nonexperimental or nonscientific, it must be done on some basis other than that of pure operational procedures.

THE USE OF TRAINED OBSERVERS

Titchener restricted the legitimate application of the introspective procedure to trained observers, typically graduate students who had undergone hundreds of hours and thousands of trials of introspective practice. This restriction existed for a number of reasons, only two of which need be mentioned here. (Some of the other reasons will become apparent in the course of later discussion.)

First, it is not easy to introspect, even under ideal circumstances. The aim of introspection is to externalize the nature of one's immediate experience. This involves the use of language and verbal categories. The language and verbal categories that the observer uses to refer to external objects in the context of everyday life are simply too imprecise for the introspective description of the contents of private experience. Introspective training, in part, consisted of the development of a standardized vocabulary that made verbal reports comparable among a group of observers.

Second, because the process of introspection cannot occur in a conceptual vacuum—introspection is nothing in and of itself—the observer had to be trained to introspect in a prescribed manner that approximated the structuralist's rather idealistic conception of how the process of introspection should take place. There was a right way and a wrong way to introspect, and the inability of an observer to report conscious contents expectable from the structuralist paradigm was the result of introspecting in the wrong way.

Because of these two reasons for using trained observers, the structuralist rightfully can be accused of (1) preselecting data and (2) defining the good observer in terms of how well his/her verbal report approximated the expectations of the experimenter. But these two kinds of problems are not unique to structuralism. In the context of contemporary behaviorism, where overt behavior is the focus, the experimenter (1) preselects data by allowing the subject only one response alternative, or at most a choice among a restrictive set of response alternatives, and (2) defines the good subject in terms of how well his/her behavior approximates certain expectations or predictions.

Problems and/or Criticisms of Introspection

There are numerous problems and/or criticisms associated with introspection as a methodological technique, and they can be discussed from many different perspectives. We shall concentrate on four basic problems/criticisms that primarily are operational, as opposed to conceptual, in nature.

First, in introspection, the observed (what is observed) and the observer (who does the observing) reside in the same existential object in the real-time and real-space universe. The observer, as the subject in the introspective session, reports on his/her own private experience as the object of interest. This relationship between the observed and the observer in structuralist introspection will be understood better if the situation that exists in a typical behavioral study is described. In a behavioral experiment, the observed (what is observed) and the observer (who does the observing) do not reside in the same existential object in the real-time and real-space universe. In a behavioral experiment, the observer is the experimenter, or some automated piece of measuring equipment; what is observed is the behavior of the subject. The experimenter, as observer, reports on the overt behavioral activity of an entirely separate organism, called the subject.

The observer in an introspective session is the self and can only be the self. The observer in a behavioral study is an independent, external agent or organism—in fact, there is no limit to the number of independent observers that can be used to decode a subject's behavior. Because of this difference in the relationship between the observer and the observed, introspective report is a private, nonpublic, subjective event; behavioral datum is a public, objective event. Consequently introspective reports are beyond the bounds of empirical reliability and/or validity assessment, whereas behavioral data are not. It is impossible to check the accuracy of introspective report; it is possible to check the accuracy of behavioral data.

Because introspective report is subjective, the structuralist is faced with a problem when two different observers, exposed to the same stimulus situation or experimental input, generate disparate results and yield conflicting introspections. For instance, in the face of stimulus object X, observer A might report a *green* color sensation, and observer B a *yellow* color sensation. Which observer is correct? There is no way of finding out! There is no way of externalizing either observer's experience for public scrutiny by a truly independent, impartial observer or experimenter, or measuring device. The use of additional introspective observers (such as C, D, and E) does not arbitrate the issue because they merely are reporting on their own private experience.

In all fairness to structuralist methodology, it should be noted that behavioral data are not objective in an absolute sense. The degree of objectivity associated with a given instance of behavior depends both on the nature of the behavior and on the measuring agent. For instance, the latency of a response in a classical conditioning experiment as recorded by an automatic timer is quite objective; how cohesive the interaction is among a group of subjects in a social psychology experiment, as measured or rated by two or three human observers, is quite subjective. Subjectivity and objectivity are merely opposite ends of the same continuum. Introspective reports are located toward the subjective end of the continuum and possess more subjective than objective components. Behavioral data are located toward the objective end of the continuum and possess more objective than subjective components. The basic advantage of a behavioral study over introspection is one of principle: A highly refined measuring device or a very large number of human observers can be brought into an experimental situation to increase objectivity, and thereby reliability and validity.

Since the structuralist cannot eliminate or reduce the subjectivity of introspective reports directly, trained, even highly overtrained, observers must be used to reduce interobserver disagreement, or increase interobserver agreement. (The need to increase interobserver agreement served as another reason for Titchener's insistence on the use of trained subjects.) The use of highly trained introspectors leads to another problem—namely, the lack of generalizability of results beyond the restrictive, highly trained subject population from which they were obtained. Structuralist psychology amounted to a psychology of the immediate experience of highly practiced university students. It cannot be assumed that the nature of the introspective reports of the untrained university student or of the lay person would be the same.

Behavioral studies also use highly trained observers to increase interobserver agreement, especially in contexts that require the observer to rate or categorize the more subjective aspects of behavior. In this case, however, it is the experimenter, or measuring agent, and not the subject, that is overtrained. Classical behaviorism also suffered from the indictment of lack of generalizability, but for different reasons. For many years, behaviorism amounted to a psychology of the overt behavior of the rat.

Titchener discovered that not every graduate student could operate as a good introspector or be trained to be a good introspector.

There were good introspectors and bad introspectors, and the latter were encouraged to leave the discipline of psychology. This notion of good and bad introspectors is quite suspicious. What is characteristic of a good introspector is not true necessarily for a bad introspector. A contemporary analogy exists in the context of parapsychological research, where there are good and bad ESPers in extrasensory experiments and good and bad PSIers in psychokinesis experiments. The fact that a given parapsychological phenomenon is exhibited only by a small proportion of the subjects tested and the fact that the good performance is attributed to a special ability possessed by the subject reduce the scientific credibility of the phenomenon.

A second problem associated with introspection relates to what Titchener called the *stimulus error*. This is the act of reporting on the content of mediate experience, instead of on the content of immediate experience. A subject reporting on the content of mediate experience makes the error of reporting on the nature of the external, physical stimulus itself. The stimulus error is the dominant interpretive response made by the organism in the context of everyday life and is characteristic of the naive, untrained introspector in the laboratory. A subject needed to be trained not to make the stimulus error during an introspective session. (This is another reason for Titchener's insistence on the use of practiced subjects.)

The stimulus error is more than a mere operational inconvenience for the structuralist. It highlights the essential arbitrariness of the basic subject matter of structuralism. The immediate "givens" of current awareness are meaningful physical stimulus objects, not rudimentary sensations. Granted we do not perceive or experience environmental events in and of themselves—all that we can experience directly are the sensations corresponding to the environmental events—mediate experience, and not immediate experience, constitutes the initial, *unanalyzed* content of consciousness. It is arbitrary as to whether perceptual objects or sensory attributes serve as the fundamental subject matter of psychology. The classical school of Gestalt psychology argued that it was more meaningful and pragmatic to focus on the immediate givens of current awareness, that is, on mediate experience, meaningful perceptual objects, or organized wholes. Gestalt psychology replaced direct, critical introspection with a freewheeling, unrestrained phenomenology, in which simple, naive responding using the vernacular was perfectly acceptable.

Third, introspection requires the use of a subject who can follow Titchener's dictum of strained attention and express subtle sensory, imaginal, and affective distinctions in words. For Titchener, the ideal introspector was an educated, specially trained, motivated, verbally facile, adult psychology graduate student. Given these characteristics of an ideal introspector, it was impossible for a structuralist to utilize direct introspection to investigate the content of the immediate experience of a preverbal child, of an adult member of the so-called abnormal population, such as a mental retardate or chronic schizophrenic, or of a nonverbal animal.

Two courses of action became available to the structuralist with respect to this problem. Children, retardates, and animals could be declared, by fiat, as being beyond the legitimate bounds of psychological investigation, or some indirect technique could be devised by which the immediate experience of such organisms might be externalized. Some structuralists took the first course of action and delimited structuralism to the normal, verbal, human adult. For them, structuralism was to be a pure or basic psychology, with no practical application aspects and no relevance for members of the abnormal population. Other structuralists took the second route and devised an indirect way of, presumably, externalizing the content of immediate experience. This technique, *introspection by analogy*, employed a standard, highly trained observer who attempted to introspect for an organism that could not introspect for itself. Titchener was not exactly comfortable with this solution. It is just as well, because introspection by analogy is manifestly ridiculous.

A fourth problem of introspection derives from the belief that the observation or measurement of a given empirical phenomenon interferes with, changes, or even destroys that phenomenon. Introspection especially is susceptible to this criticism because both the observer and the observed are a property of the same existential entity. The specific self-observational context in which this criticism is most telling is that of introspecting about the content of one's immediate emotional consciousness. The act of analyzing one's current emotional state (fear, anger, etc.) disrupts the state. The structuralist solution to this problem involved the use of *introspection by retrospection* or *memory*. The subject had to wait until the basic emotional experience ceased and then attempt to reconstruct if from memory. Such a procedure is open to a host of criticisms relative to the possibility of forgetting, distortion, bias, or time errors.

The problem of reactive measurement can be dealt with, in principle, in behavioristic psychology because the observer and the observed constitute independent existential entities: In many behavioral contexts, it is possible to separate the act of observing from the object of observation, either physically, as in a learning experiment, or symbolically, as in a social psychology experiment involving sham instructions. But it should be noted that the use of deceit or trickery in a social psychology experiment raises certain ethical questions.

Introspection at a Conceptual Level

There are numerous conceptual limitations associated with introspection. Two of them are noted briefly.

First, many significant events of psychological relevance to the individual simply do not occur in consciousness. The content of current awareness is the mere tip of the iceberg of the individual's total ongoing activities. This limitation should not be construed to mean simply that introspection is irrelevant for dealing with the individual's overt behavior. Many psychological processes and events, as emphasized by the Freudian psychoanalytic approach, as well as various physiological and neuronal processes and mechanisms, and even cognitive events and processes, such as thinking, information processing, and language or speech recognition, do not take place in consciousness and are not subject to introspection.

The only way Wundt and Titchener could handle this conceptual limitation was by arbitrarily decreeing that such nonconscious events do not constitute proper objects of concern for structuralist psychology. Other structuralists, such as Külpe, did attempt to investigate thinking via introspection and established the notion of imageless thought. They assumed that thinking occurs, but is not controlled by an element appearing in consciousness. Rather, thinking is regulated by some nonconscious mental set or determining tendency. Külpe's brand of structuralism, known as the Würzburg school, is put into perspective in Chapter 8 in the context of analyzing the historical precursors of cognitive behaviorism.

Second, there are many philosophers who, although they admit the existence of the mind, deny that the mind can serve as an object of analysis for the mind. The mind simply cannot investigate itself; it cannot serve as both observed and observer. Direct, critical structuralist introspection is conceptually vacuous in the context of this view.

The Fate of the Structuralism–Introspection Connection

No other classical school was as wedded to its methodology as was structuralism. Structural psychology can be termed introspective psychology, and the prototypical case of an introspective psychology is structuralism. The mutually contingent relationship of structuralism and introspection doomed them both. Structural psychology, by arbitrarily focusing on immediate experience as its exclusive object of study, formally raised introspection to a hallowed status. But once immediate experience devolved to an ancillary concern for the psychologist, introspection became trivial. The introspectionists, by claiming (1) exclusiveness, and (2) generality or universality for their methodology, legitimatized the structural program. Once it was demonstrated, though, that introspection possessed only limited validity and value, structuralism became viewed as a sterile, dead-end system.

Chief Historical Figures: Wundt and Titchener

To understand the basic nature and character of Wundt and Titchener, it is important to remember that structuralism was the first academic psychology. Both men were academicians in the traditional, Germanic sense of the term. Both identified with and achieved prestige and recognition from the university system structure. They regaled in formally lecturing, in academic garb before adoring students; they published voluminously at the highest level of scholastic excellence; they directed research laboratories and supervised countless doctoral theses. In terms of professional demeanor, both men were dogmatic, somewhat humorless, aloof, and untiring and systematic workers, who were very protective of their time. Today we think of psychologists as outgoing and friendly. But the subject matter and methodology of structuralism required a certain air of stuffiness or aloofness, or a need for privacy or isolation on the part of its practitioners. In their private lives, both men were courteous and sociable with many friends, were happily married, and enjoyed art, music, and the discussion of current events. Both overcame great odds to become the standard-bearers of a psychological school, having endured less-than-ideal childhoods and years of academic struggle and nonrecognition. Wundt served as a Dozent in physiology and as the laboratory assistant of the renowned Helmholtz at Heidelberg for nearly ten years. He also was an "associate professor" at Heidelberg for ten years before achieving full professorial chairs in philosophy at Zurich and then Leipzig. Titchener spent his entire professional life at Cornell University, but he never felt accepted by the American psychological establishment and was constantly on the defensive with respect to American functionalistic and behavioristic thought.

Brief, highly selective, descriptive biographies of Wundt and Titchener follow.

Wilhelm Wundt (1832–1920)

Wundt was born in 1832 in Neckarau, a small village in the Baden district of Germany. His father was a Lutheran minister, and his early education was entrusted to a vicar who served as his father's assistant. Wundt's childhood was not particularly exciting or stimulating. His only surviving sibling was a brother, 8 years older than he. After a number of abortive attempts at higher education, Wundt finally earned a medical degree at Heidelberg in 1856, spurred on by the death of his father and pecuniary circumstances. In 1857, Wundt became a Dozent in physiology at Heidelberg and, from 1858 to 1864, served as the laboratory assistant of Hermann von Helmholtz. He was promoted to a position analogous to associate professor in 1864 and was able to relinquish his assistantship job. Elected to the Baden legislative chamber in 1866, he soon resigned the office because it took too much of his time. In 1867, Wundt was permitted to offer a psychology course (entitled "physiological psychology") for the first time. Out of this course developed his two-volume *Principles of Physiological Psychology (Grundzüge der Physiologischen Psychologie)*, published in 1873–1874. Wundt accepted a full professorial chair in philosophy at Zurich in 1874 and a similar position at Leipzig the following year, where he remained until his retirement in 1917.

It was his years at Leipzig, now Karl Marx University in East Germany, that established Wilhelm Wundt as the founder of structuralism. A small demonstration laboratory was created there in 1875, and in 1879 it was converted to a legitimate research laboratory. This Psychologische Institute became the mecca of experimental psychology and attracted countless students, many of them Americans, and is recognized as the model for subsequent psychological laboratories. Students at the Institute included Edward Bradford Titchener, James McKeen Cattell, G. Stanley Hall, Lightmer Witmer, Frank Angell, Edward Scripture, Charles Judd, James Baldwin, Mary Calkins, Vladimir Bekhterev, Charles Spearman, Emil Kraepelin, Hugo Münsterberg, Oswald Külpe, and Karl Marbe. Cattell served as Wundt's first, self-proclaimed psychology assistant and presented Wundt with a typewriter to facilitate his writing endeavors. Wundt was the most prolific writer psychology has ever known. In 1881, he founded the journal *Philosophische Studien*, later renamed the *Psychologische Studien*, as an outlet for the voluminous research generated by the Institute. Wundt died in 1920, only eight days after completing his autobiography.

Edward Bradford Titchener (1867–1927)

Titchener was born in Chichester, England, in 1867. Although his father died when Titchener was a child, Titchener was able to attend Malvern College and Oxford University, graduating from the latter with a degree in philosophy in 1890. Titchener then went to Germany to study at Wundt's Psychologische Institute and earned his doctorate just two years later, in 1892. After returning to England and finding the climate at Oxford hostile to experimental psychology, Titchener accepted a position at Cornell University in Ithaca, New York, at the invitation of Frank Angell, who was moving to Stanford University. Titchener remained at Cornell, where he literally created a Wundtian Institute in miniature, until his death in 1927 from a brain tumor. Titchener became a charter member of the American Psychological Association in 1892, but eventually resigned over a matter of ethics. In 1904, an informal group of psychologists sympathetic to structuralism, "the Experimentalists," was formed. Between 1901 and 1905, Titchener published his four-volume *Experimental Psychology*, which amounted to a series of laboratory manuals. Some psychologists regard this four-volume set as the most scholarly and erudite work ever written by an "American" psychologist. Titchener's *Textbook of Psychology* was published in 1910. He also translated many of Wundt's works, forever frustrated because Wundt already had written the next edition by the time the translation of the current edition was completed. Titchener served as an associate editor of the *American Journal of Psychology* from 1895 to 1921, when he assumed sole editorship. This journal was the primary outlet for structuralist introspective research in America. Because he engaged in joint authorship, the number of publications under his name alone does not come near Wundt's output.

Titchener never renounced his British citizenship; his isolation from the American psychological establishment increased as he aged, and his productivity decreased sharply during the last few years of his life. It is interesting to note that Titchener, a personal friend of John Watson, maintained cordial relations with him, even though he established the rival school of behaviorism. Titchener found behaviorism wanting basically for philosophical reasons, and he believed that it could never last. Titchener's students at Cornell included Edwin

G. Boring, Karl Dallenbach, Margaret Washburn, Walter Pillsbury, and J. P. Guilford.

Characteristic Experimentation; Primary Research Areas

The research program associated with a given system of psychology can be characterized in terms of (1) problem areas, (2) experimental techniques, and (3) technical apparati. The structuralist research program was neither unique nor original. It studied problems that were logical extensions of prior research conducted by physiologists and physicists. It used and, in some cases, refined specific techniques that had been devised by its forebears. The equipment it employed was sophisticated for its day, but certainly not original. The significance of structuralist research derived from two sources.

First, most of the European research was conducted at Wundt's Leipzig laboratory, which represented a coalescence of all the prior psychological research conducted by spatially isolated scientists who did not identify themselves as psychologists. For the first time in history, research was being conducted by a group of scientists who regarded themselves as experimental psychologists in an institutionalized laboratory setting explicitly designed to measure the mental events of the human organism with the express intention of creating a bona fide science of conscious experience.

Second, Wundt's laboratory was equipped with all the paraphernalia, gadgets, and esoteric devices needed for making mental measurements under controlled conditions, and constituted the model for future experimental psychology laboratories. Wundt's laboratory was so well equipped that structuralism became overidentified with its instrumentation, and its detractors caricatured the system as brass instrument psychology.

We shall describe briefly the research areas, experimental techniques, and instrumentation characteristic of Wundt's laboratory.

Research Areas

Wundt and his students focused on sensation and perception, reaction time, attention, feeling, and association—phenomena that are distinctly mental in nature or aspects of conscious experience that can be construed as directly involving the mind. At least half of the studies related to sensation and perception, with the remaining studies more or less equally distributed among the other categories. The primary sensory focus was the visual modality and involved research on color mixture, color contrast, color blindness, peripheral vision, afterimages, and the like. Auditory and tactile sensations also were studied. Perceptual research concerned visual size, optical illusions, and the duration of time, or the time sense. Reaction-time experimentation assessed the conscious events that accompanied the performance of various simple and complex reaction tasks. Attention research concentrated on the focus and periphery of the content of attention as different aspects of current experience. Both the range and fluctuation of the focus were studied, with the work on attention ultimately culminating in the measurement of the immediate memory span. An attempt was made in the feeling research to correlate various feeling states with pulse rate, breathing, and muscular strength. The concept of association was operationalized in terms of word association, and Wundt and his students focused on the many constraints that determined the content of specific verbal associations. For instance, *loud–soft* is an inner association because of the intrinsic or logical connection between the two terms, whereas *table–chair* is an outer association because of the accidental or noncontingent relationship between the two terms.

Experimental Techniques

Introspection constituted the basic methodology of structuralism, and the manner in which the structuralists adopted this age-old technique already has been described. However, this was not the only generic experimental technique employed by the structuralists. Introspection had to be superimposed on or supplemented by other experimental techniques in order to investigate adequately the five content areas discussed previously. These other techniques served as specific procedural contexts in which introspection was conducted. The Weber–Fechner psychophysical methods were used in sensation and perception studies. Structuralists adopted and refined the basic procedures developed by Helmholtz and Donders for investigating reaction time. Degrees of feeling states were determined by using the method of paired comparison. Wundt's association research employed and refined Galton's word association technique.

Instrumentation

A partial list of the standard pieces of apparati stocked by the Psychologische Institute is presented here. Note that some of the equipment is specified in Germanic terminology. The purpose of a given device is indicated parenthetically where necessary.

Hipp chronoscope (for measuring time)
Fall chronometer (for measuring time)
Chronograph (for measuring velocity and time)
Fall apparat (for visual display of a word or letter)
Sprecht contact apparati (human-voice-activated device)
Zeitsinnapparat (time-sense apparatus)
Metronome
Color mixer
Electric chronographic tuning fork
Afterimage apparatus
Reaction apparat (for reaction time studies)
Rotation apparat (for color mixing)
Pendulum (for visual stimulus presentation)
Kymograph (for measuring pressure)

Historical Legacy

As already intimated in the introduction to this chapter, it is possible to take either a hard or soft view with respect to the fate of structuralism.

Hard View

No contemporary experimental psychologist would claim that immediate conscious experience is the only legitimate or proper object of study of psychology or that introspection is the canonical psychological investigative method. Structuralism, as a recognized or acceptable system of psychology, is dead, with no significant contemporary residues. The structuralist era lasted approximately from 1875 to 1930.

The ultimate demise of structuralism was not unpredictable.

Wundt spent the last 20 years of his life developing his *Völkerpsychologie*; he constantly was beset by criticisms from other laboratory centers in Germany, which, although nominally structural or introspective in orientation, professed a more functional or act-oriented approach to experience. Also, the growth of Gestalt psychology in Germany during the last decade of Wundt's life was irreversible. In America, Titchener spent the last ten to 15 years of his life in virtual social isolation. His productivity decreased significantly and he dismissed the newly created Watsonian behaviorism as sheer philosophical folly.

The end came simply because the original, first-generation progenitors of structuralism died, and the system did not possess enough internal or institutionalized momentum to endure. Wundt's and Titchener's status as exemplary scholars, intellects, and philosophers was not sufficient to sustain structural psychology once the force of their personalities was stilled forever. Remember that structuralism was a tightly knit approach that actively resisted any assimilation by nonstructural psychological approaches. Structuralism simply was overwhelmed by evolutionary forces that it neither understood nor cared about.

Structuralism can be venerated, but only as a historical relic. It was the first academic/experimental psychology. It served as a necessary link in the chain of evolutionary processes begetting contemporary psychology, regardless of its specific systematic form. Structuralism may be socially or symbolically significant to the contemporary psychologist, but it no longer possesses any substantive or intellectual relevance for contemporary psychology.

Soft View

Certain aspects of structuralism survived the demise of the school as a whole and persist as relevant concerns of contemporary psychology. For example:

1. A psychology and psychophysiology of sensation and perception still exist.
2. Concern for mental imagery is undergoing a revival.
3. Feelings or complex emotional states are objects of current interest.
4. Attention is a legitimate notion in cognitive behaviorism.
5. Association persists as a principle of synthesis.
6. Adult human subjects still engage in verbal report.
7. Contemporary cognitive behaviorism is concerned with the

nature of the mental apparatus intervening between the stimulus input and the response output.

The thrust of this view basically is semantic. It is problematical whether structuralist concepts and phenomena possess the same denotation in a functionalistic or behavioristic context. For instance:

1. Sensation and perception currently are interpreted in a receptor system or information-processing context, not as aspects of conscious experience.
2. Mental imagery currently is treated from the perspective of mediating function and meaningful content.
3. Feelings or complex emotional states currently are conceptualized as functional, motivational, or physiological entities.
4. Attention currently is regarded as a functional process, not as a repository of focused experience.
5. Association no longer constitutes the principal mode of synthesis.
6. Verbal report currently is conceptualized merely as another kind of discriminative response, subject to quantification and measurement by independent, external observers.
7. The cognitive behaviorist's construction of a mental apparatus bears only a superficial resemblance to the structuralist's fundamental units of consciousness.

Origin; Specific Historical Antecedents

Since structuralism was the first recognized academic/experimental psychology, focusing on its origin amounts to a consideration of the origin of experimental psychology. This entails two separate subquestions:

1. Why was the first experimental psychology an epistemological system, as opposed to an action or combined system?
2. Why did experimental psychology begin in Germany, as opposed to such countries as France, Great Britain, or the United states?

The first question requires reference to the presystemic or intellectual roots of experimental psychology: What was the nature of the presystemic phase of modern psychological history? The second question requires an analysis of the possible pragmatic or sociological roots of structuralism. The presystemic roots are presented first, followed by a discussion of the pragmatic roots. A final synthesis section will put the historical antecedents of structuralism in analytical perspective.

Presystemic Roots: Psychology During the Presystemic Phase

Prior to the twentieth century, the boundary lines between the various scientific disciplines, as well as those between science and philosophy in general, were not distinct. For example, Helmholtz can be classified as a physicist, a physiologist, or a psychologist, although he always considered himself a physicist. Wundt was both a philosopher and a physiologist, in addition to being a self-proclaimed psychologist. Thus it can be appreciated that an implicit focus on psychological phenomena already existed in pretwentieth century science and philosophy, so that other prior academic/intellectual disciplines served as the natural roots of structuralism. Specifically, these were the three p's: philosophy, physiology, and physics. Experimental psychology, in the form of structuralism, can be regarded as the inevitable by-product of the three-way synthesis of mental philosophy, experimental physiology, and sensory psychophysics. The presystemic roots can be specified even more precisely: (1) British mental philosophy (British empiricism or associationism), (2) German experimental physiology, and (3) German sensory psychophysics.

Two interrelated intellectual themes or questions set the stage for the eventual appearance of experimental psychology in the context of the three presystemic roots: (1) What is the nature of man? (2) How does man acquire knowledge? Each of these questions ultimately is philosophical in nature. Each, however, can be addressed empirically, via the scientific disciplines of physics and physiology, in the context of certain philosophical resolutions of the questions. Seventeenth century Cartesian philosophy (Descartes often is referred to as the key figure in the transition between medieval and modern philosophy) made each question at least partially empirical in nature, and British empiricism made both questions completely empirical. We begin the discussion with the philosophical roots.

PHILOSOPHICAL ROOTS

CARTESIAN PHILOSOPHY. René Descartes (1596–1650) was the first great, if not prototypical, rationalist of the modern era of epistemological philosophy. He espoused the doctrine of innate ideas and resolved the mind–body problem in terms of an interactionist dualism: Both mind and body exist and functionally interact with, or influence, each other. Interactionist dualism often is called Cartesian dualism. Descartes even postulated the exact physiological locus of mind–body interaction to be the pineal gland, primarily because to his knowledge it was the only unduplicated structure in the brain. The primary relevance of Descartes' ideas for experimental psychology derives from his treatment of the nature of man. Descartes assigned fundamentally different metaphysical properties to body and to mind, with far-reaching consequences.

Descartes, unlike his contemporaries, had an intimate knowledge of physiology, and he regarded man's body and bodily processes as real-space and real-time entities in the natural universe, subject to physical, causal laws and mechanical forces. In effect, Descartes took an essentially *mechanistic* or *materialistic* approach to the corporeal aspects of man. Man's body was a machine or physical system—composed of receptor, neuronal, and muscle systems—responsive to external stimulation. Descartes' description of this system—his physiology—in retrospect was fanciful, but it established the principle that man's overt bodily movements and the contents of conscious experience, including sensation and perception, were due to external stimulation and amounted to empirical phenomena. Descartes' conception of bodily movements as reflexes foreshadowed behaviorism. His conception of sense experience as a physiological event led to structuralism—the sense organs, nervous system, and the brain became legitimate objects of scientific analysis and made experimental physiology a necessary component in the overall understanding of man's nature.

Descartes' conception of the mind (that is, of higher order cognitive or mental events) was transcendental, in the medieval tradition. Mind was still beyond the bounds of the natural universe and was considered an autonomous phenomenon, subject only to philosophical/metaphysical analysis. This accounted for his rationalism and his doctrine of innate ideas. It required later French materialists, such as LaMettrie and Cabanis, and the British empiricists to make cognitive events physically and experientially sourced events, subject to scientific investigation.

BRITISH EMPIRICISM. The British school of mental philosophy, known as British empiricism or associationism, began in the late sixteenth century under Thomas Hobbes and extended up to the end of the nineteenth century under Alexander Bain and Herbert Spencer. Philosophers associated with this school included Thomas Hobbes,

John Locke, Bishop George Berkeley, David Hume, David Hartley, James Mill, John Stuart Mill, Alexander Bain, and Herbert Spencer. The school was multifaceted, and its influence was all-pervasive. Over this 300-year period, the basic concepts of the school evolved and were transformed. In the early years the school was basically an epistemological system, and in later years it amounted to a surrogate psychological/cognitive system. British empiricism not only served as the explicit philosophical progenitor of structuralism, but also as a philosophical precursor of functionalism and behaviorism.

The relevance of British empiricism for experimental psychology derives from its conception of how man acquires knowledge. As the name of the school implies, sense experience is the only recognized source of knowledge. Locke's concept of *tabula rasa* epitomizes this approach. The human mind is regarded as a blank slate or tablet at birth, which can only be filled by information coming in through the various sensory modalities. Locke's distinction between primary (physical) and secondary (psychological) qualities antedated the structuralist's mediate experience–immediate experience dichotomy. Primary qualities exist in the external, physical stimulus objects themselves; secondary qualities only exist in the consciousness of man. As a gross oversimplification, the British empiricists divided the elements of consciousness into (1) sensations, senses, or sense impressions, and (2) ideas. The external world gives rise immediately to simple sense impressions. The mind then operates on these to form simple ideas. Finally, complex ideas are constructed from simple ideas through association. The operational and conceptual aspects of association have already been described in the context of the "how" question.

It would not be incorrect to state that Wundt and the structuralists brought British empiricism into the laboratory.

PHYSIOLOGICAL ROOTS

The physiological roots gave empirical substance to the Cartesian concept of the human body as a physical entity. They also delineated the possible physiological mechanisms and processes through which knowledge or experience in the British empirical sense was derived. Nineteenth century experimental physiology successfully resolved the physiological basis of man's experience—and actions—at the neuronal level. Thus the history of nineteenth century experimental physiology is characterized by monumental developments with respect to (1) the essential structure and function of the external receptors or sense organs, especially the visual and auditory ones; (2) the nature and speed of neuronal conduction; and (3) the existence of various projection areas of the brain associated with localization of function.

GERMAN EXPERIMENTAL PHYSIOLOGY. The establishment of experimental physiology as an academic discipline antedated that of experimental psychology by approximately 50 years, and provides an interesting parallel to the later founding of structuralism. Experimental physiology became separated from the study of medicine in the 1830s under the aegis of Johannes Müller, who founded the first institute of experimental physiology, and assumed the first professorship in physiology, at the University of Berlin. Müller wrote the classic text in physiology of his time, *Handbuch der Physiologie des Menschen*, and is most famous for his formalization of the doctrine of specific nerve energy. His students included Émile du Bois-Reymond and Hermann von Helmholtz, the latter usually credited with being the greatest research scientist of the nineteenth century. Müller's steadfast adherence to a vitalist conception of physiology, as opposed to a mechanistic conception favored by his students, reminds one of Wundt's refusal to broaden structuralism to accommodate the more general psychological interests of his students. (Incidentally Wundt spent a few months in 1855 studying at Müller's institute.)

THE NEURONAL BASIS OF THE SENSING AND PERCEIVING ORGANISM. The achievements of nineteenth century experimental physiology are summarized in the following list.

1. The Bell–Magendie law. The Englishman Bell in 1811 and the Frenchman Magendie in 1822 independently discovered that the dorsal roots of the spinal cord are sensory in function, whereas the ventral roots are motor in function. This discovery was important because it demonstrated that different structural/neuronal correlates existed for different mental/psychological functions.

2. Neuronal conduction. Although Galvani demonstrated in 1791 that neuronal conduction is electrical in nature, it was not until 1850 that the German physiologist Helmholtz actually measured the speed of neuronal conduction. Prior to Helmholtz, no one had attempted to quantify the speed of neuronal conduction for two interrelated reasons. (a) It simply was assumed that the speed of neuronal conduction approximated or even exceeded the speed of light—probably as a negative carry-over from the classic assumption that the mind or soul acted instantaneously on the body. (b) Neuronal conduction at such a speed could not be measured by the then-available technology. Helmholtz simply, but ingeniously, stimulated an isolated leg muscle of a frog from different distances on the limb and through subtraction estimated the speed of conduction to be about 90 feet (30 meters) per second. Later research showed that the speed of neuronal

conduction is a function of the diameter of the nerve and other factors; however, the crucial fact that neuronal conduction is a finite and time-dependent event had been amply demonstrated.

3. Neuronal transmission. By 1891, a Spanish histologist, Santiago Ramón y Cajal, was able to put together the elements of a synaptic theory of neuronal transmission. A given neuronal tract is really a sequence of functionally and anatomically distinct nerve cells, called neurons, and neuronal transmission is synaptic in the sense that electrical activity must be repropagated at the synaptic junction between successive nerve cells.

4. Doctrine of specific nerve energy. Johannes Müller formalized the notion that the characteristic sensation, or sense experience, associated with a given physical stimulus, such as light or sound wave, is attributable to the specific type of nerve that is stimulated, not to any special property of the physical stimulus itself.For instance, we experience a visual sensation when the optic nerve is stimulated, regardless of the physical stimulus involved (light, pressure, acid, etc.). Müller's doctrine implies that each type of sensory nerve is special or different, each with its own kind of energy. Later physiologists preferred to correlate the sensation characteristic of a given physical stimulus with the specific brain projection area that ultimately is stimulated. Nevertheless Müller established the basic principle that the qualitative content of a given sensory experience is dependent on the underlying neurology involved.

5. Doctrine of specific fiber or receptor energy. This is a logical extension of item 4 and is primarily due to Helmholtz. The doctrine states that the visual and auditory sense organs (the eyes and ears) contain different types of receptors that are maximally responsive to different kinds of physical stimulation. This is implicit in the Young–Helmholtz theory of color vision and Helmholtz's theory of pitch perception. The Young–Helmholtz theory describes the differential color receptors as three types of cones: red, blue, and green. The differential pitch receptors were assumed to be differently tuned hair cells in the cochlea of the inner ear.

6. Theories of sensation. The doctrine of specific receptor energy amounted to a theory of sensation. Nineteenth century physiological research established the essential nature of the sense organ or receptor associated with each type of sensory modality. Visual, auditory, olfactory, gustatory, tactile, and temperature receptors were anatomically isolated and correlated with specific attributes of the corresponding external physical stimulus. The physiological or neuronal basis of the elementary sensations was thus established long before structuralists attempted to measure the content of the sensations themselves, as

the fundamental datum of an experimental psychology.

7. Stimulus intensity coding. The doctrine of specific nerve energy only encompasses the qualitative aspect of sensory experience, such as color or pitch. The quantitative aspect of sensory experience, such as brightness or loudness, must be accounted for by some other neuronal mechanism. Since neuronal transmission is all-or-none in the context of the synaptic theory, stimulus intensity coding is a problem. All-or-none transmission refers to the fact that the individual neuron fires at a fixed rate as long as the proximal stimulus intensity is above the absolute threshold of the neuron, regardless of the specific intensity of the proximal stimulus. The English physiologist Edgar Adrian postulated that the intensity of the external physical stimulus is represented by the total number of neurons that are activated and by the frequency of firing associated with each neuron. The more intense the physical stimulus, the greater the number of neurons that are stimulated and the greater frequency of firing of the individual neurons involved. The latter is related to the absolute and relative refractory periods of a depolarized neuron.

8. Localization of function in the brain. Descartes established the brain as the principal organ of the body in his physiology. The rather fanciful notions of faculty psychology and phrenology also helped to strengthen the belief that specific parts of the brain underlie or are correlated with specific psychological functions. Pierre Flourens, a French physiologist, performed ablation or extirpation (surgical excision, or lesion) studies on pigeon brains in 1820 and found limited evidence for localization of function. Because of this, Flourens preferred to believe that the brain acted as a whole. It was not until 1861 that Paul Broca, a French surgeon, localized a motor speech area in the third convolution of the left frontal lobe of an institutionalized aphasic. Gustav Fritsch and Eduard Hitzig, both German physiologists, were able to investigate localization of function in brain-damaged soldiers during the Franco-Prussian War. In 1870, they isolated the motor projection area of the dog using both extirpation and direct electrical stimulation techniques. David Ferrier, a Scottish physiologist, isolated the sensory area of the monkey in 1876. Later research demonstrated that brain functions were organized both in a mass action or holistic manner as well as in a localization-of-function format. Nevertheless the basic fact that psychological functions and/or experience possessed some definitive form of representation in the brain had been established.

PSYCHOPHYSICAL ROOTS

Knowledge of the physical properties of light, sound, and other types of stimuli was necessary to conduct the nineteenth century experimental physiological investigations of the various sensory systems. Such knowledge concerning the nature of an external physical stimulus is a property of physics or of mediate experience in the language of structuralism. In the seventeenth century, Galileo investigated some of the basic properties of both light and sound; in the late seventeenth century, Isaac Newton, the great English physicist, broke white light down into its component wavelengths, or colors, by a prism; and in the mid-nineteenth century, Georg Ohm, a German physicist, applied Fourier analysis to complex sound waves.

Descartes had postulated that the sensory systems were physical entities. The British empiricists had professed that the sensory systems were the only source of knowledge. Nineteenth century experimental physiology had revealed the neuronal basis of such systems. Only one more intellectual component was necessary for the advent of a structuralist psychology: empirical investigation of the exact relationship existing between a specific external physical stimulus and the sensory experience or *psychological reaction* it created in the sensing, perceiving organism. This was done in the early to mid-nineteenth century at Leipzig by two German scientists—Ernst Weber, a physiologist, and Gustav Fechner, a physicist with medical training.

The relationship existing between the physical stimulus and its corresponding psychological sensation is called a *psychophysical relation*, and this area of investigation is termed *psychophysics. Psycho* refers to the sensory or psychological component; *physics* refers to the external stimulus component. In effect, Weber and Fechner founded German sensory psychophysics which, because of the psychological nature of the dependent variable, many historians of psychology regard as the first true experimental psychology. Psychophysics continues today as a technical subarea of sensory psychology. The classic psychophysical methods, either originated or systematized by Fechner, constitute a significant component of the methodology of the contemporary psychologist. Remember that such cannot be said of structuralism and its methodology!

GERMAN SENSORY PSYCHOPHYSICS. Psychophysical research focused on the physical attribute of intensity because this property of a stimulus varies continuously and is easily quantified. The sensory modalities most often involved in the study of psychological reactions to intensity changes are the tactile and kinesthetic (muscle) senses. A small weight can be placed on the open hand of a subject (tactile sense) or the subject can be required to lift a weight with the hand (tactile sense plus kinesthetic sense). The lightness or heaviness of the weight represents intensity, unconfounded by any qualitative sensation. A blindfolded subject can make judgments with respect to (1) the presence or absence of a weight or (2) the discriminability of two weights, that is, whether they are the same or different. The first kind of judgment generates the notion of an "absolute threshold," and the second the notion of a "difference threshold" or "just noticeable difference." The absolute threshold is the minimal physical stimulus intensity that can be sensed by a subject along some stimulus dimension such as light, sound, or weight. The just noticeable difference is the minimal amount of physical stimulus intensity change that must occur before a subject can experience or sense a change in magnitude along some stimulus dimension.

In his pioneering research on weight discrimination, Weber expressed the just noticeable difference for a given weight as a function (or percentage) of the magnitude of the weight—the so-called Weber ratio. He found that this ratio remains constant as the magnitude of the weight varies. Fechner later formalized this relationship in terms of an equation, which he called the Weber law:

$$\frac{\Delta I}{I} = C$$

where I is the magnitude of the standard or original weight, ΔI is the just noticeable difference, and C is a constant. Later research showed that (1) the value of C varied with the sensory modality tested, with vision being the most sensitive modality, by virtue of having the lowest value of C; and (2) the law only holds for stimuli of medium intensity.

Fechner derived his basic psychophysical function for stimulus intensity coding from the Weber law:

$$S = K \log I$$

where S is the sensed or psychological intensity of the stimulus, I is the physical intensity of the stimulus, and K is a slope constant of proportionality. This equation can be interpreted in various ways:

1. Psychological sensation grows as the log of physical intensity.
2. To add a unit of sensation, it is necessary to multiply the stimulus energy by a constant amount.
3. Psychological sensation grows arithmetically as the physical stimulus grows geometrically.

4. Equal additions on the sensory scale correspond to equal ratios on the physical scale.

Weber is also known for his work on the two-point cutaneous threshold. A blindfolded subject is stimulated by the two tips of a compass-like device on a certain area of the skin. Whether the subject in fact senses two points, as opposed to one, depends on the distance between the tips and which part of the body is being stimulated. The two-point threshold is the minimum physical distance between the tips at which the two points can be detected by the subject. Distances within this minimum are reported as one point, and there is also a region of uncertainty in which the subject cannot definitively detect one or two points. The significance of this work can be appreciated if the structuralist terminology of mediate and immediate experience is used. When the physical distance between the two tips is within the threshold region, there is a discrepancy between mediate and immediate experience.

The total amount of psychological work generated by Fechner was voluminous. His basic findings and his methodology—the three classic psychophysical methods of limits, constant stimuli, and adjustment—were published in his *Elemente der Psychophysik* in 1860. This book greatly impressed Wundt, and he credited Fechner with the first truly experimental psychological research in history. Fechner and Wundt were associates at Leipzig and cross-fertilized each other's research efforts.

Fechner was just as much a mystic and philosopher as he was a psychophysicist. He always believed that psychophysics represented the quantitative relationship existing between mind and body. Fechner spent his later years attempting to apply psychophysical methods to the study of esthetics for the purpose of creating an experimental science of esthetics.

Pragmatic Roots

The pragmatic roots encompass the social factors responsible for the initial appearance of structuralism in Germany, rather than in such other countries as France, Great Britain, and the United States. Two sociologists, Joseph Ben-David and Randall Collins, have constructed a model of the social factors required for the transformation of psychology from a strictly intellectual notion to that of a bona fide academic profession and have applied it to these four countries. Implicit in the following analysis is the assumption that any of these countries possessed the *intellectual* potential to found a scientific psychology, but only Germany fulfilled the minimal set of *social* conditions necessary for the creation of an academic discipline of experimental psychology.

THE BEN-DAVID/COLLINS MODEL

The model assumes that the beginning of experimental psychology was occasioned by the sociological mechanism of role hybridization. Specifically, experimental psychology represents the merger of the roles of philosopher and physiologist. A combination of three social factors is postulated as necessary for this role hybridization to occur:

1. An academic, as opposed to amateur, status for both philosophers and physiologists.
2. A better competitive situation in philosophy than in physiology, encouraging the mobility of individuals and methods into philosophy from physiology.
3. An academic standing of philosophy below that of physiology, requiring the physiologist to maintain scientific status by applying empirical methods to the materials and problems of philosophy.

The first condition translates into university status, with its incumbent professional specialization, departmental structure, and doctoral-degree-granting power, for both philosophy and physiology. The second condition means that better job opportunities, such as more faculty position openings, greater chance for advancement, and/or higher salary levels, exist for philosophers than for physiologists. The final condition implies that the prestige associated with being a physiologist is greater than that of a philosopher.

APPLICATION OF THE MODEL

Ben-David and Collins concluded that during the 1870s only Germany fulfilled all three conditions. One of the conditions, academic status, was partially fulfilled in France. Great Britain and the United States fulfilled none of the conditions.

GERMANY. By 1870, Germany had evolved a codified, institutionalized, professional graduate school system and university structure such that professional recognition and certification as a philosopher or physiologist could come only from identification and association with this system/structure. In this context, recall that Wundt was a trained physiologist and occupied junior-level faculty positions at Heidelberg for some 17 years (1857–1874). The competitive situation was such that he could not get appointed to a full professorial chair in physiology, so he accepted a full professorship in philosophy at Zurich in 1874 and moved to an analogous position at Leipzig the following year. At Leipzig, Wundt established the first institution-alized experimental psychological laboratory, thereby applying his experimental physiological training to the materials and problems of philosophy—specifically, the nature of conscious experience, or knowledge, as originally defined by the British empiricists. To retain the prestige associated with experimental physiology when he was appointed to a chair in philosophy, Wundt applied the methodology of his original profession, physiology, to the problems/questions of his new profession, philosophy, and created the role hybrid of ex-perimental psychologist.

FRANCE. During the 1870s in France, a central intellectual elite existed whose status was dependent on a diffuse evaluation of ex-cellence rather than on regular university appointments and special-ized professional attainment. This elite consisted of a reference group of relatively nonspecialized intellectuals and philosophers. The lines of demarcation between disciplines were unclear, precluding any se-rious role conflicts among people of ideas. Prestige adhered to and resided in the individual, not the discipline; the person appointed to a chair determined the nature of the chair. In short, the French system was suited to absorbing intellectual innovations by specific individ-uals, but was not suited to fostering movements attempting to create a new discipline.

GREAT BRITAIN. According to Ben-David and Collins, the Brit-ish university system was a shambles in the 1870s. It amounted to an upper-class intellectual backwater. A person could only achieve prom-inence in science or philosophy as an amateur, and the first-rate British scientists and philosophers existed outside of the university system. The situation in Great Britain is described in greater detail in Chapter 3 in the context of the historical antecedents of functionalism.

UNITED STATES. As of 1870, the United States possessed a few religiously oriented schools. These institutions were too small for professional specialization, and there were no facilities for research. The extant psychology was moralistic in nature and a variant of the eighteenth century Scottish school of philosophy, characterized by associationism and an emphasis on mental capacities or faculties—so-called faculty psychology. A vigorous development of experimental psychology, derivative of the German movement, was not possible until the founding of the first graduate schools in 1876.

A Final Synthesis

Remember that structuralism amounted to the systematic investigation of the content of conscious experience by means of introspection. The object of study, conscious experience, came from philosophy; the methodology, introspection, came from experimental physiology. Prior to the formal founding of structuralism by Wundt, much philosophical theorizing, as well as laboratory experimentation, occurred, which could be characterized as psychological in nature. This included the Cartesian conception of the nature of man, the British empiricist approach to knowledge and experience, nineteenth century experimental neurophysiology, and sensory psychophysics. But the initial self-conscious application of the scientific method to the investigation of mental phenomena was occasioned by certain social conditions in Germany during which the roles of experimental physiologist and philosopher fused in the person of Wilhelm Wundt, yielding the role hybrid of experimental psychologist.

Bibliography

Ben-David, J., and Collins, R. Social factors in the origin of a new science: The case of psychology. *American Sociological Review*, 1966, 31, 451–465.

Fechner, G.T. *Elemente der Psychophysik*. Leipzig: Breitkopf & Härtel, 1860. (*Elements of Psychophysics*, 2 vols. New York: Holt, Rinehart, & Winston, 1966.)

Müller, J. *Handbuch der Physiologie des Menschen*, 3 vols. Coblenz: Hölscher, 1833–1840. (*Elements of Physiology*, 2 vols. London: Taylor & Walton, 1842.)

Titchener, E.B. *Experimental Psychology: A Manual of Laboratory Practice*, 2 vols. New York: Macmillan, 1901, 1905.

Titchener, E.B. *A Text-book of Psychology*. New York: Macmillan, 1910.

Wundt, W.M. *Grundzüge der physiologischen Psychologie*. Leipzig: Engelmann, 1873–1874. (*Principles of Physiological Psychology*. London: Swan Sonnenschein, 1904.)

3

Functionalism

Introduction

Functionalism was the primary competitor of Titchenerian structuralism in the United States for at least two decades, approximately 1892 to 1912. However, its historical importance basically stems from the fact that it served as a transitional school between structuralism and behaviorism. Functionalistic psychology contains both structuralistic and behavioristic elements and has acted as a necessary conceptual link between Titchener's and Watson's brands of psychology.

Functionalism is the most loosely formulated classical school of experimental psychology. It is more of a generalized attitude than a self-conscious, prescriptive system. Functionalism has no definitive founder, no monolithic set of tenets common to every professed functionalist, and no particular theoretical axe to grind. Functionalism is a low-key, tolerant approach to psychology. It is an open-ended and eclectic system in which practically any problem or issue can be regarded as psychological in nature or as possessing a psychological component. It is inherently optimistic, in the sense that any psychological problem or issue is assumed to admit of a final experimental resolution. Functionalism did not criticize structuralism at a conceptual level; rather it simply found the structuralist program and goals to be sterile and lacking in any real utility. In many respects, functionalism is a common-sense psychology and approximates the layman's conception of what a psychology is or should be. Functionalism still possesses a certain charm. Although its ultimate goals and orientation have been absorbed by behaviorism, any contemporary experimental psychologist with an "open mind," working close to the data in a parametric framework, can call himself/herself a functionalist.

The origin of functionalism can be related to various nineteenth century intellectual developments in England, such as the Darwinian theory of evolution and Galton's work on individual differences and so-called mental testing. Functionalism, however, is basically indigenous to America where such philosopher–psychologists as William James and John Dewey fostered a pragmatic/utilitarian attitude toward life and philosophy. Although most American universities, with the exception of Cornell, were functionalistic in orientation to some degree at the turn of the century, two schools stand out as the primary centers of functionalistic thought and research: the University of Chicago, under John Dewey, James Angell, and Harvey Carr; and Columbia University, under James McKeen Cattell, Robert Sessions Woodworth, and Edward L. Thorndike. Clark University, under G. Stanley Hall, and Yale University, under George Ladd and Edward Scripture, also should be given honorable mention as hotbeds of functionalism. Carr's version of functionalism is usually regarded as most representative of functionalism in its final form, and our discussion focuses on Carr's brand of functionalism as a transitional psychology between structuralism and behaviorism.

Object of Study; Basic Subject Matter

Nothing illustrates the hybrid nature of functionalism better than its purported subject matter. Functionalism focused on the mind, not its content or structure, but its dynamics or functioning. The object of study for functionalism was the operations and functions of consciousness. The goal of the functionalist program amounted to an abstraction of the mind in terms of various mental activities. Mental activity refers to such processes as thinking, feeling, imagining, and perceiving. Each of these processes is a distinct category of mental activity of which the individual organism is aware and which can serve as the object of introspective report. Like the structuralist, the functionalist focused on mental events; unlike the structuralist, the functionalist observed what the mind was doing, or the activities subsumed by consciousness.

The functionalist was not interested in conscious activity as an end in itself. Mind was the primary instrument allowing the individual organism to adapt to its environment. The functionalist fundamentally was interested in the actual working of consciousness as it guides and directs the individual in adjusting to the environment. This focus on the instrumental, adaptive function of mind made the functionalist an implicit behaviorist. What is organismic adaptation or adjustment to the environment, if not behavior? In effect, functionalism analyzed conscious processes as the antecedent conditions of overt behavior. Recall that the structuralist's analysis of mental contents, particularly sensations, required reference to an external reference point: the external physical stimulus or mediate experience. The functionalist's analysis of mental activities also requires reference to an external reference point—the consequences of mental activity, in an adaptation framework. Another term for this concept is response output or behavior.

Note the reference to the term "environment" in the preceding paragraph. The concept of an external environment served as another direct link to behaviorism. Another label for environment is stimulus situation. Carr actually used the terms stimulus and response, the two fundamental building blocks or units of analysis of classical Watsonian behaviorism. Functionalism basically was interested in the mind as the intermediary between stimulus and response events. The specific aspect of the organism which allowed it to adjust to a specific stimulus situation was consciousness. All that Watson did to create classical behaviorism was to remove any reference to this mental intermediary. Classical behaviorism focused an overt behavior as a direct function of the environmental input. Later behaviorists returned to the use of mediators between the stimulus and response terms. The mediators were, however, specified in physiological or strictly psychologically mechanistic language.

The functionalist concern for organismic adaptation stemmed from Darwin's evolutionary theory. Because of this, functionalism was biologically, rather than physiologically, oriented. Evolution is a theory of biological adaptation. Functionalism merely extended the notion to a psychological level. The proper object of study of psychology should be psychological adaptation, or how the organism adapts to changes and pressures in the stimulus environment. Functionalism implicitly was carving out organismic behavior, or the relationship between overt behavior and the environmental input, as the specific class of empirical phenomena that should serve as the unique focus of attention of a science of psychology.

Functionalistic psychology was inherently practical or applied. The constant emphasis on working, function, and adaptation made the organism a real-time and real-space entity. Functionalist study of consciousness, unlike that of structuralism, was not divorced from its actual, day-to-day functioning. In many ways, functionalistic writing amounted to sermonizing. The *how*, *what*, and *why* of consciousness had to be conceptualized in a pragmatic or utilitarian framework. True psychology, it was assumed, concerned activity and function, not content and structure.

In retrospect, Carr's general account of organismic or psychological adaptation seems surprisingly contemporary. His two primary theoretical mechanisms for describing adaptation were (1) the reflex arc concept and (2) the notion of a motivational sequence. The reflex arc concept is merely a logical extension of the age-old notion of reflex, but Carr interpreted it in a holistic adaptation context. The notion of a motivational sequence is quite similar to Clark Hull's analytical description of instrumental response activity or conditioning: stimulus situation ◊ drive or motive ◊ instrumental response activity ◊ incentive ◊ consummatory activity ◊ drive or motive reduction. (Hull was a behaviorist who dominated learning theory from the late 1930s to the early 1950s.) The notion of a motivational sequence still serves as one of the primary theoretical approaches to the concept of motivation.

Method of Study; Permissible Methodology

Permissible methodology was not a key analytical dimension in the context of functionalism. Despite this fact, the functionalists were methodologically sophisticated and realized the limitations and problems associated with specific experimental techniques. Functionalists attempted to generate data on mental activities, and accepted the fact that there was no one monolithic or ideal way to do this.

Carr made a fundamental distinction between objective and subjective investigation of mental activity. Objective investigation entails the inference of the mental activities of a person X through the observation of person X's overt behavior by another person Y. Subjective investigation amounts to the self-report of a person X's mental activities by person X. The former procedure is analogous to physical experimentation; the latter is equivalent to introspection. Carr realized that the content of introspective report is beyond the bounds of a reliability and/or validity assessment and that introspection was not applicable to animals, children, and members of the abnormal population. He also accepted all the criticisms that had been leveled at the structuralist brand of introspection.

The ultimate source of a piece of data relating to a mental event is irrelevant for functionalists. They accepted introspective reports *per se*, introspective reports generated while the subject performed some experimental task (such as memorizing a list of words or reacting to a stimulus as in a reaction time experiment), as well as data from such sources as anthropological reports, literature, and art. They even used lesion/ablation techniques to correlate mental activity with underlying neurology and physiology, and photographs of eye movements were used to make inferences about the mental activity underlying perception.

Implicit in this discussion is the fact that, in most cases, the functionalist was observing and recording overt behavior, such as reaction time, eye movements, and verbal responses, or the products of overt behavior, such as art and literature. All that Watson had to do to transform functionalist data into behavioristic data was to strip it of its mental trappings. The conceptual eyeglasses of the functionalists made them "see" mental activities or the results of mental activities; the conceptual eyeglasses of the behaviorists made them "see" physical activity, devoid of any mental tag or any status as a mental event marker.

Origin; Specific Historical Antecedents

Since functionalism was a rather heterogeneous collection of various subapproaches to pyschology and did not have an explicit, formal founding, it is arbitrary how one conceptualizes its origin and specific historical antecedents. The basic problem is one of distinguishing between essentially prefunctionalistic and immanently functionalistic work and thought such that the prefunctionalistic developments can be regarded as specific historical antecedents. We need a criterion for prefunctionalistic developments, and a number of different alternatives present themselves.

1. The first criterion would be a geographical one: the Atlantic Ocean. Any British work and thought would be prefunctionalistic, and any American work and thought would be functionalistic.

2. A second criterion would be the primary professional identi-

fication of the historical figure contributing to functionalism. By this criterion, the contributions of the philosopher–psychologists, William James and John Dewey, would be classified as prefunctionalistic in nature because they primarily regarded themselves as philosophers.

3. A third criterion would make the onset of functionalistic work and thought coincident with the ascendence of the four primary schools associated with functionalism. Ascendence can be defined operationally as the physical arrival of the first functionally oriented figure associated with the school and/or establishment of the psychological laboratory at the school. For example, Hall arrived and founded a laboratory at Clark in 1889; Cattell arrived and founded a laboratory at Columbia in 1891; Ladd founded a laboratory at Yale in 1892, although he had been there since l881; and Angell arrived at Chicago in 1894, although the laboratory was established in 1892.

4. A fourth criterion would be a combined temporal and self-identification one—namely, that point by which functionalism definitively had achieved a self-conscious identification as an active competitor of structuralism. According to this criterion, 1898–1903 would be the approximate dividing line between prefunctionalistic and functionalistic developments because in this period (a) Titchener coined the term functionalism and contrasted it with structuralism and (b) Angell formally reacted to Titchener's dichotomy.

5. A final criterion would be the appearance of functionalism in its fully developed form, an event coincident with Carr's publication of *Psychology* in 1925 and his ascendency to the chairmanship at Chicago in 1926.

The first criterion is too lax; the fifth criterion is too strict; the third criterion is too unwieldy. Either the second or fourth criterion would be acceptable at a conceptual level. However, we shall adopt the second criterion because the fourth one assigns most of the work and thought associated with the four schools during the decade of the 1890s to the prefunctionalistic phase. In the context of the professional identification criterion, functionalism can be viewed as having two classes of historical antecedents: (1) various nineteenth century intellectual developments in England and (2) the philosophical/psychological contributions of William James and John Dewey.

British Antecedents of Functionalism

The British antecedents include (1) Charles Darwin's theory of evolution, (2) the multifaceted work of Francis Galton, and (3) contributions to animal psychology by George Romanes and C. Lloyd Morgan.

CHARLES DARWIN'S THEORY OF EVOLUTION

In 1859 the English biologist Charles Darwin (1809–1882) published *The Origin of Species by Means of Natural Selection*, in which he formally stated his doctrine of evolution: it was a combined theory of (1) variation, (2) natural selection, and (3) survival of the fittest. Darwin postulated that (1) the members of a given species vary in their characteristics and (2) the natural environment selects certain values or combinations of the characteristics, such that (3) those particular members of a species exhibiting the most adaptable, or selected, characteristics have the highest probability of survival. In this way, the offspring of each succeeding generation gradually changes, and new species slowly evolve from prior species. Darwin formalized the applicability of the evolutionary doctrine to the origin of man in his *The Descent of Man*, published in 1871.

Although the concept of evolution was not original with Darwin, he was the first person to both supplement the doctrine with actual empirical data and elaborate on its extraordinary implications. Much of his data was obtained on a six-year trip to various South Sea islands where he was able to observe the adaptation of isolated plant and animal life to the environment. Darwin even went so far as to accumulate empirical data on the relationship existing between the expression of emotion in man and animals. Darwin's theory of evolution stimulated his cousin, Francis Galton, to embark on his numerous and wide-ranging psychological investigations. Darwin's evolutionary doctrine ranks with the Copernican and Newtonian revolutions in changing man's fundamental conception of himself and of his place in the universe. We shall limit our discussion to the strictly psychological implications and consequences of evolution.

PSYCHOLOGICAL RELEVANCY OF THE EVOLUTIONARY DOCTRINE. The psychological relevancy of the evolutionary doctrine includes the following:

1. Man officially became a part of nature or the natural universe.
2. The basic continuity between man and the animal was restored, reversing the fundamental Cartesian dichotomy between the two.

3. Because Darwin was a dualist, the animal–human continuity was assumed to exist at both the physical level of body and physiology, as well as at the mental level of conscious processes and activity.

4. The basic issue of the existence of animal consciousness was opened up. The immediate effect of the restoration of the continuity was to make the animal more like the man rather than to make the man more like the animal. It required the later appearance of classical behaviorism to banish consciousness as a basic comparative reference point and make the animal the model of man.

5. Study of animal morphology and activity became relevant for understanding man, and comparative psychology began to flourish.

6. The importance of variation made the observation and measurement of individual differences in man a matter of empirical concern.

7. Biological adaptation was extended to the psychological level, thereby establishing the functional utility of an organism's consciousness (mental activities).

8. The nature versus nurture issue became a cornerstone of psychological research and debate.

9. Observation and recording of overt activity, or behavior, became indispensable for a psychological understanding of man.

These nine implications/consequences of Darwin's evolutionary theory either served as necessary preconditions for the eventual development of functionalistic doctrine or operated as actual empirical themes that extended throughout the functionalist program.

THE WORK OF FRANCIS GALTON

Francis Galton (1822–1911) was a brilliant Englishman of independent means with an undergraduate degree in mathematics and some medical training. He made significant empirical contributions in many areas, including geography, anthropology, meteorology, and criminology, besides conducting investigations that now would be called psychological in nature. His specific psychological contributions included the following.

1. Impressed by Darwin's doctrine of evolution, Galton conducted a series of studies on the hereditary basis of general mental ability. In his classic *Hereditary Genius*, published in 1869, Galton demonstrated that genius or accomplishment in any one of the professions—law, science, medicine, and the like—tended to follow family lines. He concluded that heredity, as opposed to the environment,

was primarily responsible for the distribution of genius in the general population. Unfortunately, Galton preselected his data from upper-class English families, so that heredity was confounded with a benign environment, and neglected the working-class elements of English society whose family connections allowed accomplishment only in business and commerce. In retrospect, Galton should be credited with making the nature versus nurture issue an empirical one and making the notion of individual differences in ability an accepted and acceptable cultural phenomenon.

2. Galton measured mental capacity or intelligence, operationally defined in terms of certain sensory and motor tests. He established an anthropometric laboratory at the International Health Exhibition in London in 1884, which was transferred later to the South Kensington Museum. (James McKeen Cattell served as one of his assistants at the museum.) In 1903, Galton organized a project to measure intelligence and other abilities in English school children.

3. Galton invented the word association technique to study individual differences in associability, with himself as the initial subject. He studied both the logical relationship existing among the responses and the ultimate source of the responses. He discovered that repetition in the responses was primarily associated with events from childhood, while unique responses usually derived from relatively recent experience.

4. Galton studied mental imagery, primarily visual imagery, through the pioneering use of the questionnaire or survey technique. He was amazed to discover the existence of great individual variation in this phenomenon and the fact that many prominent scientists of his day were incapable of such imagery.

5. At a statistical level, Galton is associated with the first application of the Gaussian curve, or normal distribution curve, to mental traits, as well as being credited with creating different measures of variability for expressing individual differences. He also originated the concepts of bivariate frequency distribution or scatter plot, regression, and correlation, although the now-standard correlation coefficient formula was devised later by Karl Pearson.

Galton's concern for individual differences, his measurement of mental capacity, and his statistical tools were absorbed by American functionalistic psychology, especially by Hall at Clark University and Cattell at Columbia.

BRITISH COMPARATIVE PSYCHOLOGY

Although British comparative psychology dates from the early nineteenth century, the doctrine of evolution gave a new impetus to the study of animal behavior. For the first time, there were specific reasons for cataloguing the various skills and activities that different organisms on the phylogenetic scale could exhibit: (1) to determine to what degree a given type of animal possesses reason, consciousness, or the capacity to think; and (2) to determine to what degree this capacity extends down the phylogenetic ladder.

George Romanes (1848–1894) was the initial popularizer of animal observation and study. He was a personal friend of Darwin and, like all the British figures considered so far, was wealthy and did not have to work for a living. Romanes collected anecdotal reports on animal behavior and also performed quite credible research. He tended to "see" mind, consciousness, or intelligence in virtually every animal activity and was accused of being overly anthropomorphic in outlook.

C. Lloyd Morgan (1852–1936) was part naturalist and part experimentalist, who spent his entire professional career at University College, Bristol. He anticipated many of the concepts and research problems that later surfaced in Thorndike's work at Columbia. Morgan used the term "trial-and-error learning," preferred habit as an explanatory mechanism, and even employed the concept of reinforcement, which he viewed as a pleasure–pain principle. Morgan is remembered best for his censure of unrestrained anthropomorphism, which has come down to us as Morgan's canon: A given instance of behavior should be explained in terms of the simplest or lowest level mechanism possible.

The direct influence of British comparative psychology on American functionalism is evidenced not only by Thorndike's research at Columbia, but also by the fact that when John Watson was a student at Chicago under Angell, he already preferred to use animal subjects and was influenced by courses from the German biologist, Jacques Loeb. Loeb had resolved the question of the existence of animal consciousness in terms of associative memory: If an animal possessed associative memory, it had consciousness.

WHY FUNCTIONALISM DID NOT DEVELOP AS A SYSTEM IN ENGLAND

Since the empirical work of Darwin, Galton, Romanes, and Morgan was functionalistic in nature, it is legitimate to inquire why functionalism did not develop as a system in England. Recall from Chapter 2 that one of the prerequisites of a classical school of experimental psychology is that it be associated with an academic setting. None of the figures discussed in the context of British prefunctionalistic developments was an academic (they were amateurs in the sense discussed in Chapter 2), except for Morgan—and he moved into educational administration in 1910.

Prior to World War II, only three full chairs/professorships of psychology had been established in England: King's College, London (1906); University College, London (1928); and Cambridge (1931). A chair in psychology was not created at Oxford until 1947. An experimental psychology laboratory was founded at Cambridge in 1891 by Ward and at University College in 1897 by Sully, but these basically were seminal or symbolic efforts.

The Philosophical–Psychological Contributions of William James

William James (1842–1910) holds a unique position in the history of American psychology. Although he never studied psychology formally in Europe, he is considered by many to be America's greatest psychologist. Although he was an empiricist who disliked performing experiments himself, he is credited with establishing the first psychology laboratory in America, at Harvard. And although he profoundly influenced the course of development of psychology in America, his ultimate professional identification was that of philosophy. He was America's greatest philosopher during the last 20 years of his life.

James' only formal degree was in medicine, earned at Harvard, the only American institution of higher learning with which he ever was associated. In 1872, James taught a course in physiology at Harvard; and in 1875, he taught his first course in psychology at Harvard, on the relationship between physiology and psychology. Among James' students were four of the functionalists mentioned in the introduction: Hall, Angell, Thorndike, and Woodworth. The laboratory James established eventually was turned over to Münsterberg, a Wundt Ph.D., who had reacted against the master's strict structuralism. James was one of the charter members of the American Psychological Association, founded in 1892, as well as its president in 1894 and again in 1904.

James' profound influence on psychology derives from the fact that he was a great popularizer of the discipline as well as the author of the most successful psychology book ever written. James signed a contract with Henry Holt and Company in 1878 to write an introduction to psychology. It was 12 years before it was published, in 1890, as the two-volume *Principles of Psychology*. This book was a compendium of functionalist thought, in which James expressed his dislike of the Germanic structuralist approach and program. It contained James' classic descriptions of (1) consciousness as a stream, (2) habit as the flywheel of society, and (3) emotion as the derivative of an organism's initial physical/physiological response to a situation—the James–Lange theory of emotion. The book club to which my wife belongs recently read *Principles*; but it was read from the perspective of being an introduction to *contemporary* psychology, a fact that illustrates both the common-sense and layman orientation of functionalism and the cultural saliency which James' work still enjoys.

At a philosophical level, James was an implicit mind–body interactionist dualist and an avowed pragmatist, both of which positions found expression later in functionalism's focus on the utility value of consciousness in relation to the organism's adaptation to the environment. James was also a firm believer in determinism. However, paradoxically, he found it necessary to act as if his own behavior were free. Residues of this general attitude can be seen in functionalism's dual concern for nomothetic laws, applicable to a group of subjects or the statistical subject, and for individual differences: Although aspects of an organism are mechanistically determined, each organism in some sense is unique or a unique combination of physicochemical factors.

The Philosophical–Psychological Contributions of John Dewey

John Dewey (1859–1952) was basically a pragmatically oriented social philosopher who profoundly influenced education in America. He was the father of the progressive education movement, with its stress on education as life, learning by doing, and student-oriented instruction. These phrases sound familiar today, but they were distinctly novel at the turn of the century when knowledge of the classics was equated with the notion of a well-rounded education, learning was by rote memorization, and instruction was teacher-oriented.

Dewey obtained the Ph.D. degree in philosophy in 1884 from Johns Hopkins, where he did some studying under G. Stanley Hall and also worked in Hall's laboratory. Although he published a philosophically oriented text, entitled *Psychology*, in 1886 and served as president of the American Psychological Association in 1899–1900, his basic contribution to psychology relates to his association with the Chicago school of functionalism from 1894 to 1904. Dewey minimally is credited with being the immediate philosophical inspiration of the

Chicago brand of functionalism and maximally is credited with being the creator of functionalism as a formal system of psychology.

In 1896, Dewey published an article in the *Psychological Review* on the reflex arc concept, in which he criticized the traditional molecular, elementaristic interpretation of the reflex. This article set the basic tone of functionalism for years to come. Dewey argued that one could not meaningfully break down a reflexive act into various sensory and motor components, just as one cannot break down the content of consciousness into static units. If a reflex is to be considered adaptive in nature, it must be treated as a holistic or functionalistic entity. Dewey viewed the reflex arc as a complete circuit, which provided the organism with positive feedback, such that later activations of the reflex would occur in a changed environment or in a stimulus situation that had a different meaning for the organism.

Chief Historical Figures: Hall, Cattell, and Angell

The most prominent functionalists included Hall, Cattell, Angell, Carr, Thorndike, Woodworth, Ladd, and Scripture. Because functionalism was such a loosely knit and diverse entity, it is not meaningful arbitrarily to assign certain of these individuals to a special class labeled "founder." Unlike the other three classical schools of academic/ experimental psychology, functionalism did not possess a definitive founder or set of founders. Brief professional biographies of three of these men—Hall, Cattell, and Angell—are presented here primarily because individually they made significant contributions to the establishment of psychology as an institutional and professional force in America.

G. Stanley Hall (1844–1924)

Hall can be credited with three organizational firsts. He was (1) the organizer and first president of the American Psychological Association in 1892, (2) the self-conscious creator of the first graduate school or department of psychology in America at Clark University in 1888, and (3) responsible for the institutionalization of educational and developmental psychology.

Hall studied at Williams College from 1863 to 1867 and earned an undergraduate degree there. He received the Ph.D. degree in psychology in 1878 from Harvard under the tutelage of William James.

Later, he studied under Wundt at Leipzig (1879–1880). Hall's first academic appointment in the United States was at Johns Hopkins University in 1881, and he held a full professorship in psychology there from 1884 to 1888. He established a laboratory at Johns Hopkins in 1883 and founded the *American Journal of Psychology* in 1887. In 1889, Hall became president of Clark University—where, as a professor of psychology, he created a research-oriented graduate school of psychology. Over the next 32 years, Clark University graduated 81 Ph.D.'s in psychology, most of whom eventually assumed administrative positions in psychology and education. In 1891, Hall founded the *Pedagogical Seminary*, which later became the *Journal of Genetic Psychology*. In 1915, he founded the *Journal of Applied Psychology*. Hall's books include the two-volume *Adolescence* (1904), which underwent a number of later revisions, and the two-volume *Senescence* (1922). Hall organized the American Psychological Association in 1892 and served as its first president; he also served as its president for a second time in 1924, the year he died and four years after retiring from the presidency of Clark.

James McKeen Cattell (1860–1944)

It was Cattell who (1) institutionalized American psychology's concern for individual differences, (2) fostered psychology as an applied discipline by organizing the Psychological Corporation, (3) solidified academic psychology by serving as professor and head of the Psychology Department at Columbia University for 26 years, and (4) experienced the prestige of being the first psychologist elected to the National Academy of Sciences.

Cattell graduated from Lafayette College in 1880. He studied under Wundt at Leipzig for three years and served as Wundt's first self-proclaimed graduate assistant, before being awarded a Ph.D. degree in 1886. Cattell also had a peripheral association with Hall at Johns Hopkins and served as Galton's assistant at the South Kensington Museum. Cattell's initial academic appointment in America came in 1888 at the University of Pennsylvania, where he served as a professor of psychology. In 1891, Cattell moved to Columbia University, where he remained for 26 years as a professor and head of the Psychology Department. More Ph.D.s, specifically 344, were awarded at Columbia during Cattell's tenure than at any other American school. Cattell cofounded the *Psychological Review* with James Baldwin in 1894; this journal later became an official publication of the American Psychological Association. In 1895, Cattell acquired the rights to a scientific monthly called *Science* and also served as the president of the American Psychological Association. Cattell helped found the American Association of University Professors (AAUP), still the primary professional organization of American college instructors. He was elected to the National Academy of Sciences in 1900. Cattell's association with Columbia University ended in 1917 because of his pacifistic stand with respect to World War I. In 1921, Cattell organized the Psychological Corporation, which still is a giant in the U.S. testing industry. Cattell used it as a base of operations throughout the remainder of his active professional life.

James Angell (1869–1949)

Angell is important because of (1) his conscious identification with and stern defense of the functionalistic, as opposed to structuralistic, approach to consciousness; and (2) his 25-year chairmanship of the Psychology Department at the University of Chicago.

Angel studied under John Dewey at the University of Michigan, where he earned his undergraduate degree. He also earned a master's degree at Harvard under William James in 1892. Although Angell did further graduate study under Erdmann at Halle in Germany, he never acquired a doctorate; but over the course of his professional career he was awarded 23 honorary degrees. After teaching at the University of Minnesota for a year, he assumed the chairmanship at Chicago in 1894. Among Angell's many students at Chicago was John Watson, the founder of behaviorism, and Harvey Carr, who eventually succeeded him and supervised 150 doctorates. In 1904, Angell published his own introductory text, *Psychology: An Introductory Study of the Structure and Function of Human Consciousness*. By 1908, this work had undergone four separate editions. Angell served as the American Psychological Association president in 1906. He assumed the presidency of Yale University in 1921, serving in that capacity until 1937. Angell later became an officer of the National Broadcasting Company (NBC).

Characteristic Experimentation; Primary Research Areas

Because functionalism established the basic principle that the dynamic, adapting organism as a whole should be the object of experimental analysis, the characteristic research of the school, in retrospect, seems contemporary. Functionalistic research subsumed learning, problem solving, perception, and motivation, as well as the more directly applied areas of child and educational psychology. Functionalism's emphasis on psychological adaptation and mental activity made (1) learning and (2) individual differences in mental capacity the two primary research areas, the former at Chicago and the latter at Columbia.

Functionalism's stress on learning was adopted later by behaviorism, and thus the Watsonian and Skinnerian behavioristic approaches amounted to virtual learning psychologies, and learning became the dominant research area of American experimental psychology. In general, American experimental psychology can be characterized as a learning one, as opposed to European or Continental experimental psychology, which basically is perceptual. This state of affairs can be directly attributed to functionalism's credo of the utility of consciousness.

The Chicago functionalists studied learning and problem solving in both animals and humans. Carr primarily was concerned with applied, educationally oriented research and explicitly studied guidance or tuition. The Chicago school fostered a parametric or dimensional analysis of learning, in which the rate of learning or the nature of the acquisition function was related to the specific physical conditions or variables that comprised the experiment. This method of conducting learning research, unsurprisingly, has come to be called the functional approach to learning phenomena. The later functionally oriented work of McGeoch, Underwood, and Melton on verbal learning and retention is a direct outgrowth of the Chicago brand of functionalism.

At Columbia, Cattell catalogued individual differences in terms of reaction time, psychophysical judgments, memory span, and other variables. Cattell is credited with founding the mental testing movement in America, although his tests of mental capacity did not possess the same operational denotation as those devised by Binet and Terman, the progenitors of the verbal intelligence-quotient concept. Thorndike's life-long research program at Columbia concerned such matters as animal intelligence, trial-and-error learning, the laws of learning, the spread of effect, punishment, and transfer of training. His work could be classified as functional in nature, although he is usually categorized as an associationist or connectionist learning theorist. Thorndike's experimental work was inherently practical and made a sizable contribution to educational psychology. G. Stanley Hall at Clark University, however, is more often credited with being

America's first educational psychologist. Hall pioneered the use of the questionnaire method in the United States and studied child, adolescent, and senescent development.

Historical Legacy

The historical legacy of functionalism is implicit in its status as a transitional school between structuralism and behaviorism. If we represent structuralism as an S–(mind) psychology, functionalism as an S–(mind)–R psychology, and behaviorism as an S–R psychology, the transitional role of functionalism becomes apparent. All three schools make reference to the external, physical stimulus situation. Only structuralism and functionalism allude to mind and consciousness; only functionalism and behaviorism refer to overt physical activity and behavior. The structuralists were only interested in the structure or content of consciousness, presumably as established by an underlying external, physical reality: they merely maintained and extended the British empiricist's focus on the epistemological aspects of mind. Functionalism reoriented psychology's concern for mind into an action or utilitarian focus by emphasizing the dynamics and functioning of consciousness, primarily in relation to the adaptation of the individual organism to the environment. Thus the basic reference point for resolving mind in the functionalistic approach is behavior, or the R term, not the S-input situation. Essentially what Watsonian behaviorism did was to dispense with any reference to mind or consciousness, as an internal mediator, and relate behavior directly to the antecedent S conditions. The basic S–(mind)–R paradigm of functionalism thereby devolves to the basic S–R paradigm of behaviorism, when the reference to mind and all its trappings, such as introspection, is eliminated.

The primary historical legacy of functionalism was the establishment of the behavior or ongoing adaptive activity of the organism, either man or animal, as the proper aspect of the organism for psychology to study. This is true regardless of how the organism is studied, whether experimentally or anecdotally, and regardless of what explanatory concepts are used—the functionalists originally used everyday language and common-sense concepts. Contemporary academic/experimental psychology basically is behavioristic in orientation. Its essence can be captured by either behavioristic or functionalistic labeling: (1) soft behaviorism, (2) hard functionalism, (3) functionalistic behaviorism, or (4) behavioristic functionalism.

You may recall that it was difficult to pinpoint a specific starting date for functionalism; it is also difficult to assign a specific termination date to functionalism as a conceptual approach to psychology. Although Watson effected the behaviorist manifesto around 1912, functionalism survived as an independent and coherent approach to psychology until at least the early 1930s. Even though Watson viewed functionalism as a competitor of behaviorism, such functionalists as Angell and Carr did not regard behaviorism as a competitor of functionalism. Since functionalism was never as tightly knit or doctrinaire as structuralism, or even behaviorism, it eventually was absorbed by a more aggressive and polemical Watsonian behaviorism.

Many of the aspects and concerns of functionalism have survived intact in the context of behaviorism. Many of the characteristics of functionalism, as the original expression of the American predilection for a psychology of adaptation, remain in behaviorism, America's current dominant form of adaptive psychology. These include the following:

1. A concern for practical problems and practical application.
2. Interest in individual differences.
3. A bona fide psychology of the child or preverbal human.
4. Members of the so-called abnormal population, such as retardates and schizophrenics, as proper objects of psychological concern and study.
5. Animal research, both as an end in itself and as a means of understanding the human organism.
6. Learning as the most representative or relevant psychological process for analyzing the nature of the organism.
7. The process of evolution as the primary biological boundary condition or context for interpreting organismic activity.

In many respects functionalism is a common-sense psychology, approximating the layman's conception of what psychology is or should be. If one were to ask an incoming college freshman what psychology is, the student probably would say that it is the study of how a person adjusts as a function of his/her own conscious actions, thoughts, beliefs, and the like—assuming the respondent had not already been indoctrinated as a Freudian by a misguided high school teacher. Analytical categories and philosophical presuppositions aside, what this demonstrates is the continued relevance and salience of the basic functionalistic conception of psychology in American culture.

Bibliography

Angell, J.R. *Psychology: An Introductory Study of the Structure and Function of Human Consciousness.* New York: Holt, 1904.

Carr, H.A. *Psychology: A Study of Mental Activity.* New York: Longmans, Green, 1925.

Darwin, C. *Origin of Species by Means of Natural Selection or the Preservation of Favored Races in the Struggle for Life.* London: Murray, 1859. (New York: Washington Square Press, 1963.)

Darwin, C. *The Descent of Man and Selection in Relation to Sex,* 2 vols. London: Murray, 1871. (Chicago: University of Chicago Press, 1965.)

Dewey, J. *Psychology.* New York: American Book, 1886.

Dewey, J. The reflex arc concept in psychology. *Psychological Review,* 1896, 3, 357–370.

Galton, F. *Hereditary Genius: An Inquiry Into Its Laws and Consequences.* London: Macmillan, 1869.

Hall, G.S. *Adolescence: Its Psychology and Its Relation to Physiology, Anthropology, Sociology, Sex, Crime, Religion and Education,* 2 vols. New York: Appleton, 1904.

Hall, G.S. *Senescence: The Last Half of Life.* New York: Appleton, 1922.

James, W. *The Principles of Psychology,* 2 vols. New York: Holt, 1890. (New York: Dover, 1959.)

4

Gestalt
Psychology

Introduction

The Gestalt system basically is a perceptual psychology, with learning, problem-solving, and motivational overtones. As a perceptual psychology, it is concerned with conscious experience; as a learning psychology, it is concerned with overt behavior. Unlike the other classical schools of experimental psychology, Gestalt psychology explicitly encompasses both the experiential and behavioral components of the organism. Based on Kantian philosophy, it rebelled against the elementarism, molecularism, analytical focus, and associationism of the other three classical schools, which owe their intellectual heritage, in part, to British empiricism. Gestalt psychologists have derisively referred to structuralism, functionalism, and behaviorism as "bundle" or "brick and mortar" psychologies. Gestalt psychology initially reacted against these characteristics of structuralism on the Continent and then later reacted against these characteristics of behaviorism in America.

Although Gestalt psychology has many philosophical and psychological antecedents, it is unique among the classical schools in that it possesses a discrete beginning in time: the experimental work of Max Wertheimer and his colleagues, Kurt Koffka and Wolfgang Köhler, on apparent movement phenomena, or the phi phenomenon, at Frankfurt between 1910 and 1912. This work explicitly demonstrated the vacuousness of the structuralist approach to conscious experience. Many historians regard Wertheimer as the sole or true founder of Gestalt psychology, but all three should be treated as cofounders of the system because they all were responsible for the dissemination of the approach throughout Germany and later in the United States. Our presentation stresses the unique founding of Gestalt psychology and shows why it was such a significant event in psychological history.

Gestalt psychology overthrew structuralism in Germany, only to be persecuted by the Third Reich; however, it has enjoyed somewhat of a rebirth in postwar Germany. In the United States, Gestalt psychology competed with Watsonian and other variants of behaviorism in the 1930s and 1940s, and ultimately was absorbed by cognitive behaviorism. I know of no contemporary psychologist who is willing to argue that Gestalt psychology currently constitutes a viable, independent system in America: it merely lives on in the framework of a more liberal behaviorism.

Object of Study; Basic Subject Matter

Initial Overview

The German word *Gestalt* roughly translates into English as shape, form, or configuration; the plural form is *Gestalten*. The term is evaluatively neutral; it does not mean *good* shape, form, or configuration. Since the basic natural phenomena of interest to Gestalt psychology typically possess an inherent structure or immanent organization, the concept of good often is mistakenly attached to that of Gestalt. Gestalt psychology divines structure or organization in its subject matter: Its basic objects of interest come in prepackaged forms or appear as meaningful wholes. This statement presages the fact that the Gestaltists did not use the terms experience and behavior in the same way as the structuralists and behaviorists did. Perhaps the most neutral way to characterize the basic object of study of Gestalt psychology is in terms of phenomenal experience as related to underlying psychophysical processes or fields. Phenomenal experience subsumes both the content of conscious experience of some observer as well as the overt activity of some experimental subject. Both experience and behavior are construed in a field orientation. We now must analyze the exact denotative meanings the Gestaltists assigned to experience and behavior and also describe their notion of psychophysical processes or fields.

Experience

Since Gestalt psychology is basically a psychology of perception, what the Gestaltist essentially means by experience is perceptual experience—the objects of our perceptual awareness. This is the exact opposite of the structuralist conception of experience, conceptualized in terms of fundamental sensations. Recall the distinction between immediate and mediate experience described in Chapter 2. Structuralism focused on the immediate contents of sensory awareness and regarded the ultimate source of these to be a property of mediate experience. Gestalt psychology focuses on the objects of mediate experience and treats these as the natural or immediate givens of conscious experience. A Gestalt psychologist assumes that a subject (observer), stimulated by an external, physical object, immediately and directly experiences the object, not the isolated sensory attributes of the object. For instance, a table is reacted to as a table *qua* table, not as a collection of such sensory attributes as brown or dark; a triangle is reacted to as a triangle *qua* triangle, not as a collection of lines.

What the Gestalt psychologist means by the content of conscious experience is exactly what the general public means. They describe the content of current awareness in terms of meaningful stimulus objects using the English vernacular. In the Gestalt perspective, the content of consciousness must be described in common-sense, ordinary, everyday, meaningful descriptive terms. We react to stimuli as having an innate organization or as existing in a holistic pattern. This structured or organized perceptual experience must be accepted as such. It must not be analyzed into subparts in a structuralist, introspective manner.

Consider the following two sequences of dots, *A* and *B:*

$A: .$ . . . . .
$B: . .$ . . . .

As a matter of structuralist introspection, both sequences encompass the same conscious awareness: six distinct patches of color, brightness, and so on. As a matter of Gestalt perception, we react to line *A* as consisting of six separate, equidistant dots and to line *B* as composed of three separate pairs of dots.

The Gestalt conception of experience, as the content of one's immediate perceptual awareness, has a far-reaching prescriptive consequence for psychology. Since our perceptual experiences (1) usually come in prepackaged forms and shapes—a triangle, for example—or constitute an independent level of reality describable in object-thing language, such as a table, and (2) must be accepted as such, we cannot explain them by a simple structuralist process of analysis by synthesis. A perceived Gestalt possesses its own immanent level of reality and cannot be explained by analytical reduction. The way the Gestalt psychologist usually expresses this is by saying that the whole, or resultant, is greater than or different from the sum of its parts. Certainly line *B* is more than the simple linear aggregation of six individual dots. Line *B* encompasses a certain shape, configuration, or Gestalt, which is independent of its immediate constituents. Since the nature of a Gestalt cannot be resolved by atomistic reduction, we have the problem of explaining its existence. Why does phenomenal reality consist of meaningful wholes or Gestalten? The answer must await our discussion of psychophysical processes or fields.

Because structuralists admitted the validity only of the sensory level of consciousness, it was necessary to demonstrate instances of Gestalten that had no sensational components existing in consciousness. This is exactly what Wertheimer, Koffka, and Köhler did in the context of the phi phenomenon, an event described in detail later in the chapter.

Behavior

While admitting the existence of such simple reflexive activities as leg flexion or eyelid closure, Gestalt psychologists view instances of behavior as possessing Gestalt-like properties. By analogy to the perceptual situation, behavior is a holistic, organized molar activity or pattern of movement that has no parts. What is meant by parts in this context, of course, is molecular, conditioned response (CR) units, as construed by the behaviorist. A legitimate piece of behavior is not reducible to a linear string of component CR units. In a sense, a piece of behavior is the physicalization or external representation of some internal, central plan. For instance, take the seemingly prosaic act of pedaling a bicycle. A behaviorist would analyze it in terms of a series of subunits or subhabits. A Gestaltist views it as an emergent phenomenon, transcending any simple physiological reality. For a behaviorist, a leisurely pedal to the grocery store and hectic pedaling in a bicycle race amount to the same generic type of behavior, that is, they involve the same subcomponents. For a Gestaltist, they can constitute two entirely different molar activities, with different intentions, plans, strategies, underlying organizations, and the like.

The difference between the behavioristic and Gestalt conceptions of behavior can be amplified by describing the prototypical situation for investigating behavior in the two approaches. For a behaviorist, the prototypical experimental situation for studying overt behavior is learning in general and conditioning in particular, especially instrumental reward training. Examples of this include Thorndike's classic puzzle box experiments with cats and Skinner's operant conditioning technique with rats and pigeons. In these situations, the subject's overt activity is viewed as a blind or mechanical function of its consequences, usually reward or positive reinforcement. Specific functionally defined response classes are selected out of the organism's total response repertoire by the particular reinforcement contingencies in effect. In instrumental conditioning, the subject only can discover the correct response, the one that works, by acting on the environment, presumably in a trial-and-error manner.

For a Gestaltist, the prototypical experimental situation for studying overt behavior is problem solving, the primary example of which is Köhler's classic study of food- (banana) procuring behavior by apes. Apes confined in a cage had either to secure bananas located on the outside via the imaginative use of sticks or to obtain bananas suspended from the ceiling via the imaginative use of boxes. For a Gestalt psychologist, a problem-solving situation is like a perceptual situation in that it possesses a certain structure or organization, such that the organism can discover the correct response—solve the problem—by the active cognitive restructuring of the elements of the situation. Blind trial-and-error responding is not necessarily required; the subject can engage in holistic, molar activity by taking into account the structural or organizational aspects of the situation.

Implicit in this discussion is the fact that the Gestaltist models problem solving after perception—the solution of the problem requires reference to the phenomenal experience of the subject. The typical behaviorist prefers to model problem solving after learning—as a type of task requiring positive transfer of training from prior learning experiences.

Psychophysical Processes or Fields

Both the perceptual experience and the behavioral aspects of Gestalt psychology are held together by relating them to the concept of an underlying psychophysical field. The notion of a psychophysical field is strictly metaphysical in the context of Gestalt psychology; it was borrowed from physics. The founders of Gestalt psychology, especially Köhler, were enamoured of physics and used the dominant field theory orientation of the physics of their day as their explanatory model. Many of the rudimentary phenomena in physics can be explained by fields—electrical, magnetic, or gravitational. A field is a system, or dynamic whole, composed of interacting forces, so that an alteration in one aspect or component affects all the others. A spider's web, for instance, is analogous to a field, in that what happens in any portion of the web affects the overall web. By contrast, a set of marbles scattered randomly on the floor is not analogous to a field, because an individual marble can be removed or changed in position without affecting the basic properties of the set of marbles.

Gestaltists assume that a given perceptual experience, or Gestalt, as well as a given instance of molar activity, is a function of an underlying field. Gestalt psychologists speak of both psychological and physiological fields. They amount to the same generic concept because it is presumed that a given psychological field is reducible to a physiological field or possesses ultimate physiological reality; thus the notion of a psychophysical field.

A physiological field is basically neuronal in nature and exists in the organism's brain; this kind of field is associated primarily with perceptual experience or Gestalten. Wertheimer and Köhler emphasized the neuronal fields underlying conscious experience. The notion of a psychological field is more general and can refer to the totality of causal variables, or texture, that affects an organism at a given moment; for example, specific physical stimuli, past experience, current motivational conditions, the subject's immediate goals. This kind of field is associated primarily with overt molar activity and was stressed by Koffka.

The concept of a psychological field is largely coextensive with that of behavioral environment, which should be contrasted with that of the geographic environment. The geographic environment is the objective or physical environment in which a given behavior occurs;

the behavioral environment is the subjective or psychological environment in which a given behavioral event occurs—that is, the environment as perceived by the organism. These two environments obviously need not correspond. Koffka was fond of illustrating the difference between the geographic and behavioral environments by relating the story of a traveler who passed over the ice of Lake Constance in the dead of winter (geographic environment) under the impression that he was traversing the solid footing of a plain (behavioral environment). When the traveler was informed of his misconception, he promptly dropped dead. The Gestalt psychologist assumes that a given instance of behavior cannot be understood unless the specific behavioral environment in which it occurred is known.

The explanatory value of a field is described best in the context of a physiological field and its presumed relationship to perceptual experience. Recall that a given Gestalt possesses a certain structure or organization. The ultimate source of this structure is assumed to be an underlying neuronal brain field. A brain field has a certain structure or organization. It has certain stresses and strains; it is characterized by certain dynamic and steady states; and so on. The Gestalt psychologist postulates that a perceived Gestalt and its underlying neuronal brain field exist in an isomorphic relationship. The principle of isomorphism stipulates that the nature/structure of a given perceptual experience corresponds to the nature/structure of an underlying brain field. The relationship of isomorphism does not connote complete identity or point-for-point matching. The relationship is topological, not topographical. A good analogy here is the relationship existing between a map and the specific territory it represents. Thus the basic reason we perceive reality in meaningful wholes is that there are neuronal fields in the brain possessing the same essential structure or organization.

There is no direct physiological evidence that these postulated neuronal brain fields actually exist; and attempts to verify their existence indirectly through psychological experimentation have met with mixed results. Critics of Gestalt psychology like to point out that the postulation of psychophysical fields and isomorphism serves as a redescription of the basic behavioral data at another level of reality. They are merely circularly defined concepts or nominal explanations.

In general, the Gestalt psychologist has no way of identifying and giving substance to a particular psychophysical field or behavioral environment independently of overt behavior or the report of conscious experience. The psychophysical field and the behavioral environment are response-defined or response-inferred constructs. In all fairness, it should be mentioned that contemporary psychologists in the Gestalt tradition, such as Hochberg and Attneave, are attempting to define, categorize, and structure stimuli independently of the subject's reaction to them, so that some of the basic Gestalt perceptual principles and laws are truly predictive.

Conceptual Overview

The Gestalt psychologist studies both the content of perceptual experience and the occurrence of overt molar activity. The critical feature of these phenomena for a Gestaltist is their inherent organization or structure. This structure makes a traditional atomistic analysis through reduction and synthesis irrelevant. Instead phenomenal experience is accepted at the level at which it is given and related to underlying psychophysical fields, and overt activity is resolved in terms of an individual's behavioral environment. These entities amount to metaphysical, response-inferred concepts, which serve as a source of criticism of the overall Gestaltist program.

Method of Study; Permissible Methodology

Although Gestalt psychology constitutes a fairly tight system, which revolutionized many aspects of psychology at a conceptual level, its methodology is surprisingly eclectic and continuous with that of other systems of psychology such as behaviorism, humanism, and functionalism. Since Gestalt psychology focuses on both perceptual experience and overt behavior, its methodology must be analyzed at two levels: (1) What is the proper method of externalizing perceptual experience? (2) What is the proper method of investigating molar activity? Gestalt psychology professes only one fundamental methodological prescription at each of these levels: (1) The content of perceptual experience has to be accepted as given and not broken down into subparts. (2) Behavior can be studied only in a situation that allows the subject to be aware of the critical aspects of the psychophysical field determining the behavior. The first prescription leads to the use of phenomenology, or the phenomenal description of conscious experience. The second prescription entails the use of low-level physical experimentation, or naturalistic observation. Both phenomenology and physical experimentation, as practiced by the

Gestaltist, have the same fundamental goal, which is best left unstated until the techniques have been discussed individually.

Phenomenology

The nature of the phenomenal description of conscious experience is implicit in the foregoing discussion of the Gestalt conception of experience. The observer externalizes the content of his/her consciousness at the same level as it is given. This entails the use of meaningful object or thing words from the observer's standard vocabulary. No special or elaborate training is required for phenomenal description. The observer is not "looking for" anything special or forced to use restrictive categories of report, as in the case of structuralist introspection. In fact, in phenomenal description the categories of descriptive self-report are subject derived; and it is possible for two different observers to disagree when faced by essentially the same objective situation.

The use of phenomenology is not original to Gestalt psychology. It has a long history, as well as a slightly different connotation, in the context of German philosophy and the German literary establishment. A more restrictive phenomenal description also is implicit in behavioristically oriented studies of perception, although the term phenomenology rarely is used or acknowledged by a behaviorist.

Physical Experimentation

The Gestalt approach to physical experimentation can be described as low level, informal, nonquantitative, nonstatistical—constituting virtually naturalistic observation. The typical Gestalt study exhibits more of the properties of an informal demonstration than of a formal, analytical experiment. Manipulation of the independent variable is qualitative, as opposed to quantitative; Gestalt experimentation does not encompass elaborate control groups or the parametric variation of the input variable. An analogous statement can be made with respect to the nature of the dependent variable or behavioral data. The output data rarely are in numeric form.

Traditionally Gestalt psychologists have not been interested in quantification, measurement, or statistics. To some degree, initially this was a conscious decision on their part because they believed that it was much too early in the development of psychology as a science to bother with precise measurement and mathematical equations. Sheer numbers mean nothing to a Gestalt psychologist, at either the input level or output level of an experiment. It is not the number of elements in a given input situation that is relevant, but rather the relationship between them. A given behavioral phenomenon either is or is not exhibited by the subject—that is, it exists in an all-or-none sense, not in a probabilistic sense.

An example of typical Gestalt experimentation would be Köhler's investigation of problem solving in apes, in which an ape was exposed to a general input situation whose critical elements (sticks, boxes, bananas) were difficult to specify and vary in a quantitative manner. In such a situation, the ape either displays or does not display the basic phenomena of interest—insight, and/or problem solution.

In general, the Gestalt psychologist places a subject in a specific experimental situation to see what kind of behavior is exhibited. The situation entails some psychophysical field, behavioral environment, or perceptual structure; the organism either displays some appropriate molar activity or does not (for any of a number of different reasons). A successful experiment serves as a demonstration that can be analyzed according to the Gestaltist interpretive categories. Gestalt psychology simply is not interested in treating a specific input situation as one point in a space of many such situations, nor is it interested in interpreting the specific response output as one value along a continuum of such values.

A Conceptual Comparison

The ultimate goal of the Gestalt use of both phenomenal description and informal physical experimentation is the attainment of an *experimentum crucis*; namely, a simple, but convincing, demonstration of some observed generality. Much of Gestalt research merely illustrates or physicalizes the general laws and precepts of Gestalt psychology. Phenomenological investigations are particularly convincing because they involve the immediate perceptual experience of the observer, and the conclusions to be drawn from them are arrived at instantaneously. For instance, many of the Gestalt laws of perceptual organization achieve instant validity in the context of simple physical demonstrations, such as those involving figure–ground or grouping.

Origin; Specific Historical Antecedents

Since Gestalt psychology basically is an intellectual statement (as opposed to cultural statement, à la functionalism) and originated in the confines of the Germanic university system, it is not difficult to pinpoint its numerous historical antecedents. The antecedent influences on Gestalt psychology are so vast that we shall not be able even to begin to consider the more peripheral ones, such as Franz Brentano's act school of psychology or the phenomenological work of G. E. Müller and his associates (Jaensch, Katz, and Rubin) at Göttingen. (Brentano's act school is discussed in Chapter 8 as a historical antecedent of cognitive behaviorism.) Our discussion focuses on (1) Gestalt's specific philosophical progenitor, Immanuel Kant; (2) the Gestaltqualität-oriented thought of Mach, von Ehrenfels, and Meinong; and (3) the immediate psychological impetus of the Gestalt approach, Wertheimer's work on the phi phenomenon.

Kantian Philosophy

Immanuel Kant was an eighteenth century German philosopher who customarily is credited with initiating the modern phase of metaphysics. Like Descartes, Kant was a deeply religious and moral man who could not accept the intellectual and moral skepticism of the British empiricists, especially Hume. Kant's philosophy essentially was an attempt to restore moral and cognitive philosophy to a firm basis. His relative contribution to psychology probably is less than that of Descartes, and definitely is less than that of British empiricism. In fact, Kant argued that a science of psychology is philosophically impossible, and he hindered the development of experimental psychology in Germany for many years. But what Kant meant by psychology was the science of the mind or conscious experience, specifically that type which later was characteristic of the structuralists. Most contemporary interpreters of Kant do not find any potential antinomy in his approach to behaviorism, that is, psychology construed as the science of behavior.

THE NOUMENAL VERSUS PHENOMENAL WORLD

Kant made a fundamental distinction between two different kinds of worlds: the noumenal and the phenomenal. The noumenal world consists of things or objects in and of themselves; the phenomenal world consists of things or objects as we experience them. The noumenal world is presumed to exist behind the phenomenal world, but the contents of the noumenal world are unknowable. Kant regarded the essence of mind to be in the noumenal world; that is why psychology, construed as structuralism, was impossible. Because he found it convenient to assume that events in the noumenal world are uncaused or undetermined, Kant assigned the moral aspects of man to this world: Man can be held responsible for his actions because man's moral freedom exists in the noumenal world. The physical events of the natural universe, as objects of study of such sciences as physics and chemistry, and man's body and overt behavior are properties of the phenomenal world and are knowable—they constitute elements of our phenomenal experience. Kant accepted causality or determinism in the phenomenal world, and thus the validity of behaviorism as an approach to psychology.

Kant's basic contribution to psychology in general, and Gestalt psychology in particular, relates to his account of how phenomenal experience derives from the noumenal world. Kant's treatment of the origin of phenomenal experience, in principle, underlies the Gestalt approach to perception.

KANT'S INFLUENCE ON GESTALT PSYCHOLOGY

Descartes was a rationalist and admitted the existence of innate ideas, whereas British epistemological philosophy was empirical in nature, accepting only sense experience as the sole or ultimate source of ideas. Kant, part rationalist and part empiricist, rejected both these extremes. He postulated that the content of our phenomenal or perceptual experience arises when sense impressions from the noumenal world are processed by an innate set of a priori categories existing in the mind. Since perception was a subset of cognitive knowledge for Kant, he believed that cognitive knowledge in general arises when sense impressions are processed by these innate a priori categories.

The set of a priori categories includes space, time, and causality, among others. Our phenomenal experience is structured in spatial, temporal, and causal form because of these categories. Space, time, and causality do not exist in the external world. They are not absolute properties of the naturally occurring universe, nor a property of the noumenal world.

Because the categories are innate, they are not the result of past, associational experience. The categories are logically and temporally prior to experience. We cannot have experience or structure without them. According to Kant, no rationalistic or empirical validation of the existence of these categories is either possible or necessary. We intuit the existence of these categories.

Gestalt psychology accepted the basic principle underlying Kant's postulation of an innate set of a priori categories: phenomenal experience is, in part, the product of innate brain or cognitive mechanisms. With respect to perceptual theory, the brain mechanisms are operationalized in terms of dynamic, neurophysiological fields. With respect to cognition in general, the stresses and strains of the underlying psychophysical field must be taken into account. Thus the overall Gestalt approach to perception and cognition is nativistic, as opposed to empiristic, in orientation because of the influence of Kantian philosophy.

THE FATE OF KANT'S CATEGORIES

Kant's space, time, and causality categories eventually fell into disrepute because of the specific denotational properties that he assigned to them. Kant identified space and time with the Newtonian conception of an absolute space and time, based on Euclidean geometry; and he interpreted causality as a physical, mechanical process. Later, in the context of Einstein's theory of relativity, in which space and time are relative phenomena and the universe is based on Riemian geometry, and of purely probabilistic or functional interpretations of causality, Kant's absolutist interpretation of the categories became anachronistic; and this tended to generalize to his assumption of an overall conceptual a priori category system.

The Notion of Gestaltqualität

The notion of *Gestaltqualität* serves as an immediate intellectual precursor to that of Gestalt. Gestaltqualität means form quality, and *Gestaltqualitäten* is the plural form. The term was devised by Christian von Ehrenfels in 1890 to apply to a concept that first was articulated by Ernst Mach, a physicist. Von Ehrenfels and Alexius Meinong, a student of Brentano, merely elaborated on this concept; but we shall take the liberty of associating the term with all three men while describing the basic concept from a Machian perspective.

MACH'S NOTION OF SPACE FORM AND TIME FORM

Mach was a descriptivist (see Chapter 5) and reduced the content of all science and knowledge to sensation(s). In the course of his analysis, Mach noted that certain visual and auditory experiences—a geometric figure or a melody, for example—possess forms or qualities that are different from their constituent sensational elements. A triangle has a perceived shape over and above its color, size, and the like; and a particular melody has a perceived quality over and above its constituent notes. Mach postulated that this feature of such an experience was the result of a separate, independent sensation, one not contingent on the other constituent sensations. He called this sensation a space form in the context of the visual modality, and a time form in the context of the auditory modality. Thus any coherent visual or auditory experience has a space form or time form associated with it.

Mach argued for the independence of a space form or time form on the basis of the fact that they remain constant when the other sensory aspects of the perceptual experience, such as size and color, change. There was also some question as to whether a space form or time form constituted an actual sensation. Von Ehrenfels, unlike Mach, regarded a Gestaltqualität as an artifactual construction of the mind, and not as a sensation *per se*.

RELATION TO GESTALT PSYCHOLOGY

The notion of a space form or time form becomes more comprehensible when it is realized that the concept is analogous to the notion of a Gestalt, as a perceived meaningful whole. The reason a space form or time form—a Gestaltqualität—does not have the same existential status that a Gestalt does is that Mach, von Ehrenfels, and Meinong were structurally oriented: The Gestaltqualität existed on the same level as the other sensory attributes, such as color, size, pitch, and loudness, and merely combined with them in an additive manner to generate the coherent perceptual experience. The notion of Gestaltqualität was an aspect of the traditional reductionist and analysis by synthesis approach, decried by Gestalt psychology. Gestalt psychologists made the whole greater than the sum of its parts and conceived of the whole as being logically prior to its parts, so that in their hands the Gestaltqualität became a true or functional Gestalt with emergent properties.

The Immediate Psychological Impetus of Gestalt Psychology: Wertheimer's Work on the Phi Phenomenon

In 1912, Max Wertheimer published an article in the *Zeitschrift für Psychologie*, entitled "Experimentelle Studien über das Sehen von Bewegung" (Experimental Studies of the Perception of Movement), reporting on his two-year experimental investigation of the phi phenomenon. The appearance of this journal article marked the formal beginning of the Gestalt approach as a classical school of academic/experimental psychology.

THE PHI PHENOMENON

The phi phenomenon is best characterized generically. It is successively a perceptual phenomenon, a visual phenomenon, a movement phenomenon, an apparent movement phenomenon. Apparent essentially means illusory. The subject, or observer, experiences visual movement through space, although there is no actual physical movement present. As such, the phi phenomenon is a movement illusion. By definition, real movement occurs when some object actually moves through space and stimulates successive points on the observer's retina. Illusory/apparent movement takes place when a subject phenomenally experiences movement in the absence of this successive stimulation.

The phi phenomenon actually refers to a class of related experimental effects; that is, there are numerous ways in which the basic phenomenon can be physicalized. The minimal display setup requires the use of two distinct, physically separated light sources. Both dots of light and bars of light have been used. The critical experimental manipulation involves the successive activation of the two light sources. This can be accomplished by means of a stroboscope, a tachistoscope, or a Hunter interval timer. The specific time interval between the successive onsets determines what the observer experiences. Wertheimer isolated three types of intervals, each with its own characteristic phenomenal effect. (There is no point in presenting the time range for each of these interval types because the range depends on such factors as the distance between the light sources, the light intensity, and the distance between the display apparatus and the observer.)

1. If the time interval is *too slow*, the subject experiences exactly what is occurring in the physical environment: the successive onset and termination of the two light sources.

2. If the time interval is *too fast*, the subject experiences the simultaneous illumination of the two light sources. This is an illusion, in the sense that there is a discrepancy between the events occurring in the objective, physical environment and the phenomenal experience of the observer. But this is *not* the phi phenomenon.

3. If the time interval is *just right* (optimum or ideal, not too fast or too slow), the subject experiences the first light source moving through space and ending at the second light source. This *is* the phi phenomenon.

There are many variants of the phi phenomenon. If the light sources are dots, a dot is seen to move through space. If the light sources are bars, the bar is seen to move through space. If one bar is vertical and the other is transposed 30 degrees, the bar is seen moving down in space like a second hand on a watch. If the two light sources are used in an alternating fashion, the subject experiences back-and-forth movement. If a readily identifiable obstruction is placed between the two light sources, a circular movement (arc) is produced, which seems to jump over the impediment. If three light sources are used properly with the middle one activated first, the subject experiences a movement in both (opposite) directions simultaneously. Under certain circumstances, pure movement per se is experienced; that is, the observer does not experience an object as such moving through space, just movement. Wertheimer calls this a pure phi.

SIGNIFICANCE OF THE PHI PHENOMENON

The significance of the phi phenomenon lies in the fact that a structural, atomistic interpretation in terms of a combination of underlying sensory elements is not applicable. Unlike the case with real movement, successive points on the retina are not stimulated. There are no sensory elements associated with the phi phenomenon that can be isolated through direct, critical structuralist introspection. Wundt attempted to postulate implicit kinesthetic sensations caused by implicit eye movements, but these are impossible when the phi phenomenon is physicalized by using three light sources, giving rise to simultaneous movement in opposite directions.

Wertheimer's explanation of the phi phenomenon captures the inner essence of the Gestalt approach. The phi phenomenon should be accepted at the level at which it is experienced. It does not need explaining in any analytical sense. The phi phenomenon is a true Gestalt. Basically it is a central, as opposed to peripheral, phenomenon. There is an underlying brain field which corresponds to the phenomenal experience. At a physiological level, there is no distinction between real and apparent movement. Whatever the nature of the external, physical stimulus situation, the same underlying central neuronal processes occur. Wertheimer even demonstrated that an observer could not distinguish phenomenally between real and apparent movement.

Chief Historical Figures: Wertheimer, Koffka, and Köhler

Gestalt psychology is unique in that it possesses a trio of bona fide founders. Both Koffka and Köhler were more than just students of Wertheimer. Wertheimer was only 6 years older than Koffka and 7 years older than Köhler; and their professional lives were intricately intertwined. It is impossible to write a descriptive biography of any one of the three without referring to the other two.

All three men contributed to the initial, pioneering work on the phi phenomenon, which was conducted at the Psychological Institute in Frankfurt between 1910 and 1912. Each had been a student of Carl Stumpf at Berlin. Stumpf was a phenomenologically oriented psychologist who made significant contributions to auditory perception and the psychology of music. He also set up the first psychological laboratory at Berlin. Berlin eventually became a center of the Gestalt movement because either Wertheimer or Köhler, or both, were there from 1916 to 1935. All three jointly founded the *Psychologische Forschung*, the primary organ of Gestalt psychology, in 1921, along with Kurt Goldstein and Hans Gruhle. This journal lasted until 1938, its demise occasioned by Nazi persecution and the exodus of the Gestalt founders to America.

There were virtually no intellectual or jurisdictional disputes among Gestalt's three founders. Each specialized in different areas of psychology and made complementary contributions to the Gestalt movement at an intellectual level, as well as in terms of personality and life-style. These specializations and complementary contributions should be considered in some detail, before presenting brief biographies of the founders.

Specializations and Complementary Contributions

Wertheimer served as the inspirational and creative catalyst of the Gestalt school. It was he who originated the basic outline and substance of Gestalt psychology. Koffka and Köhler were not informed of the purpose of the phi phenomenon research until it was completed. Wertheimer had a knowledge of and interest in both law and philosophy; and he attempted to extend Gestalt principles to logic, ethics, and various social issues. There was a strong moral overtone to Gestalt psychology in Germany that did not survive the journey to America. Wertheimer specialized in perception, problem solving, and thinking, the last encouraged by his friendship with Albert Einstein. Wertheimer laboriously attempted to reconstruct the thought processes and phases Einstein experienced while developing his theory of relativity. Of the three Gestalt founders, Wertheimer published the least, but he was a warm, friendly, outgoing person whose basic influence came through his lectures and personal contact with others. He was the only founder who had not visited the United States at least once prior to his final departure from Germany. He found it difficult to adjust to the English language, and his productivity declined the last ten years of his life.

Koffka was the organizer and systematizer of Gestalt psychology. His *Principles of Gestalt Psychology*, published in 1935, is considered to be the definitive work on Gestalt psychology, but it is so scholarly and erudite that its impact was limited strictly to professionals. Koffka worked out the implications of Gestalt psychology for cognitive and perceptual development, child psychology, and learning (in the behaviorist sense of the term). He first introduced America to Gestalt psychology in a 1922 *Psychological Bulletin* article, "Perception: An Introduction to the Gestalt-Theorie." Koffka always seemed a little more aloof than the other founders, and he was the only one of the three who never had some kind of official appointment at Berlin. He migrated to America before the Nazis took over Germany, at least six years before either of the other founders.

Köhler served as the popularizer of Gestalt psychology and eventually became the best known founder, at least in America. He outlived both Wertheimer and Koffka by a quarter of a century, and his interest in anthropoid intelligence, as recounted in *Mentality of the Apes*, had a great intuitive and popular appeal. Köhler was elected president of the American Psychological Association and also was granted a Distinguished Scientific Contribution Award by this organization. He was an expert on acoustics, and this led to his later specialization in auditory perception. He also functioned as the physicist and physiologist of the Gestalt movement. As a student of Max Planck, the physicist who originated quantum theory, it was natural for Köhler to be concerned with the ultimate physical and physiological bases of Gestalten. He served as the bridge between Gestalt psychology and the physical sciences, and saw Gestalten in everything, even chemical and physical phenomena. For Köhler, the notion of Gestalt served as the best hope for a fundamental unity of the sciences. Köhler was the last founder to leave Germany, after valiantly defying Nazism at the University of Berlin for at least two years. He was a methodical and meticulous man who had no problems in adjusting to America.

Max Wertheimer (1880–1943)

Wertheimer was born in 1880 in Prague. After studying law for two and a half years, and after some exposure to philosophy under von Ehrenfels at Prague, he eventually earned a *summa cum laude* Ph.D. degree in 1904 under Külpe at Würzburg during the zenith of the short-lived Würzburg (imageless thought) school (see Chapters 2 and 8). Not much is known about Wertheimer during the period from 1904 to 1910, beyond the fact that he spent time in Prague, Vienna, and Berlin. One of Wertheimer's earliest publications was on word association in 1905. From 1910 to 1912, he conducted research on the phi phenomenon at the Psychological Institute in Frankfurt at the invitation of one of his former teachers, Friedrich Schumann. Wertheimer remained at Frankfurt from 1912 to 1916 as a Dozent in psychology, assuming an analogous position at Berlin in 1916, where he was promoted to the assistant professorship level in 1922. His famous paper on the laws of perceptual organization was published in 1923. Wertheimer left Berlin in 1929 to assume Schumann's former chair at Frankfurt, and remained there until 1933 when he came to America. Wertheimer spent the last decade of his life at the New School for Social Research in New York. His classic book, *Productive Thinking*, was published posthumously in 1945.

Kurt Koffka (1886–1941)

Koffka was born in 1886 in Berlin, and obtained the Ph.D. degree under Stumpf at Berlin in 1908. He served as an assistant of Külpe and Marbe at Würzburg for a time, and was Schumann's assistant at the Psychological Institute in Frankfurt when Wertheimer arrived in 1910. The following year, in 1911, he accepted a Dozent position at the University of Geissen, only 40 miles from Frankfurt. He remained on the faculty there for the rest of his professional life in Germany, ultimately achieving full professorial status. During World War I, Koffka did research on brain-damaged and aphasic patients. His *Growth of the Mind*, which really was a book on child psychology, was published in German in 1921 and in English in 1924; his article introducing America to Gestalt psychology appeared in the *Psychological Bulletin* in 1922. Koffka was a visiting professor in America on two occasions: at Cornell University (1924–1925) and at the University of Wisconsin (1926–1927). He resigned from Geissen in 1927 and became a full professor at Smith College in Northampton, Mass., where he remained until his death. On a research expedition to central Asia in 1932, Koffka contracted an illness from which he never fully recovered. His classic *Principles of Gestalt Psychology* appeared in 1935.

Wolfgang Köhler (1887–1967)

Köhler was born in 1887 in Revel, Estonia; his parents brought him to Germany when he was 5 years old. He was graduated from Berlin in 1909 with a Ph.D. degree under Stumpf. An assistant at the Psychological Institute in Frankfurt from 1909 to 1911, he then held a Dozent position there for the next two years. In 1913, Köhler became director of the anthropoid research station of the Prussian Academy of Science located on Tenerife, one of the Canary Islands, and remained there until 1920 because of the exigencies of World War I. During this period, he conducted his classic work on learning and problem solving in chickens and chimpanzees. A report of this work originally appeared in German in 1917, and was published in English in 1924, as *Mentality of the Apes*. Köhler served as a full professor of psychology at Göttingen in 1921–1922. His *Die physischen Gestalten* was published in 1920, but never was translated into English. As a result of this book, Köhler assumed Stumpf's chair at Berlin in 1922. *Gestalt Psychology*, his first book in English, appeared in 1929. In the United States, Köhler held visiting professorships at Clark University (1925–1926) and at both Harvard and the University of Chicago (1934–1935). He resigned from the faculty at Berlin in 1935, to begin a long tenure at Swarthmore College. His American books included *The Place of Value in a World of Facts* (1938), *Dynamics in Psychology* (1940), and a second edition of *Gestalt Psychology* (1947). Köhler served as president of the American Psychological Association in 1959, after being awarded a Distinguished Scientific Contribution Citation in 1956. He eventually retired to the seclusion of Enfield, N.H., where he was associated with Dartmouth College as an adjunct professor.

Characteristic Experimentation; Primary Research Areas

Although the Gestalt system is basically a perceptual psychology, the Gestalt research program subsumed most of the significant classical research areas of experimental psychology in addition to perception: learning, thinking, motivation, and memory. Gestalt experimentation had two fundamental goals: (1) to determine the ultimate nature of Gestalten and articulate the basic laws of perception, especially those underlying perceptual organization; and (2) to extend the dynamics of Gestalten and the laws of perception to the customarily conceived nonperceptual areas indicated above. Gestaltists modeled virtually every psychological phenomenon or process after perception. Specific experimental areas that were beyond the bounds of such a conception by and large were ignored in Gestalt research: for instance, sensation, emotion, and physiological and comparative problems. (Such areas as social and personality are commented on in the next section.)

Evaluation of the Gestalt Research Program

Any evaluative statements relative to the success of the Gestalt research program must be made at two levels: (1) interpretive and (2) descriptive.

1. Any attempts to validate experimentally the basic underlying explanatory concepts of Gestalt psychology—for example, isomorphism, brain fields, stress and strain (equilibria, disequilibria) in the behavioral environment—were doomed to failure, for two basic reasons. The state of development of experimental technology was still woefully inadequate and did not permit the assessment of the validity of such concepts. Also, these hypothetical phenomena could be investigated only indirectly: even if the experimental data came out as predicted, other theoretical interpretations were possible. In all fairness to the Gestaltists, it should be noted that they realized this. However, such attempts were made anyway, primarily in the context of isomorphism and brain fields (e.g., satiation and figural aftereffect research).

2. Attempts to demonstrate that the content of phenomenal experience is holistic and structured and that behavior can be a function of how the subject interprets the experimental environment were extraordinarily successful: Gestalt psychology did a credible job of demonstrating fundamental structure at the experiential and behavioral levels.

At the experiential level, there are (1) the basic laws of perceptual organization or grouping, such as proximity, similarity, continuity, and closure, all of which are subsumed by the fundamental principle of Prägnanz; (2) figure–ground and ambiguous or reversible figure–ground phenomena; (3) the various perceptual constancies, such as color, size, and shape; and (4) various illusions, such as the phi phenomenon and the Müller–Lyer. This Gestalt "perceptual material" is all the more impressive because much of it has auditory analogues, besides being implicitly visual in nature.

At the behavioral level, an illustrative sampling would include (1) transposition and the von Restorff effect in learning; (2) insight, set (*Einstellung*), and fixation in thinking/problem solving; (3) the Zeigarnik effect in motivation; and (4) memory trace distortion/leveling effects in retention phenomena.

All these experiential and behavioral phenomena, especially the last, had to be absorbed by the mainstream of American psychology, particularly behaviorism. Thus we find (1) in the 1940s a Hull–Spence absolute or algebraic view of transposition pitted against a Gestalt–Krech relational view of transposition; (2) a continuing American functionalistic interference view of memory pitted against a Gestaltist organizational trace view of memory; and (3) a current Harlow experiential learning set interpretation of problem solving pitted against a Gestalt insight interpretation of problem solving.

Historical Legacy

The analytical dimension of historical legacy is infinitely descriptive in the context of Gestalt psychology. An exhaustive description of the legacy of the Gestalt movement would entail a characterization of the state of contemporary psychology as a whole. Significant residues of Gestalt psychology can be found in contemporary behavioristic thought, as well as in the contemporary humanistic, phenomenological approach. Significant residues also can be found in both academic/experimental psychology and clinical or applied psychology.

The view expressed in the preceding paragraph is the current dominant interpretation of the legacy of the Gestalt movement. It has been absorbed successfully, or successively, by American behaviorism. Gestalt psychology, as a school, reached its zenith in Germany in the 1920s and 1930s, and in the United States in the 1930s and 1940s. It now lives on in the form of a more liberalized behaviorism.

More recent interpretations of the legacy of Gestalt psychology, attributable primarily to such second-generation Gestalt-oriented psychologists as Henle (a student of Köhler) and Luchins (a student of Wertheimer), indicate that Gestalt psychology really has not received a fair hearing in America. I do not agree with this interpretation, and it will be worthwhile to consider briefly some of the specific contributions that the Gestalt movement has made to contemporary psychology.

Specific Contributions of the Gestalt Movement to Contemporary Psychology

Of the four contributions discussed, the first two relate to representative content areas of psychology and the third involves a principle used in theory construction. The fourth basically is semantic in nature: categorization of Lewin's field theory approach and Goldstein's psychopathology as offshoots of Gestalt psychology.

1. The Gestalt movement revolutionized the psychology of perception. The traditional empiristic, associational, sensation-based paradigm has been replaced by a nativistic, holistic, irreductionist, emergent paradigm. No longer is perceptual psychology the handmaiden of sensory psychology. Sensation and perception now constitute two separate substantive areas of psychology. Sensory research has become increasingly neurophysiologically and mathematically oriented, while perceptual research largely has been absorbed by the information-processing orientation of cognitive behaviorism.

2. Gestalt psychology aided the cognitive or expectancy interpretation of learning, as typified by Tolman, in combating the strict, mechanical S–R associational view of learning characteristic of the Guthrian contiguity and Hullian effect approaches. Gestalt psychology broadened the behaviorist's operational criteria as to what constitutes a legitimate learning phenomenon. The boundary lines separating a strictly learning or conditioning phenomenon and a strictly problem-solving phenomenon became blurred, so that the conception of a learner as a passive, receptive organism was replaced by the view that a learner is an active, constructive organism. Conditioning ceased to be the prototypical form of learning and the basic reference point for explaining all other forms of learning.

3. Recall from Chapter 1 that the basic creative efforts of contemporary psychologists reside at the level of theory construction, not system formation. The residual effects of Gestalt psychology's basic principle—that Gestalten exist or the whole is different from the sum of the parts—primarily reside at the theory construction level. Contemporary theoretical efforts in the hard-core experimental areas, such as verbal learning, conditioning, memory, perception or object rec-

ognition, concept formation, and discrimination, invariably involve modeling, either directly in terms of mathematics or indirectly in terms of computer simulation or analogies. Contemporary models are constructed in such a way that they implicitly provide for the fact that the whole is not necessarily the mere sum of its parts: the output is not necessarily a simple linear function of the input. This implicit recognition of the fundamental Gestalt principle increases in prominence as the basic psychological phenomenon or process of interest increases in complexity: Contrast the mathematical modeling of simple CR formation by means of some Markov process with the computer simulation of complex language behavior by means of some hierarchical information-processing program.

4. The last specific contribution to be considered involves the question of whether the Gestalt movement has had any effect on personality theory, social psychology, clinical psychology, or applied psychology in general. The answer depends on whether Lewin's field theory approach to personality and social processes and Goldstein's approach to psychopathology are categorized as offshoots of Gestalt psychology. Kurt Lewin taught at Berlin from 1921 until 1932 and was influenced strongly by Wertheimer and Köhler; Kurt Goldstein taught at Frankfurt from 1916 to 1930 and was a cofounder of *Psychologische Forschung*.

There is no pressing reason for not regarding Lewinian field theory and Goldsteinian psychopathology as offshoots of Gestalt psychology and, therefore, as part of the historical legacy of the Gestalt movement. Since Lewin's work ultimately led to the sensitivity training or T-group phenomenon and Goldstein's views emphasized self-actualization of the individual, the legacy of Gestalt psychology even extends to aspects of contemporary humanistic psychology.

There is no substantive difference between an organism performing in a behavioral environment, a Gestalt notion, and an organism living and working in his/her own subjective world of private experience, the focus of interest of humanistic psychology. In both Gestalt and humanistic psychology, the individual can be understood only in terms of its own frame of reference.

Bibliography

Koffka, K. *Die Grundlagen der psychischen Entwicklung eine Einführung in die Kinderpsychologie.* Osterwieck: Zickfeldt, 1921. (*The Growth of Mind.* London: Routledge & Kegan Paul, 1924.)

Koffka, K. Perception: An introduction to the *Gestalttheorie*. *Psychological Bulletin*, 1922, 19, 531–585.

Koffka, K. *Principles of Gestalt Psychology*. New York: Harcourt, Brace, 1935, 1963.

Köhler, W. *Intelligenz-prüfungen an Menschenaffen*. Berlin: Springer, 1917. (*The Mentality of Apes*. Translated by E. Winter. London: Kegan Paul, 1924; New York: Harcourt, Brace, 1925, 1927.)

Köhler, W. *Die physischen Gestalten in Ruhe und im stationären Zustand (Static and stationary physical configurations)*. Erlangen: Weltkreisverlag, 1920.

Köhler, W. *Gestalt Psychology*. New York: Liveright, 1929, 1947.

Köhler, W. *The Place of Value in a World of Facts*. New York: Liveright, 1938.

Köhler, W. *Dynamics in Psychology*. New York: Liveright, 1940.

Wertheimer, M. Experimentelle Studien über das Sehen von Bewegung. *Zeitschrift für Psychologie*, 1912, 61, 161–265. (Translated as Experimental studies on the seeing of motion. In T. Shipley (Ed.), *Classics in Psychology*. New York: Philosophical Library, 1961.)

Wertheimer, M. *Productive Thinking*. New York: Harper, 1959.

5

Overview of Behaviorism

[See page 112 for Figure 5-1
Derivation of the Basic Forms of Behaviorism.]

Introduction

As is the case with functionalism, behaviorism is a rather heterogeneous collection of various subapproaches to psychology. The most prominent contemporary behaviorist, B. F. Skinner, considers behaviorism to be a philosophy of science concerned with the subject matter and methods of psychology. The central theme extending through all the variants of behaviorism is a focus on behavior as the primary datum of psychology. Behavior is assumed to be an objective, public event in the universe, as opposed to consciousness, which is subjective and private in nature. Psychology, conceptualized as behaviorism, is supposed to be a true science, on a par with such traditional physical sciences as physics and chemistry.

In most forms of behaviorism, the focus on behavior serves as an end in itself: The goal of behavioristic psychology is the prediction and/or control of behavior. Prediction connotes knowledge of the antecedent conditions of which the behavior is a function. Control connotes the active manipulation of behavior, presumably for the betterment of the organism, as well as, on occasion, for making a

101

specific experiment better controlled on a methodological level. An exception to the typical behaviorist's end focus on behavior is cognitive behaviorism. This variant of behaviorism is interested only in behavior instrumentally, specifically as a means of inferring the nature of the organism's cognitive processes. Cognitive processes still are regarded as physical, or material, events. No contemporary cognitive behaviorist treats cognitive processes as mind *per se*, in the Cartesian dualistic sense of the term. The central theme extending through all the variants of behaviorism perhaps is expressed better as a focus on the physical, material aspects of an organism, interpreted either as behavior or as information-processing capacity. In no form of behaviorism is the focus on experience or consciousness.

It was fashionable during the period from 1930 to 1960 to characterize any American experimental psychologist operating in the overall functionalist tradition of organismic adaptation as a behaviorist. In a loose interpretation of the term, any experimental psychologist concerned with behavior was called a behaviorist. With the rise of humanistic, phenomenological psychology, as well as the recent appearance of dialectical psychology, this use of behaviorism no longer is appropriate. There are bona fide contemporary experimental psychologists who would disclaim the label "behaviorist." Therefore, it is necessary to make some critical distinctions and formally derive the basic forms of behaviorism, so that the essential topical coverage of the next three chapters can be delimited and previewed.

Derivation of the Basic Forms of Behaviorism

Figure 5-1 presents a branching tree diagram representing the basic forms of behaviorism. The notion of basic form exists in two senses: (1) the different conceptual types of behaviorism—such as metaphysical, descriptive, or analytical—and (2) the specific content variants of behaviorism—such as Watsonian or Skinnerian. The different conceptual types of behaviorism are generated by using five binary-valued analytical dimensions, linked together in a logical or nested sequence, such that successive nodal point values identify the different conceptual types. The different content variants of behaviorism are represented by the many branches of the tree diagram: A specific path through the diagram terminates in the generation of a given content variant of behaviorism. Note that the termination of each path is parenthetically labeled with a specific content variant of behaviorism.

Figure 5-1 actually consists of two branching tree diagrams: A and B. Diagram A constitutes the superordinate one; diagram B is subordinate, serving as the continued output for two of the three branches generated in diagram A. A given content variant of behaviorism is characterized by the specific denotation of the nodal point values appearing along its path. For instance, Skinner's behaviorism is classified as both a descriptive and a radical behaviorism by diagram A; Tolman's purposive behaviorism is classified as a metaphysical *or* methodological, logical, cognitively oriented, analytical behaviorism by diagrams A and B in combination.

It is necessary to discuss the nature of the five nested analytical dimensions and their associated values—the conceptual types of behaviorism—before briefly previewing the content variants of behaviorism generated by the various branches.

Nature of the Analytical Dimensions: Conceptual Types of Behaviorism

DIMENSION ONE

The first dimension is a philosophical one and relates to the mind–body issue. A behaviorist must be some kind of monist with respect to this issue, and two variants of monism are relevant in this context: material or physical monism and mental epiphenomenalism.

Material or physical monism is associated with metaphysical behaviorism. A metaphysical behaviorist denies the existence of mind or consciousness, in the Cartesian dualist sense of the term.

Mental epiphenomenalism does not deny the existence of mind per se; however, in this approach, consciousness and mental events are strictly epiphenomenal in nature: They are purely the by-products or derivatives of having a body. In no way are mental phenomena ever causative or efficacious. Mental epiphenomenalism is associated with two different conceptual forms of behaviorism, as generated in the context of nested dimension two.

DIMENSION TWO

The second dimension relates to whether mind and consciousness, in the epiphenomenal sense, are relevant for psychology. Two different interpretations of the dimension exist: no relevance, and relevance as possible objects of empirical study.

The no-relevance interpretation generates the notion of methodological behaviorism. A methodological behaviorist conducts experimentation, at a methodological level, and interprets the behavioral data, at an explanatory level, without any reference to consciousness and mental events. In methodological behaviorism, mental phenomena are irrelevant for the prediction and/or control of behavior.

The relevance interpretation establishes the notion of radical behaviorism: Granted that mind and consciousness are never causative or efficacious, they can serve as a focus of empirical concern in their own right, as possible dependent variables. The radical behaviorist B. F. Skinner, for instance, conceptualizes mental epiphenomena as private experience, composed of internal, covert stimulus/response events, to which only the experimental subject itself has direct introspective access. The epiphenomenal covert stimuli and responses involved in consciousness are private events, not amenable to public/objective observation as are overt, physical stimuli and responses. Skinner, however, assumes that by proper training through the use of appropriate reinforcement contingencies a subject can be conditioned to label and externalize the content of his/her current awarenesses. In Skinner's radical behaviorism, the concept of behavior, or dependent variable, is applied to events occurring both within and outside of the organism's skin.

CONCEPTUAL SUMMARY OF DIAGRAM A

Diagram A generates three basic conceptual forms of behaviorism: (1) metaphysical, (2) methodological, and (3) radical.

The distinction between the metaphysical and methodological forms of behaviorism by and large is purely semantic. In both cases, experimental psychology is a monistic enterprise, dealing exclusively with physical, material behavioral events; in neither interpretation is mind, consciousness, mental phenomena, and the like relevant for the prediction or control of behavior. Note that diagram B extends from both the metaphysical and methodological branches in diagram A. It is irrelevant whether a given behaviorist is metaphysical or methodological in orientation with respect to the content of diagram B.

The distinction between radical behaviorism and the other two conceptual forms of behaviorism is significant. A radical behaviorist is willing to conceptualize so-called mental epiphenomenal events occurring within the skin as behavior, and therefore amenable to experimental analysis. The radical behaviorism branch does not extend to diagram B—but not because the nature of radical behaviorism inherently prevents such an extension. Skinner, the primary adherent of the radical behaviorist position, is also a descriptive behaviorist.

It is the latter aspect of his behaviorism that makes extension to diagram B irrelevant.

Skinner's behaviorist position, in general, is very difficult to derive. He denies the existence of mind, but refuses to be called a metaphysical behaviorist. He employs all the basic presuppositions of the methodological behaviorist with respect to the irrelevance of mind, but he refuses to be classified as such. His avowed position of radical behaviorism could be derived only by extending the domain of behavior to include consciousness or elements of private experience.

DIMENSION THREE

The third dimension is the primary analytical dimension of diagram B and is essentially psychological in nature. This dimension relates to the presumed locus of the primary determinants of behavior and determines, in large part, the characteristic psychological flavor associated with a given content variant of behaviorism.

A behaviorist is a determinist and seeks the causes of behavior in the physical, external environment. Behavior, as one kind of physical event in the universe, is related to environmental events, as another kind of physical event in the universe. The behaviorist relates two different kinds of external, objective events to each other. This statement can be true in either of two senses: immediately (directly), or ultimately (indirectly). These two senses make the presumed locus of the primary determinants of behavior a relevant analytical dimension and establish two more conceptual forms of behaviorism.

1. In the immediate interpretation, the behaviorist relates behavior only to external, environmental events, thereby excluding the use of any operationally definable internal mediators connecting a physical stimulus event and a physical response event. This practice amounts to a descriptive behaviorism in which psychological explanation consists solely of the discovery of empirical laws stated in strict S-R terminology. Note that classical Watsonian behaviorism is derived as a form of descriptive behaviorism.

2. In the ultimate interpretation, the option is open to use operationally definable internal mediators between overt stimulus and response events. The practice of using one or more hypothetical constructs or intervening variables between the stimulus input situation and the response output situation amounts to a logical behaviorism. Logical behaviorists take a prescriptive approach to psychological explanation and construct higher order theories of behavior. Most of

the specific content variants of behaviorism entailed by the logical behaviorism branch amount to theories of learning, at least in the traditional sense of the term.

Logical behaviorism is related historically to the philosophical doctrine of logical positivism, or operationism, in which any unobserved/unobservable mediating construct must be reducible to one or more empirical terms that can be measured directly. The operations involved in measuring the hypothetical construct exhaust the scientific meaning of the construct. Any postulated intervening construct that cannot be defined and assessed operationally possesses no scientific explanatory or predictive value.

The doctrine of operationism has been subject to much philosophical criticism, and also is contradicted by many of the actual practices of the physical scientist. This, in part, explains why most of the content variants of logical behaviorism, exclusive of contemporary cognitive behaviorism, are now largely passé. Operationism currently functions as an informal methodological guide for the conduction of experimental research; it no longer serves as a fundamental principle involved in higher order theory construction.

DIMENSION FOUR

The fourth dimension relates to the primary locus of the internal mediators in the context of logical behaviorism. Two distinct loci are possible: peripheral and central. These generate the two traditional approaches to learning theory: the S–R associational approach and the S–S cognitive approach.

1. Many logical behaviorists prefer peripheral or peripherally oriented explanatory mechanisms. These mechanisms directly involve the muscles and the glands (the response effectors) or physiologically specifiable receptor events (stimulus detectors). Peripheral mechanisms less directly involved with the response effectors or stimulus detectors still must be ultimately specifiable in terms of overt stimulus or response entities. Logical behaviorism stressing peripheral mechanisms subsumes the classical Hullian effect and Guthrian contiguity S–R associational theories of learning.

2. Many logical behaviorists prefer central or centrally oriented explanatory mechanisms. These central mechanisms amount to cognitive processes (true brain events), such as cognitive maps, expectancies, and hypotheses. Tolman's purposive behaviorism or S–S cognitive theory of learning is derivable ultimately from this branch of logical behaviorism.

DIMENSION FIVE

The final dimension is applicable to S–S cognitive psychologies in the logical behaviorism context and concerns whether the central mediators are reducible to behavioral or peripheral terms. Two interpretations of this dimension are relevant: reducibility and irreducibility.

1. In the reducibility interpretation, any central mechanism or cognitive event is presumed to be translatable to a behavioral or peripheral event. More generally, any explanatory statement containing central referents is presumed reducible to a corresponding statement containing only behavioral referents. This interpretation gives rise to the notion of analytical behaviorism, in which any cognitive statement is reducible to a statement involving only behavioral dispositional terms. Tolman's purposive behaviorism is classified as a type of analytical behaviorism because such peripherally oriented S–R psychologists as Hull and Guthrie were able to reduce his cognitive mechanisms to strict S–R or peripherally oriented terms. The classic confrontations between Hullian S–R effect learning theory and Tomanian S–S contiguity learning theory, which occurred from the late 1930s to the early 1950s, ultimately devolved into mere semantic squabbling.

2. In the irreducibility interpretation, explanatory statements containing central mechanisms or involving cognitive processes are not presumed translatable to explanatory statements consisting of lower level or peripherally oriented constructs. Cognitive processes are not reducible to more basic conditioning or purely associational processes; they are physical, material events that are emergent in nature. For instance, thought is not reducible to a linear string of implicit CR habits. These cognitive processes operate as mind, in the everyday conception of the term. This branch of logical behaviorism generates contemporary cognitive behaviorism, in which the primary determinants of overt behavior are assumed to be internal, mediating cognitive processes. The most popular variant of contemporary cognitive behaviorism is the information-processing approach, in which the human mind is modeled after the computer and computer-based processes.

CONCEPTUAL SUMMARY OF DIAGRAM B

Diagram B generates four conceptual forms of behaviorism: (1) descriptive, (2) logical, (3) analytical, and (4) cognitive, the latter two being subtypes of logical behaviorism. The distinction between descriptive and logical behaviorism is significant and not merely semantic. The distinction between analytical behaviorism, in which no irreducible cognitive processes exist, and cognitive behaviorism, in which cognitive processes constitute emergent phenomena, also is significant and not merely semantic. Note that every content variant of behaviorism, with the exception of Skinnerian radical behaviorism, is derivable in the context of diagram B. Unlike diagram A, which operates more as a philosophical filtering device, diagram B functions as a psychological/operational classification scheme, involving the critical decision-making dimensions/options faced by a metaphysical or methodological behaviorist.

Content Variants of Behaviorism

CLASSICAL WATSONIAN BEHAVIORISM

Watsonian behaviorism is a methodological *or* metaphysical descriptive behaviorism: Watson vacillated between the two forms of monism. His brand of behaviorism usually is labeled classical behaviorism because it initiated the behaviorist revolt against consciousness and is the original, germinal version of behaviorism. Watson was a dynamic figure. Under his stimulation as a writer and publicist, behaviorism extended beyond the rather limited confines of the academic establishment and achieved wide-ranging public recognition. Watsonian behaviorism dominated American experimental psychology from approximately 1913 to the mid-1930s. All the other content variants of behaviorism generated by the branching tree diagrams are post-Watsonian and usually are referred to collectively as neobehaviorism, although they are not labeled as such in Figure 5-1.

Watsonian behaviorism is characterized by (1) extreme environmentalism (as opposed to nativism), (2) an emphasis on empirical S–R laws (its descriptive orientation), (3) elementarism or associationism, (4) conditioning (specifically Pavlovian or classical) as the primary source of behavioral change, and (5) the classically conditioned response (CR) as the unit of habit. The more amorphous or elusive psychological phenomena, such as emotion, language, and thought, were interpreted by Watson strictly in terms of peripheral mechanisms.

Chapter 6 analyzes Watsonian behaviorism in depth.

SKINNERIAN RADICAL BEHAVIORISM

Skinnerian behaviorism is a radical descriptive behaviorism. Skinner is the immediate intellectual heir of Watson, and his radical behaviorism is a logical extension of Watsonian behaviorism, although it amounts to a completely independent system. Skinner differs from Watson in at least three significant respects: (1) Skinner formally distinguished between classical (respondent) conditioning and instrumental (operant) conditioning, making the latter (along with the operational principle of reinforcement) the cornerstone of his system. (2) Skinner allows no theoretical constructs whatsoever; his extreme descriptivism excludes any kind of intermediary—cognitive, mental, physiological. (3) Skinner will deal with consciousness or private experience as an epiphenomenal response event.

Radical behaviorism can be dated from 1938 when Skinner published *The Behavior of Organisms*, although the system did not begin to influence American psychology significantly until after World War II. A prolific writer, Skinner enjoys extensive recognition in the overall American culture. Skinnerian psychology is all-pervasive. It has tremendous practical application and behavioral technology value, and also constitutes a virtual social philosophy. As an experimental psychology, Skinner's approach is known as the experimental analysis of individual behavior. The nature and focus of operant conditioning research have changed since the 1930s; however, the basic core of Skinnerian doctrine, as originally expressed in *The Behavior of Organisms*, still persists. Radical behaviorism currently is a significant force in American experimental psychology; in fact, it is the only content variant of behaviorism generated by Figure 5–1, exclusive of contemporary cognitive behaviorism, to survive intact to the present time.

Skinnerian behaviorism is analyzed in Chapter 7.

LOGICAL BEHAVIORISM: LEARNING MACROTHEORIES

The logical behaviorism branch of Figure 5–1 generates a class of neobehavioristic variants that usually are identified and analyzed collectively as approaches to the psychology of learning or learning theory. This class includes (1) Hull's hypothetico-deductive effect system; (2) Spence, Neal Miller, Mowrer, and other neo-Hullian approaches in general; (3) Guthrie's contiguity theory; and (4) Tolman's purposive behaviorism or cognitive learning theory. Any content variant of behaviorism essentially is a learning psychology, either in a mechanical or cognitive sense; however, the members of this class are known more as learning theories than as versions of behaviorism.

From the mid-1930s to the early 1950s, Hullian effect theory, Guthrian contiguity theory, and Tolmanian cognitive theory competed with each other. This 20-year period can be referred to as the macrotheoretical era of learning psychology, in which each of these approaches attempted to account for the entire range of learning phenomena in terms of a fundamental set of learning laws and postulates. The three approaches differed in their degree of formal theorizing, but they all employed an extensive explanatory intervening variable apparatus, with Guthrie's being more informal than the others.

These macrotheoretical learning systems, in a sense, represent the maturing of behaviorism as a science. They originated in the logical postivistic tradition and intentionally were modeled after theory construction in the physical sciences. The macrotheoretical approach to learning phenomena precipitously declined following the deaths of Hull, Guthrie, and Tolman, all within the relatively short period from 1952 to 1959. The learning macrotheories were replaced by even more formal, but less comprehensive, theoretical efforts: the mathematical model approaches of Estes, Suppes, Bower, Atkinson, Bush, Mosteller, Restle, and others. These contemporary mathematical model approaches to learning are even less identified with behaviorism than their macrotheoretical forebears, and no attempt was made to derive them in the context of Figure 5–1. (See page 112.)

Certain aspects of the macrotheoretical variants of logical behaviorism, as well as their mathematical model successors, are treated in Chapters 6–8; however, spatial limitations will not permit an indepth consideration of learning macrotheory as a system.

CONTEMPORARY COGNITIVE BEHAVIORISM

The logical behaviorism branch of Figure 5–1 also generates contemporary cognitive behaviorism. This form of behaviorism represents a re-emergence of the historic interest in the central processes underlying behavior after many decades of neglect attributable to (1) the descriptive prescriptions of Watson and Skinner, and (2) the dominance of the formal, peripherally oriented, conditioning-based logical behaviorism (learning macrotheories) of Hull, Guthrie, and the neo-Hullians in general. As a result of new developments in computer science, communication theory, and modern linguistic theory, behaviorists turned their attention to the possible internal, central sources of behavior in the early to mid-1960s.

Cognitive behaviorism is referred to more generally as cognitive psychology, and it should be noted that not every cognitive psychologist is a behaviorist—for instance, the late Jean Piaget, the renowned Swiss, French-language, genetic epistemological psychologist. Cognitive psychology is not new. Structuralism, act psychology, Gestalt psychology, and Tolman's purposive behaviorism were cognitively oriented systems.

Contemporary cognitive behaviorism, but not necessarily cognitive psychology in general, is essentially an information-processing approach to behavior, in which the computer and computer-based processes serve as the basic model for the prediction and explanation of behavioral events. As presaged in Chapter 4, no longer does conditioning serve as the fundamental source of behavioral change; rather, cognitive processes perform this function, even to the point of subsuming the basic learning and conditioning processes.

Cognitive behaviorism is briefly characterized in Chapter 8.

Bibliography

Atkinson, R.C., Bower, G.H., and Crothers, E.J. *An Introduction to Mathematical Learning Theory.* New York: Wiley, 1965.

Bergmann, G., and Spence, K.W. Operationism and theory in psychology. *Psychological Review,* 1941, 48, 1–14.

Broadbent, D.E. *Behavior: A Survey of Twentieth Century Behavioristic Psychology.* New York: Basic Books, 1963.

Erwin, E. *Behavior Therapy: Scientific, Philosophical, and Moral Foundations.* Cambridge, England: Cambridge University Press, 1978.

Hilgard, E.R., and Bower, G.H. *Theories of Learning,* 4th ed. Englewood Cliffs, N.J.: Prentice-Hall, 1974.

Hilgard, E.R., and Marquis, D.G. *Conditioning and Learning.* New York: Appleton-Century-Crofts, 1940 (Revised edition by G.A. Kimble, 1961).

Hillner, K.P. *Psychology of Learning: A Conceptual Analysis.* Elmsford, N.Y.: Pergamon, 1978.

Hillner, K.P. *Conditioning in Contemporary Perspective.* New York: Springer, 1979.

MacCorquodale, K., and Meehl, P.E. On a distinction between hypothetical constructs and intervening variables. *Psychological Review,* 1948, 55, 95–107.

Marx, M.H. Intervening variable or hypothetical construct. *Psychological Review,* 1951, 58, 235–247.

Skinner, B.F. *The Behavior of Organisms.* New York: Appleton-Century-Crofts, 1938.

Spence, K.W. The methods and postulates of "behaviorism." *Psychological Review,* 1948, 55, 67–78.

Spence, K.W. Cognitive versus stimulus-response theories of learning. *Psychological Review,* 1950, 57, 159–172.

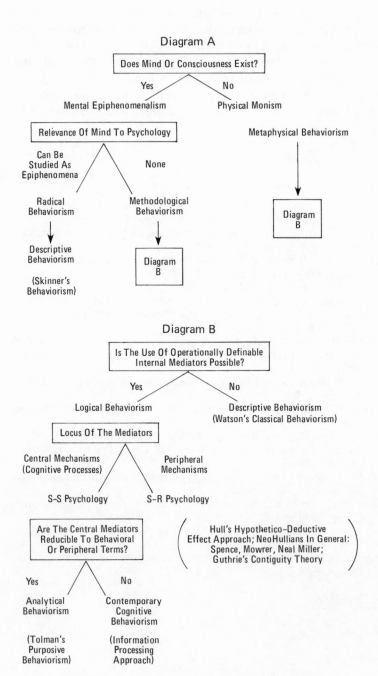

Figure 5-1: Derivation of the Basic Forms of Behaviorism

6

Watsonian
Behaviorism

Introduction

Watsonian behaviorism is not the only form of classical behaviorism. Among other psychologists who espoused some variant of behaviorism and who coexisted with Watson were Walter S. Hunter, Albert P. Weiss, Karl S. Lashley, Edwin B. Holt, Z. Y. Kuo, and Max Meyer. These men made significant contributions to the behavioristic movement in the United States. Watson's system of psychology, however, usually is treated as the prototypical form of classical behaviorism and serves as the basic comparative reference point for assessing the more contemporary versions.

John B. Watson rightfully can be credited with transforming America's functionalistic adaptation psychology into a behavioristic one. He was a dynamic leader and polemicist. He did not mince words, and what he lacked in terms of precise definition or conceptualization and supportive empirical data, he compensated for by a rabid and unswerving faith. Watson advocated behaviorism as others advocate religion. It is fashionable now to criticize Watson for his blind adherence to and overstatement of the behaviorist position, but what is forgotten is that he had legitimate reasons for attacking both structuralism and functionalism, as well as specific goals in mind by promulgating a behavioristic position.

Watson's basic aim was the acceptance of psychology as an objective science, one comparable to physics and chemistry. Consciousness, either in the structuralist content sense or in the functionalistic utility sense, simply did not serve as a source of public, verifiable data. Instead of blaming introspective observers for the irreplicability and unreliability of introspective report, Watson dismissed the method of introspection itself from the realm of objective, scientific methodology. Trained as an animal psychologist, he preferred running animal subjects—animal psychology, in America at least, had always been objective. Watson had trouble introspecting and was uncomfortable with human subjects in introspective sessions. He eventually reached the point where he found it impossible to resolve his interest in objective animal behavior with the overall field of psychology defined as the study of human consciousness, and he took the logical step of extending the objective approach to animal behavior to the domain of the human being. Watson turned psychology around. Psychology became the study of objective organismic (animal or human) behavior, and consciousness became irrelevant.

Watson's descriptive orientation is a natural consequence of his desire to rid psychology of any reference to mind and its trappings. Pure objectivity required relating behavior to external, environmental events and downplaying any internal mediators/sources of behavior. He dismissed mental events, either as input (causes) or output (epiphenomena), from psychology by fiat. Watson's descriptivism is basically reactional in nature, as opposed to Skinner's descriptivism, which is more positivistic and philosophical in orientation.

Watson's position on the relevancy of physiology for psychology is a logical extension of his approach to mind. To him the brain was a "mystery box," to be avoided as a determinant of behavior. He focused on the peripheral nervous system and the muscles and glands; and any psychological phenomenon occurring within the skin, such as thought, was interpreted strictly in terms of peripheral mechanisms. He conceptualized psychologically relevant internal events, in general, as implicit or covert peripherally based behaviors.

The positive aspect of Watson's descriptive orientation is his extreme environmentalism. The significant source of behavioral change is learning, specifically classical conditioning. The classically conditioned response serves as the unit of habit; and any complex behavior or behavior sequence, in principle, can be broken down into subhabits. Watson de-emphasized possible hereditary or nativistic sources of behavior. Inherited capacities, talents, and temperaments were illusory in his approach. Watson found no need for a theory of motive or internal motivation. He accepted the existence of some rudimentary reflexes and of three basic forms of emotion at birth; but even these became intertwined with learned habits, such that emotional expression in adulthood primarily was a matter of acquired components. His approach to instincts evolved over the years, eventually reaching the point where he denied their existence. The only reason he had to be concerned with the concept of instinct in the first place was the cotemporary prevalence of McDougall's purposive or hormic psychology, in which instincts served as the primary determinant of overt behavior.

Any descriptive behaviorism implicitly is applied in orientation, and Watsonian behaviorism is no exception. Watson presaged Skinner with his "experimental ethics," in which behaviorism served as a "foundation for saner living" and encompassed a program of social control and betterment. Watson also focused on child development, both as a subject of his own research program and as the topic of writings designed to inform the general public of the benefits of applied behaviorism. After Watson left academia in 1920, he made a career for himself in advertising, the quintessence of an applied psychology.

Although Watson vehemently attacked structuralism, it is interesting to note that his descriptive behaviorism amounts to a sensationistic, descriptive Titchenerian structuralism at a different level of reality. In Chapter 2, we pointed out that structuralism focused on the how, what, and why of conscious experience and dealt with the analysis and synthesis of mental elements. Watsonian behaviorism focused on the how, what, and why of overt behavior and dealt with the analysis and synthesis of reflexive units of behavior. Watsonian behaviorism was just as molecular, atomistic, elementaristic, and associationistic as structuralism. Only the basic object of analysis changed: from mental elements to overt responses and/or stimulus–response connections.

Since Watsonian behaviorism constituted a transitional school between functionalism and subsequent forms of neobehaviorism, its historical antecedents overlap those of functionalism, and its primary historical legacy relates to the formation of more contemporary versions of behaviorism. Our analysis, therefore, emphasizes the problems indigenous to the basic subject matter and methodology of Watson's system as a behavioristic psychology.

Object of Study; Basic Subject Matter

Initial Description

The basic natural phenomenon of concern for Watson was behavior—overt or covert, external or internal, explicit or implicit. Behavior was assumed to be determined, specifically by antecedent or concurrent environmental events. Watson used the term stimulus for environmental causes and the term response for behavior: His behaviorism is a descriptive S–R psychology. In the context of the stimulus and response terminology, Watson described the goal of behaviorism as (1) given the stimulus, to predict the response, and (2) given the response, to predict the stimulus.

The notions of stimulus and response constitute the fundamental units of analysis in Watsonian behaviorism, just as sensation, image, and feeling do in the context of structuralism. As is the case with the analytical units of any system of psychology, the notions of stimulus and response are metaphysical entities. They are definable or resolvable at any level of reality that the psychologist considers convenient or pragmatic. They are assignable any number of existential properties that the psychologist finds necessary for an adequate descriptive account of the basic natural phenomenon of interest.

Watson was informal in his characterization of stimulus and response units. He used the terms in a consistent manner; however, he was not concerned with their formal definition or denotative properties. Thus he could be quite flexible in their usage. Three basic metaphysical practices/assumptions seem to pervade Watson's descriptive S–R psychology:

1. The behaviorist program of translating mentalistic terms into behavioristic language essentially involves transforming them into stimulus and/or response terminology. A traditional mentalistic concept has to be pushed into a stimulus or response category, primarily the latter. (The response category serves as the critical metaphysical repository for every variant of behaviorism, with the possible exception of cognitive behaviorism.)

2. A given stimulus or response event can be resolved at any level of reality desired. A stimulus can be simple or complex—an isolated instance of physical energy affecting a specific sensory receptor, such as an auditory tone, or a complicated stimulus situation, such as a specific social situation. A response can be molecular or molar—the activation of a given response effector (the movement, physical activity, or secretion encompassed by such an activation) or

a functional act having some effect on the environment or achieving some goal. For instance, leg flexion as a reflexive response is a molecular event, whereas the act of driving a car is a molar event.

3. All behavior ultimately is assumed to be reducible to molecular muscular movements or glandular secretions. Molar responses are assumed to be reducible to molecular ones. In general, the whole is equal to the sum of its parts; and the basic combination process involves molecular S–R associations formed by (classical) conditioning.

There follows a description of Watson's approach to stimulus and response events, an account of his program of converting mentalistic concepts into behavioristic language, a consideration of the role of habit and classical conditioning in his system, and a characterization of the nature of Watson's determinism.

Stimuli

In the context of Watsonian behaviorism, the notion of stimulus merely serves as a convenient descriptive label. It was a functional substitute for the notion of cause and possessed no real meaning beyond this. For Watson, the term stimulus was applicable to whatever aspect of the environment was discovered to be controlling the specific response of current concern. Unlike later behaviorists, he did not assign any function to stimuli other than that of pure elicitation or causation: Stimuli did not possess reinforcing, motivational, or discriminative functions.

Watson more or less took over the physiologist's conception of a stimulus as that specific physical event which elicits physiological activity in an organism. Since the physiologist primarily is interested in isolated physiological activity, Watson assigned a psychological level of reality to stimuli, so that he could accommodate the fact that the behavioral psychologist is interested in the integrated activity of the whole organism.

Beyond giving the notion of stimulus a psychological level of reality, Watson did not have a formal conceptualization of stimulus events. He allowed both external and internal stimulus events, the latter primarily physicalized in terms of response-produced stimuli associated with peripheral response activity—for example, kinesthetic stimulation produced by muscle movement or organic stimulation produced by visceral activity. Since behaviorism is not a perceptual psychology, or is not concerned with the structure of conscious experience, Watson did not require an elaborate theory of stimulus identification. In his early days as a graduate student at Chicago, Watson studied the kinds of stimulus cues that controlled a rat's responding. Later, at Johns Hopkins, Watson, along with Yerkes, studied the discriminative visual capacity of various organisms. This research caused no conceptual problems with respect to stimulus definition because it basically was sensory, as opposed to perceptual, in nature. Watson had no problems with sensation because he conceptualized it as a kind of discriminative response.

Although Watson could avoid a formal characterization of a stimulus event at a conceptual level, he could not avoid an operational problem associated with every type of behaviorism: How do you know whether or not a given event X taken at random from the environment can serve as a stimulus? This is the problem of stimulus specification, and it cannot be resolved without appeal to the behavioral level of reality. The only way to determine whether event X is a stimulus is by assessing its effect on behavior: If event X elicits a response or comes to control response occurrence, it is a stimulus. This operational requirement makes it very difficult to construct a conceptualization of stimulus events that contains no reference to response events, and critics of behaviorism like to point out that the concept of a stimulus is circular. In its most general form, the circularity relates to the fact that neither a stimulus event nor a response event can be defined or identified without reference to the other. Given a specific stimulus–response occurrence, or pair, only one of the two terms is independent. Most behaviorists accept this fact and assume that a given stimulus–response pair is only one independent existential event: Distinguishing between stimulus events and response events is convenient descriptively, but does not amount to anything conceptually.

Responses

Recall that in most variants of behaviorism the response category serves as the crucial metaphysical repository. Virtually every psychological phenomenon subsumed by Watsonian behaviorism possesses the status of some form of response event. Watson distinguished among four types of responses: (1) explicit (external) learned, (2) implicit (internal) learned, (3) explicit unlearned (innate), and (4) implicit unlearned. The third and fourth types assumed less and less significance as his system evolved over the years.

Any response occurrence, by definition, involves one or more of the response effectors: the muscles and glands. The striped or skeletal muscles were associated with external responses; the unstriped or smooth muscles were associated with internal responses. The glands generally entail internal responses, except for those instances where the glandular secretion can be externalized directly, as in the case of salivary gland activity, such as occurs in the classical conditioning of salivation in the dog.

At a more analytical level, Watson implicitly distinguished between molecular and molar responses. In making this distinction, he attempted to have the best of two worlds. The notion of a molecular response directly corresponds to the conception of a response as effector activity, and also serves as the ultimate explanation for molar response occurrence. The notion of a molar response describes what an organism is doing (Watson was fond of characterizing behavior as doing) and involves the everyday verbal terminology of the public; that is, responses encompass meaningful, purposeful, or intentional acts.

Watson had no problem of response specification in the context of molecular activity. Response specification simply is the reverse of stimulus specification, as described previously: How do you know when a given molecular response occurs? How do you recognize instances of its occurrence? Since a molecular response is defined as muscular movement or glandular secretion, it is pure physiological activity. That physiological activity simply is given direct psychological status, or immediate psychological representation, as a response event. Note that most molecular responses are reflexive in nature and are elicited by simple stimuli: The identification of a given physiological event as a molecular response is not independent of the stimulus level of reality, and molecular responses are defined circularly. The notion of a simple stimulus elicitor and that of a reflexive molecular response merely constitute two sides of the same coin: They refer to the same existential event and cannot be distinguished independently.

Watson did have problems of response specification in the context of molar activity, and that probably is why molar response occurrence was explained by reduction to a concatenation of molecular level responses. A molar response is not simple reflex activity, elicited by the presentation of a specific stimulus; it cannot be specified in terms of a psychological representation of physiological activity. A molar response appears to have meaning or to be intentional—it accomplishes some goal or has an effect on the environment. The stimulus associated with a given molar event usually is some complex stimulus situation: The more complex the behavior, the more recessed is the actual controlling stimulus event. A given molar activity certainly cannot be specified in terms of preceding or concurrent stimulus events. It can be identified only in terms of succeeding or consequential stimulus occurrences—the goal or ultimate environmental change. This smacks of teleology.

Unlike such later behaviorists as Skinner and Hull, Watson assumed no response-contingent reinforcing function of a stimulus event, nor did he postulate the existence of a class of instrumental responses amenable to reinforcement. He could not define a molar response as an instrumental response event, specifiable in terms of its effect on the environment or reinforcing consequences. He could not engage in functional response specification: A given instance of behavior is a member of molar response class X if it results in the accomplishment of environmental change X or in the procurement of reinforcing stimulus X. The reason a functional response specification of molar activity is not teleological is that it is assumed that a given instance of molar activity occurs because it has been reinforced for happening in the past: The controlling variable is past reinforcement history, not the attainment of a future goal or instance of reinforcement.

In sum, Watson *explained* the occurrence of molar activity by reduction to molecular events. However, he could not operationally *specify* the occurrence of a given instance of molar activity in terms of the stimulus elicitation of a molecular response, nor did he make the critical distinction between an elicited response and a reinforceable instrumental response that would have allowed him to engage in functional response specification of molar activity.

Watson's Reduction of Mentalistic Phenomena to Behavioral Terms

To maintain a consistent material monistic approach to psychological phenomena, Watson had to reduce many mentalistic concepts to physical terms. Many psychological phenomena, which traditionally were regarded as mentalistic in nature, had to be translated into peripheral stimulus or response events to make them continuous with other publicably observable, physical events. Any mentalistic notion impervious to such a reduction is irrelevant for an objective psychology and is functionally meaningless. Watson not only gave a behavioristic interpretation to the three fundamental mental elements of the structuralist program—sensation, image, and feeling—but he also gave a physical interpretation to such symbolic processes as language and thought, and to such internal motivational states as emotion and instinct. Most of these reductions involve the response category and the postulation of implicit responses.

SENSATION

For Watson, the structuralist notion of a sensation as embodying the inner essence of the content of one's immediate awareness is meaningless. Sensation viewed as an absolute category of experience is vacuous. In the context of classical behaviorism, sensation reduces to an external discriminative response. For instance, if a subject responds differently in the presence of a green stimulus and a red stimulus, the experimenter infers that the subject reliably can distinguish between the two stimulus colors, even though the content of the sensed experience of the subject is a private event beyond public scrutiny. Saying "yes" in the presence of a green stimulus and "no" in the presence of a red stimulus are discriminative responses. These discriminative responses are objective, publicably observable events. The use of such responses allows the behaviorist to investigate various aspects of sensory capacity: absolute thresholds, difference thresholds, just noticeable differences, and so on. Even an animal psychophysics, assessing the range and sensitivity of the various sensory modalities, is possible in the behavioral context through the use of classically conditioned motor responses. (The ultimate in animal sensory research currently involves the use of operant conditioning in the framework of Skinnerian radical behaviorism.)

IMAGERY

We shall confine our comments to visual imagery. In structuralism, a visual image is the residue of a prior visual sensation and constitutes an absolute category of experience. Watson reduces the notion of visual imagery to kinesthetic stimuli set up by minute or implicit eye movements occasioned by the subject's attempt to imagine a certain object or event. Thus a centralized mentalistic image is translated into an implicit peripheral response-produced stimulus event. Such a conception of a visual image is not relevant for the prediction or control of overt behavior, and Watson did not investigate visual images. His conversion here is hypothetical, and merely illustrates what the behavioral approach can accomplish.

FEELING

For the structuralist, one of the concomitants of conscious experience is a subjective feeling state or affection, which can be described qualitatively as pleasant or unpleasant. Watson performed a hypothetical reduction of pleasant and unpleasant feelings in terms of internal, response-produced stimulation occasioned by the activation of the sexual organs and related erogenous areas. The onset of sexual arousal produces pleasant feelings; the termination or interruption of sexual arousal produces unpleasant feelings. Watson accounts for the capacity of an originally neutral stimulus object, one not inherently associated with sexual stimulation, to elicit a pleasant or unpleasant feeling through the process of (classical) conditioning.

LANGUAGE

By language, Watson essentially meant speech or verbal behavior. The speech utterances of an organism, although symbolic in nature, are no different from other external, motor responses. There is no fundamental difference between oral speech sounds and communication involving physical gestures. Language amounts to a system of acquired verbal habits. Individual words are (classically) conditioned in children, and extended utterances consist of implicit S–R chains.

Although Watson's approach to verbal behavior was quite primitive and simplistic, his basic behavioristic orientation was carried on by Skinner in his more definitive and sophisticated analysis of verbal behavior conducted in an operant conditioning framework.

To be more specific about verbal behavior in a behavioristic context, we must distinguish between the ability to encode (produce) and decode (comprehend) speech. Watson's approach to language primarily concerned the production aspect. Language comprehension involves the notion of meaning, the behavioristic approach to which is described later in the context of radical behaviorism.

THINKING

Although orthodox structuralists did not study thinking (it was imageless), it represents the quintessence of a mentalistic concept. The primary activity associated with the traditional concept of mind is thinking or the generation of new ideas. Watson proposed a strictly peripheralistic interpretation of thought. He made it a subset of language. Thinking is a kind of behavior; thinking amounts to implicit verbal responses; thinking is subvocal speech. When an organism thinks, he/she essentially is talking to himself/herself. Thinking simply is another kind of implicit habit, specifically an implicit laryngeal habit. Watson had an elaborate description of how thought, or thinking behavior, is internalized. His associates attempted to record implicit tongue movements while a subject was thinking, and even tried to record implicit hand movements while a deaf mute was thinking (a deaf mute speaks with the hands).

Watson's conception of thinking provides for one of Freud's basic notions: the unconscious. The content of the unconscious in general is unlabeled or unlabelizable experience. The vast store of experiences accumulated by an individual during infancy are said to reside in the unconscious, and consequently are irretrievable. For Watson, such experiences occur before the child can verbalize his/her experiences; they are stored as unlabeled material and, therefore, are inexpressible later in life.

EMOTION

Although emotion is not necessarily a mentalistic notion, it customarily is treated as an elusive, internal psychological state, not subject to direct observation on the part of the psychologist. Watson reduced an emotional state to a peripheral reaction, primarily involving the visceral and glandular systems. An emotion was conceptualized as a combined explicit and implicit response, with the latter predominating. In the course of studying the expression of emotion in human infants, Watson discovered that certain stimuli, as UCSs, elicit characteristic innate patterns of responding, as UCRs, which could be characterized as emotional in nature. Watson empirically isolated the sufficient stimuli and characteristic identifying responses for three basic types of infantile emotion: rage, love, and fear. He considered adult emotional expression to be an extension and modification of the three basic infantile emotions: The emotional expression of an adult also involves learned components, acquired through the process of (classical) conditioning. (Watson's overall research program on emotion is described later in this chapter.)

INSTINCT

The notion of instinct is one of the most pervasive, as well as elusive, psychological concepts in the history of psychology. Watson's thought with respect to the nature of an instinct evolved through at least three separate stages. Initially he believed instincts were a concatenation of innate reflexes. Later he allowed this concatenation of innate reflexes to be overlaid with learned habits. Finally he denied the very existence of instincts.

The Role of Habit and Classical Conditioning in Watson's System

Although Watson was an environmentalist, he had no formal theory of learning. He rejected Thorndike's law of effect as too subjective because of its reference to satisfaction and dissatisfaction, and he was not influenced by Thorndike's connectionism or learning research (see Chapter 3). Watson's learning notions were essentially pre-Thorndikian in nature and were adopted from British empiricism. The two basic factors in learning were frequency and recency. The correct or learned response, as in a maze, tends to be the most frequent one as well as the most recent one. Together these two factors reduce to a law of exercise or pure repetition, in which contiguity between stimulus and response events plays a crucial role.

For Watson, all learning generically was a form of conditioning; and what he meant by conditioning was Pavlovian classical conditioning. (Skinner did not distinguish formally between the classical and instrumental forms of conditioning until the 1930s.) Classical conditioning played two crucial roles in Watsonian behaviorism.

1. It served as the primary source of behavioral change at a conceptual level, and in this context the notion of a conditioned response served as the unit of habit. Watson reduced practically everything to some type of learned habit, and a habit simply was viewed as a classically conditioned response.

2. It served as a methodological research technique by which animal and nonverbal or preverbal human behavior could be studied objectively. Classical conditioning is to Watsonian behaviorism what introspection was to structuralism. In effect, Watson replaced introspection with classical conditioning as the fundamental methodology of experimental psychology and enhanced behaviorism's claim to objectivity.

Watson's emphasis on classical conditioning often leads to the mistaken belief that classical Watsonian behaviorism and (classical) conditioning possess an inherent relationship, whereas, in actuality, no such relationship exists. Watson promulgated his behaviorist manifesto before he even became aware of Russian objective psychology—Pavlov's and Bekhterev's work on classical conditioning. Watson's behavioristic notions simmered for at least a decade before they were published formally in a 1913 *Psychological Review* article, and he did not announce conditioning as the fundamental component of his behaviorism until a 1915 speech accepting the presidency of the American Psychological Association.

Watson never conducted theoretical or parametric classical conditioning research. He simply accepted the Russian experimental work on classical conditioning at face value and made conditioning the fundamental explanatory principle of his behaviorism. What he did do was to use classical conditioning in illustrative, practically oriented research. He demonstrated, for instance, that fears could be conditioned and deconditioned through appropriate pairings of CSs and UCSs.

The Nature of Watson's Determinism

Watsonian descriptive behaviorism can be construed as advocating a traditional, strict, or unidirectional interpretation of determinism, in which causation is assumed to be physical or mechanical in nature: Cause and effect constitute an explicit, automatic sequence. Mechanical systems, in which the activity or movement of one physical body (as cause) imparts the necessary force or energy for the activity or movement of another physical body (as effect), serve as the model for this kind of determinism.

Watson made extreme environmentalism the cornerstone of his system, in part, to justify his objective approach to human behavior. Of course, stimuli did not lead to responses in a direct, mechanical, transformation of energy sense; however, Watson's emphasis on the reflex made the organism a prisoner of its environment. Although he did not appeal to underlying physiology to explain overt behavior, he assumed the classic, push–pull conception of a reflex in which response output is an automatic function of a telephone-type neuronal hookup system. For Watson, the primary source of new responses, or behavioral change, was classical conditioning, an automatic process over which the organism had no real control. Both the unconditioned response (UCR) and the conditioned response (CR) were regarded as involuntary.

Method of Study; Permissible Methodology

Watson, like Wundt, was extremely conscious of methodology. His behaviorist revolt was in large part methodological—an objective psychology required objective methods. The subject matter of psychology could not be objective unless its methods also were objective. But, again like Wundt, Watson contributed no new research techniques, with the possible exception of the method of verbal report, which amounted to a reinterpretation of introspective data. His basic methodological contribution relates to the expressed goal of objectivity, which requires an enhanced recognition of and higher standards for what constitutes an acceptable behavioral research technique.

The basic principle underlying all behavioristic research is the use of experimental conditions that allow objective observation. In the context of this principle, Watson advocated only four specific research techniques: (1) observation with and without experimental control, (2) the conditioned reflex method, (3) the method of verbal report, and (4) mental testing.

Observation With and Without Experimental Control

This technique does not require extensive comment. Observation with experimental control refers to the standard laboratory situation in which the input conditions, or independent variables, are under the explicit control of the experimenter. Observation without experimental control refers to naturalistic observation, as it usually occurs in field studies. This category is indicative of the nature of the overall orientation taken by contemporary experimental psychologists with respect to acceptable experimental methodology.

The Conditioned Reflex Method

The conditioned reflex method is synonymous with classical conditioning, interpreted as a research technique. Watson did not study the process of classical conditioning; rather, the conditioned reflex method merely served as a convenient instrument for studying behavior objectively. The conditioned reflex method is to classical Watsonian behaviorism what the operant conditioning technique is to radical Skinnerian behaviorism: (1) a method of behavioral control or (2) a reliable tool by which to demonstrate some of the abstract principles of the system. For instance, it was used to study the range and sharpness of various sensory capacities, as well as the limits of various response capacities; and it was used to demonstrate that fears can be learned. Animals, preverbal or nonverbal humans, and various members of the abnormal population had to be studied with the conditioned reflex method. In the context of the normal human adult subject, it served as a surrogate for introspection or verbal report. In sum, Watson promulgated the conditioned reflex method and made it the cornerstone of his methodology because it afforded a nonmentalistic description of most of the psychological phenomena in which he was interested.

The Method of Verbal Report

The method of verbal report implicitly was previewed in the context of describing Watson's conception of sensation. This technique served as Watson's behavioristic analogue for structuralist introspection. A behavioristic experiment involving verbal report and a structuralist introspective session are similar in many respects; however, the purpose and interpretation of the two techniques are vastly different.

1. The purpose of an introspective session is to externalize the contents of an observer's consciousness. The purpose of verbal report is to generate language responses, which serve as substitutes for nonverbal motor responses. In many experiments involving adult humans, it simply is more convenient to accept the subject's verbal expression as physical discriminative responses than to use a conditioned motor response. In a simple task involving a highly restrictive verbal response category system, such as "yes" or "no," the verbal response is equivalent to pushing a button or raising a hand.

2. At an interpretive level, in an introspective session the subject or introspector observes his/her own consciousness. In a behavioristic study involving verbal report, the experimenter, or some automated recording device, observes and tallies the verbal responses emitted by the subject. Introspective report is private and subjective, not amenable to reliability and/or validity assessment, whereas verbal report is public and objective, amenable to reliability and/or validity assessment. See Chapter 2 for a more detailed discussion of the differences between an introspective session and the typical behavioral study.

The method of verbal report makes a behavioristic psychology of sensation and/or perception feasible. The content of verbal report serves a discriminative, indicative function, just as does a physical motor movement or a pointer reading on a dial of an instrument. Classical behaviorists did not go overboard in their use of verbal report. They allowed only a restricted number of verbal report response categories in order to maintain a high level of objectivity in an experiment. A classical behaviorist would find complete, unrestricted verbal report, such as occurs in the descriptively elaborate responses given in the presence of a Rorschach inkblot card, largely uninterpretable. The classical behaviorist typically did not allow free-wheeling phenomenological description in the Gestalt sense.

Mental Testing

In accepting the objectivity of mental tests, Watson merely was facing reality. A mental testing movement already had mushroomed in America in the context of functionalistic psychology, and was solidified by World War I. Watson himself worked on personnel assessment problems after being drafted into World War I service: He ran an examining board for aviators. Watson gave a behavioral interpretation to mental tests: What a test measured was behavior, or overt responses, not mental qualities. The importance of mental testing as a research technique increased for Watson after he left academia and entered the business world.

Origin; Specific Historical Antecedents

Behaviorism, as a formal system of psychology, was announced by Watson in his 1913 *Psychological Review* article, "Psychology as the Behaviorist Views It." This article was based on a series of lectures he had given at Columbia University the previous year, at the invitation of Cattell. Watson's founding of behaviorism is similar to Darwin's establishment of the evolutionary doctrine (see Chapter 3). Both intellectual movements possessed numerous historical precursors and represented the culmination of a lengthy process of evolution. Both Watson and Darwin were consummators or completers, who fused relevant historical trends into a separate, identifiable conceptual entity.

Since Watsonian behaviorism is a direct intellectual descendent of American functionalism, the historical antecedents of functionalism discussed in Chapter 3 are relevant in the context of behaviorism. These are not reviewed here, and the reader is invited to refer to that chapter. The historical input into behaviorism is multifaceted; to delimit the discussion, we concentrate only on those historical antecedents that are related directly to behaviorism's fundamental characteristic—its objectivism or material monism.

Three explicit roots of behaviorism's objectivism/material monism can be identified: (1) various philosophical trends, (2) objective animal psychology, and (3) Russian objective psychology. Many aspects of the initial two roots already have been covered implicitly in the text, so they need be discussed only briefly. The third root must be analyzed in some depth.

Philosophical Trends

The philosophical influences on Watsonian behaviorism included materialism or the mechanistic doctrine, the British empirical school of epistemological philosophy, and the doctrine of positivism.

MATERIALISM

Watsonian behaviorism is the logical culmination of materialism in general and French materialism in particular. The mechanistic/materialistic doctrine postulates that human beings are like any other natural phenomenon in the universe and can be explained in strict physical–chemical terms. Recall from Chapter 2 that Descartes began the trend to mechanism in French philosophy. Although a dualist, Descartes was an implicit mechanist because he assigned the body—simple sensory functioning and simple physiologically based reflexes, for example—to the material world. He was a total mechanist with respect to the behavior and psychological nature of animals. Later French philosophers, such as LaMettrie and Cabanis, were material monists and expunged any reference to mind and consciousness. They viewed the human organism simply as another animal, or even as a type of machine. They were total mechanists. Thomas Hobbes, one of the early British empiricists, was a mental epiphenomenalist, and also advocated a total materialistic/mechanistic view of the human being.

BRITISH EMPIRICISM

Although the British empiricists, except for Thomas Hobbes, were not generally materially monistic in orientation, two aspects of Watson's psychology are direct descendents of British empirical thought: environmentalism and associationism.

1. The British empiricist's notion of *tabula rasa* and stress on the

experiential source of knowledge translates into an extreme environmentalism in Watson's behaviorism. Watson extended the British empiricist environmentally based epistemology to the totality of behavioral
expression on the part of the human organism.

2. The British empirical doctrine of associationism was absorbed
by Watson *en masse*. He merely changed the basic content of an association from one of mentalistic ideas to one of physical stimulus
and response events. In general, any S–R behavioristic theory of learning is a direct outgrowth of British associationism, with respect to
both the content of learning (an S–R association) and the physical
factors mediating learning (contiguity, recency, frequency, similarity,
and so on).

POSITIVISM

The modern version of the doctrine of positivism essentially was
originated by the nineteenth century Frenchman, Auguste Comte.
Positivism primarily is an epistemological statement that equates truth
with public, objectively verifiable knowledge. Comte criticized the
notion of consciousness and the method of introspection long before
Wundt ever entered the laboratory. His positivism also functions as
an implicit philosophy of science because it delimits the proper subject
matter and bounds of science, and in this context scientific objectivity
can be viewed as a form of positivism. Watson's goal of creating a
truly objective psychology, interpreted as the science of behavior, is
a logical outgrowth of Comte's positivism. Comte's positivism ultimately led to both Mach's extreme descriptivism or sensationism (see
Chapter 4), which had a marked effect on Skinner's radical behaviorism, and the Vienna Circle's logical positivism, which influenced
the logical behaviorism of such neobehaviorists as Hull, Guthrie, and
Tolman.

Objective Animal Psychology

An objective animal psychology existed long before behaviorism
was promulgated by Watson. Recall from Chapter 3 that Darwin's
theory of evolution stimulated a rebirth of British comparative psychology, and that Morgan's comparative psychological work influenced Thorndike's animal experimentation at Columbia. For all
practical purposes, Thorndike was an implicit behaviorist: he analyzed behavior in strict stimulus and response terms and emphasized
connectionism or associative shifting. Although his law of effect did

not influence Watson, it is the cornerstone of Hullian and Skinnerian psychology.

Watson was introduced to animal psychology, as a graduate student at Chicago, by Angell and Donaldson. At Chicago, he also was influenced by the German objective biologist, Loeb. Later, at Johns Hopkins, he collaborated with Yerkes, an animal psychologist, and took courses from Jennings, a biologist. Watson performed comparative and/or animal psychological research for at least a decade prior to his publication of the behaviorist manifesto. This manifesto merely represented the extension of an objective orientation that he already possessed in the context of animal psychology to the overall field of psychology itself, especially human psychology. He transformed human psychology from a psychology of subjective consciousness to a psychology of objective behavior.

Russian Objective Psychology

A physicalistic psychology existed in Russia some 50 years before classical Watsonian behaviorism began in America, although it was known neither as a behaviorism nor as a psychology. In retrospect, it is called Russian objective psychology, a term that refers collectively to the psychological systems and thought of Ivan Sechenov (1829–1905), Ivan Pavlov (1849–1936), and Vladimir Bekhterev (1857–1927), who were all associated in some capacity with the Military–Medical Academy at St. Petersburg University. Of the three, only Pavlov retains any contemporary cultural salience, primarily because of his classical conditioning of the salivary reflex in the dog. But merely associating Pavlov with a dog's salivating to the sound of a bell is a caricature of his real significance in the history of psychology.

If Russian objective psychology is analyzed in depth, analogues can be found in it for practically every facet of Watsonian behaviorism—material monism or mechanism, extreme environmentalism, associationism, language and thought as physically based reflexive activity, and so on. The appearance of a Russian physicalistic psychology analogous to behaviorism during the latter part of the nineteenth century is amazing when one considers that Russia was a non-Western, nonindustrialized, totalitarian (czarist) society. Although Sechenov, Pavlov, and Bekhterev studied at one time or another in the West, specifically Europe, they were not impressed by European psychology, which they found too mentalistic, too subjective, and too introspective. What they meant by European psychology was an amalgamation of structuralism, Gestalt psychology, and Freudian psychoanalysis.

The key to understanding Russian objective psychology is the fact that all three men were experimental physiologists with medical training backgrounds. Of the three, only Bekhterev came close to identifying himself as a psychologist; Pavlov maintained throughout his life that he was not one. Russian objective psychology did not even have a concept of behavior. The object of analysis of Russian objective psychology was physiological activity/processes, specifically nervous activity, especially that occurring in the brain; the fundamental analytical unit was the reflex. It is very difficult to characterize the inner essence of Russian objective psychology: In general, it is a systematic orientation in which any psychologically significant or relevant phenomenon, such as our consciousness or behavior, is resolved in terms of underlying physiological reflexes. The term reflex is more general than in American psychology and carries connotations of central cortical activity. Sechenov is considered the father of Russian objective psychology; Bekhterev's system often is referred to as reflexology; and Pavlov labeled his subject matter the psychophysiology of higher nervous activity.

Although Bekhterev and Pavlov were colleagues at St. Petersburg for a time, they were fierce competitors. Pavlov and his system eventually gained dominance over Bekhterev and his version of objective psychology, both inside and outside of Russia. Pavlov achieved an international reputation for his work on the digestive processes in the dog and received a Nobel prize in medicine and physiology in 1904, before he even began systematic investigation of canine salivary secretion. Pavlov's laboratory was comparable to that of Wundt's and attracted approximately 200 research collaborators over the years. The Soviet (Communist) government eventually recognized the psychophysiology of higher nervous activity as the officially sanctioned psychology of the state. Bekhterev's reflexology was condemned and passed from the scene after his death.

Pavlov's psychophysiology of higher nervous activity encompassed the neurophysiological underpinnings of classical conditioning and anything that could be related to it.

1. Pavlov's empirically researched classical conditioning phenomena included acquisition, extinction, spontaneous recovery, generalization, and discrimination. He accounted for these in terms of underlying hypothetical cortical brain processes, such as excitation, inhibition, and irradiation.

2. Examples of psychological phenomena that Pavlov was able to relate to classical conditioning included:

a. Behavior pathology (experimental neurosis) as created by a too-difficult discrimination.

b. Individual differences (personality types) based on differential nervous system typologies.

c. Sensory analyzing systems in the brain (our sensation and perception).

d. Speech and thought, as products of the second signal system (symbolic CSs).

The metaphysical or physiological trappings of Russian objective psychology did not have an influence on American behaviorism. But what influenced American psychology was its methodology or basic research focus: classical conditioning. Pavlov published an article on the conditioned reflex in a 1906 issue of *Science*. Yerkes and his Russian student, Morgulis, translated some of Pavlov's papers reporting the discovery of the conditioned reflex, and these appeared in a 1909 *Psychological Bulletin* article. Bekhterev focused on learned motor responses, interpreting them as association reflexes; Pavlov studied learned salivary responses, referring to them as psychic secretions. The American learning establishment ultimately absorbed Bekhterev's specific research focus (motor responses) and Pavlov's operational terminology (CS, UCS, CR, UCR) and prototypical behavioral phenomena (acquisition, extinction, and the like). Watson, of course, adopted the classically conditioned response as the unit of habit, equated Pavlovian conditioning with learning, and made conditioning the primary source of behavioral change.

Chief Historical Figure: John Broadus Watson (1878–1958)

Watson was born near Greenville, S.C., in 1878. His mother was very religious, and he endured a fundamentalist upbringing. Watson was a rebellious youth who often got into trouble with the police; scholastically, he was a mediocre student. However, at the age of 16, he matriculated at Furman University, and would have graduated with the B.A. degree in 1899 except for the fact that he submitted a term paper to an instructor with the pages in reverse order. He remained at Furman another year and was graduated with an M.A. degree in 1900.

After his mother died, Watson was able to pursue his interests in philosophy and psychology; and he went to the University of Chicago, primarily because John Dewey was there. Watson did not understand Dewey and found him to be a great disappointment. He became more attracted to psychology, and focused his studies under James Angell, the functionalist, H. H. Donaldson, an expert on the nervous system of the rat, and Jacques Loeb, the German biologist. Watson felt at home in the animal laboratory, and came to prefer animal research over human research, which required introspection. One of his best known studies from this Chicago period involved the removal of various sensory systems from a white rat who was attempting to learn a maze. He discovered the primacy of kinesthetic cues for the rat in traversing the maze. Watson worked hard at Chicago, both in and out of class. He labored at numerous part-time jobs, including one as caretaker of Donaldson's rat colony, to support himself. He suffered a nervous breakdown because of his overactivity, but overcame it after a short vacation. Watson earned his Ph.D. degree in only three years, graduating in 1903 as the youngest doctorate Chicago had produced to that time. His Ph.D. dissertation, supervised by Angell and Donaldson, was entitled "Animal Education: The Psychical Development of the White Rat." In this study, he demonstrated a correlation between the increasing complexity of behavior in the young albino rat and the growth of medullation in the central nervous system. Watson remained at Chicago after obtaining his doctorate, working as an assistant in experimental psychology for two years and then as an instructor for two years. Chicago promoted him to the assistant professorship level, but, when Johns Hopkins offered him a full professorship at an annual salary of $3500, Watson left Chicago, in 1908, to begin the most celebrated period of his academic life.

It was during the Johns Hopkins years that Watson made his indelible mark on American psychology. In 1909, he became chairman at Hopkins and also was appointed an editor of the *Psychological Review*. He took courses from Jennings and collaborated with Yerkes in developing an apparatus for testing an animal's visual (color) capacities. Perhaps Watson's most famous Ph.D. student at Hopkins was Karl Lashley, who later renounced the strict molecular associationism of his mentor's behaviorism. Watson performed the famous little Albert experiment with Rosalie Rayner, tested various fear removal techniques with Mary Cover Jones, and studied emotional expression in a large sample of infants at the Harriet Lane Hospital in Baltimore.

Although Watson talked of objectivity as early as 1903 with his colleagues at Chicago and had discussed it at a colloquium at Yale in 1908, it was Cattell's invitation to deliver lectures at Columbia in 1912 that crystallized his thinking on the subject. These lectures developed into the 1913 *Psychological Review* article proclaiming the behaviorist revolution: "Psychology as the Behaviorist Views It." His first book, *Behavior: An Introduction to Comparative Psychology*, published in 1914, focused on animal behavior. *Psychology from the Standpoint of a Behaviorist*, which appeared in 1919, focused on human behavior. Watson was elected president of the American Psychological Association in 1915, and in his acceptance speech he introduced the conditioned reflex as a primary concept in his behaviorism. In 1916, he published an article in the *Psychological Review* entitled "The Place of the Conditioned Reflex in Psychology." Watson's tenure at Johns Hopkins was interrupted by World War I; he was drafted, ran an examining board for aviators, and was scheduled to enter the intelligence service for disciplinary reasons until the Armistice made the transfer moot. Watson had to leave Johns Hopkins in 1920 because of a messy divorce and his remarriage to Rosalie Rayner. Rosalie died in 1936, an event from which Watson never fully recovered.

After leaving Johns Hopkins, Watson joined the J. Walter Thompson advertising agency in New York City, and by 1924 had become a vice-president there. He switched to William Esty and Company in 1936, and remained with this firm until his retirement in 1946 to a small farm outside of New York City. During his advertising years, Watson continued to write books and popular articles, and even give occasional guest lectures at universities, but his creative endeavors as the founder of the behavioristic movement essentially were over. Watson's post-1920 writings are characterized by a questionning of and an attack on such cherished, traditional beliefs as those concerning child rearing, marriage, religion, and sex. A book entitled *Behaviorism*, which was based on lectures given at the New School for Social Research, was published in 1924 and achieved great popular success. In 1928, Watson and his wife published a child-rearing guide, *Psychological Care of Infant and Child*. A revised edition of *Behaviorism* appearing in 1930 was Watson's last book on psychology *per se*, and marked his formal departure from psychology. He published an autobiography in 1936.

Watson spent his last few years in declining health, and he died in 1958. The psychological/academic establishment had treated him rather shabbily following his divorce, and in a partial attempt to rectify the situation an effort was made by the American Psychological Association to recognize Watson as a past president at its 1957 convention in New York City. Watson traveled to New York, occupied a hotel room, but never managed to attend the convention.

Characteristic Experimentation; Primary Research Areas

Watson's research program derived from two related sources: his belief in environmentalism and his desire to separate learned (acquired) and unlearned (innate, hereditary) components of behavior; thus his interest in child development and child-rearing practices, and in the active manipulation of the child's environment. His research program was a combination of the genetic, developmental approach and the experimental laboratory approach, with the human infant as the primary subject type. This program can be illustrated by considering three specific topical area studies performed by Watson and/or his co-workers: (1) infant emotion, (2) fear conditioning, and (3) fear deconditioning.

Recall that Watson also had an active animal research program; however, most of his animal studies preceded the 1913 *Psychological Review* article proclaiming the behaviorist manifesto. After the manifesto, Watson's basic aim was to demonstrate the relevance of the objective approach to human behavior.

Infant Emotion

Watson observed over 200 babies at Harriet Lane Hospital in Baltimore to determine whether there were any distinctive innate components of behavior. He noted a whole repertoire of reflexive activity, such as sneezing, grasping, crying, and blinking. Somewhat later, in an attempt to separate the learned and innate components of emotion, Watson discovered that an infant is capable of only three basic forms of emotional expression: rage, fear, and love. Rage is evoked by restricting the infant's natural movements and is manifested by holding of the breath, stiffening of the body, and slashing movements of the arms and hands. Fear is elicited by a loud sound or the sudden loss of support and involves crying, lip puckering, breath catching, and eyelid closure. Love is related to the stroking, patting, or general manipulation of sensitive bodily areas and is shown by smiling, cooing, gurgling, extension of the arms, and so on.

These stimulus and response events are objective entities; the identification of the specific emotions associated with them is a subjective inference on the part of the experimenter. Later research demonstrated that an experimenter could not identify a given emotional reaction through observation of the physical response alone, without accompanying knowledge of the specific eliciting stimulus.

Watson postulated that other emotional states, such as shyness, hate, jealousy, anguish, pride, and shame, develop out of the three basic forms of infantile emotional expression. The innate rage, fear, and love responses are modified by conditioning such that adult emotional expression has significant social/cultural components: In adulthood, a person can exhibit unwarranted rage, ungrounded fears, or unreasonable love attachments. Watson empirically demonstrated that a fear response can be learned—that is, conditioned to an initially neutral stimulus event, as described below.

The Case of Little Albert: Fear Conditioning

Perhaps the most famous of Watson's laboratory demonstrations is his and Rosalie Rayner's creation of a conditioned emotional fear response in an infant male named Albert. They paired an initially neutral stimulus event for Albert, a white rat, with a known elicitor of fear, a loud sound. After approximately seven pairings, the rat also elicited fear responses in Albert. Watson and Rayner also demonstrated that the conditioned fear generalized to stimuli similar to the white rat: rabbit, dog, fur coat, cotton wool, human hair, and Santa Claus mask.

The creation and generalization of a learned fear on the part of Watson and Rayner demonstrate the viability of classical conditioning as an agent of behavioral change, in particular, and the utility of the environmentalism doctrine, in general. Behaviorists who faulted the Freudian psychoanalytic explanation of unwarranted fears, or emotional responses in general, in terms of repressed childhood sexual impulses and experiences had empirical data supporting their environmental approach.

Contemporary interest in the case of little Albert revolves around two things: (1) Watson and Rayner's demonstration probably is the most misdescribed and misrepresented laboratory phenomenon in the history of American psychology. This state of affairs is attributable partly to Watson himself, because he presented numerous versions of the study over the years. (2) Little Albert's acquired fear was never actively extinguished, because his mother removed him from the hospital before this could be attempted. Today, the failure to do this, if not the entire demonstration, would be considered unethical. Mary Cover Jones, under the direction of Watson, did actively engage in the deconditioning of an acquired fear in the laboratory, but not Albert's, as described below.

The Case of Peter: Fear Deconditioning

Three years after the case of little Albert, Mary Cover Jones deconditioned fear responses of unknown specific origin that a boy named Peter exhibited in the presence of a white rabbit. She used a technique that today would be called the method of toleration. Peter was fed lunch (entailing an appetitive UCS) in a room that contained a caged white rabbit (the aversive fear elicitor) at a distance. Over a period of days, the caged rabbit was brought closer and closer to Peter. Eventually Peter actively played with and fondled the rabbit while eating his lunch. Peter's fear responses were deconditioned or extinguished by the conditioning of approach responses occasioned by the pleasant meal. Mary Cover Jones also demonstrated that the approach response generalized to other, similar stimuli.

The case of Peter virtually went unnoticed, in comparison with that of little Albert. It constitutes an instance of the use of a behavior modification technique. Behavior modification did not become a significant aspect of American applied psychology until 30 years later, in the mid-1950s, under the impetus of Skinnerian radical behaviorism.

Historical Legacy

The historical legacy of classical Watsonian behaviorism is represented implicitly by Figure 5–1: the many variants of neobehaviorism. Skinnerian radical behaviorism is the most direct descendent of classical behaviorism and is the version of neobehaviorism bearing the greatest similarity to the Watsonian approach at a conceptual level, primarily because of Skinner's adherence to an extreme descriptivism and environmentalism, that is, primacy of conditioning processes. The various forms of logical behaviorism still stressed the importance of learning/conditioning, but they attempted to fill in the gap between overt stimulus events and response events, either peripherally (Hull, Guthrie, neo-Hullians) or centrally (Tolman).

Classical Watsonian behaviorism maintained and solidified many of the concerns it absorbed from functionalistic psychology: (1) an implicit interest in overt behavior, (2) the inherent practicality of an adaptive psychology, (3) an optimistic attitude about the future of man, and (4) a subject matter not divorced from the social/cultural milieu in which man finds himself. Watson made these concerns permanent features of American experimental psychology. Through his initial, germinal efforts and Skinner's later refinements, American behavioristic psychology came to serve as a social philosophy.

Watson's, and later Skinner's, descriptivism made experimental psychology a truly self-contained and independent science. Watsonian behaviorism broke experimental psychology away from two of its three presystemic roots: philosophy and physiology. By denying both the substance and utility of consciousness and refraining from any appeal to mentalism, psychology is divorced from its original or immediate philosophical base. Declaring that knowledge of internal physiology is irrelevant for the prediction/control of behavior prevents any ultimate reduction of psychology to biology. The third presystemic root, physics, was enhanced by the advent of behaviorism. Watson sought the objectivity characteristic of physics. Skinner limited relevant psychological truth to the empirical, physical input–output laws characteristic of physics. The logical behaviorists modeled their theory construction efforts after those practiced by physicists.

Watsonian behaviorism changed the fundamental focus of experimental psychology. Man no longer was studied as an experiencing organism, but as an acting organism. No longer a strictly epistemological entity, man became an object in time and space, generating physical output that affects the environment. The classic research areas subsumed by experiencing, epistemological man, sensation and perception, were superseded by those research problems associated with an action-oriented man, learning and conditioning. At a philosophical level, the advent of behaviorism represents the triumph of materialism or mechanism in psychology.

Watson's behaviorist manifesto set the stage for the beginning of contemporary experimental psychology. Granted that classical behaviorism, as a system of psychology, did not survive the decade of the 1930s, the residues of Watsonian behaviorism permeate the very essence of contemporary psychology. It was behaviorism that absorbed functionalism and Gestalt psychology, not vice versa. Contemporary experimental psychology must be characterized as some form of behaviorism, even if it is a more liberal, tolerant, or loose behaviorism. In Skinnerian radical behaviorism, everything is behavior, even the act of being conscious or reporting on the content of consciousness. In the contemporary mathematical model approach, the basic predictive focus still is on various response classes. Even in contemporary cognitive behaviorism, intervening cognitive/information-processing activities are physical, material events that ultimately must be related to or relevant for overt behavior.

Bibliography

Pavlov, I.P. The scientific investigation of the psychical faculties or processes in the higher animals. *Science*, 1906, 24, 613–619.

Watson, J.B. Psychology as the behaviorist views it. *Psychological Review*, 1913, 20, 158–177.

Watson, J.B. *Behavior: An Introduction to Comparative Psychology*. New York: Holt, 1914.

Watson, J.B. The place of the conditioned reflex in psychology. *Psychological Review*, 1916, 23, 89–116.

Watson, J.B. *Psychology from the Standpoint of a Behaviorist*. Philadelphia: Lippincott, 1919, 1924, 1929.

Watson, J.B. *Behaviorism*. New York: Norton, 1925, 1930.

Watson, J.B. *Psychological Care of Infant and Child*. New York: Norton, 1928.

Yerkes, R.M., and Morgulis, S. The method of Pavlov in animal psychology. *Psychological Bulletin*, 1909, 6, 257–273.

7

Skinnerian Behaviorism

Introduction

If we search the history of psychology for any system that has survived for at least half a century, there are three: the Freudian psychoanalytic approach, Piaget's genetic epistemological psychology, and Skinner's radical behaviorism. The longevity of Skinner's system can be attributed to the fact that it is infinitely descriptive and has been institutionalized.

1. Radical behaviorism as a system:

a. Is a general philosophical world view, an approach to the philosophy of science, and a social philosophy.

b. Is an explicit experimental technique and a sophisticated form of behavioral control, usually termed the experimental analysis of individual behavior or operant conditioning.

c. Serves as the source of an applied behavioral technology that includes behavior modification, programmed learning, and psychopharmacology.

d. Has achieved the status of a true paradigm in the Kuhnian sense of the term, according to many commentators on the psychological scene.

2. Radical behaviorism as an institution:

a. Comprises a separate division of the American Psychological Association: Division 25, the Division for the Experimental Analysis of Behavior.

b. Supports three separate in-house journals—*Journal of the Experimental Analysis of Behavior* (JEAB), *Journal of Applied Behavior Analysis* (JABA), and *Behaviorism*—founded in 1958, 1967, and 1973 respectively.

c. Possesses a large number of dedicated, rabid adherents scattered throughout the American educational establishment.

d. Is represented by an operant conditioning laboratory in virtually every experimental psychology department in the country, even if it is only a Skinner box for instructional purposes.

Skinner—a gentle, unassuming, nondirective man—probably did not consciously set out to found a system of psychology. For certain reasons, Skinner became interested in the concept of behavior. He discovered ways in which behavioral occurrence could be controlled and measured meaningfully, and he came up with certain behavioral principles that seemed to work and to be applicable to virtually every psychological problem. In a sense, Skinner's achievements are the result of operant conditioning itself. He was the right man, in the right place, at the right time; the environment continually kept reinforcing his responses.

Skinner's system inherently is pragmatic and adaptable. As it evolved, only those aspects of it that worked survived. Although a sophisticated philosopher, Skinner never really attempted to justify his system philosophically. Skinnerian principles simply work—they may lack true or ultimate explanatory power; they may be circular in part and self-correcting; they may be irrelevant for understanding the inner essence of man—but they work, and that is the only justification they need. Whenever a student takes off on Skinnerian psychology in class in a critical direction, I simply respond with the query: "How else can you deal meaningfully with a mental retardate?" It is as if Skinnerian psychology breaks up life, or the environment, into digestible chunks for the retardate and also slows them down, so that he/she can begin to exhibit responses bearing some resemblance to those that traditionally are labeled normal and adaptive. Skinnerian psychology is a psychology for the tinker, the technician, the mechanically gifted. Skinner himself is probably the greatest tinker psychology has ever known. It takes gadgets to implement Skinnerian principles, and Skinner was the past master at constructing them: Skinner box, baby crib, teaching machine, and so on.

As a logical extension of Watsonian behaviorism, radical behaviorism is both descriptive and environmentalistic; however, Skinner's descriptivism and environmentalism are more sophisticated than Watson's.

As a descriptive entity, radical behaviorism is a pure black box or empty organism approach. No internal referents of any kind are tolerated: cognitive, mental, physiological, neuronal, even genetic. Any significant or relevant psychological event is resolved in terms of a stimulus or response. A reflex is simply a correlation between an external stimulus and an overt response. The organism merely is a locus of variables. One of Skinner's favorite analogies involves a person having, or constructing, a poem just like a mother has, or constructs, a baby. So-called mental events and the contents of consciousness are behavior, that is, covert responses that can be externalized under the right circumstances. Skinner denies the efficacy of a cognitive apparatus because it stands between the organism and its experience of the environment. Skinner prefers to construe the organism as being in direct contact with the environment. Prediction and/or control of behavior is possible by merely taking into consideration the nature of the external contingencies that are in effect. Skinner is particularly critical of the mental apparatus used by the Freudian psychoanalytic approach: The apparatus is circular and merely redescribes the relevant external psychological factors, or psychological history of the organism, at another level of reality.

Correlative with his descriptivism, Skinner claims to be atheoretical; but he is only atheoretical in the sense that he denies the relevance of logical behaviorism (learning macrotheories), in general, and the hypothetico-deductive method, in particular. Skinner sees no value in constructing elaborate theories and then deriving testable hypotheses from them. What if the hypothesis is not confirmed experimentally? Theories just cover up ignorance of the true controlling variables. These are discoverable only through induction. Skinner's descriptive S–R laws are induced through experimentation. When sufficient experimentation has been completed, then summary laws can be formulated; but the concepts embodied by the laws have no meaning beyond the operations used to physicalize them. Skinner makes many theoretical assumptions, many of which are explicit; but they are not derived from a formal theory. Skinner has a metatheory, which functions as his theory; but it is not a theory in the traditional sense of the term. Skinner can be dubbed one of the greatest learning theorists of the current century, but he has no learning theory *per se*.

Skinner's environmentalism is focused around the concept of an operant and its reinforceable properties. The primary source of behavioral change is operant conditioning, not Pavlovian conditioning as in the case of Watsonian behaviorism. The notions of an operant conditioning contingency and reinforcement serve as the crux of Skinner's system. They embody the environmental circumstances that the organism faces in real life, that is, they serve as models for what occurs in the natural environment. The natural environment both selects and reinforces certain response classes (actually reinforcement entails selection), and these response classes are strengthened and endure. Skinner's environmentalism is pure Darwinism on an individual organism, or ontogenetic, level.

The focus of radical behaviorism has evolved and changed since its inception in the 1930s. It is difficult to present a specific chronology because there usually was a time lag between when Skinner first worked in a given area and when his work had a significant effect. For instance, *The Behavior of Organisms* was published in 1938, but did not affect learning psychology until after World War II; *Walden Two* was published in 1948, but the Skinnerian doctrine did not have an impact on social engineering until much later; *Verbal Behavior* was published in 1957, but it was based on his 1948 William James lectures at Harvard, which, in turn, were based on a 1941 manuscript. Therefore the following statements only encompass a rough chronology. Between 1930 and approximately 1955, Skinner concentrated on animal research, defining the basic parameters and concepts of operant conditioning and competing with the macrotheoretical learning approaches. Between 1955 and 1960, Skinner began to apply his principles to the human organism, specifically its verbal behavior. During the decade of the 1960s, a pure behavioral technology in terms of behavior modification and programmed instruction was developed. In the 1970s, Skinner became a virtual social philosopher, extending his principles to the proper composition and functioning of a humane society.

The pure laboratory aspects of radical behaviorism—the experimental analysis of individual behavior—also has changed appreciably over the years. From an initial concern for (1) the original shaping or acquisition of a piece of behavior, (2) the isolation of specific reinforcing events, (3) the delimitation of simple schedules of reinforcement, and (4) the functioning of conditioned reinforcers and discriminative stimuli, the focus of operant conditioning research has switched to (1) steady-state aspects of behavior and choice behavior, (2) relational properties of reinforcing events, (3) complex reinforcement schedules, and (4) relational properties of conditioned reinforcers and discriminative stimuli. Skinner's original formulation of the descriptive law of effect has been replaced as the fundamental empirical relationship in operant conditioning by Herrnstein's so-called matching law. Since Skinner retired from the active conduction of operant research and closed down his laboratory, the experimental analysis of individual behavior has been carried on by a second, even third, generation of active, dedicated Skinnerians. Contemporary operant psychologists no longer are reinforced by merely observing and measuring physical behavior in the raw as revealed by a cumulative record, but rather by articulating the verbalisms and higher level symbolic relationships that such activity permits. No longer does JEAB publish reproductions of cumulative records; the basic response datum is abstracted and expressed in symbolic mathematical equation form. The matching law is an equation; specifically, a class of related equations.

Radical behaviorism possesses such longevity that it can be compared meaningfully with classical Watsonian behaviorism as well as with contemporary cognitive behaviorism. Our analysis must highlight both of these aspects of radical behaviorism, as well as describe the evolutionary changes in operant conditioning research.

Radical behaviorism has been subjected to much criticism, much of it irrelevant or silly. Skinner ordinarily does not respond to his critics: He claims to be misunderstood and has better use to make of his time. There are only two crucial issues relevant to the viability of radical behaviorism as a system: (1) Does it adequately account for verbal behavior or language, thinking, meaning, and cognition in general? (2) Can it meaningfully be implemented as a form of social control; that is, who should serve as the controller, or philosopher-king in Plato's terminology, and what should be the goals of a society organized according to Skinnerian behavioral principles? Our discussion, it is hoped, will shed some light on these issues.

Object of Study; Basic Subject Matter

Initial Description

As an extension of classical behaviorism, radical behaviorism (1) focuses on behavior in relation to its controlling variables, (2) uses stimulus and response events as the fundamental units of analysis, (3) assumes a complex behavioral act is reducible to individual stimulus and response subevents, (4) regards conditioning as the primary source of behavioral change, and (5) assigns no causative role to mental events. However, Skinnerian behaviorism possesses only a superficial similarity to Watsonian behaviorism:

1. Control does not have the same connotations for Watson and for Skinner.
2. Skinner conceptualizes stimulus and response events differently than Watson.
3. Skinner's combinatorial rules for generating complex behavior do not correspond to Watson's.
4. Operant conditioning serves as the primary source of behavioral change for Skinner, while classical conditioning performs this function for Watson.
5. For Skinner, so-called mental events are epiphenomenal in nature and can be studied empirically as a form of behavior, while Watson prefers to reduce all mentalistic phenomena to conceptual peripherally based stimulus or response events.

As a laboratory endeavor, radical behaviorism is known as the experimental analysis of *individual* behavior. Skinnerian methodology permits an analysis of the behavior of an individual organism, not in an idiographic sense, but strictly for functional purposes: An attempt is made to discover the controlling stimuli for the responses associated with a single organism. An individual subject's behavior is resolved in terms of (1) S–R correlations (reflexes), (2) R–S contingencies (reinforcement control), and (3) S–R–S contingencies (discriminative stimulus control).

For Skinner, stimuli and responses are functional entities, defined operationally in terms of extrinsic or relational properties. A stimulus is not a form of physical energy, for example, a light wave; a response is not a muscular movement or glandular secretion, for example, leg flexion or salivation. These can be intrinsic properties of a specific stimulus or response event, but they are not used to operationally define a stimulus or response event. The notions of stimulus and response are class concepts for Skinner. A given stimulus or response occurrence is a member of a larger, functionally defined class of stimuli or responses. For instance, a given bar-press response occurrence is a member of the response class "bar pressing," and a given flash of light is a member of the stimulus class "light." The stimulus class or response class, as a whole (not the individual members), is defined in terms of certain operations performed by the experimenter. The goal of Skinnerian psychology is to establish correlations between response classes and specific antecedent or consequent stimulus classes.

Skinner makes a fundamental distinction between two different types of responses: respondents and operants. Each type of response (1) is associated with a different kind of conditioning, (2) bears a different functional relationship to stimulus events, and (3) enters into different kinds of contingencies. These two response types serve as convenient organizational units for analyzing the basic subject matter of radical behaviorism.

Respondents: Eliciting Stimuli, S–R Reflexes, S–S Contingencies, and Classical Conditioning

A respondent is a response that is elicited from an organism by a specific stimulus. For instance, leg flexion is elicited by a tap to the knee; salivation is elicited by placing meat in the mouth; a startle reaction is elicited by a sudden, unexpected sound. In Pavlovian terminology, a respondent is an unconditioned response (UCR) elicited by an unconditioned stimulus (UCS). A respondent and its eliciting stimulus, or a UCR and its UCS, are not independent events—collectively they define the notion of a reflex. A respondent merely is the response element of a given S–R reflex. If the UCS is a biological elicitor of a respondent, the reflex is said to be an unlearned or ·biological one; if the UCS is an acquired elicitor of a respondent, the reflex is said to be a learned or conditioned one.

Skinner assumes that a respondent only is amenable to classical conditioning (respondent conditioning in his terminology). The way in which an original neutral stimulus (nonelicitor) is transformed into an acquired elicitor of a respondent is through respondent conditioning. Respondent conditioning involves the use of an S–S contingency, in which the first S term is an original neutral stimulus (eventual CS or conditioned stimulus) and the second S term is a UCS (either a biological or acquired response elicitor). In respondent conditioning, a new respondent is not created; rather the respondent-eliciting capacity of a given stimulus merely is transferred to another stimulus event.

The general public would call a respondent an involuntary response. Since a respondent is stimulus elicited and stimulus specific, it is relatively easy to produce and control; however, the notion of a respondent plays only a trivial role in Skinner's system, for two basic reasons:

1. Skinner more or less equates a respondent with internal physiological activity, that is, autonomically mediated smooth muscle or
glandular activity. Respondents do not operate on the environment
and are not behavioral acts in the everyday sense of the term.

2. Skinner does not regard classical conditioning as a significant
source of behavioral change. Granted that classical conditioning occurs in the natural environment, the S–S contingency subsumed by
respondent conditioning is inflexible. The relationship between the
UCS and the UCR (respondent) is predetermined (either biologically
or through prior conditioning), and a desired alteration in either the
UCS or UCR event requires a change in the other event also. A respondent can change only if the elicitor changes, and the desire to
switch from the conditioning of one kind of respondent to another
requires an entirely new UCS or S–S contingency.

Operants: Reinforcing Stimuli, R–S Contingencies, and
Operant Conditioning

An operant is a response that simply is emitted by the organism.
An operant is assumed to occur in some stimulus situation; however,
the functional aspect of the stimulus situation is unknown and is left
unstated. For instance, bar pressing, key pecking, maze running, and
wheel turning are operants. An operant more or less corresponds to
the everyday conception of a behavioral act and appears to be vol-
untary in nature. An operant can affect the environment. An operant
can have consequences. If these consequences are physicalized in
terms of positive reinforcing stimuli, the so-called operant conditioning paradigm is generated. The simplest form of operant conditioning
involves an R–S contingency, in which the R term is the operant
response and the S term is the positive reinforcing stimulus. Operant
conditioning entails the selective positive reinforcement of response
occurrences from a specific, predetermined operant response class,
the result of which is an increase in the frequency of occurrence of
the members of the operant response class.

For Skinner, the most significant components of the behavioral
repertoire of an organism are operant responses, and operant conditioning constitutes the primary source of behavioral change in his
system. In the laboratory, a whole host of operant responses have
been conditioned: the bar press of the rat, the key peck of a pigeon,
the lever pull of a monkey, the button push of a human. In the natural
environment, a whole host of significant behaviors can be construed
as operant responses, amenable to operant conditioning: any physical

movement involved in a sporting or recreational event, for example, batting a ball or shooting a basket; self-care activities, such as eating, drinking, dressing, grooming; symbolic or verbal activities, such as reading, studying, listening, writing, speaking. Complex spatially or temporally organized behaviors in the natural environment, such as playing a piano or driving a car, can be conceptualized as chains of operant responses.

The R–S contingency subsumed by the simplest form of operant conditioning inherently is flexible. There is no predetermined connection between the R and S terms of the contingency. The relationship between the R and S terms merely is functional, arbitrary, or temporal. The individual R and S terms are independently manipulatable and substitutable. For instance, a bar press response can be reinforced by food, water, or sexual contact; or food can be used as a reinforcer for bar pressing, key pecking, lever pulling, or button pushing. In the natural environment, a retardate's correct dressing behavior can be reinforced by a token, a toy, a piece of candy, elaborate praise and attention; a token can be used to reinforce a retardate's proper dressing, proper tooth brushing, proper reading of the hands on a clock, and so on.

We are now in a position to discuss the more technical aspects of Skinner's operant psychology in the context of an expanded three-term S–R–S contingency.

The S–R–S Contingency: Stimulus, Response, and Reinforcement Definition and Specification

In operant conditioning, there is one response event and two stimulus events, one of which is optional. The response event, of course, is operant in nature. The mandatory stimulus event is the presentation of a positive reinforcer; the optional stimulus event is a specific physical stimulus in whose presence the operant is reinforced, for instance, a light. Such a stimulus usually is called a discriminative stimulus. Using CR, $+S^R$, and S^D as symbols for an operant response, positive reinforcer, and discriminative stimulus, respectively, the abstract S–R–S contingency translates into an $S^D - CR - +S^R$ contingency. The three elements of the $S^D - CR - +S^R$ contingency cannot be defined and specified independently.

THE OPERANT RESPONSE (CR)

In the laboratory, Skinner chooses the operants he investigates with some care: not every response that the organism emits qualifies as an operant. An operant is a functionally defined response class that possesses certain characteristics.

A functionally defined response class is a set of individual response activities that result in the same ultimate environmental change or have the same consequence. For instance, a rat in a Skinner box with a depressible bar as the response manipulandum can emit response instances from only two functional response classes: (1) the bar-press response and (2) the non-bar-press response. The bar-press response class consists of those response activities that fully depress the bar: these can involve the left front paw, the right front paw, the head, the whole body, and so on. The non-bar-press response class consists of those response activities that do not depress the bar: these include exploring, grooming, sleeping, and eating. Note that the intrinsic properties of the members of the functional bar-press and non-bar-press response classes are irrelevant for the definition of the response classes. The effect of a given instance of response activity, or its relationship to some external object, determines its response class membership.

Not every functionally defined response class can serve as an operant response. In addition to being a response class functionally defined in terms of a response manipulandum independent of the organism, an operant response must possess at least four other characteristics: spontaneity, autonomy, isolatability or measurability, and lawfulness. Spontaneity essentially means that members of the response class are easily performable by the organism, already constitute part of the organism's natural response repertoire, and even conceivably occur with an operant (i.e., prereinforcement) rate greater than zero. Autonomy means that members of the response class are not a component of a larger, more comprehensive, significant behavioral activity; for instance, they must not be components of the organism's natural eating, drinking, or mating behavior. Isolatability or measurability requires that the topography of the members of the response class be clear-cut and unambiguous so that occurrences of the members of the response class are obvious and easily or discretely countable. Lawfulness means that members of the response class, as defined, must partake in meaningful functional or correlational relationships: They must occur in a consistent, predictable manner under the influence of a particular controlling variable. As Skinner would say, the members of the response class must generate smooth curves.

To some degree, operant responses are species-specific and contingent on the underlying biology of the organism. The bar-press response constitutes an indigenous operant for the rat; it is not so for the pigeon. Likewise a key peck constitutes an indigenous operant for the pigeon; it is not so for the rat. There are many operant responses indigenous to the human being; button pushing simply is more convenient procedurally than others.

It is the fourth characteristic, lawfulness, which makes an identification of an operant response, independent of the two other terms in the contingency, impossible. The primary controlling variable, to which a functionally defined response possessing the first three characteristics is related, is reinforcement, the third term of the contingency. Operant responses cannot be identified independently of reinforcing stimuli. A functionally defined response exhibiting spontaneity, autonomy, and isolatability or measurability, but not amenable to the effects of reinforcement, is not an operant response. For Skinner, the notion of an operant response minimally implies the notion of a reinforceable functionally defined response.

THE REINFORCING STIMULUS (+ S^R): THE WEAK OR EMPIRICAL
LAW OF EFFECT

Reinforcement constitutes the canonical controlling variable of which responding is a function in operant conditioning. Specific aspects of a reinforcing stimulus that can come to control operant responding include: (1) amount, quantity, magnitude, or size; (2) hedonic quality; (3) immediacy of delivery; and (4) schedule, with the last having the greatest effect on the frequency and patterning of responding.

Skinner takes a purely descriptive approach to reinforcing events. There is no absolute list of reinforcers that possess some theoretical property in common: For instance, the macrolearning theorist Hull postulated that only stimulus events allowing primary drive reduction can serve as reinforcers. Skinner must define a reinforcing event strictly in terms of its effect on behavior. Since operant conditioning involves response-contingent reinforcement—that is, a reinforcer cannot be delivered unless a member of the appropriate response class occurs—the possible reinforcing property of a given stimulus event can be assessed only in terms of its effect on the operant response, the second term of the contingency. A given stimulus is a positive reinforcer if its presentation increases the frequency of emission of the members of the operant response class upon whose occurrence its delivery is contingent. (Negative reinforcers are stimuli whose termination conditions priorly occurring responses; for many reasons, Skinner did not advocate the use of negative reinforcement.)

Skinner's descriptive principle of reinforcement sometimes is called the weak or empirical law of effect. This law is supposed to function as a powerful control technique; however, it is circular for those operant response classes that are used to establish the reinforcing properties of a given stimulus in the first place. For instance, assume that we know that stimulus X is a reinforcer because it conditioned operant response Y. Then we cannot turn this statement around and say that operant response Y was conditioned because it was reinforced by stimulus X. There are a number of ways in which this circularity can be minimized or completely broken and which need not be mentioned here, but there is no way to resolve the fact that a reinforcer cannot be defined and specified independently of the response term of *some* R–S or S–R–S contingency. The empirical law of effect also suffers from another criticism: It is irrelevant for explaining the behavior generated by simple and complex schedules of partial reinforcement.

THE DISCRIMINATIVE STIMULUS (S^D): STIMULUS CONTROL AND STIMULUS DISCRIMINATION

Although operant conditioning can proceed in the context of a general, amorphous stimulus situation that is given tacit recognition (i.e., the internal confines of the appropriate Skinner box), on occasion it is convenient or pragmatic to bring the operant response under explicit stimulus control. This is accomplished by having an explicit physical stimulus in the environment—for example, a light on—associated with the delivery of reinforcement. Recall that such a stimulus is called a discriminative stimulus: S^D (S-dee). Having a specific discriminative stimulus present during an entire operant conditioning session is singularly uninteresting and not all that different from the simple situation in which no specific discriminative stimulus (i.e., the amorphous, tacit stimulus situation) is used. The usual procedure is to alternate random-length discriminative stimulus intervals with intervals during which the discriminative stimulus is absent. The absence of the discriminative stimulus amounts to the presence of another stimulus, called the nondiscriminative stimulus: S^Δ (S-delta). In the simplest case, the S^Δ—for example, light off—is associated with the nonavailability of reinforcement (the extinction procedure).

An S^D sets the occasion for responding, and an S^Δ sets the occasion for not responding. Operant responding is reinforced in the presence of the S^D; operant responding is not reinforced in the presence of the S^Δ. The S^D and S^Δ come to control responding and nonresponding respectively. Once the organism learns to behave appropriately in the presence of the two stimuli, the organism is said to have formed a stimulus discrimination. The notion of stimulus control or stimulus discrimination has extensive application to the natural environment where attempts are made to bring appropriate or desirable behaviors under explicit environmental control. Note that an S^D and S^Δ are not elicitors of responding and nonresponding. They do not function as UCSs in the context of respondents. They merely function as informational stimuli, signaling when reinforcement is available or unavailable, or signaling which specific contingency currently is in effect.

It is impossible to define the concept of a discriminative stimulus, or a nondiscriminative stimulus, without reference to the operant response and the reinforcing stimulus, the other two elements of the three-term S–R–S contingency. It is impossible to identify whether a given stimulus—for example, light, buzzer, tone, colored disc—taken at random from the environment can serve as a discriminative stimulus, or a nondiscriminative stimulus, independently of its effect on operant response occurrence.

A CONCEPTUAL CONCLUSION

Recall the discussion in the context of Watsonian behaviorism to the effect that stimuli and responses constitute circularly defined and specified events: A stimulus is an event that produces or is associated with a response, and a response is an event that is produced by or associated with a stimulus. Any purely descriptive behavioristic psychology encounters the problem of the codefinition and codetermination of its fundamental units of analysis. In Skinnerian radical behaviorism, this problem arises at three different levels: (1) cospecification of eliciting stimuli and respondents, (2) cospecification of operant responses and reinforcing stimuli, and (3) cospecification of discriminative, informational stimuli and operant responses.

Language, Meaning, and Verbal Behavior: Extension of the Operant to the Symbolic Level

INITIAL DESCRIPTION

Skinner analyzes overt verbal behavior, not language. Verbal behavior subsumes oral speech, the written word, and even physical gestures. These kinds of stimulus/response events possess some symbolic significance over and above their pure physical form. Language entails the logical, cognitive, or rule-governed system that presumably, for the linguist at least, stands behind verbal behavior. Skinner construes verbal behavior as simply another class of behavior that is under discriminative stimulus and reinforcement control. Verbal behavior is perfectly analogous to purely physical or motor behavior—bar pressing, for example—which ordinarily possesses no symbolic meaning.

Skinner explicitly focuses on speech as a functional system, that is, the dynamics of speaking. His goal is to explain speech activity functionally, specifically its momentary, deterministic occurrence and content. Unlike the linguist, he is not interested in the long-term statistical, or distributional, structural aspects of speech. Skinner distinguishes among five different kinds of verbal operants: (1) mands, (2) tacts, (3) echoics, (4) textuals, and (5) intraverbals.

MANDS

A mand is a verbal operant that functions as a request or command; for example, "milk," "give me milk," or "milk please." A mand can consist of one word, as is typical of a child's request, or of many words expressed in a socially polite manner, as is characteristic of the adult. At a grammatical level, a mand is equivalent to an imperative sentence. It is a surrogate for an actual physical procurement or reaching response. Procurement of the desired object is not accomplished by the individual's own physical activity; rather, delivery of the object is mediated by the behavior of the person affected by the mand.

What can serve as the relevant reinforcing event for the expression of a mand is entailed by the content of the mand itself; for instance, procurement of milk for "milk please." This fact makes the mand an ideal verbal operant for shaping by an adult member of the verbal community: Unless the verbal request (speech sound) is of a specific, acceptable form, it need not be reinforced. A parent can reinforce occurrences of "milk," but not occurrences of "mik," "meke," or the like. Ordinarily a mand is not under strict external stimulus control, although selective reinforcement of a mand in the presence of different human mediators can make the expression of a mand more probable in some situations than others. For instance, grandmothers typically reinforce a mand such as "candy" more than mothers do. The expression of a mand is more directly related to the current motivational state of the organism; for example, "milk" has a higher probability of occurrence when the requester is thirsty than when he/she is not thirsty.

TACTS

A tact is a verbal operant that functions to describe or label a given situation or the nature of the immediate environment. For instance, a one-word tact "elephant" emitted by a child at a zoo identifies the animal immediately in front of the child. A complete sentence, such as "It sure is a nice day," can describe the nature of the current stimulus situation. At a grammatical level, a tact is equivalent to a declarative sentence. A tact is not a surrogate for some physical, motor response; we ordinarily do not physically act out representations of an elephant or of a nice day. (The game of charades and other situations precluding auditory communication, such as sneak attacks, are obvious exceptions.) Tacts play a significant role in Skinner's system because, as we shall see later, the externalization of the content of one's immediate perceptual or conscious awareness involves tacting.

The relationship of a tact to reinforcement and to discriminative stimulus control is the reverse of that of the mand. The stimulus class that can reinforce a tact is open ended. A tact involves nonspecific, generalized reinforcement. Typically some form of recognition or approval response by the hearer of the tact is sufficient for reinforcement. The expression of a tact is under fairly strict discriminative stimulus control: The nature of the current physical stimulus determines the appropriateness or content of a given tact.

ECHOICS

An echoic is a verbal operant that mimics or repeats the content of the specific verbal operant that served as its immediate stimulus. For instance, a mother might say "doll"; her child's immediate repetition of "doll" would then constitute an echoic. Echoics are strictly stimulus-bound; however, their reinforcement is open ended and generalized.

TEXTUALS

A textual is a verbal operant occasioned by a visual stimulus, such as a picture, printed word, or written word. The content of the textual amounts to a decoding of the stimulus. Textuals are like echoics in that they are stimulus-bound and receive open-ended, generalized reinforcement. The most significant application of the notion of a textual is to reading. Reading involves explicit (aloud) or implicit (silent) textuals, reinforced by explicit social recognition and praise, as in school, or by implicit events, such as an increase in knowledge or intellectual appreciation in an adult.

INTRAVERBALS

An intraverbal is a verbal operant that is under the stimulus control of another, previous verbal operant. For instance, after a conversation begins between two people, much of the speech activity that occurs following the first verbal operant is intraverbal. An intraverbal emitted by person *X* reinforces the preceding intraverbal emitted by person *Y* and serves as the discriminative stimulus cue for the next intraverbal emitted by person *Y*: An intraverbal possesses both reinforcing and cue functions. Conceptualizing a conversation as a string of intraverbals highlights the functional or chain character of extended speech. The onset of the conversation probably is occasioned by a specific physical environmental circumstance, and its cessation probably is occasioned by the explicit delivery of physical reinforcement or the promise of such reinforcement, but the maintenance of the internal dialogue requires intraverbals performing dual reinforcement and cue functions.

MEANING

The existence of verbal behavior presumes that meaning exists: Speech sounds have and carry meaning. The speaker encodes (produces) meaning, and the listener decodes (comprehends) meaning.

Descriptive behaviorists such as Skinner and Watson must account for the existential status of meaning in a nonmentalistic way. They have two choices: Meaning can be construed as a stimulus event or as a response event. In an extended conversation, meaning can exist in each form simultaneously. In the context of speech decoding, meaning is a response event. The meaning of a stimulus word is whatever response the stimulus word elicits from the organism. In the context of speech encoding, meaning is a stimulus event. The meaning of an encoded response word is whatever stimulus property or significance it possesses for an observer.

Skinner presumes the inseparability of the meaning of a word and its use. The meaning of a word is given by the specific stimulus/behavioral situation in which it occurs, many of which entail reinforcement contingencies. The meaning of a word is established by the objects and relations for which it serves as a surrogate. Let us attempt to illustrate these rather abstract statements in both a decoding and an encoding context.

First, suppose a child responds, either physically or verbally, to the word *dog*. We can infer that the word has meaning for the child. But we cannot infer the specific content of the child's meaning—that is mentalistic and subjective. Meaning exists only in the sense that the verbal stimulus elicits consistent responses from the child. These consistent responses ultimately derive from how the word *dog* is used by the verbal community and the reinforcement of its correct usage. In large part, the meaning of a word is conditioned by the past reinforcement history of the organism.

Second, suppose a child speaks the word *dog*. We can infer that the word has meaning for the child, but not the specific content of the child's meaning, if the use of the term is appropriate to the stimulus situation. An actual physical stimulus instance of a *dog* need not be present. The appropriateness of usage of the word *dog* in the particular stimulus situation is, in part, a function of the commonality between the past reinforcement history of the child and that of the verbal community to which the child belongs.

Skinner's approach to meaning in relation to verbal behavior merely amounts to the consistent use and occurrence of words in specific stimulus–response correlations. Words have meaning if they are decoded consistently or encoded appropriately; they have meaning to the degree that purely verbal operants are susceptible to the same type of reinforcement contingencies that purely motor or physical operants are.

Consciousness: Extension of the Tact to Private Events

Recall from Chapter 5 that one of the basic features of radical behaviorism is the assumption that mental events can be studied profitably as epiphenomena. Skinner assumes that events occurring within the skin are relevant for psychology, not as possible physiological mediators of behavior or as possible cognitive processes determining behavior, but simply as another form of behavior. Skinner construes the content of current perceptual awareness and current introspective awareness as behavior, that is, internal, covert behavior to which only the experiencing organism has direct access. In effect, Skinner presumes that phenomenological experience, either in the Gestalt or humanistic psychology sense, exists and can be empirically studied.

Perceptual awareness refers to phenomenological experience in the presence of an external, physical stimulus; introspective awareness refers to phenomenological experience in the absence of an external, physical stimulus: The source of the experience must be some internal, private stimulus event. Either type of awareness is a private event, as opposed to a public event. Only the individual has direct access to these events. Skinner presumes that the individual learns to react discriminatively to these private events occurring within the skin, just as he/she does to the public events occurring in the external world outside the skin, under certain contingencies of reinforcement. The verbal community reinforces self-descriptive responses, just as it does motor responses and verbal operants (speech) referring to external events. Technically these self-descriptive responses are tacts—the externalization of the content of consciousness involves tacting. Since the verbal community cannot reinforce self-descriptive responses consistently, an individual cannot tact about events occurring within the skin as subtly and precisely as he/she does about events occurring in the external, physical environment. Unlike the humanist/phenomenologist, Skinner does not assume that the content of private experience is easily knowable or labelable; that is, internal, private stimuli are not easily discriminable.

Skinner's account of perceptual and introspective awareness can be extended to the phenomenon of self-awareness. Self-awareness is the state of being aware; self-awareness is being conscious of one's consciousness. Self-awareness involves the knowledge of being conscious and of being able to reflect on it. Since expressions of perceptual or introspective awareness involve self-descriptive tacting responses, expressions of self-awareness involve self-descriptive tacting responses *about* self-descriptive tacting responses. As in the case of self-descriptive tacting awareness responses, self-descriptive tacting self-awareness responses are a function of the reinforcement contingencies arranged by the verbal community.

Distinguishing between awareness and self-awareness raises the interesting question of whether it is possible for an organism to be aware without being self-aware. In the context of Skinner's analysis, the answer would have to be in the affirmative: The existence of an awareness tacting response does not logically imply the existence of an additional self-awareness tacting response. It is conceivable that an animal such as an ape, as well as a human chronic schizophrenic, is aware without being self-aware.

Skinner's account of the distinction between awareness and self-awareness leads to another interesting question, one that cannot be resolved realistically in the context of his system. Suppose a bird, such as a parrot, is conditioned to say "I know that I am in pain," when it is in obvious pain by all external behavioral indicators. Is the parrot self-aware of its pain? By all the extant criteria in Skinner's system, the answer would have to be "yes"; however, on the basis of considerations external to his system, most psychologists would argue that the parrot is not self-aware.

Skinner's willingness to treat different kinds of awareness as amenable to behavioral analysis is not about to revive an experimental psychology of consciousness, that is, a latter-day structuralism. The controlling variables/stimuli for such mental phenomena as imagery and feeling are amorphous and private (i.e., inaccessible to the verbal community that must reinforce their consistent labeling), so that a psychophysics of these kinds of experiences is highly unlikely.

The Status of Mental Events in General: Skinner's Aversion to Cognitive Behaviorism

As in the case of Watson, Skinner has developed a behavioral language for resolving erstwhile mentalistic concepts:

1. Sensation and/or perception involve the discriminative stimulus control of descriptive verbal operants such as tacts.
2. Imagery and feeling amount to self-descriptive tacting responses under the reinforcement control of the verbal community.
3. Verbal behavior/speech constitutes a symbolic operant response system under discriminative stimulus and reinforcement control.
4. Thinking amounts to covert, or internalized, tacting responses.
5. Emotion reduces to the content of self-report in the face of certain operations performed with reinforcing stimuli; for instance, presentation of a positive reinforcer can cause joy, removal of a positive reinforcer can cause depression, presentation of a negative reinforcer (aversive stimulus) can cause fear or anxiety, and removal of a negative reinforcer can cause relief.

In addition to his characteristic behavioristic reduction of mentalistic notions, Skinner also actively argues against a cognitive psychology of any form. Although Skinner perenially has advocated the purging of mental causes from psychology, his extreme descriptivism currently stands in bold relief against the recent resurgence of cognitive behaviorism. Skinner's aversion to the use of any cognitive apparatus to explain behavior can be abstracted in terms of the following points.

1. The proper reference point to be used for explaining behavior should be the external contingency, usually reinforcement contingency, that currently is in effect. The notion of an external contingency is a given for Skinner, that is, it is directly observable. The existence of an internal cognitive process caused by or corresponding to the external contingency is strictly hypothetical in nature. For instance, many psychologists "see" association formation occurring in a situation involving a reinforcement contingency. For Skinner, the existence of an association is inferred, going beyond the observational, sensationistic givens of the situation. Skinner claims that the subject on whom the contingency is acting does not internalize the contingency *per se*.

2. The prototypical cognitive processes, such as association, storage, comparison, discrimination, identification, and abstraction are based on physical analogies. They are externally sourced and amount to redescriptions of physical processes at another level. Cognitive descriptions always are reducible to behavioral or physical descriptions for Skinner. The use of a cognitive description ultimately is circular and adds nothing new to a pure behavioral/physical description.

3. Skinner's basic aim is the control of behavior, which only can be fostered meaningfully by an appeal to the reinforcement contingencies subsumed by the current physical situation. The postulation of a cognitive apparatus contributes nothing toward the achievement of this goal. If anything, such cognitively oriented concepts as intention, purpose, and will point toward the future and carry teleological overtones. Behavior that appears to have intentional, purposive, or goal-directed aspects can be resolved in terms of the past reinforcement history of the organism. For instance, it might seem reasonable to say that a rat is pressing the bar in a Skinner box because it *expects* food. But what is an expectation? For Skinner, it is merely a redescription at another level of the past reinforcement history of the rat with respect to the food.

4. Skinner considers the notion of a cognitive information-processing system to be fanciful. For instance, one component of this system, memory, is accounted for by an appeal to various storage and retrieval processes. He concedes that it sounds nice to say verbal behavior is stored as lexical memories, but how is eating behavior stored, or how is a visit to a friend stored? Skinner believes that the whole field of information processing can be reformulated in terms of changes in the control exerted by various stimuli.

5. Cognitive psychology likes to emphasize so-called rule-governed behavior. Such behavior is explained by pointing to the fact that it follows some rule. Instances of rule-governed behavior vary from the simple response of stopping at a stop sign to using grammatical rules to construct a well-formed sentence. Skinner basically treats a rule as a device to short-circuit a contingency. A rule is a way of summarizing a contingency or a way of representing an organism's past experience with a contingency. Rules are poor copies of a contingency for Skinner, and are less efficient in generating and controlling behavior. He has no fundamental conceptual problems with a rule, because it always can be reduced to a physical contingency.

6. Cognitive psychology requires internal representations of the external world to stand between the world and the organism's experience of it. Skinner prefers to assume that the organism is in direct

contact with the environment. For instance, in the cognitive approach seeing amounts to a process of construction or representation; in Skinner's system, seeing is an actual behavior, one under direct stimulus control.

The Nature of Skinner's Determinism

Skinner's radical behaviorism subsumes a more liberal interpretation of determinism than Watson's system does. The basic goal of Skinnerian psychology is the establishment of correlations between classes of stimulus events and classes of response events. Stimuli and responses are assumed to be related to each other or covary; that is, they exist in some functional relationship that does not necessarily connote actual physical causation. Skinner's system affords such a peremptory degree of control over an individual organism's behavior only because he focuses on only one response variable, rate, and manipulates only two kinds of operational contingencies, reinforcement and stimulus discrimination.

Like Watson, Skinner assumes that organismic behavior exclusively is controlled by the environment; but unlike Watson, he also assumes that the organism can change the environment. The environment and organismic behavior mutually influence each other: Determinism is reciprocal or bidirectional, as opposed to unidirectional, in nature. In prototypical laboratory operant conditioning, the experimenter is conditioning the subject, but the subject is also conditioning the experimenter. The subject's response rate increases as a function of reinforcement delivery, and the experimenter's rate of reinforcement delivery increases as a function of the subject's responding. At an applied level, the basic theme of Skinner's *Walden Two* and *Beyond Freedom and Dignity* is the design and construction of environments that encompass benign contingencies for the control of human behavior.

The application of Skinnerian operant conditioning principles to certain applied settings, such as behavior modification, can be interpreted as involving a contractual determinism whereby the organism yields certain power and authority to the psychologist through a kind of social agreement. The behavioral psychologist assumes control over the means of access to reinforcement and its delivery for the betterment of the organism. (Behavior modification specialists engaged in private practice are encouraged to use actual *physical* contracts specifying the terms, goals, and techniques of the treatment program.) The arbitrariness of control in this setup is demonstrated by the fact that the terms of the social contract can be resisted and changed, for any number of reasons.

The ultimate in behavioral control is self- or personal control, as opposed to external or social control. For example, the best way to prevent crime is not by having police officers stationed every 50 feet in one's environment, but rather by conditioning people to refrain from criminal behavior regardless of the state of the external stimulus situation. Skinner's admission of internal stimuli, which can be discriminated through proper training, and of self-planned and self-generated reinforcement, makes the individual organism more than a mere prisoner of his/her immediate physical surroundings. The object of many behavior modification programs is self-improvement through self-control: improved study skills, weight reduction and maintenance, efficient use of work or recreational time, extinction of smoking behavior, and so on.

A NOTE ON DETERMINISM IN LOGICAL BEHAVIORISM

The kind of determinism entailed by the many variants of logical behaviorism (learning macrotheory) is much closer to the liberal, functional relationship interpretation, characteristic of Skinner, than it is to the strict, mechanistic interpretation, favored by Watson. Unlike the Watsonian and Skinnerian systems, logical behaviorism encompasses both descriptive and theoretical explanation: Overt behavior is related to both environmental events and theoretical constructs intervening between the overt stimuli and responses. The many possible interactions and hypothetical relationships existing among the intervening theoretical constructs admit an element of randomness and unpredictability into any experimental situation. Hull even built a formal randomness or oscillation factor into his system. The kind of experiments that learning macrotheorists performed did not afford a high degree of control over the organism's behavior, and the learning macrotheorists had to absorb the consequent lack of predictability into the theoretical level of analysis. The mathematical model approach, as an extension of logical behaviorism, constructs statistical models of learning and explicitly makes response probability the primary dependent variable for representing behavioral occurrence.

Method of Study; Permissible Methodology

The experimental analysis of individual behavior is as wedded to a specific methodology as structuralism was to direct, critical introspection. In no other contemporary system of psychology is methodology as important or such a significant aspect of the approach. For many people, Skinnerian psychology is identified primarily as a specific experimental technique. This probably is attributable to the fact that Skinner's system is atheoretical and descriptive. The most popular name for this specific experimental technique is operant (or Skinnerian) conditioning, the physical embodiment (or heart and soul) of which is the so-called Skinner box, a piece of laboratory equipment that has acquired legendary status.

Generically, operant conditioning is free-responding or continuous-time instrumental reward conditioning. In instrumental conditioning, the delivery of reinforcement is response-contingent; reward means that reinforcement is positive (as opposed to negative) in nature; free responding or continuous time should be interpreted as the opposite of the use of discrete trials. In operant conditioning, there are no trials and intertrial intervals. The response manipulandum is available continuously, and as the subject can respond anytime it wants, every moment after the experimental session begins is real time.

Although the use of an instrumental conditioning procedure is not original to Skinner (it was first used in America by Thorndike), Skinner was the first American learning psychologist to distinguish formally between respondent (classical) and operant (instrumental) conditioning. The physical realization of instrumental reward conditioning in terms of operant conditioning and the physical embodiment of operant conditioning in terms of the Skinner box situation are original to Skinner. Skinner did not invent his box and the myriad contingencies it subsumes in any systematic or deductive way. The Skinner box and its attendant, peripheral equipment, as well as the contingencies that can be physicalized by its use, slowly evolved over the years in the context of Skinner's attempt to refine the notion of behavior and to control its actual occurrence. In a sense, the development of the Skinner box is the result of an operant conditioning process: Skinner was reinforced for the creation of a succession of different experimental apparati, which slowly, but surely, came ever closer to an approximation of the final design that now subsumes the notion of a Skinner box.

We shall (1) describe the prototypical experimental setup used to investigate operant conditioning in the laboratory, (2) abstract the critical features of the operant conditioning situation, and (3) illustrate the tremendous flexibility of Skinnerian methodology by alluding to some of its procedural and conceptual extensions.

The Prototypical Laboratory Setup for Operant Conditioning Research

A sophisticated, professional operant conditioning setup consists of three separate components, each of which is commercially available: (1) various programming equipment, (2) a cumulative recorder, and (3) some type of Skinner box chamber—a rat, monkey, or pigeon Skinner box. The three components constitute a system whose primary feature is automation. Between the moment the subject is first placed in the experimental chamber and the time the subject is removed, all events are automated: stimulus presentation, response recording, reinforcement delivery.

The programming equipment functions as the control/regulation element of the system: It determines the specific contingency (or contingencies) to which the subject is exposed by scheduling the delivery of the relevant stimulus and reinforcement events and regulating response recording. The programming equipment establishes the basic input situation for the subject and serves as a surrogate experimenter. Programming equipment can include relays, interval timers, tape devices, digital displays, even minicomputers, and thus the programming aspect of operant conditioning amounts to an electrical engineering technology in its purest form.

The cumulative recorder is an automated response-recording device that produces a picture of the subject's cumulative responding over time. A response line is traced on a moving piece of paper, so that the subject's behavior is expressed in terms of a rate curve or cumulative record. The specific details involved in the generation of a cumulative record need not concern us, except to point out that response rate is the *only* dependent variable that Skinner allows.

The Skinner box chamber comprises the immediate physical environment of the subject. A sophisticated Skinner box consists of three basic components: (1) one or more stimulus generators, such as a white light or colored lights; (2) a response manipulandum, such as a depressible bar; and (3) a reinforcement delivery device, such as a pellet dispenser or water tube. The nature of the internal confines of the chamber and of the three basic components are contingent on the type of subject being used: There is a characteristic rat, monkey, and pigeon Skinner box.

A specific operant conditioning laboratory can encompass more than one experimental setup—the three basic components of the system can be varied independently or duplicated. Any number of Skinner boxes and cumulative recorders can be plugged into different components of the programming equipment, thus allowing numerous operant conditioning experiments to be conducted simultaneously. The operant conditioning laboratory is a throwback to Wundtian brass instrument psychology. However, nobody calls it this, probably because it represents a triumph of modern technology and behavioral engineering.

Critical Features of the Operant Conditioning Situation

The basic aspect of the operant conditioning situation is time; this is true for both the stimulus input events and the response output events. The Skinner box is essentially a temporal situation, as opposed to the spatial environment characteristic of a maze. The contingencies are temporally defined, and the subject remains in one spatial location and merely operates on the response manipulandum over time to receive a reward. On the response side, the Skinner box facilitates sheer frequency counts of the members of a repetitive response class over time and measurement of the all-or-none, digital aspects of responding.

Recall that operant conditioning is a free-responding or continuous-time procedure: The stimulus input events and response output events are interminably intermixed in time. The stimulus events and response events are cofunctions of each other. The presentation of the stimulus events is a function of the responding, and the responding is a function of the presentation of the stimulus events. This aspect of operant conditioning serves as the source of both its methodological strengths and weaknesses.

STRENGTHS

On the strength side of the ledger, the operant conditioning situation affords a peremptory degree of control over the subject's responding: discriminative stimulus control, reinforcement control, or both. This control is physical or actual, as opposed to statistical, in nature. The environmental contingencies are in virtually constant contact with the behavior, and the behavior is in virtually constant contact with the environmental contingencies. This peremptory degree of control is what primarily distinguishes Skinnerian methodology from traditional behavioristic learning methodology. The subject's rate of responding is so susceptible to any variation in the environmental contingencies that Skinner can generate interpretable, meaningful data by the use of one subject—the so-called single-organism approach. A cumulative record serves as a magnifying glass, revealing the temporal properties of a single organism's behavior. Skinner does not need to use multigroup designs generating average, summary data that are not necessarily characteristic of the individual organism. He does not need to use formal statistical tests to determine whether obtained group differences in performance are significant. Skinnerian methodology does make informal use of statistical decisions. For example, how do you know when a subject's response rate has stabilized or achieved a certain characteristic pattern?

When a subject's response rate is so variable that it is uninterpretable, it is assumed that the subject's behavior is not under control. Traditional methodology absorbed variability into the theoretical entities that were presumed to intervene between the overt stimulus and response events. A certain degree of randomness was built into behavioral occurrence by using theoretical constructs; a certain degree of randomness was explained away or tolerated by the use of learning theory. Since Skinner's approach is descriptive and atheoretical, variability cannot be explained away or tolerated. Variable data are bad data, and bad data do not constitute behavior. At this level, Skinnerian methodology is just as prescriptive as structuralist introspective methodology. Bad data dictate a change in the environmental conditions to bring the responding back under control.

BASIC WEAKNESS

On the weakness side of the ledger, the operant conditioning situation confounds response-produced effects and the effects of the experimental contingency. The future input (stimulus events) is a direct function of the current output (responding): Rate of responding and rate of reinforcement are confounded. As a consequence, the specific source of a given psychological phenomenon cannot be inferred unambiguously. Does it arise from the rate of reinforcement or from the rate of responding?

It is possible to separate response-produced effects and the effects of the experimental contingency by using some kind of yoked control procedure or subject. One subject, the experimental subject, is exposed to a standard operant conditioning session. Another subject, the yoked control, also is exposed to an operant contingency, but the nature of this contingency is determined by the behavior of the experimental subject: The delivery of the stimulus events is contingent on the responding of the experimental subject. The responding of the yoked control subject is nonefficacious and irrelevant; the delivery of the critical stimulus events, such as reinforcement, to both subjects is contingent on the responding of the experimental subject only. In the yoked control subject, the future input is not a direct function of the current output; rate of responding and rate of reinforcement are not confounded.

Some Procedural and Conceptual Extensions of Skinnerian Methodology

The standard Skinner box contains one response manipulandum and a two-state stimulus generator (light on; light off). While this allows the investigation of numerous behavioral phenomena, a Skinner box equipped with two or more response manipulanda and two or more multistate stimulus generators (multicolored key lights or discs) increases the flexibility of the operant conditioning situation enormously. Much of the current conceptually oriented pure, as opposed to applied, operant conditioning research involves a multiresponse setup or a multistimulus setup.

Operant conditioning makes an animal psychophysics feasible. Stimulus control is so great that various psychophysical functions can be generated. Absolute and difference thresholds can be determined, visual or auditory acuity can be assessed, color vision can be investigated, and so on.

Responding in the operant conditioning situation can be used as a baseline for assessing the effect of an independent variable, or experimental operation, which is not part of the immediate physical contingency controlling the responding. For instance, after extended exposure to a variable interval (VI) schedule of reinforcement, the subject exhibits a smooth, steady rate of responding. This can be employed as a baseline for assessing the specific behavioral effect of the administration of a certain drug or of the institution of a certain brain lesion or ablation. The use of multiple baselines (different reinforcement schedules under differential stimulus control) in the context of the same experimental session allows the assessment of possible interaction effects between the externally imposed operation and the specific contingency controlling behavior. Operant psychology initiated the modern phase of both psychopharmacology and brain–behavior correlational research.

Operant conditioning can be applied to any problem situation or used in any physical environment in which behavioral control is necessary. These entail the status of operant conditioning as a behavioral technology: programmed instruction or learning, behavior modification or therapy, token economies or reward systems, various self-control techniques, experimental communities, and the like.

Origin; Specific Historical Antecedents

Because radical behaviorism is the direct intellectual heir of classical Watsonian behaviorism, any extensive consideration of the historical roots of Skinner's system would be redundant. The comments previously made in the context of discussing the specific historical antecedents of classical Watsonian behaviorism, as well as those pertaining to the origin of functionalism, are equally applicable here. Consequently we focus only on the two basic intellectual influences that shaped Skinner's thought.

Intellectual Influences on Skinner's Thought

Although Pavlov's and Watson's psychological thought motivated Skinner's initial psychological work, they do not consitute the primary intellectual influences on his system. Watson absorbed Pavlov's emphasis on the classically conditioned reflex; however, Skinner did not absorb Watson's stress on the CR as the unit of habit. Skinner was not enamoured of respondents and respondent conditioning; he considered them too limited to serve as the primary source of behavioral change. What Skinner did absorb was (1) the functionalist's stress on adaptation and Darwin's evolutionary doctrine, as exemplified in Thorndike's animal work on instrumental learning, and (2) the radical empiricist orientation of such predecessors as Ernst Mach and Bradford Titchener.

DARWIN'S EVOLUTIONARY DOCTRINE AND THORNDIKE'S LAW OF EFFECT

Thorndike's associative connectionism, emphasizing stimulus and response events, and his law of effect, which stresses the importance of the consequences of behavior for the creation of learned responses, are implicit in Skinner's operant psychology. Skinner retained Thorndike's basic stimulus, response terminology and adapted Thorndike's law of effect: A consequential satisfying state of affairs became positive reinforcement, and a consequential dissatisfying state of affairs became a punishing event. Stress on the consequences of an individual organism's behavior is an adaptive notion and applies Darwin's evolutionary doctrine, originally stated at the species level, to the behavior of an individual organism. The effects of reinforcement on responding amounts to Darwinism on an individual, or ontogenetic, level. Adaptive (successful) responses are retained (operantly conditioned); nonadaptive (unsuccessful) responses drop out (are extinguished).

RADICAL EMPIRICISM

The doctrine of radical empiricism underlies Skinner's descriptivism. This doctrine entails an extreme form of empiricism, in which the immediate units of observation constitute the only legitimate level of reality. What is observed directly exists and is real. Inferences based on the observational entities, especially those to a higher theoretical level of reality, are not allowed. The specific form of radical empiricism that antedated Skinner's behavioral descriptivism is called sensationism, because the fundamental psychological object of analysis at the time was subjective experience. Both Ernst Mach (cf. Chapter 4) and Bradford Titchener (cf. Chapter 2) were sensationists. The immediate givens of subjective consciousness were sensations. Mach was a physicist, and he advocated sensationism in a philosophical sense; Titchener, a Wundtian structuralist, advocated a sensationistic psychology. Skinner merely applied the doctrine of radical empiricism to the basic object of interest of a truly physicalistic psychology—behavior. For Skinner, there are immediately given, noninferential, objective stimulus and response events; and that is all.

Chief Historical Figure: Burrhus Frederic Skinner (1904–)

B.F. Skinner (Fred to his friends; he dislikes the name Burrhus) was born in 1904 in Susquehanna, Pa. His father was a self-taught lawyer with no formal college degree; his mother was a pleasant, popular person who was quite strait-laced. Like Watson, Skinner came from a rather subdued, religiously oriented family; and he rebelled. Unlike Watson, who was physically rebellious, Skinner rebelled at an intellectual or symbolic level, by playing practical jokes and being somewhat of a comedian. As a child, Skinner was an accomplished musician and delighted in tinkering with and constructing things, a harbinger of things to come later in the context of the psychology laboratory.

Skinner's earliest intellectual ambitions were literary, and he entered Hamilton College in Clinton, N.Y., in 1922. He majored in English, studied some philosophy and biology, earned a Phi Beta Kappa key, but never took a formal psychology course as an undergraduate. During the summer before his senior year, Skinner attended a writer's workshop at Middlebury College, where he attracted the attention of Robert Frost, who encouraged his literary ambitions. Skinner spent the first year after graduating from college unsuccessfully attempting to write the great American novel. Through reading Bertrand Russell he discovered Watson and behaviorism, and his long journey in psychology began.

Skinner entered Harvard University as a graduate student in psychology in 1928 and, because of his prodigious work schedule, received his Ph.D. degree in only three years. At the time, Harvard was not explicitly behavioristic in orientation, but it was tolerant of a self-starter such as Skinner. His Ph.D. mentor was Edwin G. Boring, and his dissertation involved part of his work on the reflex. He remained at Harvard from 1931 to 1936, where he served as a postdoctoral fellow and later as a Junior fellow. It was during these initial Harvard years that Skinner formulated his descriptive approach to the concept of reflex, distinguished between respondent and operant conditioning, and performed the studies that laid the foundation for *The Behavior of Organisms* (1938).

Skinner accepted an academic appointment at the University of Minnesota in 1936, and was promoted to an associate professorship in 1939. At Minnesota, he influenced William K. Estes and collaborated with him on some classic punishment/anxiety studies. (Estes later became a significant figure in the mathematical model movement in learning and ultimately applied mathematics to cognitive processes; however, Estes still retains Skinner's functional, or operational, approach to stimulus, response, and reinforcing events.) During World War II, Skinner worked on an army project in which he trained pigeons to guide the flight of a missile. Although this project never "got off the ground," it demonstrated the viability of his approach to behavior.

Skinner left Minnesota in 1945 to become full professor and chairman of the psychology department at Indiana University, where he remained until 1948. At Indiana, the first of a series of annual meetings on the experimental analysis of behavior was held in 1946; these meetings eventually led to the establishment of Division 25 of the American Psychological Association in 1956.

Since 1948 Skinner has been associated with Harvard University. Although now formally retired, he still maintains an office there, and Harvard still serves as the home base of his professional activities. It was during this second period of affiliation with Harvard that Skinner became one of the leading experimental psychologists in America. Like Watson, Skinner published voluminously. (He even plotted his day-to-day writing progress in terms of a cumulative record.) In addition to countless journal articles, his books include the following, listed in order of publication: (1) *Walden Two* (1948), a utopian novel, written in seven weeks, which inspired many experimental communities and which became a popular best seller in the 1960s; (2) *Science and Human Behavior* (1953), Skinner's version of an introductory level psychology text; (3) *Schedules of Reinforcement* (1957), coauthored with Charles B. Ferster, which reported on their extensive research program on partial reinforcement schedules; (4) *Verbal Behavior* (1957), based on Skinner's 1948 William James lectures at Harvard, which in turn were based on a 1941 manuscript; (5) *Contingencies of Reinforcement* (1969), a conceptual analysis of his system; (6) *Beyond Freedom and Dignity* (1971), a popularly oriented work that formalized Skinner's social philosophy; and (7) *About Behaviorism* (1974), a defense of his brand of behaviorism.

In 1958 Skinner received a Distinguished Scientific Contribution Award from the American Psychological Association. He published an article entitled "Behaviorism at 50" in *Science* in 1963 to commemorate the 50th anniversary of Watson's founding of behaviorism. Skinner was awarded a National Medal of Science by the United States government in 1968. The American Psychological Foundation presented him with a gold medal in 1971.

Skinner still remains professionally active, giving visiting lectures, appearing at conventions, and serving as a guest on occasional TV talk shows. For the past decade, Skinner has assumed the role of a social philosopher. His system has become an object of analysis for contemporary philosophy, and his writings are continually being textually analyzed by philosophically oriented psychologists. He is best remembered by the undergraduate psychology student as the rather unassuming, soft-spoken man who appeared in a number of educational movies putting pigeons through their paces. This probably is how Skinner himself prefers to be recalled.

Characteristic Experimentation; Primary Research Areas

The experimental analysis of individual behavior primarily focuses on learning, as a substantive content area of experimental psychology; however, its methodological tenets and techniques of behavioral control have affected research in virtually every experimental and applied area of psychology. Since the nature of operant conditioning research is infinitely descriptive and also has changed over the years, it would be unrealistic to attempt an in-depth analysis of the basic operant conditioning research program conducted during the last half century. Instead we present an abstraction of the essential features of operant research (1) as carried out by Skinner during the early years and (2) as performed by contemporary (post-1960) second and third generation Skinnerian psychologists.

Traditional Experimentation

The initial impetus to operant conditioning research was Skinner's view that respondent conditioning and operant conditioning constituted two distinct forms of learning. Great stress was put on the nature of the operant as an emitted response and the arbitrariness of the reinforcing operation. The original acquisition of the operant response—that is, its shaping or the increase in its frequency of occurrence above the initial operant rate—was the focus of attention. Research determined exactly what constituted the reinforceable dimensions of the operant response: shape, duration, intensity or force, interresponse time (IRT), and so forth. Analogous parametric investigation of the reinforcement variable identified the effective dimensions of the reinforcer, usually food in a properly deprived organism: amount or quantity, hedonic quality, immediacy of delivery, schedule of delivery, and the like. The schedule of reinforcement turned out to be the most meaningful property of a reinforcer, both during original acquisition and later during extinction exposure; and a voluminous amount of research data was generated in the context of the four basic types of simple partial reinforcement schedules: fixed interval, fixed ratio, variable interval, and variable ratio. The concept of a reinforcer was absolute or transsituational, but no attempt was made to specify the fundamental, or theoretical, defining properties of a reinforcing event. Bringing an operant under stimulus control—the formation of a simple stimulus discrimination—and the relationship between a discriminative stimulus and a secondary, or conditioned, reinforcer was of great experimental interest. Operant conditioning also was used as a baseline for assessing the effects of various external experimental manipulations, especially drug-related and lesion-related ones. The choice of the specific operant responses and reinforcers to be used in the laboratory was done with some care, according to a few implicit criteria as to how operant conditioning research ideally should be carried out; however, possible biological or hereditary constraints on learning and various ethological considerations were not a matter of concern.

Contemporary Experimentation

The contemporary basic operant conditioning researcher is no longer concerned with the original acquisition or shaping process. This process now is of interest strictly to the applied operant conditioning specialist operating in the behavior modification or therapy context. No longer does JEAB publish pictorial representations of cumulative records, the trademark of traditional operant conditioning research. With their demise, Skinner in 1976 published an editorial, or virtual obituary, in JEAB entitled "Farewell, My LOVELY." Currently the maintenance, terminal, steady-state, or asymptotic rate of responding is the focus of analysis. Fine-grain analysis of transition states or behavior constitutes a related current interest. Steady-state behavior primarily is studied in a relational context such that switching behavior and/or choice behavior constitute derivative concerns. The matching law has become the most general empirical relation yielded by operant conditioning research—the relative rate of responding associated with a given response alternative is equal to the relative rate of reinforcement associated with the response alternative. The study of complex schedules of reinforcement has replaced the use of single simple schedules of reinforcement, and positive and negative contrast and induction effects have become basic experimental phenomena of interest. Simple schedules of reinforcement are being modeled as modified complex schedules of reinforcement. Current stimulus discrimination and reinforcement research stresses the relational nature of such events. Discrimination research now focuses on conditional discrimination, errorless discrimination training, and conditional matching-to-sample. Most contemporary operant psychologists accept Premack's relativistic or nontranssituational descriptive approach to reinforcement, which makes reinforcement and punishment, or the positive and negative laws of effect, merely opposite sides of the same coin. Stimulus change per se and brain stimulation now constitute prototypical reinforcing events. A renewed interest exists in relating operant conditioning to respondent conditioning, as manifested in (1) the use of operant conditioning baselines to assess presumed CSs, (2) the operations of autoshaping and negative automaintenance, and (3) the control of schedule behavior by the use of interspersed or intercalated neutral stimuli. Operant conditioning has been extended to internal autonomic responses, once only believed controllable by respondent conditioning reinforcement operations. Biological and hereditary concerns and issues, as well as those of the ethologist, are starting to creep into operant psychology; and the contemporary operant researcher is beginning to worry about the relationship between the operant response and the reflexive consummatory activity elicited by the reinforcing event (food).

Historical Legacy; Contemporary Significance

The historical legacy of Skinnerian radical behaviorism is implicit in the introduction to the chapter: Skinner's system is infinitely descriptive and has been institutionalized. Granted that the era of the classical schools of experimental psychology is over, and granted that no contemporary system of psychology is accepted monolithically by every psychologist, Skinner's approach to psychology is the best contemporary example of the rather idealized notion of a system, as defined and characterized in Chapter 1. Radical behaviorism simultaneously (1) can serve as an object of philosophical analysis, (2) entails a specific experimental methodology, and (3) subsumes a sophisticated behavioral technology.

We shall highlight the contemporary significance of Skinner's system by focusing briefly on its behavioral technology aspects and on its consequences for social control and the design of a culture or society.

Behavioral Technology

The behavioral technology aspects of Skinner's system can be abstracted in terms of four nonmutually exclusive areas: (1) programmed learning/instruction or teaching machines, (2) behavior modification or therapy, (3) psychopharmacology, and (4) commercial animal training. In the first two areas of application, the focus is on the human being, and the ultimate goal is an environmental change involving consistent and/or beneficial contingencies, such that the organism's behavior is improved and made more adaptable. In the last two areas of application, the nonhuman organism is the focus, and the behavioral control principles inherent in operant conditioning are rather mechanically exploited for commercial purposes. (The prior statement is intended as a descriptive one, not an evaluational one.)

PROGRAMMED LEARNING/TEACHING MACHINES

Skinner is credited with beginning the contemporary phase of programmed learning/teaching machine activity. A teaching machine is a device that presents an individual student with a specific course of study that is broken down into discrete steps, better known as a program. Programs are designed around Skinner's learning principles. The program presents and tests information on a frame-by-frame basis, such that error responses are minimized, the learner receives immediate reinforcement, and progress through the program is self-paced. Teaching machine is a generic term that can refer to a simple mechanical device, a computer, or simply a pile of cards (frames). Likewise, a program is a generic term that can refer to a pile of cards, a roll of printed paper, a book in programmed learning form, or a computer programming tape. Programmed learning techniques are particularly relevant for the instruction of slow learners and for the acquisition of highly repetitive, rote learning material characteristic of introductory level courses. Although the boom days and initial evaluation phase of programmed learning largely are over, the techniques still are accepted widely as teaching aids and adjunct educational tools by the American educational establishment.

BEHAVIOR MODIFICATION

Behavior modification involves the application of respondent and operant conditioning principles to meaningful and socially relevant behavior occurring in the home, school, work, or therapeutic environment, as well as to problems of self-control and self-improvement. Behavior modification now consitutes a virtual independent subdiscipline of psychology, with its own conceptual and certification problems. The number of behavior modification textbooks on the market is voluminous, and most psychology departments in the country have a behavior modification course. Each of these areas of application amounts to a subspeciality, for example, behavior therapy in the therapeutic environment or contingency management in the industrial context.

The most extensive application of behavior modification techniques has been in the therapy context: private practice and institutional settings such as mental hospitals and centers for the developmentally disadvantaged. Behavior therapy is in direct competition with such more traditional forms of therapy as chemotherapy and psychoanalysis. "Behavior modification specialist" constitutes a legitimate job slot/title in many institutional settings. Over the past few years, behavior therapy has become increasingly more cognitive in its orientation, as well as the source of some critical ethical issues.

PSYCHOPHARMACOLOGY

Psychopharmacology is a behavioral technology in the purest sense of the term. Performance in the Skinnerian operant conditioning situation serves as a direct means of assessing the behavioral effect(s) of a new drug or chemical compound; the operant conditioning technique serves as a true measuring instrument. The rapid and efficient development of new drugs by the American pharmaceutical industry would be impossible without Skinnerian conditioning techniques.

COMMERCIAL ANIMAL TRAINING

This application of Skinnerian principles amounts to behavior modification in an animal context—socially significant behaviors and behaviors with entertainment value are conditioned in animals. Lay terminology for such behaviors is tricks. This use of operant conditioning is epitomized by the late Keller Breland and his wife Marion Breland, who established a training farm for animals in Alabama more than 20 years ago. The Brelands became famous for their discovery of specific instances of organismic behavior that are intractable to Skinnerian behavioral control—so-called misbehaviors. Misbehaviors present no conceptual problems for Skinner because they are such from the trainer's perspective, not from the animal's perspective. Skinner never claimed that all behavior is operantly conditionable or free of prepotent hereditary influences. For instance, the fact that a raccoon prefers washing a couple of tokens instead of depositing them into a box to obtain reinforcement does not vitiate Skinner's principles of behavioral control.

Radical Behaviorism as a Social Philosophy

In his 1948 novel, *Walden Two,* and his more recent book, *Beyond Freedom and Dignity* (1971), Skinner discusses the implications of his principles for social control and a just society. In *Walden Two,* Skinner extols the virtues of a society based exclusively on positive reinforcement; in *Beyond Freedom and Dignity,* Skinner argues that the cultural myth of the existence of freedom and dignity retards the establishment of a truly enlightened and just society based on radical behaviorist principles.

Skinner assumes that all behavior is determined, or controlled, by environmental contingencies, such that the locus of behavioral change must reside in the external physical and social environment. The fundamental question is not whether control does or should exist;

the basic problem is one of benign and efficient control. The use of aversive contingencies (punishment, negative reinforcement) should be eliminated completely, and the use of inefficient reward contingencies (positive reinforcement) also should be eliminated.

The typical person does not accept the notion of control. This is evidenced by the way in which the culture or "literature" uses the terms freedom and dignity. Freedom is the escape from aversive contingencies and negative forms of control. Dignity derives from the praise one receives for exhibiting good works in the absence of the knowledge of what is controlling them. Skinner argues that these views are paradoxical because (1) people do not seek to escape from reward contingencies and positive forms of control, yet (2) people do not emit praise when desirable behavior is under known positive contingencies.

Skinner is aware of the fact that a behavioristic approach to social control is open to two basic queries: (1) Who does the controlling? (2) What are the ultimate goals of control? Skinner has no absolute answer to these questions, but he does reject the notion that his principles implicitly justify a totalitarian state. What Skinner does present is a general interpretation. Society is evolving; its structure is evolving; its goals are evolving. Skinner assumes that society implictly will evolve desirable goals and benign forms of control if people are made aware of the fact/necessity of control. Skinner is an instrumentalist and utilitarian, in the philosophical sense. He considers it perfectly reasonable to assume that people can decide on goals in a democratic manner, change their environment in a rational way, and partition control responsibilities among different segments of society. Skinner also emphasizes that the best way to guarantee the nonabuse of control is to design sources of countercontrol in the system. For instance, the basic reason mistreatment occurs in some institutional settings is that the patients/residents lack any significant means of countercontrol.

Bibliography

Ferster, C.B., and Skinner, B.F. *Schedules of Reinforcement*. New York: Appleton-Century-Crofts, 1957.

Skinner, B.F. *The Behavior of Organisms*. New York: Appleton-Century-Crofts, 1938.

Skinner, B.F. *Walden Two*. New York: Macmillan, 1948, 1962.

Skinner, B.F. *Science and Human Behavior*. New York: Macmillan, 1953.

Skinner, B.F. *Verbal Behavior*. New York: Appleton-Century-Crofts, 1957.

Skinner, B.F. Behaviorism at 50. *Science*, 1963, 140, 951–958.

Skinner, B.F. *Contingencies of Reinforcement: A Theoretical Analysis*. New York: Appleton-Century-Crofts, 1969.

Skinner, B.F. *Beyond Freedom and Dignity*. New York: Bantam/Vintage, 1971.

Skinner, B.F. *About Behaviorism*. New York: Knopf, 1974.

8

Cognitive
Behaviorism

Introduction

In Chapters 6 and 7, we assumed that the explicit object of interest for a behaviorist is overt behavior and were able to describe this interest in the context of two fairly closely-knit descriptively oriented systems of behaviorism in which the fundamental units of analysis are stimulus and response events. It now is necessary to change gears: In contemporary cognitive behaviorism, the primary object of interest is not overt behavior, and it is impossible to characterize contemporary cognitive behaviorism as a fairly closely-knit system associated with only one, or even a few, principal adherents. Because the content of contemporary cognitive behaviorism is so vast, this chapter necessarily must be less detailed and more abstract than the discussions of classical and radical behaviorism.

We also are faced with two immediate conceptual problems: (1) Exactly what is the domain of cognitive psychology? (2) Is it meaningful to claim that cognitive behaviorism is a viable approach to or component of cognitive psychology? The answer to the second question by and large is contingent on how the first question is answered.

At least two views of the domain of cognitive psychology exist. In one view, the domain of cognitive psychology is coextensive with the domain of psychology as a whole: Any and every psychological phenomenon can be construed as involving at least one cognitive process. Every content subarea of psychology is a part of cognitive psychology, or cognitive psychology is relevant for every content subarea of psychology. Cognitive psychology subsumes perception, attention, imagery, learning, memory, thinking, problem solving, concept formation, language, and so on. This view of cognition is reflected in the general statement that psychology, as a whole, seems to be getting more cognitively oriented these days. In the other view, the domain of cognitive psychology is limited strictly to epistemic meaning, the laws of thought, propositional knowledge, or reasoning in general. Cognitive psychology encompasses a unique and specialized subject matter: the categories and forms of human symbolic thought. Perception, learning, memory, and the like can supply the objects of analysis to which cognition is applied, but these psychological phenomena are not continuous with or components of cognitive phenomena. Perception, learning, memory, and so forth are not cognitive activities in and of themselves.

The contemporary human information-processing approach to cognition, and computer modeling thereof, presumes the first view of cognitive psychology. The structural approach to cognition, characteristic of the linguist Noam Chomsky and the genetic epistemologist Jean Piaget, presumes the second view of cognitive psychology.

The restricted-domain, structural interpretation of cognitive psychology precludes the existence of a cognitive behaviorism: Chomsky and Piaget are cognitive psychologists, but the notion of cognitive behaviorism cannot be used to characterize their approaches or any significant components of their approaches. The unlimited-domain, information-processing approach to cognitive psychology can be construed as a cognitive behaviorism. A cognitive behaviorist is concerned with filling in the conceptual void existing between overt stimulus and response events with an explicit cognitive apparatus, one that is irreducible to peripheral mechanisms or strict behavioral terms. A cognitive behaviorist assumes that an emergent, physical or material, cognitive system intervenes between overt stimulus and response events. A cognitive behaviorist treats all the traditional areas of experimental psychology, not from a learning, conditioning, physiological, or perceptual viewpoint, but from a general cognitive or information-processing viewpoint. An illustrative, but not complete, sampling of contemporary cognitive behaviorists would include George Miller, Herbert Simon, Donald Norman, Gordon Bower, Lyle

Bourne, Wayne Wickelgren, Allen Newell, Saul Sternberg, Donald Rumelhart, and Earl Hunt.

Our analysis of contemporary cognitive behaviorism focuses on its physical and conceptual dependence on the computer and on its emergence as a variant of behaviorism in the early to mid-1960s.

Object of Study; Basic Subject Matter

The fundamental assumption of cognitive behaviorism is that response output is not a simple linear or automatic product of the stimulus input. A strict descriptive approach is insufficient for the prediction and/or control of behavior. Even the simplest stimulus—a light, for example—must be decoded; and even the simplest response—for example, a knee jerk—must be encoded. An individual organism's cognitive apparatus makes unique and undeniable contributions to its overt behavior and view of the world.

Skinner resolves an S–R reflex in terms of a functional S–R correlation; the cognitive behaviorist resolves an S–R reflex in terms of some significating structure underlying the overt S–R correlation. A physiological reflex is a function of the organism's beliefs, expectancies, or current level of awareness. Skinner resolves behavioral change in an operant situation in terms of the automatic effect of reinforcement and the specific physical contingency that is in effect. The cognitive behaviorist resolves operant response acquisition in terms of some significating structure underlying the physical contingency. Is the subject aware of the contingency? Does the subject believe there is a connection between its responding and the rewarding consequences? Does the subject verbalize the abstract rule subsumed by the contingency?

Focusing on the cognitive effect of a given stimulus input amounts to an experimental epistemology, in the structuralist sense of the term. Many cognitive behaviorists like to define cognition as the science of knowledge: (1) how it is coded and represented, and (2) how it is processed, acquired, stored, used, and so forth. Cognitive behaviorism studies the form and acquisition of knowledge.

Since the cognitive events occurring between an overt stimulus and response are arbitrary and infinite in number, the information-processing approach to cognition requires some conceptual scheme after which cognitive processes can be modeled. The distinguishing feature of the information-processing approach is that the computer serves as the basic model: The mind is analogous to a computer; the computer serves as the metaphor for the mind. The content of contemporary cognitive behaviorism amounts to a collection of computer-based analogies.

A computer, at an informal level, is an electronic device that is capable of processing symbolic or coded information at an exceedingly high rate of speed. At a more technical level, a computer is the central control component of a larger, more comprehensive, electronic information-processing system that also includes peripheral input and output components. The actual physical makeup of a computer, as a machine, need not concern us, except to point out that it must possess some monitoring, processing, and storage capacity. The storage capacity does not have to be structural in nature, that is, functional access to an independent tape storage system is all that is required. A computer has great flexibility because its activities are under the control of a program. Unlike a simple adding machine or electronic calculator, which are manufactured with only one or a few built-in programs, a computer can be programmed to perform an infinite number of tasks. While a computer basically is an information-processing device, its function at a given moment usually is identified in terms of the use to which the information is being put. For instance, a computer can be printing out a payroll, solving a problem, guiding a missile, monitoring the operations of a nuclear power plant, analyzing scientific data, or organizing Social Security records.

It is not the physical computer itself, but the larger functional information-processing system of which it is a component, that serves as the explicit model for human cognition. This system receives information, classifies inputs, recognizes patterns, manipulates symbols, stores items in memory, retrieves items from memory, solves problems, makes decisions, organizes material for efficient display and output, and so forth. The basic structural components and functional operations encompassed by the computer-based information-processing system constitute the object of study or basic subject matter of contemporary cognitive behaviorism. By analogy, the human being is assumed to possess certain structural information-processing mechanisms that perform certain operations, such that human cognition involves a hierarchically organized simultaneous and/or successive series of information-processing stages and substages.

A typical cognitive experiment or cognitive model focuses only on one stage of the overall information-processing system—such as perception, memory, problem solving, concept formation, language decoding or encoding—or on selected substages—for example, selective attention, pattern recognition, iconic storage, or critical feature analysis in the context of perception.

No overall monolithic model for human cognition exists because the total number and content of the stages and substages, as well as their interrelationships, are contingent on the methodological ingenuity and sophistication of the experimenter. Cognitive behaviorists are discovering what functionally and parametrically oriented verbal learning psychologists have known for years: The human organism is capable of performing in experiments of infinite parametric variation. This should not be interpreted to mean that certain performance constants and limitations in cognitive capacities do not exist. Reaction time to one stimulus is always faster than reaction time to a multistimulus display; a conjunctive concept is easier to learn than a disjunctive concept; the capacity of the short-term memory span is 7 $\pm$ 2 chunks of information; the duration of the iconic image is approximately 200 ms under standard conditions. Sophisticated laboratory research has demonstrated that there is no natural limit to the number of hierarchical substages and no natural lower bound to the time frames of their occurrence.

Method of Study; Permissible Methodology

A cognitive behaviorist can use any experimental technique that permits a tie-up between a presumed cognitive process or operation and some measure of objective performance. Newell recently enumerated 59 separate techniques used by cognitive behaviorists. The focal point of cognitive methodology relates to modeling, of either the mathematical or computer simulation variety. There is no absolute difference between a mathematical and a computer model: A mathematical model can be expressed in computer program form, and a computer model can involve predictive equations. Of the two kinds of modeling, only computer simulation is indigenous to cognitive research. Mathematical models are used to test various S–R associational theories of learning.

Just as the information-processing approach to cognition, as a system of psychology, is conceptually dependent on the computer, the empirical assessment of various models of cognition is physically dependent on the computer. This use of the computer is called computer simulation, and is described briefly below.

Computer Simulation

Assume that a psychologist devises a cognitive model for a specific cognitive task, such as pattern recognition. The model is a detailed description of the specific stages and/or operations the typical subject is presumed to go through to perform the task. These stages/operations can involve counting, sorting, selecting, matching, identifying, and so on. The model, especially if it does not involve predictive equations, is transformed into a computer program. The original cognitive model now has become a computer model. The actual physical form of the computer model is that of some technical computer "language," such as FORTRAN. Recall that a computer can be programmed to do any one of an infinite number of tasks. When a computer is being controlled by a program based on a cognitive model, it is programmed to mimic a human being and simulate the human's presumed cognitive processes.

The empirical assessment of the cognitive model entails the comparison of a set of data generated by human subjects performing the cognitive task and the response output generated by a computer that performs the same task (i.e., processes the same information) according to the dictates of the computer model/simulation program. The comparison can result in any one of three logically distinct outcomes:

1. The computer's performance essentially matches the performance of the human subjects. This is a successful simulation. More than likely the original cognitive model is a good representation of what the human subject actually does at a cognitive level while performing the task.

2. The computer's performance is worse than the performance of the human subjects. This is an unsuccessful simulation. The original cognitive model does not encompass enough of what the human subject actually does at a cognitive level while performing the task.

3. The computer's performance is better than the performance of the human subjects. This is an unsuccessful simulation. The original cognitive model ascribes too much to the human subject at a cognitive level while he/she is performing the task.

Artificial Intelligence

The third outcome requires an additional comment. In principle, it is possible to program a computer to perform better than a human in the context of certain cognitive tasks, such as retrieval from memory or perceptual scanning, but this is not the goal of computer simulation. On the other hand, we do not have to degrade a computer's capabilities in those areas where it is superior to the human: We can be interested in a computer's performance in a specific cognitive task in an absolute sense, independently of the human's capabilities as a comparative reference point. This general area of research is called artificial intelligence, in which the attempt is made to determine whether a computer can be programmed to solve problems, act intelligently, act creatively, and so forth. The use of the computer in artificial intelligence research is just as significant and important as its use in computer simulation research. Since the computer-based information-processing system constitutes the model for the information-processing approach to human cognition in the first place, artificial intelligence research serves as the source of fruitful hypotheses about human cognition.

Origin; Specific Historical Antecedents

In a sense, there always has been a cognitive psychology, regardless of whether it was philosophical (rational) or empirical (experimental) in orientation. The nature of experiencing man, the form and acquisition of his knowledge, and man in relation to epistemology have been key themes of intellectual history. Consequently contemporary cognitive behaviorism (1) merely constitutes one phase of the human being's perennial interest in cognition and (2) is embedded in a historical context rich in antecedents. We shall present a very brief and selective sketch of this historical context, the substance of which somewhat overlaps material detailed in other chapters of the book.

The most significant question relative to the origin dimension pertains to why cognitive psychology re-emerged in the form of an information-processing approach to human cognition in the early to mid-1960s, after interest in the epistemological aspect of man had been dormant for a half century under the suppressive effects of descriptive behaviorism and peripherally oriented logical behaviorism. The conditions responsible for this re-emergence must be analyzed.

The Historical Context

The historical context of cognitive behaviorism can be abstracted in terms of (1) specific philosophical precursors, (2) the cognitive relevance of prior schools/systems of experimental psychology, and

(3) the specific contributions of two individuals, Hermann Ebbinghaus and Frederick C. Bartlett.

PHILOSOPHICAL PRECURSORS

The philosophical precursors include Cartesian philosophy, British empiricism, Kantian philosophy, and the eighteenth and nineteenth century Scottish school of philosophy. Each of these philosophical approaches amounts to an implicit cognitive system, with British empiricism related to the unlimited domain interpretation of cognitive psychology and the other three more directly related to the restricted domain interpretation of cognitive psychology.

1. Descartes' dualism and incipient mechanism partitioned the human cognitive system into two parts. Lower order cognitive events, such as sensation and perception, were material events subject to natural law. Higher order cognitive events, such as memory and thinking, were mental events that transcended natural law. Descartes' emphasis on rationalism and innate ideas influenced the structural approach to cognitive psychology. Chomsky's approach to linguistics often is referred to as Cartesian linguistics, and Piaget's genetic epistemological system stresses a fixed developmental sequence of exclusively maturationally based cognitive stages.

2. British empiricism already has been characterized as a surrogate psychological theory of cognition. The British empiricist account of cognition amounts to an implicit human information-processing approach, in which learning and/or memory constituted the pivotal component. All ideas result from sense experience, and specific physically sourced stimulation is processed successively as sensations, simple ideas, and complex ideas. Contemporary information- processing models downplay the importance of association, but the basic relationship between British empiricism and contemporary cognitive behaviorism still holds.

3. Kantian philosophy postulated the existence of a set of innate, a priori categories that structure our cognitive experience. Although these categories are grossly analogous to the structural components of contemporary information-processing systems, Kant's basic influence is on the structural approach to cognition, primarily because of his nativistic orientation. Structurally oriented cognitive psychologists admit the existence of metaphysically based cognitive categories that largely are independent of experience.

4. The eighteenth and nineteenth century Scottish school of philosophy competed with British empiricism and was characterized in Chapter 2 as the source of American prefunctionalistic psychology.

The three most prominent members of this school were Thomas Reid (1710–1796), Dugald Stewart (1753–1828), and Thomas Brown (1778–1820). The school took a nonskeptical, common-sense approach to metaphysics and epistemology, replaced association with suggestion, and emphasized moral philosophy. At a cognitive level, Scottish philosophy is important because of Reid's postulation of approximately 20 mental powers. These powers are more generally called faculties, and Scottish philosophy initiated the modern phase of faculty psychology. Each faculty amounts to a separate mental ability. Faculty psychology had a pervasive effect on phrenology, localization of function concepts and research, and educational practice and theory (i.e., the need to train the faculties by rote practice). The notion of a faculty is indigenous to the structural approach to cognition.

PRIOR SCHOOLS/SYSTEMS OF EXPERIMENTAL PSYCHOLOGY

The relevant prior conceptual approaches to experimental psychology include structuralism, Külpe's Würzburg school, Brentano's act psychology, functionalism, Gestalt psychology, and Tolman's purposive behaviorism. The first three schools and Gestalt psychology focused on the organism's private experience or consciousness and constituted implicit cognitive systems; functionalism and Tolman's purposive behaviorism related cognitive processes to overt behavior.

1. Structuralism focused on the content of consciousness. Wundt assumed that lower order cognitive phenomena, such as sensations and images, were amenable to direct, critical introspection, and he made the higher order cognitive processes, such as thinking and language, part of his *Völkerpsychologie*. Contemporary psychologists again are focusing on mental imagery, but from a more functional orientation. It now is recognized that Wundt's conception of language anticipated many of Chomsky's basic linguistic notions. Titchener took a more descriptive approach to mental phenomena than Wundt did and denied the existence of thought as a separate element of consciousness. Thinking had to be represented in consciousness as a kind of or property of an image; imageless thought simply did not exist. Titchener's approach to cognition is more reminiscent of Skinner's radical behaviorism than it is of cognitive behaviorism.

2. Külpe's Würzburg school was referred to briefly in Chapter 2 as a variant of structuralism in the context of imageless thought. Oswald Külpe (1862–1915) was trained as a structuralist and worked under Wundt at Leipzig for eight years. His short-lived Würzburg school (1894–1909) focused on thinking. Külpe's brand of introspection admitted the existence of imageless thought, that is, thought

occurred, but it was not represented in consciousness as a mental element. Wundt's and Titchener's denial of imageless thought and Külpe's acceptance of imageless thought constituted a continuing structuralist controversy that never was resolved satisfactorily before the matter became moot because of the disappearance of the structural approach. The Würzburg school also demonstrated that more than association was involved in the generation of mental elements. Külpe and his students related the directed nature of thought to set, determining tendency, or *Einstellung*, in experiments in which association was constrained, and not free. The notion of set still persists in the context of contemporary cognitive research on perception, memory, and problem solving.

3. Brentano's act psychology was referred to briefly in Chapter 4 as a historical antecedent of Gestalt psychology. Franz Brentano (1838–1917) was more of a philosopher than a psychologist. His psychology was more empirical than experimental. For Brentano, a mental event was not a passive content to be observed; rather it was an act on the part of the observer that involved reference to an external object. In comparison with Brentano's act psychology, Wundtian and Titchenerian structuralism was a content school. Brentano's approach to consciousness is reminiscent of later American functionalist psychology, and also influenced the unlimited-domain interpretation of cognitive psychology.

4. American functionalism can be construed as a cognitive psychology, primarily because it related overt behavior to the operations of consciousness. Granted it did not focus on cognitive activity as an end in itself, cognitive processes were instrumental in the organism's adaptation to the environment. The status of cognitive events in functionalist psychology is continuous with the status of cognitive events in contemporary cognitive behaviorism.

5. Gestalt psychology basically was a perceptual psychology and constituted an implicit cognitive system. Its stress on organization/structure in perception, learning, memory, problem solving, thinking, and so on derived from Kantian philosophy. It was Gestalt psychology that kept the cognitive tradition and the importance of central processes alive during the heyday of descriptive behaviorism and peripherally oriented logical behaviorism. Recall from Chapter 4 that relevant aspects of Gestalt psychology have been absorbed by contemporary cognitive behaviorism.

6. Tolman's purposive behaviorism was derived as a centrally based logical behaviorism in Chapter 5. His system basically is a cognitive approach to learning. Tolman is credited with establishing the intervening variable concept, but, unlike Hull and Guthrie, he

stressed cognitive mechanisms: Both classical conditioning and instrumental learning involved expectancy (S–S association) formation. In classical conditioning, the CS becomes a sign that the UCS, as significate, is forthcoming, and the subject behaves appropriately. In instrumental learning, as physicalized by discrete-trial reward conditioning in a maze, the subject (rat) forms a cognitive map of the maze, and its behavior is under the control of spatial contingencies, internalized in the form of behavioral expectancies. Tolman also is credited with originating the technical distinction between learning and performance. Cognitive learning can be occurring, but need not be exhibited in behavior (performance) unless sufficient incentive conditions make it worthwhile for the organism to act on its expectancies.

Tolman's purposive behaviorism had only an ancillary effect on contemporary cognitive behaviorism for a number of reasons: (1) He never took himself or his system seriously—his primary goal was to have intellectual fun. (2) Hull was able to adapt his peripherally based effect approach, so that it accommodated most conceptual and empirical problems posed by Tolman's research. (3) Tolman was more action oriented than epistemologically oriented, that is, he was interested in the same kind of overt behavior that Hull was: goal-directed behavior of the rat in a maze situation.

THE CONTRIBUTIONS OF EBBINGHAUS AND BARTLETT

Neither Ebbinghaus nor Bartlett was associated with a formal school of experimental psychology, and their respective contributions to the history of psychology can be treated in any one of a number of contexts. Ebbinghaus single-handedly founded the experimental psychology of verbal learning and memory, and Bartlett anticipated the information-processing approach to organization and structure in memory and thinking.

HERMANN EBBINGHAUS (1850–1909). Ebbinghaus' relevance for cognitive psychology derives from the fact that he demonstrated that an experimental psychology of human long-term memory is feasible. Since the precise measurement of long-term retention requires a preliminary original learning phase, Ebbinghaus also implicitly created an experimental psychology of verbal learning. His achievement in the area of learning/memory can be compared to that of Fechner in the area of sensation: Fechner founded psychophysics (cf. Chapter 2). Both Fechner's psychophysical methods and Ebbinghaus' verbal learning/memory assessment techniques survive virtually intact today and still subsume legitimate subareas of experimental psychology.

Ironically Ebbinghaus' immediate impetus for the creation of a quantitative approach to memory was his perusal of Fechner's classic work *Elemente der Psychophysik*, which he bought in a secondhand bookstore in Paris. Ebbinghaus became determined to do for the higher mental processes what Fechner did for sensation. Between 1879 and 1884, before he became affiliated with any (German) university, Ebbinghaus meticulously generated learning and retention curves for nonsense syllables, using himself as the sole subject. This research was published in his classic *Über das Gedächtnis (On Memory)* in 1885.

Ebbinghaus' work delineated the basic parameters of and created the basic methodology for verbal learning/memory research: (1) He invented the nonsense syllable (the CVC) to control for the meaningfulness of the verbal material. (2) He devised the trial-by-trial method of presentation of the verbal items of a list for the original learning phase, and in so doing established repetition as the basic structural variable in verbal learning research. (3) He created operational criteria for quantifying degree of original learning. (4) He initiated massed versus distributed practice acquisition procedures. (5) He formalized time out after original learning as a retention interval. (6) He invented the relearning or savings method of assessing retention.

Although contemporary cognitive behaviorists do not conduct memory research that is as functionally oriented as Ebbinghaus' and do not place as much emphasis on the notion of an association, the information-processing approach to human cognition would be impossible without Ebbinghaus' pioneering work on human memory.

FREDERICK C. BARTLETT (1886–1969). Bartlett was a British psychologist who held the chair in psychology at Cambridge University from 1931 until his retirement in 1952. He had a tremendous effect on British psychology administratively because, as of 1960, two-thirds of all the chair holders of psychology in England were his former students.

Bartlett was a cognitive psychologist in the contemporary sense of the term. He was influenced by Ward and Stout, who were anti-British empirical and associational in orientation: They espoused concepts similar to the basic Gestalt notions. Bartlett was particularly interested in memory and thinking. His classic text *Remembering* originally appeared in 1932, and his *Thinking* was published in 1958.

Remembering reported on his memory research, which began during World War I and continued throughout the decade of the 1920s. Bartlett's approach to long-term memory is indistinguishable from that of the contemporary information-processing theorist. Unlike Ebbinghaus, who took a strictly quantitative approach to the retention of meaningless material, Bartlett focused on narrative memory for meaningful material, such as connected discourse, at a qualitative level. Subjects were tested for their memory of a given story line or theme weeks, months, and even years after their initial reading of the material. The results convinced Bartlett that memory is a reconstruction process, as opposed to a reproduction or automatic retrieval process. A subject coded and recalled the material in terms of schemata—a subject's own personalistic organizational categories based on past experience, current attitudes, and so forth. Bartlett's conception of memory is reminiscent of the Gestalt view with its emphasis on distortion and leveling.

In *Thinking* Bartlett assumed a functional orientation to thought, treating it as a high-level ability comparable to motor skills. He regarded thinking as a social phenomenon, the study of which could not be divorced from the culture and society in which it occurred. This is reminiscent of Wundt's *Völkerpsychologie*.

The Re-emergence of Cognition as Information Processing

The question of why cognitive behaviorism emerged in the 1960s as a system of psychology reduces to why the human mind and cognitive processes again became acceptable objects of concern for experimental psychologists. The answer requires a two-level response, involving (1) the state of neobehaviorism or orthodox behaviorism in the 1960s, and (2) various post-World War II developments outside of psychology that served as theoretical and methodological influences on behaviorism.

NEOBEHAVIORISM IN THE 1960S

Most nonbehaviorists or antibehaviorists like to argue that behavioristic psychology had become sterile by the 1960s. Watson's descriptive behaviorism had been rejected as too simplistic and extreme; the comprehensive macrotheoretical learning systems of Hull, Guthrie, and Tolman had either failed or simply run their course. Skinner's radical behaviorism was still flourishing, and the mathematical model approach to learning research was at its height. But the detractors of behaviorism did not appreciate either the subtle or substantive differences between Skinner's and Watson's brands of behaviorism, nor did they construe mathematically based learning models to be in the mainstream of behaviorism. If the detractor's assessment of the state of orthodox behaviorism in the 1960s is correct, then a return of interest in cognitive phenomena would seem to be a natural development.

On the other hand, committed behaviorists did not consider their discipline to be in a sorry state in the 1960s. Behaviorism had changed, but it had matured. It was less optimistic, but more realistic; it was less polemical, but more confident; it was less closely-knit, but more flexible. Radical behaviorism and mathematical model learning research served as the foundation for the cognitive revival. Skinner did not deny the existence of mental events; he simply found them to be irrelevant as causal entities, but not as epiphenomenal events. Skinner simply accepts a subject's statement such as "I see a ball." The cognitive behaviorist wants to supply the hypothetical cognitive superstructure responsible for the statement. The mathematical model learning research, much of it originally concentrated in the area of human verbal learning, expanded to include such areas as discrimination, observing responses, attention, memory (both short-term and long-term), concept identification, and concept formation. The mathematical psychologist not only studied these entities as epiphenomena, but also used them as hypothetical states in models for predicting other phenomena. For instance, a mathematical psychologist not only studies memory as an end in itself via a specific model, but also uses it as a hypothetical state in a model designed to predict performance in another kind of task, for example, a paired-associate learning experiment. A mathematical model approach to these phenomena existed, independent of their absorption into a cognitive information-processing approach. It is merely a semantic question as to whether current mathematically based learning and learning-related research is cognitive or not.

EXTERNALLY SOURCED THEORETICAL AND METHODOLOGICAL INFLUENCES

One of the characteristics of science, in general, and psychology, in particular, is that its specific object of interest is contingent on theory and methodology: A specific natural phenomenon is investigated if it has meaning in the context of a given theory and if it is amenable to acceptable extant methodology. Watson had decreed mental events out of psychology for methodological reasons. Granted that theory was rudimentary in the classical schools of experimental psychology, it is not in the context of contemporary systems of experimental psychology. Various externally sourced theoretical and methodological developments made a return of interest in cognitive processes possible in the 1960s.

1. At a theoretical level, post-World War II developments in engineering, communication theory, systems analysis, and linguistics served as sources of psychological theory: for instance, cybernetics, feedback systems, information theory, signal detection theory, and transformational grammar.

2. At a methodological or technological level, post-1940 development of the computer and computer programming afforded a scientifically acceptable alternative to introspection: computer simulation and artificial intelligence.

The information-processing approach to human cognition represents the fusion of these two external influences. The human brain is treated as a communication system whose operations can be mimicked by a computer. The return of interest in cognition is only one facet of the effect of the computer on psychology; contemporary cognitive behaviorism is just one aspect of a newer, more sophisticated, more technologically oriented psychology that a computer and computer-based analogies permit. The computer also has revolutionized educational theory and practice, therapy and diagnostic evaluation, and mental testing. The influence of the computer on psychology is so pervasive that it serves as one of the sources of humanistic psychology, which in part is a reaction to a purely mechanistic approach to man.

Chief Historical Figure: Herbert A. Simon

Contemporary cognitive behaviorism possesses no one monolithic spokesperson; so many contemporary experimental psychologists identify with the information-processing approach that even a cursory biographical sketch of a small sample of them would be prohibitive. I have chosen to focus on Herbert A. Simon for three basic reasons: (1) He pioneered the use of the computer analogy in psychology. (2) His career epitomizes the influence of external sources on orthodox behaviorism. (3) His research accomplishments recently were honored by a Nobel prize in economics (there is no Nobel prize in psychology). Only two figures in the history of psychology prior to Simon achieved Nobel recognition: Ivan Pavlov (digestive processes) in 1904 and Georg von Békésy (physiological basis of hearing) in 1961, both in medicine and physiology. (More recently, in 1981, the sensory physiologists David Hubel and Torsten Wiesel were accorded Nobel recognition for their work on the neurophysiology of visual information processing in cats and macaques.)

Herbert A. Simon (1916–)

Simon was born in Milwaukee, Wis., in 1916. He received both the B.A. and Ph.D. degrees in political science from the University of Chicago, in 1936 and 1943 respectively. Although formally trained as a political scientist, Simon's education was eclectic: As a graduate student, he studied James, Freud, and Piaget; factor analysis; mathematical biophysics; and rational decision making in statistics, symbolic logic, and economics. His Ph.D. thesis concerned organizational decision making and was published in book form as *Administrative Behavior* in 1947. A second edition appeared in 1957.

From 1936 to 1939, Simon worked as a research assistant for the International City Managers' Association, and he was director of administrative measurement studies in the Bureau of Public Administration at the University of California, Berkeley, from 1939 to 1942. Simon entered academia in 1942 as a faculty member at the Illinois Institute of Technology, where he served as chairman of the Department of Political and Social Science for three years. In 1949, Simon moved to the newly created Graduate School of Industrial Administration at the Carnegie Institute of Technology, now known as Carnegie-Mellon University. At Carnegie, he served as department head, and later as associate dean.

In 1952, Simon became a consultant at the RAND Corporation's System Research Laboratory and his long, productive association with Allen Newell began. Under the influence and stimulation of Newell, Simon's interest in decision making in organizations shifted to decision making in the human being, and they began a basic research program on human thinking. By the end of 1955, Newell and Simon had designed the Logic Theorist (LT), the first heuristic computer problem-solving program. This work on the computer simulation of human thought was reported to the psychological community in their 1958 *Psychological Review* article, "Elements of a Theory of Human Problem Solving." The Logic Theorist was expanded in the 1960s and became known as the General Problem Solver (GPS). Newell and Simon's simulation research soon was extended to other psychological processes, such as verbal learning, concept formation, and perception. The shift in Simon's research interests was reflected in his formal faculty positions at Carnegie-Mellon. He was named professor of administration and psychology in 1961, and he became a professor of psychology and computer science in 1965.

Simon has served as an associate editor of a number of journals; he also has served on various governmental committees and advisory bodies. He received the American Psychological Association Distinguished Scientific Contribution Award in 1969 and was accorded the Nobel prize in economics in 1978.

Simon is a prolific writer. In addition to over 100 journal articles, he has written or coauthored a number of books, including *Administrative Behavior* (1947, 1957), *Public Administration* (1950), *Models of Man* (1957), *The New Science of Management Decision* (1960), and *Human Problem Solving* (1972).

Characteristic Experimentation; Primary Research Areas

The domain of the information-processing approach to human cognition minimally subsumes sensation, perception, pattern recognition, attention or selective attention, short-term and long-term memory, visual imagery, learning, language acquisition and comprehension, thinking, problem solving, concept formation, cognitive development, and artificial intelligence. The extent and diversity of this domain necessitate a highly selective presentation of the characteristic experimentation associated with cognitive behaviorism. We shall describe briefly the five primary classes of cognitive research.

Five Primary Classes of Cognitive Research

It is the cognitive behaviorist's task to chart the flow of information through an organism's cognitive system from input to output. As information is processed by the system, it is continually being transformed. The five primary classes of cognitive research derive from the necessity for investigating the cognitive system at those specific points at which crucial transformations in information are most likely to occur. These crucial points of information transformation are (1) transduction of physical stimulus energy, (2) physical pattern recognition, (3) symbolic pattern recognition (language decoding), (4) memorial construction, and (5) reasoning and thinking. Of these, only the first is explicitly physically or physiologically defined; the remaining four are conceptually or functionally defined in terms of specific environmentally sourced demands or experimental laboratory task demands imposed on the organism as an information processor.

1. The first point at which information transformation occurs is the interface between the external environment and the sensory receptors: Physical stimulus energy associated with the various sensory modalities must be transduced by the appropriate receptor. The primary experimental question in this context relates to the fidelity of this transduction process: How and to what degree are the physical attributes of the external stimulus represented by the neuronal response of the receptor? This question absorbs the traditional psychophysical methods used to assess qualitative and quantitative stimulus discrimination, the newer experimental techniques subsumed by signal detection theory, and various methods of psychophysiological (neuronal) response recording and analysis.

2. The second level of information transformation involves the traditional research area of perception, more commonly called the problem of pattern recognition by the cognitive behaviorist. How is the stimulus information coded at the perceptual level, and how does the organism recognize or assign an interpretation to the stimulus input at this level? Research on these questions involves the sensory iconic (visual) and echoic (auditory) stores, conceptual template matching and critical feature analysis pattern recognition systems, selective attention mechanisms, and possible context, expectation, or memorial (past experience) effects.

3. A third kind of information processing entails the transformation of physical patterns into meaningful symbolic patterns. This is the problem of language comprehension, research on which is in an embryonic stage, compared with the other four classes. Current research focuses on phonemic identification, speech perception, representation of semantic meaning and the grammar (syntax) of a natural language by a computer program, how grammatical and semantic knowledge is best combined to decode incoming sentences, sentence decoding as a function of context, and the like.

4. A fourth kind of information transformation is of interest in its own right, and also interfaces with pattern recognition, language comprehension, and reasoning or thinking—namely, memorial construction. Stimulus information can be deposited into and retrieved from two different kinds of memory stores: the short-term memory store (STM) and the long-term memory store (LTM). Memory, especially the LTM variety, has a long research history: What are the

spatial characteristics (capacity) and temporal characteristics (duration) of each store? How is material inputed into each store? How is information coded and organized in the two stores? How is material retrieved from each store? An identifying characteristic of contemporary cognitive research on memory is its focus on various mnemonic devices or memory tricks: method of loci, coined words or phrases, and pegword rhyme systems, for example.

5. A fifth level of information transformation relates to reasoning and thinking. Most reasoning and thinking involve the manipulation and rearrangement of symbols for the purpose of solving some problem, deciding on some specific course of action, inducing some relational or classifying rule, or deriving some logical conclusion. This class of cognitive research subsumes problem solving, choice and decision making, concept formation, and logical, analogical, deductive, or inductive reasoning tasks. Research on reasoning/thinking was revolutionized by the computer-based analogy and, in many respects, constitutes the glamour area of cognitive behaviorism. There is something seductive about programming a computer to play checkers and chess, prove a mathematical theorem, or make investment decisions.

Historical Legacy; Contemporary Significance

The information-processing approach has had a significant impact on psychology. Whereas conditioning served as the basic source of behavioral change in the context of descriptive behaviorism and peripherally oriented logical behaviorism, cognitive processes now serve as the primary source of behavioral change in the context of contemporary cognitive behaviorism. The information-processing approach has absorbed such traditional research areas as sensation, perception, learning, and memory. These phenomena now are viewed as properties of a more general and comprehensive cognitive information-processing system. Cognitive psychology is beginning to influence behavior modification and therapy because of its current stress on self-control and self-reinforcement. The psychology of motivation and the psychology of emotion are becoming increasingly cognitively oriented. Contemporary social psychological theory and research are cognitive in nature. Developmental psychology and cognitive psychology serve as mutual influences on each other. A cognitive approach to personality exists: Kelly's theory of personal constructs.

Cognitive behaviorism has become institutionalized to some degree. Every large undergraduate and graduate department of psychology in the country has at least one information-processing specialist on its faculty. Three cognitively oriented professional journals have been created in the past 15 years: *Cognitive Psychology* (1969), *Memory and Cognition* (1971), and *Cognition* (1973). The *Journal of Experimental Psychology: Human Learning and Memory*, a publication of the American Psychological Association, was retitled the *Journal of Experimental Psychology: Learning, Memory, and Cognition* in 1982. Carnegie-Mellon has held an annual symposium on cognition since 1964; Loyola University conducted a symposium on cognitive psychology in the years from 1972 to 1974.

Cognitive behaviorism has advanced to the point where its adherents now are standing back and evaluating its past achievements and immediate future prospects. Alan Newell is dissatisfied with the plethora of research techniques. Ulric Neisser has sounded the warning that the vast majority of cognitive studies do not possess ecological validity, that is, they are too divorced from the process of cognition as it occurs in the natural environment and everyday life. Neisser also has pointed out that the implications of the information-processing approach for behavioral prediction and control have not been fully publicized. Prediction and control constitute much more elusive and less feasible goals in the context of a cognitive psychology. It is fairly well agreed that the initial period of spectacular conceptual and methodological advances in cognitive behaviorism is now over; unless some new conceptual developments appear on the immediate horizon to revitalize the computer-brain analogy, cognitive behaviorism is in danger of stagnation.

Bibliography

Bartlett, F.C. *Remembering: A Study in Experimental and Social Psychology.* Cambridge, England: Cambridge University Press, 1932.
Bartlett, F.C. *Thinking: An Experimental and Social Study.* New York: Basic Books, 1958.
Ebbinghaus, H. *Über das Gedächtnis: Untersuchungen zur experimentellen Psychologie.* Leipzig: Duncker & Humblot, 1885. (Translated by H.A. Ruger and C.E. Bussenius, 1913; New York: Dover, 1964.)
Fechner, G.T. *Elemente der Psychophysik.* Leipzig: Breitkopf & Härtel, 1860. (*Elements of Psychophysics*, 2 vols. New York: Holt, Rinehart, & Winston, 1966.)
Neisser, U. *Cognitive Psychology.* New York: Appleton-Century-Crofts, 1967.

Neisser, U. *Cognition and Reality*. San Francisco: Freeman, 1976.

Newell, A., Shaw, J.C., and Simon, H.A. Elements of a theory of human problem solving. *Psychological Review*, 1958, 65, 151–166.

Newell, A., and Simon, H.A. *Human Problem Solving*. Englewood Cliffs, N.J.: Prentice-Hall, 1972.

Simon, H.A. *Administrative Behavior*. New York: Macmillan, 1947, 1957.

Simon, H.A. *Models of Man*. New York: Wiley, 1957.

Simon, H.A. *The New Science of Management Decision*. New York: Harper & Row, 1960.

Simon, H.A., Smithburg, D.W., and Thompson, V.A. *Public Administration. New York: Knopf, 1950.*

9

Depth Psychology: Psychoanalysis

Introduction

The historically most important and significant system for resolving and treating abnormal phenomena is Freudian psychology, better known as psychoanalysis. Psychoanalysis, as a form of therapy, grew out of the psychogenic interpretation of mental illness (specifically, the hysterical neurosis) characteristic of nineteenth century French psychopathology. Psychoanalysis is similar to radical behaviorism in that it constitutes a world view; however, the historical/cultural impact of Freud's system exceeds that of Skinner's because it transcends psychology. Freud is important in the history of psychology, but he is more important in the history of ideas. His contribution to intellectual history transcends his contribution to psychology.

Freud devised a highly personalistic system of psychology that (1) possesses an immense degree of face validity and (2) has had a tremendous impact on society and the way people view themselves. Freud's system has great practical application value and popular appeal because it can resolve practically every psychological phenomenon of interest and concern to the public at large. Freudian psychology exhausts the psychological universe for the typical person, and even many scholars. Freud's ideas have influenced literature, philosophy, theology, ethics, art, political science, anthropology, sociology, and "pop" psychology. A given phenomenon often is explained by simply stating: "It is Freudian." You never hear an analogous statement such as, "It is Skinnerian." Freud's system is so pervasive that frequently it is claimed that psychoanalysis explains everything from an erection to the resurrection.

Freudian psychology is a depth psychology: It resolves overt behavior in terms of internal mentalistic events and irrational forces, many of which are unconscious or beyond the awareness of the organism. It is successively a developmental psychology, a personality psychology, a motivational or dynamic psychology.

Both the therapeutic and general world view aspects of Freud's system evolved simultaneously in the context of attempting to relieve the psychological suffering/problems of a small sample of middle and upper class Austrian women who lived around the turn of the century. Freud's system explicitly originated in the treatment of the hysterical neurosis, characteristic of women living in an age of Victorian standards and morality.

A system of psychology based on such a sampling source is highly personalistic and beyond meaningful empirical assessment. Freud's system is more of a dogma than a set of empirical propositions. To say that the content of his system is Freud's own private, subjective view of the world is more than a circular statement. Anyone is allowed to have his/her own private view of the psychological universe; however, very few of us have had our views institutionalized, hallowed, or accepted as the ultimate revelation. Any initial adherent of Freudian doctrine who came to disagree with one or more of his fundamental notions had to leave the movement. Any instance of internal dissension could be resolved only by the nonbeliever splitting away, denying the master's authority, and creating a rival depth psychology. Freudian psychoanalysis probably spawned more offshoots than any other system of psychology, with Adler's individual psychology and Jung's analytic psychology constituting the two primary examples. Among other analysts who found themselves in varying degrees of estrangement from Freud were Rank, Ferenczi, Stekel, Breuer, and Bleuler. Space limitations will not permit an in-depth consideration of the many offshoots of Freudian psychology, beyond analyzing why they developed in the first place. As a comparative reference point, it is possible to disagree with Skinner and still remain a behaviorist.

Freud had an interesting way of responding to critics and criticism. The beliefs and intentions of a critic could be evaluated derogatively by any number of psychoanalytic principles. Criticism was given a psychoanalytic interpretation. It was viewed as resistance; and, for Freud, the degree of resistance elicited by a concept was a measure of the degree of truth value possessed by the concept. Freud was in the unique position of counting as positive evidence for his system the degree of resistance that it elicited.

Since Freud's system is personalistic and self-derived, his life has been analyzed more than that of any other psychologist in history. The boundary lines separating Freud's personality and his abstract system of beliefs are not clear-cut. Just as Skinner's system of psychology often is viewed as an example of operant conditioning, Freud's life and thought often are interpreted in a psychoanalytic framework and subjected to Freudian analysis.

Freudian psychology will be treated as a world view in the context of object of study or basic subject matter. Psychoanalysis will be analyzed as a form of therapy in the method of study or permissible methodology section. Freud's approach will be described as a logical/conceptual extension of French psychopathology in the origin and specific historical antecedents section. Some of the specific influences on Freud and his thought will be highlighted in the descriptive biography. Characteristic experimentation or primary research areas constitute a null analytical dimension for Freudian psychology; however, we shall enumerate the specific aspects of Freud's system that have influenced experimental psychology. The historical legacy section summarizes the current status of psychoanalysis and the social, cultural implications of Freud's system.

Object of Study; Basic Subject Matter

Initial Description

Like the structuralists and functionalists, Freud focused on the mind. Unlike structuralism and functionalism, Freudian psychology did not focus on the elements and activities of consciousness; rather Freud made the existence of unconscious mental activities and strivings the cornerstone of his psychology. The notion of an unconscious mental life was not original with Freud; however, the declaration that it constitutes the canonical concept for resolving the psychodynamics of the human being was original with Freud, and amounts to his greatest contribution to psychology.

Like the behaviorist, Freud observed and recorded behavior, but in an implicit manner. Freud had no formal concept of behavior, and it did not constitute his exclusive focus of concern. His interest in behavior was incidental: It allowed him to investigate the nature of the unconscious. Unlike the behaviorist, Freud related overt behavior to an elaborate internal mental apparatus and motivational system. Freudian psychology basically is a mentalistic one in comparison with the descriptive behavioristic systems of Watson and Skinner. Freud was just as much a determinist as the behaviorist. It was the individual's psychic life, however, that was determined; overt behavior was not controlled by the environment, but by the complex psychological events occurring within the body.

It is not meaningful to differentiate formally between the experiencing (mind) and reactive (behavior) aspects of the human being in the context of Freudian psychology. Freud's system focused on the nature of man as a psychological being, that is, what kind of creature is man at a psychological level? While Skinner treated the organism as a locus of externally sourced variables, Freud viewed the organism as a repository of antagonistic motivational forces and interacting mentalistic processes at various levels of consciousness, which manifested themselves in overt behavior. Freud's psychodynamics and its behavioral manifestations amounted to a closed system, and this system as a whole constituted his object of study or basic subject matter.

The content of Freud's psychodynamics, as well as the relative importance of its various subcomponents, changed over the years, and Freud never claimed to have produced a final, fixed system. This is to be expected, considering the inductive nature of his system. We shall abstract Freud's basic subject matter in terms of (1) the primary assumptions of his depth psychology, (2) the fundamental structural components of his system, (3) the kind of explanation his system afforded, and (4) the different phases of development or recognition of psychoanalysis.

The Primary Assumptions of Freud's Depth Psychology

A depth psychology resolves overt behavior and/or the primary psychological phenomena of interest in terms of internal determinants; it attempts to reconstruct an organism's inner psychic world. Freud's depth psychology is characterized by four primary assumptions.

1. The organism basically is a biological creature and is subject to various innate, instinctual forces. As a biological creature, the human being does possess physical–chemical reality, is continuous with the rest of nature, and is a product of evolution. Freud assumed mechanism/materialism, although he eventually despaired of attempting to reduce his mentalistic concepts to underlying neuronal/physiological events. Freud differed from the behaviorists by making motivational or dynamic constructs the cornerstone of his materialism: pleasure, pain, sex, aggression, and the like. His system, like many others, is a general equilibrium–disequilibrium one, in which the end goal of overall activity is the attainment of some state of balance or absence of tension.

2. The organism basically is a prisoner of its past history. Freud takes a continuity, as opposed to noncontinuity, approach to human development. Much of adult behavior, especially its salient features that are labeled abnormal or neurotic, are the direct result of certain childhood experiences. Freud has an elaborate theory of psychological development, physicalized in terms of a succession of fixed psychosexual stages, which serve as the source of a person's adult personality, whether normal or abnormal.

3. Not only is the internal psychic world of the organism determined, but also much of its contents and processes is unconscious. For Freud, the notion of the unconscious is more than a descriptive, verbal label: It is an actual location or repository of ideas, memories, wishes, strivings, conflicts, and so forth. Freud used the notion of the unconscious to resolve both normal and abnormal psychological phenomena; the explicit goal of his therapeutic and investigatory techniques was the externalization of the contents of an organism's unconscious. Much of the attraction of Freudian psychology for the general public derives from his use of the unconscious: Giving a specific psychological phenomenon a simplistic symbolic interpretation is very impressive to most people.

4. The organism basically is an irrational, as opposed to rational, creature. The irrational components of an organism's personality predominate over the rational components, especially in an individual who has not undergone an extensive in-depth analysis. In a sense, the goal of psychoanalysis, as a form of therapy, is to make the client aware of these irrational forces so that they can be dealt with rationally. Freud was bitterly criticized for revealing and emphasizing the irrational aspects of man. Although Freud's view of man and his condition was pessimistic, his vision of the future of man was not as bleak as his detractors would have one believe.

The Fundamental Structural Components of Freud's System

The fundamental structural components of Freud's system minimally consist of (1) two basic motivational constructs, (2) three levels of mind, (3) three systems of personality, and (4) five psychosexual stages of development.

THE MOTIVATIONAL CONSTRUCTS

Freud ultimately postulated the existence of two basic motivational constructs: a life instinct and a death instinct. The life instinct sometimes is called Eros; the death instinct sometimes is called Thanatos. The life instinct is associated with a specific form of energy, termed the libido, whose basic denotation is sexual in nature. The sex drive and libido are equivalent notions, although what Freud meant by libido is far more general than mere adult heterosexual motivation and contact. A child possesses libidinal energy, and Freud's revelation of childhood sexuality created a storm of protest. The death instinct is associated with a specific form of energy, which Freud left nameless, whose basic denotation is aggressive in nature. Aggression and self-destruction derive from the death instinct. The life instinct also embodies the so-called pleasure principle, while the death instinct also embodies the so-called pain principle.

THE LEVELS OF MIND

Freud postulated the existence of three levels of awareness or three states of mental activity: conscious, preconscious, and unconscious.

1. Freud's use of the term conscious is continuous with its use in structuralistic, functionalistic, and Gestaltist psychology. It consists of those mental events and activities of which the organism is immediately aware. Conscious mental events (thoughts) are governed by the laws of logic; conscious activity involves the so-called secondary process.
2. The preconscious is an intermediate state, separating the contents of the conscious and the unconscious. The content of the preconscious is not as directly accessible as that of the conscious, but is more easily retrievable than that of the unconscious.
3. The unconscious is the repository of all sorts of actively repressed material, such as unpleasant or socially tabooed childhood experiences, socially unacceptable libidinal strivings, and conflicts. The content and activities of the unconscious are not governed by the

laws of logic, but are characterized by the so-called primary process. Freud called his theory of unconscious mental functioning *metapsychology*, because academic/experimental psychology studied conscious mental events. Freud resolved the contents of dreams, slips of the tongue, memory lapses, neurotic symptoms, irrational fears, certain forms of anxiety, accident proneness, even certain types of humor and wit, in terms of the unconscious.

INVESTIGATION OF THE UNCONSCIOUS: DREAM ANALYSIS. The analysis of dreams, or dream interpretation, constitutes the prototypical situation for unraveling the workings of the unconscious for Freud. Dreams possess a manifest content and a latent content. The manifest content is a disguised representation of events as they exist in the unconscious. The manifest content is a result of the so-called dream work; the manifest content is characterized by displacement, condensation, conversion, timelessness, and so on. Through analysis of dream symbolization and the use of ancillary information about the organism, the manifest content of a dream can be interpreted, that is, transformed into latent content, the meaning of the dream at the unconscious level. Freud assumed that dreams perform a wish fulfillment function: Decoding of a dream reveals the forbidden unconscious desires of the organism. Freud ultimately postulated a set of standard, universal symbols for dream decoding: for example, climbing stairs represented sexual intercourse; a suitcase symbolized the vagina; a hat stood for the penis. This allowed the symbols in myths, art objects, and primitive cultures to be interpreted; and the whole dream interpretation enterprise accorded Freud's system a tremendous degree of cultural validity.

In addition to dream analysis, Freud externalized the contents of the unconscious by the use of free association and hypnosis (analyzed later in this chapter).

THE COMPONENTS OF PERSONALITY

Freud ultimately analyzed the structure of an organism's personality in terms of three systems: id, superego, and ego.

1. The id is the most primeval system. It is innate and consists of the primitive and unmodified sexual and biological desires/strivings of the organism. The id follows the pleasure principle, and its goal is the immediate gratification of the organism's needs. The content of the id is wholly unconscious.

2. The superego is an acquired system, inculcated through the

demands of the parents and society. It is the repository of the cultural and/or moral precepts of society and consists of two subcomponents: the conscience, in the everyday sense of the term, and the ego ideal, a representation of the ideal self, that is, what the self should be. The superego's primary function is to act as a check on the unmodified, unabashed strivings of the id. The content of the superego can exist at all three levels of awareness.

3. The ego largely is acquired and functions as a reality principle. The content of the ego can exist at all three levels of awareness; however, very little of the ego's content is unconscious. The ego operates logically, in terms of the secondary process, and serves to arbitrate between the desires of the id and the prohibitions of the superego.

THE PSYCHOSEXUAL STAGES OF DEVELOPMENT

Freud assumed a succession of five fixed stages of development, distinguished primarily in terms of what serves as the acceptable or only object of libidinal satisfaction: (1) oral, (2) anal, (3) phallic, (4) latency, and (5) genital. The attainment of a stable adult personality requires a successful progression through these stages. Fixation at or regression to one of these stages constitutes part of the etiology of a neurosis or serves as the source of a specific personality type, for example, an anal character.

1. The oral stage subsumes the individual's first two years of life. During this stage, libidinal satisfaction is obtained through the mouth—eating, drinking, sucking, chewing in general. The only object that can serve as a source of libidinal satisfaction besides the self in this stage is the mother. The adult oral character is overly concerned with such activities as eating, drinking, kissing, and smoking.

2. The anal stage encompasses the third and fourth years of life. Libidinal satisfaction is concentrated on the toileting activities: micturition and the retention or expulsion of the feces. The adult anal character is overly preoccupied with cleanliness and orderliness.

3. The phallic stage begins in the third or fourth year of life and extends through the fifth year; thus it overlaps the anal stage. In the phallic stage, libidinal energy is focused on the biological sex organs; and the object of libidinal desire is the parent of the opposite sex. Boys encounter and must resolve the so-called Oedipal complex; girls encounter and must resolve the so-called Electra complex. Successful resolutions of these complexes lead to identification with the same-sex parent and the formation of the superego. Adults disproportionately affected by events occurring during the phallic stage display

behaviors characteristic of the extreme sexual prototype: The man is excessively masculine; the woman is excessively feminine or a *femme fatale*.

4. The latency stage occurs between the fifth year and the onset of puberty, usually around the age of 12. This is a culturally defined stage, which violates Freud's basic biologically (sexually) defined typology. In this stage, the boy or girl identifies with peers of the same sex, "hates" members of the opposite sex, and comes to adopt the behavioral characteristics of the ideal sexual prototype, that is, developes the appropriate sex-role identity. Adults who do not progress beyond the latency stage never develop a libidinal interest in members of the opposite sex.

5. The genital stage commences at puberty and continues throughout the remainder of adult life. Libidinal satisfaction is obtained via the biological sex organs in a heterosexual context: The object of the libido is a member of the opposite sex. An adult who is frustrated in his/her heterosexual behavior through direct expression of libido either can repress the libidinal strivings or indirectly express them in dreams, neurotic symptoms, or perversion. Indirect expression constitutes displacement; and the most socially acceptable form of displacement is sublimation, whereby the organism channels the libido into creative artistic, scientific, or literary endeavors.

The Nature of Freudian Explanation

Although Freud constructed an elaborate conceptual system, in which an organism's psychic life was assumed to be determined, he was unable to predict behavior or any other psychological phenomenon that was significant or relevant. Freud was able only to postdict behavior and/or a psychological event; that is, he was able only to explain them after they occurred. Freud's system exclusively affords after-the-fact explanation. Given a psychological event X, the psychoanalyst only can trace its possible source back in time. An after-the-fact explanation basically is circular in nature; and a descriptive behaviorist, such as Skinner, dismisses Freud's elaborate mentalisms because they are circular.

From another perspective, the Freudian system overdetermines its basic subject matter. A given psychological event, such as a neurotic symptom or the manifest content of a dream, can result from any one of a number of mechanisms; that is, each mechanism alone is sufficient to cause the event, yet each of the mechanisms operates concurrently and jointly determines the event.

The Phases of Development or Recognition of Psychoanalysis

The evolution of psychoanalysis as a system of psychology can be divided into four distinct periods: (1) initial germination or formal founding phase, (2) consolidation phase, (3) schism phase, and (4) internationalization phase.

1. Freud was graduated from medical school (University of Vienna) in 1881, and commenced an approximately two-decade professional association (practice) with Josef Breuer the following year. Over this period of time, Freud and Breuer developed a distinctly psychogenic approach to the etiology and treatment of hysteria. In 1895, they published *Studien über Hysterie*, reporting on their work with hysteric patients. This event usually is hailed either as the formal beginning of psychoanalysis as a movement or as the explicit ending of the initial, germinal phase of psychoanalysis. Other significant events during this period included Freud's trips to France to study under Charcot and Bernheim in the late 1880s and his self-analysis in the late 1890s.

2. The next decade (1900–1910) is considered the consolidation phase of the psychoanalytic movement. Freud wrote about his work on dreams, the psychopathology of everyday life, and his theory of sexuality. The Wednesday evening discussion groups were formed, Freud attracted a substantial number of European adherents and students, and various psychoanalytic professional societies were established. Freud's ideas were published in American journals, and he was recognized by the American psychological establishment through his attendance (and receipt of an honorary doctorate) at Clark University's celebration of its 20th anniversary in 1909.

3. The period from 1911 to approximately 1918 (the end of World War I) represents the great schism of the psychoanalytic movement. Adler, Jung, and others rejected orthodox Freudian psychoanalysis and left the movement to establish systems of their own. Freud did not publish any new significant theoretical works during this period.

4. It was in the following years, from 1918 until 1939, when Freud died in England after leaving Austria because of the Nazi takeover, that psychoanalysis and its founder achieved international recognition. Freud greatly expanded the core area of psychoanalysis (id, ego, superego, Eros, Thanatos, etc.) and expostulated on the religious and social consequences of psychoanalysis. He attracted many American and English students, and psychoanalysis spread to America and England through the efforts of Anna Freud and Ernest Jones. Freud's books were translated into English in the 1920s and became a signif-

icant component of the psychological literature. In the 1930s, psychoanalysis began to rival behaviorism as a school of psychology.

Method of Study; Permissible Methodology

The methodology dimension exists at two distinct levels in the context of Freudian psychology: (1) What constitute appropriate therapeutic techniques for analyzing and treating the psychological problems/symptoms of patients? (2) What serve as legitimate tools for the inductive inference of the nature of psychological reality? The first level relates to psychoanalysis as an applied psychology, specifically as a form of therapy; the second level relates to psychoanalysis as a world view. Remember with respect to the second level that Freud was an inductive theorist, much in the manner of Skinner, although Freud's methodology and sampling sources differed greatly from Skinner's.

There is no sharp dividing line between these two aspects of Freudian methodology, either at a conceptual level or at the level of everyday practice. At a conceptual level, the two aspects had the same ultimate purpose: the inference of the content of the unconscious. At an operational level, Freud used the same techniques for therapy and theoretical induction. He performed therapy and induced the nature of psychological reality concurrently in the context of the same patient or session.

We shall analyze Freud's basic methodology in the context of the second level. It should be realized that these comments also apply to the first level, with only a minimal change in wording. We also shall present the basic characteristics of psychoanalysis as a form of therapy in this section, not from a methodological perspective, but from a clinical, content perspective.

Freud's Basic Methodology

INFORMAL AND FORMAL EVIDENCE FOR THE UNCONSCIOUS

Freud could appeal to two different classes of empirical phenomena by which to infer the existence or content of the unconscious: informal and formal.

1. The informal class consists of empirical observations made in the context of everyday life or in the natural environment and is

suggested by the title of his book *The Psychopathology of Everyday Life*, in which he gives a psychodynamic interpretation to such phenomena as slips of the tongue (i.e., Freudian slips), memory lapses, accident proneness or physical (motor) errors, and instances of verbal humor and wit. According to Freud, these specific phenomena demonstrate the existence and effects of a dynamic unconscious.

2. The formal class consists of empirical observations made in the context of the therapeutic situation, as during an actual therapy session, and includes such phenomena as dreams, neurotic symptoms, irrational fear, guilt, anxiety, and conflict. In other words, the formal class consists of the full range of so-called abnormal behaviors and psychological problems that bring the patient to the psychoanalyst in the first place. This class is important because it serves as the focus of Freud's three basic techniques for externalizing the unconscious.

TECHNIQUES FOR INVESTIGATING THE UNCONSCIOUS

Freud used three nonmutually exclusive techniques for studying the unconscious: (1) analysis of dreams, (2) hypnosis, and (3) free association. The first technique is not necessarily indigenous to the therapeutic situation—a person's dreams can be analyzed independently of the act of undergoing psychoanalysis. The second and third techniques are indigenous to the therapeutic situation and are used explicitly to unravel the etiology of specific neurotic systems. Freud eventually abandoned the use of hypnosis as a therapeutic technique, and the standard psychoanalytic therapy session came to consist of some combination of dream interpretation and free association. However, the notion of psychoanalysis as an operational form of therapy is now identified almost exclusively with the free association technique.

Freud's conception of dream analysis as "the royal road" to unlocking the secrets of the unconscious has been described in a preceding section. His use of hypnosis and how the free association technique evolved from it are discussed later. The remainder of this section focuses on the free association technique, as the dominant component of a standard psychoanalytic therapy session.

THE FREE ASSOCIATION TECHNIQUE

INITIAL CHARACTERIZATION. At an informal descriptive level, free association involves a patient lying on a couch in a relaxed manner and talking about anything that comes to mind while the analyst listens intently, takes notes, and talks back when appropriate.

The process of free association has become a stereotype in the con-sciousness of the general public and is as closely identified with Freud as the conditioned salivation of a dog is with Pavlov. (The process of free association seems to be facilitated if the analyst sports a goatee.) The general public views psychoanalysis as some kind of mysterious process, and the professional analyst does not actively discourage this conception. The analyst is the dominant figure in the session and is the source of all suggestions, insights, interpretations, and the like. It generally is assumed that the analyst cannot legitimately conduct psychoanalytic therapy without personally undergoing a prior anal-ysis.

At a technical level, there is nothing mysterious about free as-sociation. It consists of two critical psychological components: (1) verbal behavior, or self-report, on the part of both the patient and the analyst, and (2) a dynamic social interaction process. Free asso-ciation involves introspection (primarily on the part of the patient), as it occurs in a social situation. Psychoanalysts do not emphasize these two aspects of free association, probably because functionally it merely is an extension of a typical doctor–patient conversation that occurs during a routine office call. The significance of the introspective aspect of free association is highlighted once it is remembered that structuralist methodology consists of one-way introspection in a highly refined stimulus situation. The significance of the social aspect of free association is highlighted if it is realized that the content of a patient's self-report is not merely a matter of his/her clearing the mind, but also is a function of the presence of the analyst.

EVALUATION. The free association technique is subject to a number of criticisms, relative to either its internal or external validity. Internal validity involves whether or not free association functions as a legitimate source of psychological data or subsumes legitimate psy-chological processes. External validity relates to whether or not free association generates empirically meaningful data, subject to check according to one or more external criteria or representative of the true state of affairs (psychological reality).

Four specific criticisms of free association, as a methodological device, are considered here. Although they are not necessarily mu-tually exclusive, the initial two criticisms primarily pertain to external validity, and the other two primarily concern internal validity.

1. The content of Freud's system of psychology is genetic, de-velopmental, or historical in nature: It resolves current behavior/psychological phenomena in terms of past psychological ex-

perience or phenomena. The free association technique does *not* entail genetic, developmental, or historical methodology: It only generates contemporary data, from which attempts are made to construct the nature of the past events. Induction of the nature of the past from present data is a very risky business. Freud did not bother to engage in methodologically sound longitudinal studies that sampled from different time periods of an organism's life.

2. Use of the free association technique is associated with the so-called single-case study method: A voluminous amount of data is generated in the context of only one organism, or one organism exhausts the domain of study. The single-case study method is indigenous to any kind of clinical psychology or psychology with a treatment focus. Conclusions derived from a case study are not amenable to experimental evaluation by any external criterion. Freud could assess only the internal consistency of the conclusions that were based on his free association data. A conclusion derived from one specific aspect of the data could be cross-checked only with other aspects of the same data set.

3. The third criticism of free association relates to its existential status as a kind of introspection. The content of introspective verbal report is subjective and beyond reliability and/or validity assessment, a point originally made in Chapter 2 in the context of evaluating structuralist methodology. Freud's free association technique involves even less control over the milieu in which the introspection is conducted than the structuralist setup did. Freudian introspection exclusively is introspection by retrospection, which even the typical structuralist actively avoided if at all possible. Like the structuralist, Freud never applied the free association technique to children, not so much because a child is preverbal, but rather because the child has no past to which the content of free association can be related.

Freud did get burned by his rather naive acceptance of introspective data. The most famous instance of this is his so-called seduction error. His female patients reported all sorts of infantile sexual experiences, and Freud made these a critical element of his psychodynamics. It was years before Freud realized that most, if not all, of these sexual experiences merely were fantasies and wishful thinking on the part of the patients. Instead of radically changing his theory, Freud merely postulated that a wishful sexual fantasy is equivalent to an actual sexual seduction in the mind or psychological world of the patient.

4. Although the free association technique encompasses a social situation, the analyst is the sole agent of interpretation, insight, and inference. Because the analyst is subject to selective perception as

well as judgment, selective prompting of the patient's responses, and so on, the probability is very high in free association that at least part of the symptomology of the patient is an explicit invention of the analyst.

A COMMENT ON POST-FREUDIAN METHODOLOGY

Psychoanalysts who carried on in the Freudian tradition after the founder's death (neo-Freudians) and some experimental psychologists expanded the domain of acceptable psychoanalytic methodology by also focusing on normal behavior outside of the confines of the prototypical analytic session:

1. Anthropological investigations were made of the symbols, rituals, and child-rearing practices of primitive societies.
2. Laboratory experimentation was conducted, primarily animal studies of regression and fixation.
3. Tests, especially those of the projective personality variety, were used to externalize the content of the psychodynamics of the normal human adult.

The Basic Characteristics of Psychoanalysis as a Therapeutic Technique

Psychoanalysis is only one form of psychotherapy; however, it is the original, germinal form (in the context of the psychogenic approach to abnormality) from which myriad other varieties of psychotherapy derived. The following discussion is oriented toward those features of psychoanalysis that make it a distinctive form of therapy, and six basic characteristics of psychoanalysis are presented.

1. Psychoanalysis is both intensive and extensive. In the ideal case, the patient undergoes daily one-hour sessions five times a week for a period of years.
2. The purpose of psychoanalysis is to externalize the long repressed contents of the unconscious, which serve as the source of the patient's current symptoms or psychological problems. Much of this externalization process involves the recall and reliving of childhood memories and experiences. Of the many forms of psychotherapy, psychoanalysis is the one that puts the highest premium on a childhood etiology of disturbances occurring in adulthood. The specific techniques available to the analyst for facilitating the externalization

process already have been analyzed; namely, free association and dream analysis.

3. The therapist–patient relationship in psychoanalysis is an authoritarian one: The analyst is the dominant figure, possessing all interpretive power and serving as the exclusive object of emotional catharsis or agent of emotional change. The dynamics of this is described in item 4.

4. The critical psychological components/stages of psychoanalysis consist of resistance, transference, and interpretation. (The beginning phase and terminal phase of psychoanalysis also can be viewed as psychological stages, but are not emphasized here.) Resistance is demonstrated when the free association process begins to break down because the patient is close to externalizing the critical unconscious events. Transference occurs when the patient projects either positive or negative feelings/attitudes onto the analyst—the patient relives his/her past disturbing experiences with the analyst serving as the surrogate object or cause of these experiences. Transference probably is the most distinguishing characteristic of psychoanalytic therapy. Freud warns that the analyst must prevent a countertransference from occurring. Interpretation subsumes the analyst's explication of the patient's symptoms and their relationship to the causative factors and experiences revealed by the externalization process.

5. The boundary conditions for a successful psychoanalysis are quite explicit. Psychoanalysis is most appropriate for hysterical, anxiety-ridden, or obsessive-compulsive neurotics who are intelligent, educated, cooperative, and 20 to 40 years old.

6. Psychoanalysis can be conducted only by a sufficiently trained therapist. Freud urged that the professional analyst should undergo an analysis and two years of supervised internship before engaging in psychoanalytic practice. Although Freud considered psychoanalysis to be a profession independent of medicine, virtually all practicing psychoanalysts in America are psychiatrists or physicians, and a psychoanalyst without medical training usually is called a lay analyst.

Origin; Specific Historical Antecedents

Psychoanalysis can be construed as a logical or conceptual extension of nineteenth century French psychopathology, which primarily was concerned with the treatment of hysteria by hypnosis. Interest in neither hysteria nor hypnosis alone is sufficient to account for the origin of psychoanalysis. It is the fusion of interest in these two psychological entities, as represented in French psychopathology, that is uniquely responsible for the beginning of psychoanalysis.

Many detractors of Freud argue that he was not an original thinker. Numerous elements of psychoanalysis possess historical precursors. While the latter statement is true, it is unfair to regard Freud as any less an original thinker than Darwin or Watson, who also fused extant historical and conceptual trends into new intellectual entities.

This section analyzes the importance of hysteria and hypnosis for the founding of psychoanalysis, traces the origin of psychoanalysis in French psychopathology, and briefly describes some of the specific historical precursors of Freudian thought.

Hysteria and Hypnosis as Psychological Phenomena

HYSTERIA

Among the symptoms of hysteria are limb paralysis, body anesthesia, blindness, and deafness, and a given hysteric patient displays one or more of these in some combination. The unique feature of a hysterical symptom is that it possesses no traceable physiological cause. The content of a given paralysis or anesthesia does not correspond to the underlying musculature or pattern of neuronal innervation of the organism: They are anatomically aberrant. Also, specialized tests demonstrate that the blindness or deafness is not due to a sensory defect. Historically it was believed that hysteria was characteristic only of adult females, and not of adult males. The traditional somatogenic approaches to the treatment of hysteria included hydrotherapy, in which the organism is given some kind of bath, and electrotherapy, in which a mild electric current is passed through the organism's skin. (Electrotherapy is not the same thing as electroshock therapy.)

HYPNOSIS

Hypnosis is a psychological technique whereby an organism is put into some kind of trance or hypersuggestive state, through either the verbal instructions or the physical actions of a so-called hypnotist. An organism in such a trance or state can be induced either to exhibit or to refrain from certain behaviors that are beyond the immediate control of the organism prior to the hypnotic induction instructions or procedure. At a conceptual level, hypnosis amounts to a social influence process, but its entrance into and relevance for psychology derive from its use by amateur healers and charlatans as a miracle cure. Hypnotism derived from mesmerism, a social influence technique used by Franz Mesmer (1734–1815) in Vienna and Paris. The content of Mesmer's social influence process was mineral or animal magnetism. Mesmer believed that physical diseases were the result of certain fluids in the body, which could be controlled, originally by magnets (mineral magnetism), and later by the physical intercession of Mesmer himself (animal magnetism). Mesmerism involved hypnotic suggestion, but it took later medical practitioners, such as James Braid (1795–1860), to divorce it from any presumed magnetism base and make hypnotic suggestibility an internally sourced property of the reacting organism.

THE FUSION OF HYSTERIA AND HYPNOSIS

Hysteria and hypnosis individually constituted anomalous psychological phenomena. Hysteria was not resolvable in the context of the somatogenic approach to abnormality; hypnosis was such a vacuous and refractory psychological entity that it was readily exploitable by charlatans and was only grudgingly accepted by the medical establishment. French psychopathology provided the key for the ultimate resolution of these phenomena. It was discovered that hysterical symptoms could be induced by hypnotic instructions and that hypnotic suggestions could be used to remove the symptoms of a hysterical patient. The amenability of hysteria to hypnotic suggestion provided hysteria with a possible psychological base, and the use of hypnosis as a possible therapeutic technique provided hypnosis with some legitimacy.

French Psychopathology

There actually were two different centers or schools of French psychopathology: Jean Charcot (1825–1893) and Pierre Janet (1859–1947) at the Salpêtrière Hospital in Paris, and August Liébeault (1823–1904) and Hippolyte Bernheim (1837–1919) at an institute/clinic in Nancy. Each school had a different conception of hysteria and hypnosis.

THE SALPÊTRIÈRE SCHOOL

Charcot was a neurologist who initially specialized in treating such neuronal disorders as epilepsy, multiple sclerosis, and infantile paralysis. He later focused on hysteria and established its basic symptomology; however, he always remained in the somatogenic tradition. Charcot did demonstrate that hysterical symptoms were producible and removable through hypnosis, but he assumed that susceptibility to hypnosis was just another symptom of hysteria and so only hysterics could be hypnotized. Thus he viewed hypnosis as pathological. He regarded both hysterical symptoms and susceptibility to hypnosis as the result of neural degeneration.

Janet, a neurologist and a pupil of Charcot, devised the first true psychogenic interpretation of hysteria, although he never formally renounced the somatogenic approach. He established hysteria as the prototypical kind of neurosis, involving a dissociation of unpleasant childhood memories from normal consciousness. The explicit function of hypnotic treatment was the inducement of a catharsis that released the repressed memories causing the hysteria.

THE NANCY SCHOOL

Liébeault and Bernheim were not neurologists, but practicing physicians. They did not take a pathological approach to hypnosis, for instance, they did not regard hypnotic suggestibility as a symptom of hysteria. The Nancy School construed the hypnotic state to be a mere extension of the normal waking or sleeping state. Liébeault and Bernheim used hypnosis to treat other phenomena in addition to hysteria, such as bed wetting, gastric disorders, and writer's cramp.

THE INFLUENCE OF THE FRENCH SCHOOLS ON FREUD

Freud was a trained physician, who initially specialized in clinical neurology. He dealt with overt behavioral disorders that were relatable to underlying neurological deficits and degeneration. For financial reasons, Freud had to expand the domain of his medical practice and take on hysteric patients whose maladies were only superficially neurological in origin.

Freud studied hypnosis and hysteria under Charcot for six months in 1885 and 1886. He retained an incidental remark that Charcot had made about hysteria, that it always had a sexual origin. Freud also studied under, or at least consulted with, Bernheim for a few weeks in 1889. He particularly was impressed by Bernheim's use of posthypnotic suggestion, that is, the hypnotized person was able to recall, at the command of the hypnotist, the content of the hypnotic trance after it was over. Freud knew of Janet's conception of and treatment of hysteria, but he always believed that Janet did not go far enough toward breaking away from the somatogenic tradition.

Breuer, Freud's initial professional associate, independently discovered and used Janet's hypnosis-induced catharsis technique—in the context of Fräulein Anna O. Breuer treated the hysterical symptoms of Anna O. for two years (1880–1882), until she began to exhibit a positive transference to him, whereupon he abruptly terminated the treatment.

Freud used both hypnotic suggestion and the hypnotic-induced catharsis technique to treat his own hysterical patients. He called the catharsis experience an abreaction, and he evolved a more extensive psychogenic interpretation of the etiology of hysteria than Janet's. Freud's conception of hysteria constituted the initial, germinal form of his psychoanalytic psychodynamics. Recall that Freud and Breuer jointly published *Studien über Hysterie* about their work with hysteric patients in 1895.

THE EVOLUTION OF FREE ASSOCIATION FROM HYPNOSIS

Although the French pathologists, and both Breuer and Freud, used hypnosis in the treatment of hysteria, it should not be inferred that hypnosis constituted a monolithic technique. Charcot, Liébeault, and Bernheim merely used hypnotic suggestion. Janet and Breuer used hypnosis to facilitate the patient's recall and verbal expression of repressed material (the so-called talking cure) for the inducement of a catharsis reaction.

Freud initially used hydrotherapy and electrotherapy; but when he realized that the minimal beneficial effects of these treatments were the result of suggestion, he switched to the active use of hypnotic suggestion. Hypnotic commands did not lead to the permanent disappearance of symptoms, so Freud adopted Janet and Breuer's catharsis (talking cure) technique. He eventually became dissatisfied with this approach because not all patients could be put into a deep enough hypnotic trance. Finally Freud used a directed suggestion *or* directed association technique, whereby he placed his hand on the patient's forehead and requested the patient to recall events associated with or similar to the hysterical symptoms. Eventually he discontinued the use of the hand-pressing operation and merely requested the subject to talk about the symptoms. Later Freud did not even require that the initial associations be made about the symptoms themselves: This was his so-called free association technique.

Some Historical Precursors of Freudian Thought

It is impossible to trace all of the historical antecedents of Freudian thought in depth, for two basic reasons: (1) the domain of his thought is wide-ranging and all-pervasive, and (2) the content of his thought is a unique combination of polar opposites—mechanism versus dynamicism, pleasure versus pain, life instinct versus death instinct, conscious versus unconscious, physical (biological) energy systems versus mentalistic psychodynamics. The historical trends and work contributing to eight aspects of Freud's thought are considered briefly below.

1. Freud's focus on sex is not unique in the psychological literature. Krafft-Ebing, a German neurologist, dealt with sexual abnormality and pathology in his *Psychopathia Sexualis*, published in 1893. Havelock Ellis, an English doctor and editor, published seven volumes of *The Psychology of Sex* between 1897 and 1928. Ellis studied dreams and knew of the sexual content of dreams. He also was the founder of the sexual/marriage counseling movement. Janet had realized the sexual nature of many repressed memories of childhood, and, in general, the French psychopathologists knew of the relationship between sex and hysteria.

2. The key Freudian psychoanalytic concepts of repression and resistance were anticipated by Schopenhauer, a nineteenth century German philosopher.

3. Freud's psychic determinism is a direct translation of the long intellectual tradition of mechanism.

4. Freud's dynamicism derives from many sources: Leibnitz's monadology, Fechner's belief in mental energy, Brentano's focus on mental activity, Goethe's romantic view of science, and the age-old doctrine of hedonism, to name a few.

5. Freud's focus on the irrational or animal nature of man and the death instinct was anticipated by Schopenhauer and another famous nineteenth century German philosopher, Nietzsche.

6. The pleasure and pain principles are merely semantic variations of hedonism.

7. Freud's overall biological conception of man is distinctly Darwinian in nature and tone.

8. Freud's stress on the unconscious is merely one aspect of the extensive evolution of that concept. Leibnitz had postulated the existence of the unconscious and of different degrees of consciousness in the context of his monadology. Herbart had conceived of the notion of a threshold or limen of consciousness, and also developed a "mathematics" of the ideas existing in the unconscious. Fechner used the concept of the unconscious in his mystical attempt to relate mind and body. The unconscious was a critical component of Schopenhauer's and Nietzsche's transcendental philosophy. Interest in the unconscious was even a cultural phenomenon during Freud's lifetime: Von Hartmann published nine editions of his *The Philosophy of the Unconscious* between 1868 and 1882.

Recall that Freud postulated the existence of a dynamic unconscious, not a descriptive unconscious. Leibnitz and Fechner regarded the unconscious merely as a descriptive concept: An unconscious idea is one of which the organism is not currently aware. Unconsciousness is just the lack of consciousness, and an unconscious idea only has physiological trace or structural reality. Freud, along with Herbart and von Hartmann, reified the notion of the unconscious. It was an actual psychological state or location; the unconscious was a dynamic system to which ideas were actively assigned by the mechanism of repression. In essence, the descriptive unconscious is a semantic notion, while the Freudian dynamic unconscious is an actual system of repressed, seething ideas.

Chief Historical Figure: Sigmund Freud (1856–1939)

Freud was born in Freiberg, Moravia (now Pribor, Czechoslovakia), in 1856. His father was an independent businessman, variously described as a cloth maker or wool merchant, who was able to move the family to Vienna in 1860, after a sojourn in Leipzig. Freud grew up in a large household: He was the eldest of eight children, and two half-brothers his mother's age and an older nephew also lived with the family. Freud was an excellent student and intellectually curious as a boy; and his parents accorded him special treatment by assigning him a separate room as a study, lit by oil lamps instead of candles.

Freud graduated from the gymnasium (German high school) with distinction in 1873 and began his studies at the University of Vienna the same year. He spent the next eight years there and graduated with a medical degree in 1881. This eight-year period represents the critical formative years of Freud's life. The fact that he earned only a medical degree is not indicative of the depth and breadth of his education. He studied philosophy under Brentano, the act psychologist (see Chapter 8). He spent six years studying under and working for Brücke at the Vienna Physiological Institute: Brücke was one of the original signers of the mechanist manifesto, along with Helmholtz, du Bois-Reymond, and Ludwig. Freud received a thorough grounding in science, in general, and in physiology, anatomy, and neurology, in particular.

Freud would have pursued an academic career and engaged in physiological research, but his financial circumstances and Jewish background did not make this a viable option. Since the late 1870s, Freud had been befriended by Josef Breuer, and with his financial aid and psychological support, set up a private practice as a clinical neurologist (neuropathologist) in 1882. Freud also studied under Meynert, a renowned brain anatomist and expert on brain damage. Specializing in cases of organic brain damage was not sufficiently financially rewarding, and Freud had to take on hysteric patients. By the mid-1880s, Freud had given up any pretense of being an anatomist or neuropathologist and was committed to being a professional therapist, and the long road to the development of psychoanalysis had begun.

Freud studied under Charcot for six months in 1885 and 1886 and under Bernheim for a few weeks in 1889. He developed a distinct psychogenic approach to the etiology and treatment of hysteria and persuaded Breuer to publish *Studien über Hysterie* about their work on hysteria in 1895. Recall that this event usually is treated as the explicit beginning of psychoanalysis as a system of psychology.

Freud fell in love with Martha Bernays in 1882, but was not in a financial position to marry her until 1886. They had six children, and Freud was generally regarded as a good family man. One of his daughters, Anna Freud, helped establish psychoanalysis in England and became famous as a child psychoanalyst.

By the mid-1890s, Freud was convinced of the infantile sexuality etiology of hysteria and other neurotic disorders and had begun his work on dream analysis and postulated the wish fulfillment purpose of dreams. After his father's death, in 1897, Freud instituted a formal two-year program of self-analysis, and periodically reanalyzed himself throughout the rest of his life. Freud had become estranged from Breuer by 1898, because of his emphasis on sex. This was to be the first of many such estrangements.

The first decade of the twentieth century was a professionally profitable one for Freud. In 1900, he published *The Interpretation of Dreams*, by his own account the most satisfying of his books, and also his most original contribution to psychology. *The Psychopathology of Everyday Life* appeared in 1904, and *Three Essays on the Theory of Sexuality* in 1905. The *Journal of Abnormal Psychology* published a number of articles on psychoanalysis in 1906. The Vienna Psychoanalytical Society evolved from the Wednesday night discussion groups and was founded by 1907. In 1908, a Congress of Psychoanalysis was held at Salzburg, attended by Freud, Jung, Adler, Stekel, Abraham, and others. The International Psychoanalytic Association followed in 1910, with Jung as its first president. This fact was important to Freud because Jung was a gentile and an already established psychiatrist:

Jung's administrative command represented a form of external recognition for Freud. The decade ended with Freud's appearance and
honorary doctorate at Clark University's twentieth anniversary celebration. Jung accompanied Freud to America; they both lectured and
had the opportunity to meet James, Cattell, Titchener, and Hall.
Freud's lectures were published in the *American Journal of Psychology*
in 1910. Freud did not particularly care for America and its more
casual life-style and never returned to the United States.

The next decade (1911–1918) was rough on Freud, both financially
(because of World War I) and professionally. This was the period of
the great defections from the orthodox psychoanalytic movement:
Bleuler, Adler, Jung, Ferenczi. (Rank left in 1926.) Jung's defection
was particularly troubling to Freud because of the status and prestige
he brought to the psychoanalytic movement. Freud did publish *The
Introductory Lectures on Psychoanalysis* during this period (1917).

The final 20 years of Freud's life were marked by international
recognition and the ultimate acceptance of his system by the medical
establishment. In the 1920s, he attracted American and English students, and his works began to appear in English translations, eventually amounting to some 24 volumes. Freud was an excellent writer,
with a breezy and engaging style. He also engaged in voluminous
correspondence, which served as an informal means of social control
over the movement. Freud published *Beyond the Pleasure Principle* in
1920 and *The Ego and the Id* in 1923. These works represent the culmination of his efforts with respect to the hard core of psychoanalytic
theory. In *The Future of an Illusion* (1927) and *Civilization and Its Discontents* (1930), Freud extended psychoanalysis to the social and cultural arena.

As a result of smoking about 20 cigars a day, Freud contracted
cancer of the mouth in 1923, and underwent the first of 33 operations.
He was in pain for the rest of his life. With the rise of National
Socialism in Germany in 1933, Freud's books were banned and burned
in Germany: Freud, along with Einstein, was a purveyor of Jewish
science. When the Nazis took over Austria in 1938, Freud was allowed
to go to London, England, at the intercession of William Bullitt, the
American ambassador to France, after formally certifying just treatment on the part of the Gestapo. The Third Reich did gain possession
of his remaining book stock and ultimately murdered four of his
sisters, a fact that was unknown to Freud at his death. Freud was
welcomed as a hero in London and was made a member of the Royal
Society. Cancer finally overwhelmed Freud, and he died in a mor-
phine-induced coma in 1939.

Characteristic Experimentation; Primary Research Areas

This is a null analytical dimension in the context of Freudian psychology for two basic reasons: (1) The level at which or context in which most of Freud's basic propositions are stated precludes their direct empirical test. (2) Freud regarded experimental evaluation of his propositions, in the traditional sense of the term, to be irrelevant for their ultimate acceptance and validity.

Freud's insistence on the metaphysical or evaluational independence of the psychoanalytic approach successfully isolated his system from the mainstream of academic/experimental psychology. His system is absolutely impervious to any evolutionary or discontinuous changes in science. Psychoanalysis is not subject to a Kuhnian type of analysis (see Chapter 1): Any disagreement with Freud resulted in eventual banishment from the orthodox psychoanalytical movement; that is, a paradigm clash between orthodox Freudian psychoanalysis and Adlerian individual psychology or Jungian analytical psychology does not result in a refocused monolithic depth psychology, but only in an increasingly more fragmented depth psychology, the individual components of which end up appealing to an increasingly smaller number of adherents.

Although Freudian psychology is isolated from academic/experimental psychology, academic/experimental psychology is not isolated from psychoanalysis. The content of Freudian psychology is so far-reaching and pervasive that (1) it does have something to say at a theoretical level about virtually all of the basic psychological processes studied by experimental psychology, and (2) it does contain a sufficient number of low-level constructs subject to operational definition and empirical test. Very brief characterizations of these two aspects of Freud's influence on experimental psychology will be presented.

The Theoretical Influence

By focusing on the internal determinants of overt behavior, Freudian psychology complemented the external, environmentalistic orientation of functionalism and behaviorism. Freud's internal determinants were motivational, (psycho)dynamic, irrational—as opposed to cognitive or rational—in nature; and his approach can be related meaningfully to learning, memory, perception, motivation, thinking, social processes, and personality/developmental psychology. Freudian psychology is irrelevant for such experimental areas as sensation, physiological psychology, and comparative psychology.

1. Classic learning theory (i.e., Hullian macrolearning theory; see Chapter 5) stressed association formation as it occurs under the influence of the theoretical law of effect (biological drive reduction). The theoretical law of effect is simply a more specific version of the principle of hedonism or the pleasure–pain principle. While Freud did not focus on association formation *per se*, he was the first psychological theorist to provide association elicitation with a motivational base.

2. Freud made the memorial construction process (i.e., recall from some memory store) in part a motivational or emotionally laden event. Motivated forgetting, repression of unpleasant memories, selective recall, and the like are now stock concepts in the experimental study of memory phenomena.

3. Freud also made the perceptual construction process (i.e., pattern recognition, object identification, etc.) in part a motivational or emotionally laden event. Experimental psychologists now realize that we see what we want to see. The influence of Freudian psychology is most directly observed in perceptual defense research, in which some socially unacceptable or tabooed event either is not perceived at all or is perceived much more slowly in comparison with an emotionally neutral control stimulus.

4. The experimental psychology of motivation is merely a logical/conceptual extension of Freudian psychology. Granted that the life instinct and death instinct are concepts without any empirical meaning, Freud's other motivational constructs, such as libido (interpreted as the sex drive), aggression, conflict, guilt, anxiety, the defense mechanisms, and the ego (interpreted as the self), constitute critical components of the psychology of motivation.

5. The direct influence of Freudian psychology on thinking or problem-solving research is minimal, in comparison with the other areas. Freud made experimental psychologists aware of pathological and aberrant thought processes and, by and large, served a heuristic function by calling attention to the importance of nonlogical mental operations—the primary process.

6. Contemporary social psychology focuses on aggression, social norms or moral standards (as reflected by the superego), influence processes or patterns (i.e., as they occur in the Oedipal situation), leadership (i.e., authoritarian father figures), and the like, all of which are critical elements of Freudian psychodynamics.

7. Personality assessment and development have been pro-

foundly influenced by psychoanalysis. Projective personality tests, such as the Rorschach inkblot test and the Thematic Apperception Test (TAT), are direct consequences of Freudian theory. Freud's psychosexual stages of development serve as the model of virtually all contemporary theories of development: The psychological problems and interactions faced by the child at each of these stages, as originally detailed by Freud, must be resolved or absorbed by any serious developmental theorist. For instance, Neal Miller's S–R behavioristic theory transforms the oral stage into a critical feeding situation, the anal stage into the problem of toilet training, and so on.

Operational Specification and Experimental Evaluation

During a period extending from the late 1930s to the early 1950s, active attempts were made to operationally define some of Freud's lower level constructs and to evaluate them in an experimental context. Freud's concepts of objective anxiety and aggression and some of his (ego) defense mechanisms, such as fixation, regression, and displacement, were operationally definable in the context of the O. Hobart Mowrer and Neal Miller versions of neo-Hullian learning theory; and numerous animal experiments were performed to test their general validity. In general, the results of these research efforts were positive. Much research also was conducted on experimental analogues of repression with human subjects using verbal materials and/or verbal learning.

Freud's emphasis on sex, aggression, conflict, and dreams led to the empirical investigation of these phenomena, although not necessarily in a Freudian context or from a Freudian orientation, that is, the results of these investigations have no direct bearing on Freudian psychology. The neo-Freudians now actively conduct genetic/developmental observational research on infants and children, instead of relying on the verbal report of adult respondents exclusively.

Historical Legacy; Contemporary Significance

Freud died slightly over 40 years ago, but it still is possible to be a practicing, or professional, orthodox Freudian psychoanalyst. Although Freudian psychology is less monolithic than it was during the heyday of its founder, psychoanalysis still persists as a distinctive and recognizable brand of psychology. The current status of Freud as a founder of a system of psychology is similar to that of Pavlov in Russia in the context of the psychophysiology of higher nervous activity: Contemporary adherents work within the confines of the original system, making minor adjustments without performing radical revision, and continually pay homage to the creator. We shall summarize the historical legacy and contemporary significance of Freud's system of psychology by focusing on the current status of depth psychology, the overall effect of the psychoanalytic approach on psychology, and the social/cultural implications of Freud's thought.

The Current Status of Depth Psychology

If we construe Freud's system as the original depth psychology, it has engendered two kinds of offshoots: (1) depth psychologies developed by analysts who originally were orthodox Freudians, but who eventually felt obliged to leave the Freudian camp; and (2) depth psychologies that amount to mere conceptual extensions of the original Freudian approach.

INDIVIDUAL AND ANALYTIC PSYCHOLOGY

The two primary examples of the first class of depth psychology are Alfred Adler's (1870–1937) individual psychology and Carl Jung's (1875–1961) analytic psychology. Adler left the orthodox camp in 1911, and Jung left by 1914. Although the background conditions responsible for each departure differ, both Adler and Jung fundamentally disagreed with Freud's conception of and emphasis on sex. Adler's and Jung's systems constitute independent depth psychologies, with little overlap, although they both tend to take a more optimistic view of man than Freud did. Adler eventually emigrated to the United States, where his approach has been systematized and conceptually elaborated by the Ansbachers. Jung always remained a permanent resident of his native Switzerland. The depth, originality, and even intensity of Jung's thought are comparable to Freud's, although Jung's influence was eclipsed by that of Freud as long as Freud was alive. Jung's analytic system is an excellent counterexample for those who argue that a non-Freudian depth psychology is inconceivable. Both individual psychology and analytic psychology have reached the point where it is proper to speak of the existence of neo-Adlerians and neo-Jungians.

NEO-FREUDIAN APPROACHES

The second class of depth psychology subsumes the so-called neo-Freudian approaches. The most prominent neo-Freudians include Karen Horney (1885–1952), Harry Stack Sullivan (1892–1949), and Eric Fromm (1900–1980). Other neo-Freudians who have made substantial theoretical or methodological contributions to Freud's original system include Heinz Hartmann, Ernst Kris, David Rapaport, George Klein, Erik Erikson, and Lawrence Kubie. The neo-Freudian movement, as a whole, is characterized by (1) a greater stress on the environmental or social (as opposed to internal or dynamic) determinants of behavior; (2) a greater and more independent role of the ego in the psychodynamics of the organism; (3) some attempt at integration of psychoanalysis with social science in general and psychology in particular; and (4) active investigation of infant and child behavior. To demonstrate the general leavening or assimilative trend of the psychoanalytic movement, it can be pointed out that Sullivan was an American-born psychiatrist whose writings quite frequently resemble those of behaviorists, and that Fromm often is classified as a humanistic psychologist.

TRANSACTIONAL ANALYSIS

Daniel Robinson (1979) recently argued that the different varieties of depth psychology mentioned in this section are not evolutionary products of one another or conceptual advances, but merely constitute other attempts at a depth psychology. Recall from the introduction that, unlike behaviorism or any other scientifically oriented system, a given depth psychology is a personalistic system, irrationally adhered to or rejected (by faith, not reason).

A contemporary example of Robinson's basic thesis is Eric Berne's (born Bernstein) (1910–1970) transactional analysis. Berne's system merely is another attempt at a depth psychology and not a conceptual advance. Berne was a Jew, trained in orthodox Freudian psychoanalysis, who possessed the burning desire to develop a new depth system. He succeeded beyond his wildest dreams by creating the ultimate in "pop" psychology: a simplistic and indiscriminate extension of strict, traditional Freudian psychoanalysis, with overtones of Skinnerian behavior modification and Rogerian group therapy. Transactional analysis is a combination of two things: (1) group therapy (in the Rogerian sense) in which the nature of the interaction (i.e., transactions) are analyzed and classified according to a (2) dynamic structure (basically psychoanalytic in nature) stated in a populist terminology that presumably anyone can understand. The psychoanalytical elements or depth psychology aspects of transactional analysis are easily identifiable: (1) Berne's three ego states of child, parent, and adult correspond directly to Freud's concepts of id, superego, and ego; and (2) Berne's three tendencies of Sleepy, Spunky, and Spooky correspond directly to Freud's notions of death instinct, life instinct, and the reality principle.

The Overall Effect of the Psychoanalytic Approach on Psychology

While psychoanalysis is immune from psychology, experimental and applied psychology are not immune from psychoanalysis. This is a convenient spot to summarize briefly some of Freud's specific content contributions to the practice and conceptual development of psychology. A representative sampling of Freud's content contributions would have to include the following items:

1. Focus on infancy and childhood.
2. Importance of idiographic personality factors.
3. Existence of unconscious motivation and/or irrational determinants of behavior.
4. Notion of (ego) defense mechanisms.
5. Viability of projective personality tests.
6. Spawning of (psycho)therapy in the contemporary sense of the term.
7. Establishment of abnormal psychology as a legitimate subarea of psychology, that is, formal recognition of the psychogenic approach to the etiology of abnormal phenomena.

The Social/Cultural Implications of Freud's Thought

Toward the end of his life, Freud sought to specify the social/cultural implications of his system, much in the manner that Skinner did. He published *The Future of an Illusion* in 1927 and *Civilization and Its Discontents* in 1930. What Freud meant by an illusion, of course, was religion; and civilization embodied all the constraints that constitute the essential content of the superego. Because Freud concentrated on the internal determinants of behavior, the implications of his system relate more to the nature and existential status of man than to the nature and primacy of the external environment, as in the case of Skinner.

A strict interpretation of Freud's system leads to a pessimistic view of the future of humankind, on two accounts. First, the existence of the death instinct in the individual organism can lead to the eventual expression of externally directed aggression or internally directed self-destruction: Freud was affected deeply by the events precipitated by World War I, and he did not postulate Thanatos until approximately 1920. Second, the other fundamental instinctive force, physicalized in terms of an unabashed, striving libido, made the human being an animalistic creature requiring instant and indiscriminate gratification. Civilization could not exist unless these animalistic impulses were checked by an equally unabashed and irrational superego that had inculcated the demands and strictures of organized society. The clash of the id impulses and the prohibitions of the superego only could lead to fundamental unhappiness, neurotic conflict, guilt feelings, and so on.

Freud's system also makes a mockery of the so-called spiritual nature of man. Since religion is an illusion, God is not an independent being, that is, a separate and distinct metaphysical entity, serving as the source of idealistic external standards and urging the human race on to their attainment. God merely is an extension of the self. God merely is a powerful father figure, explicitly created to satisfy man's need for protection against feelings of infantile helplessness.

Skinner sometimes is criticized for making creativity and innovation an automatic, mechanical product of (1) extreme forms of response variability (2) that happen to be reinforced: A novel response simply is an extreme form of an old one that the environment happens to reinforce selectively. Freud has received analogous criticism for his account of creativity and innovation. These result from sublimation, the displacement of libidinal energy into culturally relevant artistic, scientific, or philosophical pursuits. No ultracreative person likes to be told that his/her accomplishments are the result of sexual frustration.

As in the case of Skinner's radical behaviorism, psychoanalysis is sometimes mistakenly appealed to as a justification for an authoritarian, totalitarian form of government or society: (1) A dictator would function as an extended father figure, much like God; or (2) a dictatorial form of government is necessary to keep the primitive life and death instincts under control. Psychoanalysis does not indigenously justify any particular form of government. As is true of Skinner's system, Freud's psychodynamics merely specifies the conditions that must be taken into account if a just or benign society is to be created for the benefit of all. For Freud, these factors were of internal, as opposed to external, origin.

Bibliography

Breuer, J., and Freud, S. *Studien über Hysterie (Studies in Hysteria)*. Leipzig: Deuticke, 1895. Reprinted in J. Strachey (Ed.), *The Standard Edition of the Complete Psychological Works of Sigmund Freud*, vol. 2. London: Hogarth, 1955.

Ellis, H. *Studies in the Psychology of Sex*. New York: Random House, 1936.

Freud, S. *The Interpretation of Dreams*. Leipzig and Vienna: Deuticke, 1900. Reprinted in J. Strachey (Ed.), *The Standard Edition of the Complete Psychological Works of Sigmund Freud*, vols. 4 and 5. London: Hogarth, 1953.

Freud, S. The psychopathology of everyday life. *Monatsschrift für Psychiatrie und Neurologie*, 1901, 10, 1–32; 95–143. Reprinted in J. Strachey (Ed.), *The Standard Edition of the Complete Psychological Works of Sigmund Freud*, vol. 6. London: Hogarth, 1960.

Freud, S. *Three Essays on the Theory of Sexuality*. Leipzig: Deuticke, 1905. Reprinted in J. Strachey (Ed.), *The Standard Edition of the Complete Psychological Works of Sigmund Freud*, vol. 7. London: Hogarth, 1953.

Freud, S. The Clark University Lectures. *American Journal of Psychology*, 1910, 21, 181–218.

Freud, S. *Introductory Lectures on Psychoanalysis*, 1916–1917. Reprinted in J. Strachey (Ed.), *The Standard Edition of the Complete Psychological Works of Sigmund Freud*, vols. 15 and 16. London: Hogarth, 1963.

Freud, S. *Beyond the Pleasure Principle*. Leipzig: Internationaler Psychoanalytischer Verlag, 1920. Reprinted in J. Strachey (Ed.), *The Standard Edition of the Complete Psychological Works of Sigmund Freud*, vol. 18. London: Hogarth, 1955.

Freud, S. *The Ego and the Id*. Leipzig, Vienna, and Zurich: Internationaler Psychoanalytischer Verlag, 1923. Reprinted in J. Strachey (Ed.), *The Standard Edition of the Complete Psychological Works of Sigmund Freud*, vol. 19. London: Hogarth, 1961.

Freud, S. *The Future of an Illusion*. Leipzig, Vienna, and Zurich: Internationaler Psychoanalytischer Verlag, 1927. Reprinted in J. Strachey (Ed.), *The Standard Edition of the Complete Psychological Works of Sigmund Freud*, vol. 21. London: Hogarth, 1961.

Freud, S. *Civilization and Its Discontents*. Vienna: Internationaler Psychoanalytischer Verlag, 1930. Reprinted in J. Strachey (Ed.), *The Standard Edition of the Complete Psychological Works of Sigmund Freud*, vol. 21. London: Hogarth, 1961.

Hartmann, E. von. *The Philosophy of the Unconscious*. New York: Macmillan, 1884.

Krafft-Ebing, R.V. *Psychopathia Sexualis*, 1893. New York: Pioneer Publications, 1950.

Robinson, D.N. *Systems of Modern Psychology: A Critical Sketch*. New York: Columbia University Press, 1979.

10

Humanism, Phenomenology, Existentialism

[See page 274 for Figure 10-1
The Nature and Extent of the Overlap
Between Humanism and Traditional Experimental Psychology.]

Introduction

The ultimate irresolvability of psychology's basic subject matter is highlighted by the relatively recent (post-1960) appearance of a new movement in psychology: humanism, phenomenology, or existentialism. This new movement is multifaceted in nature: It consists of heterogeneous, diverse, even conflicting components. It is both a reaction to and an extension of behaviorism and depth psychology or psychoanalysis. It is both an abstract entity and a practical guide for living. Membership in the movement is by self-proclamation, not by acceptance of a set of monolithic principles and beliefs.

The most general and neutral term for this new movement is humanistic psychology. In this context, phenomenological psychology and existential psychology can be viewed either as alternative *labels* for humanistic psychology or as specific *subkinds* of humanistic psychology. We shall use the latter interpretation in this chapter and treat phenomenology and existentialism as historical antecedents of the more recent strictly American versions of humanism professed by such psychologists as Abraham Maslow and Carl Rogers.

233

Although Maslow and Rogers were the first self-conscious humanists, they were not the first psychologists to have an essentially humanistic orientation. Elements of humanism can be found in the psychoanalytic thought of Fromm, Horney, and even Jung and Adler. European existential psychologists, such as Ludwig Binswanger, Adrian von Kaam, and Medard Boss, and the American existential psychologist, Rollo May, anticipated many of the tenets of humanism. Kurt Goldstein, a Gestalt-oriented holistic psychopathologist (see Chapter 4); Gordon Allport, the American personality theorist; Charlotte Buhler, a Gestalt-oriented developmental psychologist; and the American phenomenological psychologists Donald Snygg and Arthur Combs also functioned as implicit pre-1960 humanists.

Adherents of humanism like to refer to their discipline as the third force in psychology, behaviorism and psychoanalysis being the other two forces. The phrase "third force" connotes nothing more than the fact that humanistic psychology is different from behaviorism and psychoanalysis; the term is self-perpetuating because there is no widespread consensus relative to exactly what humanism is. Humanistic psychologists typically do not claim to be a party to a new formal system as such, replete with a rigid set of assumptions and methodology. Humanism is an attempt to reorient psychology to more person oriented (individual organism) objectives.

For a proponent of humanism, the new movement represents a return to a true concern for consciousness, after 50 years of neglect by behaviorally oriented experimental psychology and by analytically oriented depth psychology. In a sense, humanism adopted the phenomenal orientation of Gestalt psychology, but extended it from the realm of mere perceptual consciousness to cover the organism's entire personality or state of being. Humanism deals with the state of a person's awareness or conscious feelings in an understanding context.

The object of interest of humanistic psychology just as readily could be described in terms of behavior, but not in the behaviorist's sense of the term. Humanism presumes a nonmechanistic view of man, does not accept the principle of determinism, views man as subject and not object, and focuses on the holistic adaptive status of an organism's behavioral actions. Each person, or his/her behavior, is unique and must be resolved in terms of his/her own subjective conscious world view. The humanist is interested in a person's everyday life behavior as it occurs in the natural environment, not in constricted pieces of artificial behavior as they occur in the laboratory: By definition, humanism is both a world view (philosophy of man) as well as an applied psychology (psychotherapeutic approach).

Humanism is permeated (1) by such concepts as external validity, meaning, understanding, subjectivity, relevance, and value, and (2) by such goals or phenomena as authenticity, self-actualization, creativity, development of meaningful human relationships, knowledge of innermost feelings, expanding one's awareness, and love. In a sense, humanism represents (1) a return to a common-sense psychology, in which a person's goals, feelings, desires, and the like are of primary concern; and (2) a revival of interest in such Christian values as love, concern, and goodness. While humanism is not necessarily anti-empirical, it is a protest against the mechanistic, deterministic, reductionistic orientation of Lockian, Newtonian, and Darwinian science adopted by behavioristically oriented experimental psychology. Humanism's common-sense and value orientation does exist in a sophisticated philosophical framework, but it is one that derives from the German idealistic/transcendental tradition (e.g., Kant, Hegel, Fichte, Husserl, Heidegger).

Because humanistic psychology is multifaceted and can be analyzed from many different perspectives, our presentation is constructed around the following five operational assumptions:

1. Humanism is an explicit outgrowth of, or reaction to, both descriptive behaviorism and Freudian psychology.

2. The philosophical and/or historical input into humanistic psychology minimally consists of phenomenology and existentialism.

3. The most representative versions of contemporary humanistic thought are contained in the psychological approaches of Maslow and Rogers; and these two men constitute humanism's chief historical figures.

4. Humanism is more a philosophy of man and human nature (i.e., more a statement of the current condition of man) than it is a formal system of psychology in the usual sense of the term, replete with elaborate theory and detailed mechanisms for resolving the basic psychological processes.

5. Humanism inherently is an applied psychology because it focuses on the condition of man as it is given in the naturally occurring social, cultural, and political environment.

One more preview statement is necessary. The nature of humanism makes it mandatory to consider its origin and specific historical antecedents before discussing its method of study and permissible methodology.

Object of Study; Basic Subject Matter

Initial Description

The basic impetus to humanism was dissatisfaction with behaviorism and psychoanalysis at both a conceptual and a methodological level. At a conceptual level, humanism downgrades the drive reduction (homeostatic) orientation of the behaviorist and the psychoanalyst. It finds fault with the behaviorist's use of the animal or machine as the model of man and with Freud's unconscious, irrational, animalistic determinants of personality. It also discounts the historic orientation of both behaviorism and psychoanalysis, that is, the resolution of current psychological phenomena in terms of past events. At a methodological level, humanism rejects Freud's exclusive investigation of the abnormal personality (i.e., the weak, sick, or crippled) and behaviorism's piecemeal approach to the analysis of isolated behaviors: Man is much more than a concatenation of biological and learned reflexes or reflexive units.

The essential content of humanism derives from its conception of man and its use of the word *human*. For the humanist, human is a substantive, technical term. Humanness identifies the essential state, being, or condition of man; humanness is an absolute property of a certain class of living beings, called man, which distinguishes man from the animal and has very real consequences for the nature of man. By contrast, for the behaviorist, the term human is a nontechnical, nonexplanatory one, amounting to mere verbal jargon for denoting the most complex kind of organism on our planet: Nothing is gained by labeling an organism human.

Since man is human and distinct from the animal, that is, his own kind of being, man must be studied as his own kind of entity. The model of man is himself. The fundamental characteristic of man differentiating him from the animal is his self-awareness or self-consciousness: To be human is to be self-aware or conscious of self. Thus humanism's model of man is man as he knows and is revealed to himself.

The only reality for man is that which he experiences; a psychologist can only interpret a given person's psychological situation through knowledge of the individual's own view of his/her experiences; an organism's overt behavior can only be resolved in terms of his/her own experience.

Humanism focuses on the experiencing person, more specifically, the healthy person and his/her functioning, modes of living, and goals in life. The healthy person is assumed to be creative, in a constant state of striving, becoming, and potentiating. The individual person is assumed to be a unique and irreducible entity that possesses dignity. The humanist attempts to understand an organism's subjective experience and view of the world, not to predict and/or control its overt behavior.

Although humanism reacted against both descriptive behaviorism and classical Freudian psychoanalysis, it is easy to construe humanism as a latter-day form of depth psychology. Humanism evolved in an essentially applied context: Rogers is a committed psychotherapist; Maslow underwent a psychoanalysis and engaged in psychotherapy for at least a decade, although he spent virtually his entire professional life in academia; existential psychology is equivalent to a conceptual approach to psychotherapy (i.e., existential psychotherapy); psychoanalysis is the classic form of psychotherapy; and so on. Humanism is a subjective, personalistic, inner-directed approach that must be accepted on faith, as is the case with traditional analytical depth psychology. Humanism differs from classical depth psychology only in that it stresses the normal (healthy) person, assumes the efficacy of consciousness, places the self or ego at the center of the psychological universe, views man as fundamentally good, is future oriented, and is optimistic.

We shall characterize the nature of humanism's basic subject matter by considering (1) the focus of humanism, (2) the nature and extent of the overlap that exists between humanism and traditional experimental psychology, (3) the logical status of the concept of self-realization, (4) Maslow's need hierarchy and its relationship to self-actualization, (5) Rogers' self theory and its relationship to self-actualization, and (6) the relationship between Skinner's radical behaviorism and the goals of humanism, particularly as envisioned by Rogers.

The Focus of Humanism

The focus of humanism readily can be characterized in terms of its object and unit of analysis, goal or purpose, and applied orientation.

OBJECT AND UNIT OF ANALYSIS

Since humanism treats man as a unique, irreducible entity, it focuses on the individual organism as the unit of analysis; more specifically, the humanist focuses on the psychological state of the person as revealed by the nature, content, level, and degree of his/her self-awareness. For the humanist, an isolated piece of overt behavior (e.g., an eye blink, a bar press, locomotion in space) is a meaningless psychological entity; even a complex behavioral sequence is meaningless unless it is a reflection of how the individual feels or how he/she regards himself/herself. In effect, the humanist deals with the private, subjective, experiential world of the individual organism.

GOAL OR PURPOSE

To the humanist, prediction and/or control is anathema. The goal of humanism is to understand the organism's own private experiential world view. The only conceivable justification for psychological intervention is the enhancement of the organism's degree of adjustment to the environment: The goal of humanism is the enhancement of the very qualities and characteristics that make man human, the prototypical instance of which is assumed to be self-actualization.

APPLIED ORIENTATION

Stripped of its antibehavioristic and metaphysical pronouncements, humanism can be seen as a rather explicit attempt at an applied psychology. It focuses on the person, personality, ego, self, the essence of one's being and existence. Humanism is concerned with such psychological phenomena as creativity, love, self-regard, growth, autonomy, identity, responsibility, and adjustment. As a remedial or interventionist endeavor, humanism amounts to a psychotherapeutic process that strives to make the individual understand himself/herself better and be more aware, independent, open, integrated, and stable.

THE FOCUS IN PERSPECTIVE

An uninitiated observer of the psychological scene might wonder why the humanistic approach is new, or even necessary. The tenor and tone of 50 years of psychological history preceding 1960, as represented by behaviorism and psychoanalysis, neglected, if not actively repressed, this kind of psychology, or a psychology stated at this level. Neither behaviorism nor psychoanalysis regarded man as unique; and each made the organism a prisoner of uncontrollable forces, either external or internal (unconscious) in origin. Humanism placed man at the center of the psychological universe and put man back in control of his own destiny, that is, man again had control over, and was responsible for, his actions and general state of psychological well-being.

The Nature and Extent of the Overlap Between Humanism and Traditional Experimental Psychology

The degree of correspondence between humanism and traditional experimental psychology with respect to specific psychological content subareas of interest is presented in Figure 10–1, (pg. 274) in terms of two partially overlapping circles: The subareas of psychology appearing in the intersection portion of the circles are of joint concern to humanism and experimental psychology. While the content of the illustration is readily interpretable, mention should be made of some of the considerations and assumptions underlying its construction.

1. Those subareas of psychology that are of concern only for experimental psychology constitute the most easily resolvable portion of the illustration. Humanistic psychology is not interested in such classic research areas as sensation, conditioning, and comparative psychology; in fact, these areas are completely irrelevant for humanistic psychology. The irrelevance is not a simple function of the fact that these research areas focus on isolated, fragmented processes of the organism. Humanists realize that these basic psychological processes exist; but they bypass them in their approach, opting to focus on the results or products of these psychological processes (i.e., experience). Humanists can get away with this conscious neglect as long as they focus on the holistic experience of the normal and/or healthy person. The humanist can engage only in platitudes when it comes to dealing with people who have learning deficits, sensory defects, biologically based memory lapses, brain damage, physiological disorders, and the like. Rectification of these kinds of problems requires viewing the organism as a physical–chemical entity, and employing all the technical expertise that has derived from experimental investigation of the basic psychological processes.

2. Those subareas of psychology that are of concern to both humanistic psychology and experimental psychology comprise a portion of the illustration that is subject to a number of qualifications. Initially there is no problem associated with treating personality, psychotherapy, counseling, and motivation (or emotion) as foci of interest for humanistic psychology. These phenomena constitute the self-proclaimed canonical interest areas of humanism: They basically entail dealing with the organism as a whole or using the organism as the fundamental unit of analysis. These areas also constitute the basic foci of classical depth psychology and served as humanism's exclusive

focus of interest during its initial decade of development (the 1960s). There is a problem associated with treating personality, psychotherapy, and counseling (but not motivation or emotion) as interest areas of experimental psychology. Experimental (i.e., behavioristic) approaches to personality, psychotherapy, and counseling exist, but in no way do these psychological subareas comprise primary research foci of traditional experimental psychology. Their inclusion in the overlap portion of the illustration presumes a liberal interpretation of the nature of experimental psychology. The placement of social and developmental psychology in the overlap also involves a major reservation. While it is arguable that they constitute natural foci of interest for humanism, it is not readily resolvable that they constitute subareas of experimental psychology.

3. Those subareas of psychology that are of concern only for humanistic psychology comprise a portion of the illustration that is essentially indeterminate and open ended (i.e., still evolving). By no means is the listed content of this region exhaustive. Most of these phenomena are of relatively recent concern for the humanist: Humanists began to focus on them in the 1970s, primarily because of the impetus of Carl Rogers. As such, this listing amounts merely to a representative sampling of humanism's current concerns. Note the inclusion of the term "saving" in this portion of the illustration. This is my own idiosyncratic terminology for the fact that the humanist does not deal with predictable/controllable overt behaviors, but focuses on the holistic experience or adaptive state of the organism in an essentially nondeterministic framework. My use of the term "saving" is a corruption of its meaning in certain religious contexts, for example, the organism is saved by accepting Christ. By analogy, one can argue that the humanistically oriented therapist is in the saving business.

The Logical Status of the Concept of Self-Realization

One of the central themes running through virtually every version of pre- and post-1960 humanistic thought is a stress on some form of self-realization as the primary goal of life. It even is implicit in the more optimistic versions of depth psychology characteristic of Jung, Adler, Horney, and Fromm. Humanism is future or goal oriented, both as a conceptual approach to the nature of man and as a pragmatic approach to psychotherapy. The notion of self-realization serves as a convenient construct for physicalizing the humanist's emphasis on striving, creative activity, potentiating, and constructive growth.

Humanism's focus on self-realization is a logical extension of Freud's original concentration on libidinal/id satisfaction. Humanism takes a negative attitude toward the view that the satisfaction of irrational, animalistic desires constitutes the sole or dominant goal of life. Humanism's stress on the realization of creative desires and drives serves as a positive counterweight to Freud's postulation of a biologically based homeostatic state of balance.

The assumption of an end goal of self-realization has virtual axiomatic status in humanistic psychology: Its validity is not subject to empirical proof or disproof. The assumption of a tendency to self-realize operates as a fundamental orienting principle for the humanist and is analogous to the notion of Gestalt in Gestalt psychology, conditioned response or S–R association in behaviorism, and so on. Most humanists regard the striving for self-realization as innate and/or genetically given.

The humanist does not assume that the process of attempting to realize one's primary goal in life is automatic or problem-free. Many things can prevent or inhibit self-realization; we are explicit about some of these later in the context of discussing Maslow's and Rogers' approaches to self-realization. Problems can arise either from not pursuing an end goal or from failing to achieve an end goal—for example, conflicts, anxiety, guilt. These problems possess the same pathogenic existential status that they do in the context of the Freudian approach, but they are not conceptualized as resulting from Freudian psychodynamics (i.e., id–superego confrontation, etc.).

It is not necessary for us to be concerned with the specific linguistic domains of the most commonly used alternative labels for self-realization; namely, self-actualization and self-fulfillment. It is irrelevant for our purposes whether there is any substantive difference in meaning among these three terms. The label "self-actualization" dates back at least to Goldstein (1939) and was popularized by Maslow (1954). Likewise we need not be concerned with the possible *objects* of realization—needs for Maslow, potentialities for Rogers, values for Buhler, personal meaning for Frankl. The language of humanism is so descriptive and nontechnical that such an analysis very swiftly would reach the point of limited returns.

The principle of self-realization is used in the next two subsections as a vehicle for analyzing Maslow's and Rogers' specific content contributions to humanistic psychology: We focus on how they inculcate the goal of self-realization in their respective humanistic approaches.

Maslow's Need Hierarchy and Its Relationship to Self-Actualization

Maslow's most significant content contribution to humanistic psychology relates to his conceptual approach to motivation. He has devised a five-component need hierarchy, in which striving for self-realization is represented structurally as the highest order or ultimate need.

THE FIVE COMPONENT NEEDS

Maslow's five-level hierarchy comprises the following classes of needs, listed in order from lowest to highest:

1. Physiological.
2. Safety or security.
3. Belongingness or love.
4. (Self-) esteem.
5. (Self-) actualization.

1. The physiological needs subsume food, water, sexual contact, and escape/avoidance of pain (aversive stimuli)—the four primary drives of Hullian effect theory (see Chapter 5)—as well as oxygen, sleep, and elimination of bodily wastes. The satisfaction of these needs, in general, is necessary for the maintainence of the biological integrity and the physical survival of the organism.

2. The safety or security needs relate to the organism's desire to maintain a stable, predictable environment, free from anxiety, chaos, and immediate physical threat. Maslow differentiates between the realization of these needs in childhood and adulthood: The child's primary source of safety/security is his/her parents and a stable home/family environment; the adult obtains security through accumulation of tangible assets and developing belief systems or acquiring knowledge that help resolve the nature of reality.

3. The belongingness or love needs are bidirectional in nature: One not only must receive trust and affection, but also must express them. These needs are satisfied by membership in some kind of primary group: family situation, informal school clique, fraternity or sorority, social club, the encounter experience.

4. The self-esteem needs entail a feeling of respect, both for oneself and from the generalized other, that is, the social environment. Self-respect leads to a feeling of competence, adequacy, and confidence; respect from others involves recognition, acceptance, prestige, and status. In general, an organism possessing self-esteem has a feel-

ing of genuine self-worth.

5. The postulation of a need for self-actualization is Maslow's way of physicalizing the humanist's generalized focus on the realization of one's primary end goal in life. The specific domain of this need is open ended: It depends on the specific capacities, skills, and talents of a given individual. The general rule is that the individual must become what he/she can become. Lack of self-actualization is accompanied by a general malaise about the meaning of life, boredom, a repertoire of limited daily activities, and the like.

THE TWO BASIC CHARACTERISTICS OF THE NEED HIERARCHY

So far we have specified only one aspect of the principle of self-realization in the context of Maslow's approach: It is located at the top of a five-level need hierarchy. Other denotative properties of Maslow's concept of self-actualization derive from the two basic characteristics of his need hierarchy: order of fulfillment of the needs and the existence of two basic types of needs.

ORDER OF FULFILLMENT. Maslow assumes that the class of needs located at level N does not even arise until the $N - 1$ lower level needs have been satisfied: The individual does not become aware of level N needs and these level N needs do not direct behavior until all the lower level $N - 1$ needs have been provided for. For instance, a person who is hungry or thirsty is preoccupied with certain physiological needs and is unconcerned with any of the other classes of needs; safety and security become important once the physiological needs have been met; the love needs achieve salience once the organism is not hungry or thirsty, and feels secure. The consequence of Maslow's order of satisfaction assumption for the principle of self-realization should be obvious: The possibility for self-actualization does not even arise until the organism has successfully completed the other four levels of the hierarchy.

TWO BASIC TYPES OF NEEDS. Maslow divides the five component needs of his hierarchy into two basic kinds: deficient and growth. The deficient needs subsume the first two levels of the hierarchy; the growth needs encompass the top three levels of the hierarchy. The distinctive properties of these two types of needs highlight the nature of the need for self-actualization.

1. The deficient needs basically are biologically based: They involve some kind of physiological deficit that must be rectified, and the reduction of these needs involves some kind of tension reduction

or return to some kind of homeostatic balance state. The deficient needs are animal needs, in the sense that they are the only kind of needs animals possess, and constitute the only type of needs of interest to traditional experimental psychology (i.e., the behaviorist) and to Freudian depth psychology. The deficient needs are the first to appear ontogenetically and phylogenetically. They appear during infancy in the life cycle of the individual organism, and early in the overall evolutionary developmental process. Since satisfaction of the deficient needs is necessary for organismic survival, they require virtually instant gratification, and lengthy postponement of gratification can result in death.

2. The growth needs basically are psychologically based: They are future oriented and are associated with the onset of tension and striving. The growth needs are distinctively human: They appear late ontogenetically and phylogenetically. The need for self-actualization need not appear until middle age for the typical person (it takes that long to fulfill all the lower order needs), and no species below the ape displays the need for anything beyond safety or security. The growth needs establish the conditions necessary for a well-rounded, adjusted life. Since the growth needs are not related to biological survival, their gratification can be indefinitely postponed; however, their gratification involves a more complex set of environmental circumstances and is more problematical than that of the deficient needs. For instance, true self-actualization can occur only in a benign social, economic, and political climate.

THE CHARACTERISTICS OF A SELF-ACTUALIZED INDIVIDUAL

Maslow presumes that a self-actualized person (1) has certain values and (2) displays certain traits. These values include wholeness, perfection, justice, beauty, uniqueness, creativity, and truth. A complete enumeration of traits would involve a three-digit figure, but Maslow's most publicized listing consists of 15 items:

1. Efficient perception of reality and an acceptance of it.
2. Acceptance of self and others.
3. Spontaneity.
4. Problem-centered, rather than self-centered, orientation to life.
5. Need for privacy and detachment.
6. Independence from the environment.
7. Appreciation of the basic givens of life with continued freshness and pleasure.
8. Profound mysticism or peak experiences.

9. Identification with humankind.
10. Deep interpersonal relations with others.
11. Democratic personality structure.
12. Perception of the distinction between ends and means.
13. Well-developed and nonhostile sense of humor.
14. Creativity.
15. Nonconformity.

WHY MOST PEOPLE DO NOT SELF-ACTUALIZE

Maslow estimates that less than 1 percent of the American populace has satisfactorily self-actualized and that the average person has only 10 percent of his/her total actualization needs fulfilled. These figures are extremely pessimistic when weighed against the primacy that the humanist accords to the principle of self-realization. Without questioning the validity of these figures or the validity of the need for self-actualization concept itself, we are left with two basic classes of reasons for the general nonattainment of self-actualization in the context of Maslow's approach: structural and dynamic. The structural class relates to the fact that the need for self-actualization is located at the topmost level of a need hierarchy and can become salient only after the content of the lower order levels has been accommodated. The dynamic class involves the nature of the four lower order needs and the specific physiological/psychological conditions necessary for their satisfaction. Literally an infinite number of things can go wrong in a dynamic, or process, sense to prevent the fulfillment of the characteristic needs located at any one of these levels. Since the successful ascent of Maslow's motivational ladder is a multiplicative, as opposed to additive, probabilistic function, it is no surprise that very few successful completions do occur.

SOME CRITICISM AND EVALUATION

Maslow's approach to motivation, in general, and his concept of need for self-actualization, in particular, are subject to numerous criticisms, three of which will be discussed to illustrate the nature of the critical attack on Maslow's humanism.

1. Maslow's concept of a need hierarchy is not as absolutistic as it is claimed to be: It is relativistic, internally inconsistent, and admits of numerous exceptions. For instance, Maslow pays only lip service to the requirement that ascendence of the hierarchy is done in an all-or-none, discrete, stepwise fashion. He allows ascendence to occur if a need at level $N - 1$ is severely frustrated, instead of satisfied; also

the order of the need components above the safety, security level by and large is capricious. Any theoretical construct (i.e., predictive device) that is internally inconsistent and admits of numerous exceptions is beyond meaningful empirical evaluation.

2. The specific denotative content that Maslow assigns to the principle of self-realization, as physicalized in terms of a need for self-actualization, is subjective and personalistic. Maslow does not provide a formal operational definition for the need for self-actualization. The little research that he has performed on the construct is idiosyncratic, involving his own conception of what a self-actualizer should be. Since the humanist studies man as man knows himself, the model of man that Maslow imposes on his self-actualization construct is man as Maslow knows him. The denotative properties of self-actualization are more of a reflection of Maslow's own value system than they are of the nature of man per se.

3. There is a fundamental contradiction, or inconsistency, involved in humanistic psychology, which is particularly evident in Maslow's construct of a need for self-actualization. The humanistic approach assigns the ultimate responsibility for the individual organism's state of well-being to the individual organism itself; or the content of a given instance of overt behavior is always resolved in terms of the organism's conscious experience (i.e., internal mental mechanisms). In this context, the need for actualization is innate or genetically given—the specific talents and skills that the individual is supposed to develop to the fullest possible fruition are innate or given. But how can these talents and skills be developed, or how can the individual even know what his/her primary talents and skills are in the first place? The answer is "only by the supportive measures of a benign and liberal environment" or "only by interaction with the environment." Thus, although the humanist postulates the existential primacy of the self, self-creativity, self-realization, and so on, these concepts are meaningless when divorced from any substantive reference to or conceptual inclusion of the external (social) environment.

Using the Skinnerian perspective, is it the individual who self-actualizes, or is it the environment that actualizes (i.e., allows "self"-actualization to occur)? The descriptive behaviorist can get away with merely referencing the environment because the products or objective indicants of self-actualization are given at that level of reality. The humanist cannot get away with merely referencing the self or conscious experience—either in terms of investigatory subjective verbal report or in terms of ultimate explanatory etiology—because the process or products of self-actualization do not occur in an existential vacuum.

In sum, humanists take a very naive approach to the nature versus nurture issue (or to the relative contributions of the environment and heredity); and this is readily apparent in the context of their principle of self-realization.

Rogers' Self Theory and Its Relationship to Self-Actualization

Rogers' humanistic thought is more comprehensive and conceptually more developed than Maslow's. Because of this, it is not surprising that the humanistic movement has sought to associate itself with Rogerian thought more than Rogers has sought to associate himself with the humanistic movement. Rogers' system of psychology is explicitly phenomenological, and only implicitly humanistic, in nature. The most appropriate comparative reference point for assessing Rogers' conceptual approach to psychology is not Maslow's humanistic thought or any other version of humanism, but rather Skinner's radical behaviorism. Rogers' phenomenological system and Skinner's descriptive behaviorism constitute virtual mirror-image approaches to psychology and the nature of man; Rogers and Skinner have engaged in a running oral and written debate, extending over the past quarter of a century, with respect to the merits and liabilities of their respective systems. (Aspects of this rather unique relationship between Rogers' and Skinner's systems are treated later in this section.)

At a conceptual level, Rogers' phenomenology is best characterized as a self theory, although it just as easily could be interpreted as (1) a personality theory, (2) a motivational theory, (3) an approach to psychotherapy, or (4) even an implicit approach to social psychology. Rogerian psychology most often is identified as an approach to psychotherapy and is known as nondirective or client-centered therapy; however, Rogers currently prefers the more general label of person-centered therapy to accommodate his interest in the encounter (group) experience.

As is the case with Maslow's approach to self-realization, Rogers treats a tendency to self-realize as axiomatic and a conceptual given; however, its characteristics and the dynamics underlying its fruition are vastly different. It is necessary to develop some of Rogers' critical psychological constructs before his resolution of the principle of self-realization can be described.

THE SELF OR SELF-CONCEPT

The self merely is Rogers' term for that part of the content of a person's conscious awareness that becomes differentiated from the continually ongoing flow of consciousness and gets identified with the "I" or "me." The source of the self (i.e., as a differentiation) is experiential: it is attributable to past learning. By definition, the content of the self is wholly conscious. Rogers does not regard the self as a homunculus (i.e., a separate being within a being) guiding and directing overt behavior. It is purely a descriptive concept or verbal label, not a causal entity: It merely functions as a dependent variable or response category for empirical investigation. Because Rogers is a phenomenologist and focuses on the content of conscious experience, the concept of self serves as a convenient category for describing a certain segment of that experience. Rogers distinguishes between two kinds of selves: the actual, or current, self (as presently described) and an ideal, or future, self that specifies the kind of individual the person would like to be.

REGARD CONSTRUCTS

Rogers postulates the existence of six interrelated regard constructs: (1) positive regard, (2) positive self-regard, (3) conditional positive regard, (4) conditional positive self-regard, (5) unconditional positive regard, and (6) unconditional positive self-regard.

1. Positive regard is the individual's innate need for warmth, liking, respect, sympathy, and acceptance, as expressed by another person or some significant other, such as a parent or spouse.

2. Positive self-regard is a learned need for warmth, liking, and so on in the absence of a significant other. It is a derivative of positive regard. As a derived concept, it is analogous to the notion of a secondary/conditioned drive in the context of any number of peripherally oriented variants of behaviorism.

3. Conditional positive regard is the expression of warmth, liking, or acceptance by an individual X for another individual Y, when the behavior, demeanor, or actions of individual Y meet the standards of individual X. This concept is analogous to that of response-contingent positive reinforcement in Skinner's system (see Chapter 7).

4. Conditional positive self-regard is the state of liking and accepting oneself only if one satisfies the specific criteria/standards that a significant other uses to dispense warmth, liking, or acceptance. Rogers refers to such standards as conditions of worth. Thus a person

can experience conditional positive self-regard only if he/she satisfies somebody's conditions of worth.

5. Unconditional positive regard is the noncontingent expression of warmth, liking, or acceptance by an individual X for another individual Y, as occurs between a mother (X) and her newborn child (Y), or between the partners in a newly formed love relationship. It amounts to an unconditional valuation of individual Y by individual X. This concept is analogous to that of free or non-response-contingent positive reinforcement in Skinner's system (see Chapter 7).

6. Unconditional positive self-regard is an individual's ideal state of self-acceptance in the absence of any conditions of self-worth. It is attributable to the receipt of noncontingent expressions of warmth, liking, or acceptance from significant others. Rogers speculates that unconditional positive self-regard probably does not exist in reality, at least not in pure form.

ACTUALIZING CONSTRUCTS

Rogers' system possesses two different actualizing constructs: an actualizing tendency and a drive for self-actualization.

1. The actualizing tendency is Rogers' sole and all-encompassing motivational construct. It is biologically based (innate) and includes all of Maslow's component drives. Everything from the mundane act of eating a meal to the highly creative act of composing a symphony is an expression of the actualizing tendency.

2. The drive for self-actualization is a subcomponent of the actualizing tendency and represents the desire to actualize those specific aspects of experience that are associated with the self-concept: When the innate actualizing tendency becomes directed toward the attempt to realize the goals and abilities represented in the self-concept, it is referred to as the drive for self-actualization.

THE ORGANISMIC VALUING PROCESS

This is the organism's innate capacity to construe positively those experiences perceived as actualizing and to construe negatively those experiences perceived as nonactualizing. Under ideal circumstances, the organism seeks positively valued experiences and avoids negatively valued experiences, that is, self-actualizes.

WHY MOST PEOPLE DO NOT SELF-ACTUALIZE

In the context of Rogers' approach, the basic reason why people do not self-actualize is the development of an eventual conflict between the conditions of worth and the organismic valuing process. The conditions of worth replace the organismic valuing process as the basic internal guide for overt behavior. Under ideal circumstances, the organism's positive regard is maintained by unconditional positive regard: The organism is free to act in accordance with the dictates of the organismic valuing process and to seek (avoid) positive (negative) experiences. Under more typical circumstances, the organism's positive regard can be maintained only by conditional positive regard: The organism must satisfy somebody's conditions of worth. The behaviors specified by the conditions of worth can conflict with those that are chosen by the organismic valuing process, in which case the former set of behaviors prevails. In other words, the organism, especially a child, will perform behaviors that are inherently nonactualizing to earn approval, love, and acceptance from a significant other, such as the parent.

THE CHARACTERISTICS OF A FULLY FUNCTIONING PERSON

Rogerian terminology for Maslow's concept of a self-actualized individual is a fully functioning person; however, the two notions are not complete equivalents. For Maslow, self-actualization entails the attainment of some final end state; for Rogers, fully functioning is a process notion. A fully functioning person is one who is continually moving in a direction of freer expression. A fully functioning person is characterized by the following personality traits.

1. Openness to experience. The self can entertain the content of any new cognitive or emotional experience, without any feeling of threat.
2. Existential living. The self is continually evolving and changing to absorb new experiences.
3. Organismic trusting. The self makes decisions based on the validity of its own internal experientially sourced criteria, not in terms of an externally imposed code.
4. Experiential freedom. The self operates as if it were indeed free from external constraints or influences. (This basically is the assumption of free will.)
5. Creativity. The self is totally and fully creative.

SOME CRITICISM AND EVALUATION

Rogers' self theory and his resolution of the principle of self-realization are subject to numerous criticisms, only two of which will be discussed to illustrate the nature of the critical attack on Rogers' phenomenology.

1. Rogers' concept of the self is not as absolutistic as it is claimed to be: It is componential and situational. Research has demonstrated that there are many selves, and the content of conscious awareness associated with the "I" or "me" (i.e., the labeling thereof) can be broken down into distinct categories. There can be a social self, intellectual self, emotional self, religious self, and so on. Also, the content of the self at any particular moment can be situationally determined. For instance, the content of the intellectual self (i.e., the self-perception thereof) can vary, contingent on the specific intellectual task the person currently is performing. He/she might be very good at writing an English composition, but very bad at doing math problems, with corresponding effects on the self-concept.

In general, the specific content of the self or a specific kind of self in a given situation, in part, is a function of the expertise of the phenomenologically oriented researcher. The self is just as much a construction of the investigator as it is an absolute property of the experiencing organism. (The situation with respect to the self is analogous to that of symptomology in the therapeutic situation.) A descriptive behaviorist would argue that it is possible to elicit a self, and another self, and then another self, *ad infinitum*. The humanist likes to employ growth or flowering imagery. There is no logical termination rule for determining when the budding of new selves must cease.

2. The humanist's simplistic approach to the relationship between the organism (self) and the external environment is also reflected in Rogers' approach to the principle of self-realization: Any true self-actualization is exclusively due to the self-actualizing tendency under the sole guidance and control of the organismic valuing process. For Rogers, this situation exists only when there are no environmental contingencies determining the organism's behavior or self-concept—the organism's exclusive source of positive regard is unconditional positive regard. On the other hand, Rogers realizes that the organism's behavior and self-concept are under the control of environmental contingencies more often than they are not: The organism's usual source of positive regard is conditional positive regard. But the conditions of worth entailed by the conditional positive regard mitigate the effects of the organismic valuing process and prevent self-actualization. The environment can only prevent or inhibit self-actualization, never facilitate self-actualization. Thus, unlike Maslow, Rogers is willing to reference the environment, but only

from a negative perspective, not from a positive perspective. Like Maslow, Rogers is not willing to concede that the environment ever allows actualization to occur.

Skinner's Radical Behaviorism and the Goals of Humanism

B. F. Skinner was awarded the 1972 Humanist of the Year medal by the American Humanist Association. This event should serve as an indication of the fact that behaviorism and humanism are not necessarily completely incompatible conceptual approaches to psychology. Certainly behaviorism, as represented by Skinnerian radical behaviorism, and humanism, as represented by Rogerian phenomenological self theory, have diametrically opposed views of the nature of man and of the nature of the critical psychological processes. They describe the basic structure and dynamics of psychology in terms of mirror-image concepts and terminology. But this does not necessarily mean that the two systems are not isomorphic to each other, or that they do not possess the same ultimate goals.

ISOMORPHISM

It is possible to convert most, if not all, of Rogers' basic psychological concepts into Skinnerian terminology and dynamics. Positive regard is equivalent to the concept of (socially sourced) positive reinforcement. Conditional positive regard and unconditional positive regard specify the two basic ways in which positive reinforcement can be delivered: contingent or noncontingent on prior behavior. The positive self-regard constructs can be conceptualized as acquired needs or drive states, which for Skinner perform stimulus elicitational or discriminative stimulus functions. Skinner would have no problem with the self-concept; it is merely epiphenomenal (as Rogers suggests) and amounts to the organism tacting under the control of the reinforcement contingencies of the surrounding verbal community. The characteristic events of a Rogerian client-centered therapy session easily can be expressed in terms of Skinnerian dynamics.

ULTIMATE GOALS

The professed goals of behaviorism and humanism, the prediction and/or control of behavior and understanding of the conscious experience of the organism, respectively, are only superficially different. Skinner focuses on the individual organism, just as Rogers does. In this context, it is merely a semantic issue as to whether the denotative object of concern is characterized as overt behavior or as

subjective experience. The ultimate synonymity of the goals of behaviorism and humanism is obscured by the fact that the behaviorist
focuses on and specifies dynamics (bidirectional determinism, environmental contingencies, etc.), whereas the humanist focuses on and
specifies end states (teleology, principle of self-realization: self-actualization, the fully functioning person, etc.). The behaviorist typically does not specify the ultimate goals of behavioral control or
behavioral dynamics. For Skinner, these certainly are benign, and
even could be construed in self-realization terminology. Humanists
typically do not specify the psychological dynamics responsible for
self-actualization (Rogers is an exception). They cannot, because they
bypass the traditional psychological processes.

THE REAL DIFFERENCE BETWEEN BEHAVIORISM AND HUMANISM

The substantive difference between behaviorism and humanism
resides at the level of means (instrumentality), not ends (goals). For
Skinner, a fully functioning or self-realized organism is achieved by
having it operate in a situation that subsumes a set of optimal reinforcement contingencies. For instance, Skinner would exploit Rogers'
conditions of worth to condition desirable behavior. For Rogers, a
fully functioning or self-realized organism is achieved by having it
operate in a situation devoid of any kind of restrictive contingencies.
For instance, Rogers would use Skinner's positive reinforcement in
a noncontingent manner. For behaviorism, self-realization is a matter
of proper behavioral technology. For humanism, self-realization is a
matter of exhortation, preaching, platitudes, altered states of consciousness, altered self-concept. Skinner and Rogers agree on one
aspect of instrumentality: They both abhor the use of
punishment—Skinner because it is ineffective and self-defeating in
the long run, and Rogers because it constitutes an instance of a restrictive contingency.

SOME FINAL PERSPECTIVE

Both the behaviorist and the humanist go about their everyday
affairs, attempting to improve the condition of man. The behaviorist
does it in a matter-of-fact, almost indifferent fashion; the humanist
does it in such a way as to make the recipient feel special or human.
The distinction between behavioristic determinism and humanistic
teleology is overdrawn. Bidirectional or reciprocal determinism allows
future goals to be achieved through a process of successive approximation. Humanists merely pay lip service to teleology because they
typically do not supply any specific mechanisms through which future
goals can affect current behavior or consciousness. A system of psy-

chology created by the judicious combination of behaviorism and humanism would exploit the explicit aspects of each: (1) the means, dynamics of behaviorism, and (2) the goals, end states of humanism.

Origin; Specific Historical Antecedents

It is possible to treat the antecedents of humanistic psychology from many perspectives, because many disparate historical and intellectual trends coalesced in the synthesis called the third force. The input into humanistic psychology can be categorized in terms of at least four interrelated hierarchical dimensions:

1. Immediate psychological versus ultimate philosophical.
2. General psychological versus specific psychological.
3. Direct psychological versus indirect psychological.
4. Positive psychological versus negative psychological.

These categorical dimensions are listed in a nested, hierarchical order such that the first entry in each row is divisible into the two categories of the next row. Immediate psychological antecedents are divisible into general and specific; general psychological antecedents are divisible into direct and indirect; direct psychological antecedents are divisible into positive and negative. We shall briefly sketch in the content of the psychological categories and then analyze the ultimate philosophical category in some detail.

The Nature of the Psychological Input into Humanism

The immediate psychological antecedents of humanism include (1) such general psychological approaches as Skinnerian behaviorism; Freudian psychoanalysis; Gestalt psychology; Snygg and Combs' phenomenological psychology; Binswanger, Boss, von Kaam, and May's existential psychology; Dilthey and Spranger's understanding psychology; Allport's personality theory; and Goldstein's psychopathology; and (2) such specific psychological constructs as the self (e.g., James, Mead, and Snygg and Combs' approaches to a self-concept) and the principle of self-realization (e.g., Jung and Goldstein's concept of self-actualization). The first five general psychological approaches—behaviorism, psychoanalysis, Gestalt psychology, phenomenological psychology, and existential psychology—can be classified as direct influences; the last three general psychological approaches—understanding psychology, personality theory, and psychopathology—can be classified as indirect influences. Of the direct influences, Gestalt psychology, Snygg and Combs' phenomenological psychology, and existential psychology can be regarded as positive influences, in the sense that humanism absorbed the essential metaphysical and methodological assumptions associated with them; Skinnerian behaviorism and Freudian psychoanalysis can be treated as negative influences, in the sense that humanism reacted against the essential metaphysical and methodological assumptions associated with them.

The primary positive aspect of humanistic psychology is that it constitutes an expanded Gestaltist phenomenological psychology. The primary negative aspect of humanistic psychology is that it rejects the determinism, reductionism, and mechanism associated with behaviorism and psychoanalysis. The primary positive aspect of humanistic psychology ultimately is traceable to the philosophical influences of phenomenology and existentialism.

The Nature of the Philosophical Input Into Humanism

The philosophical roots of humanistic psychology are associated with the Kantian legacy, as opposed to that of British empiricism. This should not be surprising, considering the fact that humanism can be construed as an expanded form of Gestalt psychology. The Kantian legacy in Continental European philosophy included two interrelated, but distinguishable, philosophical movements: phenomenology and existentialism. Both phenomenology and existentialism are heterogeneous collections of specific subphilosophies: Phenomenology primarily is concerned with epistemology, and existentialism basically serves as an approach to metaphysics. Phenomenology is the more general of the two in the sense that a traditional existentialist takes a phenomenological approach, but not every phenomenologist necessarily is an existentialist.

PHENOMENOLOGY

Phenomenology derives from Kant's basic distinction between the noumenal world and the phenomenal world: objects as they are in themselves and objects as they exist in one's immediate consciousness (see Chapter 4). Initial forms of phenomenology, as represented in Hegel's and Fichte's thought, sought to specify how man (or mind) developed and transcended, such that objects or the world could be known noumenally. Later forms of phenomenology, characteristic of Husserl, Brentano, and Merleau-Ponty, denied that any meaningful "jump" could be made from the phenomenal world to the noumenal world, such that the phenomenal world exhausts a person's meaningful reality. Edmund Husserl (1859–1938), a German philosopher, is considered to be the founder of the latter interpretation of phenomenology; Franz Brentano (1838–1917) physicalized the notion in the context of his act psychology (see Chapter 8); and Maurice Merleau-Ponty (1908–1961), a French philosopher, is regarded as the most prominent contemporary proponent of this approach.

HUSSERL'S PHENOMENOLOGY. For Husserl, phenomenology is the canonical method of philosophy, that is, the specific epistemological tool by which reality is known. It is "deductive": it transcends science and historiography as sources of truth. The object of analysis of phenomenology is the content of one's immediate conscious experience, as intuitively given. The phenomenological observer must grasp or attend that which is immediately given in consciousness, unanalyzed by any preconceived categories. The true phenomenological observer experiences essences. Essences possess meaning or intelligible structure at their own level of reality. The Husserl notion of essence is analogous to that of a Gestalt, although the nature of a given essence need not necessarily be expressible in words. For Husserl, essences are the only indubitable and authentic data of existence.

Let us consider the notion of red, as an illustration of an essence. As a matter of structuralist introspection, red is a sensation. For a physicist, red is a color or wavelength. For a physiologist, red is neural receptor activity. For Husserl, red is an essence: It has its own meaning, structure, reality as given. The basic point of Husserl's phenomenology is that red, experienced as an essence, is the *real* red and exhausts the meaning of red for the observer.

BRENTANO'S CONCEPT OF INTENTIONALITY. The content of conscious experience is mental in nature: Phenomenological essences are mental phenomena. Thus phenomenological essences can also be characterized as objects of thought. A phenomenologically given essence, as an object of thought, need not exist in an absolute physical sense, nor need it correspond to an object occurring in physical, external reality. Brentano's term for this situation is intentionality. Essences are intentional objects; mental phenomena in general possess only intentional reality; a mental event even can be defined as an intentional event. For Brentano, the contents of conscious experience are intentional objects and possess only intentional reality.

The contemporary humanistic psychologist uses the term intentionality, but it has a different meaning: A human being possessing intentionality is one who knows himself/herself, that is, his/her motivation, personality, and self-identity, and can act meaningfully on this basis. It is possible for the humanist's intentionality (i.e., an individual in a state of intentionality) to have only intentional existence in the Brentano sense.

MERLEAU-PONTY'S PHENOMENOLOGY. For Merleau-Ponty, phenomenological essences or intentional objects do not simply appear in consciousness: They are not automatic nor do they occur in a vacuum. They basically are a product of the experiencing self. The content of consciousness is a function of the organism's perspective, frame of judgment, and the like. Merleau-Ponty primarily applied phenomenology to the organism's perceptual experience: The structure of an organism's perceptual experience is contingent on the nature of the experiencing self and what the organism brings to the situation.

PHENOMENOLOGY IN PSYCHOLOGY. The application of phenomenology to psychology involves either or both of the following assumptions: (1) The conscious experience of the organism constitutes the canonical, or most meaningful, aspect of man for psychology to study, and (2) the externalization of the content of consciousness, as given, via the use of the vernacular language, amounts to a reliable/valid psychological process or experimental technique. Humanism was not the first conceptual approach to psychology to take an essentially phenomenological orientation. Phenomenological precursors of humanism minimally include (1) Brentano's act psychology, (2) the phenomenological work of G. E. Müller and his associates at Göttingen, (3) Gestalt psychology, (4) Snygg and Combs' phenomenological approach to self and personality, and (5) Robert MacLeod's seminal efforts at Cornell University. The historical importance of humanism's use of phenomenology derives from the fact that it is associated with a focus on the individual, holistic organism as the unit of analysis, and it is intertwined with an essentially existential view of man.

EXISTENTIALISM

Existentialism essentially is a social or activist Continental philosophy that began as a protest against the metaphysical systems of

Kant and Hegel. Existentialism represents a break with philosophical tradition: It is anti-intellectual, antianalytic, and antiscientific. Existentialists abhor generalization, abstraction, symbolization, and classification. Existentialism is more of an approach to life or a life-style: The existentialist approach is one of emotional groping, grasping, or feeling. Existential thought is of such a nature that it is more easily expressed in literature, novels, plays, and the like. It focuses on the nature of being, existence, and/or man. This is why existentialism is phenomenologically oriented: If man is to be understood, he must be viewed in the light of his own world—his own phenomenal world. There is no one school of existentialism: Christian, atheistic, and social forms exist. The most prominent existential philosophers include Søren Kierkegaard (1813–1855), Karl Jaspers (1883–1969), Martin Heidegger (1889–1976), and John-Paul Sartre (1905–1980).

THE TWO BASIC TENETS OF EXISTENTIALISM. The first tenet concerns the specific metaphysical focus of the existentialist, and the second tenet relates to the existentialist conception of man.

1. Existential philosophy distinguishes between two possible metaphysical foci: reality or essence and existence or being. Traditional metaphysics was concerned with reality or essence, as distinguished from mere appearance: What is the nature of the ultimate substance(s) composing the universe? Existentialism regards the ultimate nature of reality as unknowable and, therefore, irrelevant. Of crucial metaphysical concern for existential philosophy is the nature of existence or being; specifically, man's existence or being.

2. The critical belief that the existentialist holds about the nature of man's existence or being is that man is completely free. Man's condition of freedom connotes more than the simple free will versus determinism issue interpreted at the level of overt behavior. For the existentialist, man's freedom extends to the choice of a culture, a metaphysics, and the meaning and significance of life. What the existentialist essentially means by man's condition of freedom is that there is no one, absolute, standard reason why he is a part of the universe. Man's existence or being has no inherent, preordained meaning and significance.

PSYCHOLOGICAL CONSEQUENCES OF THE TWO TENETS. According to the existentialist, once man realizes he is free, man (1) suffers anxiety, torment, or dread; (2) views life (existence) as absurd; or (3) experiences a feeling of alienation from the natural life, or universe, around him. Anxiety, absurdity, and alienation are characteristics of the existential state of man. The existentialist does not evaluate these characteristics negatively: anxiety and alienation are catalysts for personality change, development of a more authentic existence, recommitment to life, and renewed emphasis on striving and becoming. In effect, since man exists in an existential vacuum, he must create his own reality and his own reason for living.

EXISTENTIAL PSYCHOLOGY: EXISTENTIAL THERAPY. Where existential philosophy ends and existential psychology begins is indeterminate. Existential psychology is a philosophical psychology, not an academic/experimental one. It should not be surprising that existential philosophy has had its greatest effect on psychology in the area of therapy: Existential psychotherapists such as Binswanger, von Kaam, Boss, and May already have been mentioned in the chapter. The existential approach to therapy usually is called existential analysis or *daseinsanalysis*. (*Dasein* is German for the state of being aware of one's existence in a surrounding physical world.) Existential psychology is continuous with humanistic psychology: They both (1) treat man as a unique form of life in the universe, (2) take a phenomenological approach to conscious experience, and (3) emphasize such things as striving, becoming, and potentiating.

Method of Study; Permissible Methodology

Although a humanistic psychologist is not a hard-core experimentalist or a quantitative or methodological specialist in the traditional sense, the analytical dimension of permissible methodology is relevant in the context of the humanistic approach: Humanism's general approach to methodology is (1) continuous with other aspects of humanism and (2) particularily illustrative of humanism's overall value system and foci.

Even though methodology merely is a means to a certain end in every system of psychology, traditional behavioristic experimental psychology tends to lose sight of this fact and treats methodology as an end in itself. A specific research problem is chosen because it is amenable to a well-accepted/documented experimental technique, not because it is relevant for unraveling man's nature or serves as a significant contribution to the psychological literature. One could never accuse a humanist of being guilty of confusing means with ends: The sole criterion of the humanist in choosing research projects is meaningfulness. A given study is undertaken because it is psychologically relevant and pertains to the human issues and concerns, as defined by the humanistic psychologist. For the humanist, the degree of objectivity or validity afforded by a given research technique is purely a secondary matter.

Recall that humanism bypasses the traditional psychological processes. The notion of a stimulus situation, independent variable, or experimental operation is foreign to humanistic psychology. Humanism does not seek to induce or certify causal relationships. The key to understanding humanistic methodology is the realization that humanistic psychology, at a conceptual level, amounts to the combination of an expanded Gestalt psychology and a more optimistic form of depth psychology. As an expanded Gestalt psychology, humanism attempts to analyze, understand, and externalize an individual organism's consciousness, not just the content of the perceptual consciousness, but the full range of consciousness: feelings, self-concepts, goals, desires, and beliefs. This means that humanists employ phenomenological description, just as Gestaltists do. As a form of depth psychology, humanism must assess some aspect of the state of well-being of the organism, that is, level of self-actualization attained, nature of the self-concept, or degree of perceived change in a therapeutic situation. This means that humanists ideally should use developmentally focused longitudinal methodology, and also must face all the problems associated with single-case study methodology.

Phenomenological Description

The nature of phenomenological description was adequately covered in Chapter 4 in the context of Gestalt methodology; however, since the humanist focuses on holistic consciousness and the totality of personal experience, humanistic methodology adds two features to Gestaltist phenomenological analysis.

THE TWO BASIC FEATURES

The additional features of humanistic phenomenological analysis relate to (1) the relationship between the subject and the experimenter and (2) the nature of the interaction between the subject and the experimenter.

1. Since it is the humanist's purpose merely to understand an organism's experience, not to control or exploit the organism in any

way, the subject (client, patient, informer) and the experimenter (therapist, observer, researcher) are assumed to be equals. The organism is a true subject, as opposed to an object, in the context of humanistic psychology. The subject actually is the ultimate arbiter in any humanistic phenomenological investigation because the experimenter must interpret the situation only through the subject's view of the situation. The experimenter must accept the content of the subject's verbal report at face value.

2. Since the humanist must induce the subject's basic frame of reference, it is necessary for him/her actively to participate in the phenomenological session: querying, probing, and testing hypotheses. The experimenter interacts with the subject physically and verbally, unlike the case in a behavioristic study where the experimenter must act as a physically aloof, objective measuring device.

THE THERAPEUTIC SITUATION: PSYCHOANALYSIS VERSUS ROGERIAN THERAPY

Much of the phenomenological description that is of concern to the humanist occurs in the therapeutic situation. It is legitimate to inquire how humanistic therapy differs from other forms of therapy, such as Freudian psychoanalysis, as a source of phenomenological description. While Rogerian client-centered therapy does not exhaust humanistic therapy, it is considered to be the prototypical (and is the most prevalent) form. Therefore, a brief comparison of psychoanalysis and Rogerian therapy is in order.

Recall from Chapter 9 that psychoanalytic therapy basically consists of free association, which, in turn, was described as a form of introspection. The content of the patient's introspective self-report is used to infer the existence and/or nature of unconscious material. In psychoanalysis, the therapist is the dominant figure and forces his/her own interpretive categories on the patient's descriptions: The psychoanalyst even uses the patient's report to make inferences of causality. In Rogerian therapy, the therapist and client are equals. The therapist provides a totally accepting environment by issuing unconditional positive regard, and interprets the client's descriptions only at an emotional level with no cognitive assessment entailed. In other words, the therapist merely acts as an emotional echo chamber. Just as psychoanalysis can be caricatured, Rogerian therapy is aped by saying "uh-huh" or "uhm."

There are two critical differences between free association, as a form of introspection, and Rogerian therapy, as a form of phenomenal description:

1. Freud uses the content of the patient's self-report to infer the nature of an objective reality, while Rogers uses the content of the client's self-report merely to understand the client better and to increase his/her self-awareness and self-acceptance: There is no inference to an objective reality independent of the client's perceived world.

2. Freud must worry about the reliability and validity of his patient's self-report because of its use as an inductive device; Rogers need not worry about these aspects of his client's self-report because it merely denotes the client's subjective view of reality.

THE SKINNERIAN VIEW OF PHENOMENOLOGY

Recall from Chapter 7 that Skinner admits the possibility of externalizing the contents of one's immediate awareness or self-awareness: Verbal self-report amounts to tacting responses. Unlike the humanist who views the ability to engage in phenomenal description as a natural process, Skinner believes that the ability to identify and label one's experience is conditioned by the environment through various reinforcement contingencies. The conditions under which this conditioning process can and does occur are far from ideal, and Skinner regards the externalization of consciousness through phenomenological description to be a very difficult task.

Assessment of Well-Being

There is wide variation among individual humanistic psychologists with respect to the degree to which the ideal methodology for assessment of well-being is approximated; and humanistic psychology, in general, has been heavily criticized for its overall subjective approach to the assessment of organismic adaptation. We shall cite only the research efforts of Maslow and Rogers in this connection because only their conceptions of humanism are analyzed in the chapter.

MASLOW: MEASUREMENT OF SELF-ACTUALIZATION

The quantity and quality of Maslow's own research on self-actualization have been characterized in a previous section as constituting a severe disappointment; however, some of his adherents recently developed a so-called Personal Orientation Inventory (known as the POI), which can be used to assess an individual's degree of self-actualization. This is a 150-item self-report questionnaire, similar to a standard, commercially available objective personality test. The POI has been demonstrated to possess an acceptable degree of construct validity and promises to be a valuable research tool for future Maslowian-inspired research on self-actualization.

ROGERS: MEASUREMENT OF THE SELF-CONCEPT

Rogers empirically evaluates an organism's self-concept, both as an end in itself and as an indirect means of assessing the validity of his client-centered therapy. This is done through a process/technique known as the Q sort, which involves an organism placing cards containing possible self-descriptive words, phrases, or sentences in different piles, ranging from least similar to most similar. Usually a seven- or nine-category system (continuum) is used. The organism (sorter) is constricted with respect to the frequency of use of each category, such that an essentially normal distribution of cards results: Most cards must be assigned to the middle categories, and very few cards can be placed in the extreme categories. The Q sort is quite flexible. The organism can sort on the basis of the currently perceived self-concept and/or on the basis of a desired (ideal) self-concept. A comparison of these two sorts, which can be physicalized in terms of a correlation coefficient, reveals any discrepancy existing between the organism's current self and ideal self. Successive samplings with these two kinds of sorts can be done over time with an individual as an indirect test of the effectiveness of Rogerian therapy, if appropriate control measurements are also made.

It also should be mentioned that Rogers empirically has measured the effect of his therapy through content analysis. In this technique, the individual verbal statements made by a client during therapy are coded in terms of various categories; and the relative frequency of occurrence of the different kinds of category statements (i.e., favorable or unfavorable) has been shown systematically to increase or decrease over time.

Conceptual Overview: Response Constructs

Humanistic psychologists and/or phenomenologists can deal only with response or response-inferred constructs at a methodological level. Psychological reality is exclusively revealed through the self-report of the organism in a therapeutic, testing, assessment, or similar context. This heavy dependence on response constructs would lead to severe reliability/validity assessment problems if the humanist assumed that response constructs mirrored some objective reality; fortunately, the typical humanist merely uses such constructs to infer the nature of the individual organism's subjective world.

Chief Historical Figures: Maslow and Rogers

Maslow is usually credited with founding the third-force movement in America, and the humanistic movement prefers to regard Rogers as one of its own. Since Maslow's death in 1970, Rogers certainly constitutes the most renowned humanist; however, in a sense, Rogerian phenomenology has absorbed and superseded humanism.

The lives and careers of Maslow and Rogers present some interesting parallels. Both were loners and aloof, as well as scholarly, exceptional students, during childhood. They both married early against parental wishes and found marriage to be a very self-fulfilling experience. Maslow and Rogers earned their undergraduate degrees at the University of Wisconsin and studied at or were associated with Columbia University. Both underwent a "conversion" or "semiconversion" experience, which served as the impetus for their concern for the individual person. (This conversion experience is characteristic of other humanistic psychologists, such as Rollo May.)

Our biographical sketch of Maslow will be briefer than that of Rogers. Many people consider Rogers to be on a par with Skinner, and believe that they are the two greatest living American psychologists. Rogers' life and career could be meaningfully compared with that of Skinner: They both possess a self-effacing personality, mild disposition, nondirective manner, and unsought fame. They both were pioneers in their respective areas: Rogers had to fight the psychiatric establishment and establish psychotherapy as a proper function of the psychologist; Skinner had to contend with the learning establishment—the group-oriented methodology and theoretical baggage of traditional macrolearning theory (Hull, Guthrie, Tolman).

Abraham Maslow (1908–1970)

Maslow was born in Brooklyn, N.Y., in 1908. His parents were uneducated Jewish immigrants from Russia, but eventually the family owned and operated a barrel manufacturing company. Maslow's childhood can be characterized as lonely and scholarly. He began his undergraduate training at Cornell University, but transferred to the University of Wisconsin in his junior year, after marrying Bertha

Goodman. He initially became interested in psychology after discovering Watsonian behaviorism and went to Wisconsin because he believed Koffka, Driesch (a biologist), and Meiklejohn (a philosopher) were there, as announced in the university's catalogue. Although they no longer were in residence by the time he arrived, Maslow remained at Wisconsin, earning his three degrees there: B.A. (1930); M.A. (1931); and Ph.D. (1934). Maslow received a thorough grounding in experimental, comparative, developmental, and social psychology, and even did his Ph.D. dissertation under the redoubtable Harry Harlow on the sexual and dominance characteristics of monkeys. At Wisconsin, he served as an assistant instructor in psychology (1930–1934) and as a teaching fellow in psychology (1934–1935).

He became a Carnegie Fellow at Columbia University in 1935. Maslow assumed an associate professorship at Brooklyn College in 1937 and remained there until 1951. In the late 1930s and early 1940s, New York City was the center of the psychological universe because of the rise of Nazism in Europe: Such notables as Fromm, Adler, Horney, (Ruth) Benedict, and Wertheimer were available for Maslow's delectation and consultation. He underwent psychoanalysis, and his commitment to behaviorism formally died with the birth of his first daughter. America's entrance into World War II also affected Maslow's professional focus: He became overly depressed with the current state of man.

In 1951, he became chairman of the Psychology Department at Brandeis, but stepped down to a full professorship in 1961 to puruse his interests in the humanistic movement. During the 1960s, Maslow became the primary spokesman of humanism in America. Most of his books were written and published during this period. He served as one of the founding editors of both the *Journal of Humanistic Psychology* and the *Journal of Transpersonal Psychology*. He was instrumental in the creation of the American Association of Humanistic Psychology and the American Psychological Association's Division 32. He was president of the American Psychological Association in 1968. In 1969, Maslow became the first resident fellow at the W. Price Laughlin Charitable Foundation in Menlo Park, Calif. Maslow had a history of heart trouble during most of his life and died from a heart attack in 1970.

Maslow's books include the following: *Toward a Psychology of Being* (1962, 1968), the original humanist manifesto; *Religions, Values, and Peak Experiences* (1964); *Eupsychian Management* (1965); *The Psychology of Science* (1966); *Motivation and Personality* (1954, 1970); and *The Farther Reaches of Human Nature* (1971), a posthumous collection of some of his journal articles.

Carl Rogers (1902–)

Rogers was born in 1902 in Oak Park, Ill., a suburb of Chicago. His father was a civil engineer and contractor, so the family was financially secure. His mother was a fundamentalist, and Rogers experienced a Protestant ethic upbringing. When he was 12, the family moved to a farm 30 miles west of Chicago, where Rogers became responsible for many daily chores. Rogers' parents were permissive and encouraged independence, but they also had high moral standards and high expectations. Rogers was an outstanding, virtually straight A student during his preparatory years, and did his best work in English and science. He essentially was a loner and led a fairly sheltered life before leaving the homestead for college.

Rogers entered the University of Wisconsin in 1919, simply because it was the family school. Because of his farm experience and fundamentalist upbringing, he initially majored in agriculture and participated in the YMCA and other Christian groups. A religious youth trip to China liberalized and broadened his views, and he decided to study for the ministry and switched his major to history. Rogers was graduated from Wisconsin in 1924 with a B.A. degree in that discipline. At Wisconsin, Rogers took a grand total of one psychology course, and that was by correspondence.

Rogers matriculated at the Union Theological Seminary in New York City in 1924, after marrying Helen Elliott. Exposed to both psychology and psychiatry at a realistic level for the first time, his interests changed again; and he formally entered Teachers College at Columbia, where he earned an M.A. degree in clinical psychology in 1928 and a Ph.D. degree in clinical psychology in 1931. He received a fellowship from the Institute of Child Guidance at Teachers College for the 1927–1928 academic year. His Ph.D. thesis involved a test for measuring personality adjustment in children, copies of which still sell today.

In 1931, Rogers accepted a position as a staff psychologist at the Child Study Department of the Society for the Prevention of Cruelty to Children in Rochester, N.Y. For the next decade, he was very active in applied psychological service for delinquent and underprivileged children. Rogers was instrumental in forming the Rochester Guidance Center, of which he emerged as director despite strong opposition from the psychiatric establishment. This was to be the first of two battles with psychiatry over the right of a psychologist to engage in psychotherapy. During the Rochester years, Rogers developed his client-centered approach, about which he published *The Clinical Treat-*

ment of the Problem Child in 1939. This book earned Rogers an invitation to join the Ohio State University faculty in 1940.

He accepted a full professorship of psychology at Ohio State, primarily because he had found teaching a summer session at Teachers College enjoyable. At OSU, Rogers began to attract students and to achieve initial worldwide recognition. His empirical evaluation of client-centered therapy led to the publication of *Counseling and Psychotherapy* in 1942. Rogers identified more with the social work establishment during these years, and he served as vice president of the Orthopsychiatric Association in 1944 and as president of the American Association for Applied Psychologists in 1944.

After teaching the summer session at the University of Chicago in 1944, Rogers moved there in 1945 to establish and direct a counseling center based on Rogerian principles. Again he experienced flack from the psychiatric community. In 1947, Rogers served as president of the American Psychological Association, after he aided in its fusion with the American Association for Applied Psychologists. Rogers published *Client-Centered Therapy*, probably his most definitive work, in 1951, and *Psychotherapy and Personality Change*, with Dymond, in 1954. He served as president of the American Academy of Psychotherapists in 1956, and also received the American Psychological Association's Distinguished Scientific Contribution Award the same year. By Rogers' own account, this award constituted his most prized and edifying formal recognition.

Rogers became a professor of both psychology and psychiatry at his alma mater, the University of Wisconsin, in 1957. He became involved with an ill-fated, politically mismanaged, strife-ridden study of the application of client-centered therapy to schizophrenics. In 1961, he published *On Becoming a Person*. Rogers became dissatisfied with the strict, experimentally oriented, academic requirements of the Psychology Department (his graduate students had a tough time); and he eventually resigned from the psychology faculty, but retained his position in the Psychiatry Department. Rogers spent the 1962–1963 academic year as a fellow at the Center of Advanced Study in the Behavioral Sciences at Stanford.

Rogers joined the Western Behavioral Science Institute at La Jolla, Calif., in 1964. He founded and has been associated with the Center for the Study of the Person (also at La Jolla) since 1969. He edited *The Therapeutic Relationship and Its Impact* (1967) and published *Freedom to Learn* (1969) and *Becoming Partners* (1972). He received the American Psychological Association's Distinguished Professional Contribution Award in 1972. Over the past 20 years or so, Rogers has shifted his focus from client-centered therapy to a rabid involvement with the encounter group movement. As Skinner did during the sunset of his career, Rogers also has recently sought to sketch in the broad social, educational, industrial, and political consequences of his phenomenological approach. He retired from the active conduction of therapy years ago and spends much of his time cultivating his garden, the ultimate physical analogy for the humanistic conception of growth.

Characteristic Experimentation; Primary Research Areas

Humanistic psychology has not spawned a characteristic research program in the traditional sense of the term. Any number of reasons can be presented for this:

1. Humanism stresses values, ideals, and other "wholesome" entities that possess a high moral content. Such activities traditionally are not a focus of scientific research.

2. Humanism has nothing to prove, in the same sense that Freudian psychology or any depth psychology has nothing to prove. Humanistic concepts are circular and only afford after-the-fact explanation, not predictions.

3. Humanism focuses on the externalization of consciousness (just as psychoanalysis focused on the externalization of the unconscious) more or less as an end in itself: The goal merely is to understand the subjective world of the organism.

4. Humanism basically is goal oriented, future oriented, or teleological in nature. It is possible to ascertain a specific organism's perceived goals empirically, but not to relate them to overt behavior by any mechanisms subject to empirical test.

5. Humanism can focus on the whole organism as the unit of analysis only in an applied sense. A given organism's overall state of well-being and adjustment requires empirical assessment, but it is experimentally impossible to deal with the myriad psychological mechanisms and processes underlying overt behavior in a holistic manner, that is, all at once.

6. Humanism, in part, arose as a protest against the characteristically trivial, piece-by-piece research conducted by traditionally oriented experimental psychologists.

The Self-Concept

There is one humanistic concept that has been subject to an appreciable amount of experimental investigation: the self. Over the past 35 years, well over 1000 studies have been performed on the self-concept. This is not so much due to the fact that the self constitutes Rogers' canonical concept, but rather because it can be conceptualized as an intervening variable in the traditional, nondescriptive behavioristic sense of the term. This means that the self-concept can be studied both as input and output: (1) A person's self-concept can be construed as an independent variable and related to overt behavior as a dependent variable; and (2) a person's self-concept can be construed as a dependent variable and related to various etiological factors as independent variables. Reference already has been made to the general outcome of the self-concept research in the context of evaluating Rogers' self theory: the self is componential and can be situationally determined.

Prescriptive Aspects of Humanistic Experimentation

The humanistic approach has affected psychological research at a prescriptive level more than it has at a descriptive level: It specifies the characteristics of ideal or relevant research without necessarily carrying out such research. Four prescriptive aspects of humanistic experimentation are readily isolable, the first one of which merely constitutes a review in this context.

1. Research projects should be chosen strictly in terms of their relevance for revealing the nature of man as a psychological entity, not on the basis of methodological convenience or acceptability.

2. Animal subjects should not be used to study the psychological nature of man. The rationale underlying this prescription is obvious. Man constitutes a unique form of life in at least two respects. Initially, even in cases where the same psychological process is common to both the man and animal (e.g., conditioning, object recognition, etc.), there are qualitative, as well as quantitative, differences in them such that the experimental results generated by animal research are not generalizable to man. Second, the specific psychological aspects of man that are dear to the heart of the humanist (e.g., self-esteem, self-fulfillment, self-identity, creativity) either do not exist at the animal level or possess no significant analogues at the animal level.

3. The nature of man, or ultimate potential of man, can be revealed meaningfully only by studying healthy, wholesome individuals. Using more traditional terminology, psychology should focus on the normal personality, not the abnormal personality. Humanistic psychologists generally beg the question of how normal individuals can be identified operationally.

4. The nature of man is best resolved in the context of a developmental, life-cycle approach. There is a need to study the course of human life as a whole: Each person can be characterized in terms of a central developmental core. The notion of a central developmental core is analogous to that of Freud's psychodynamics: libido, id, ego, superego, psychosexual stages of development, and so forth. But humanists do not accept Freudian psychodynamics; and they treat the concept of a central developmental core as an open-ended one: The nature of a given organism's central developmental core is only discoverable through empirical investigation.

The fourth prescription is important because the humanist assumes the individual is in control of his/her own destiny: Significant experiential and behavioral changes in an individual over time are self-generated. It is this fourth humanistic prescription that has had the greatest effect on actual descriptive research. The past decade has seen a voluminous increase in developmentally oriented research on the human being. This research is being performed in the context of so-called life-span psychology, which is detailed in the next chapter as an aspect of dialectical psychology.

Historical Legacy; Contemporary Significance

As a contemporary conceptual approach to psychology, the nature and content of humanistic psychology are still evolving. We shall use the legacy/significance dimension as a means of updating the current status of humanistic psychology, primarily with respect to (1) its institutional aspects, (2) Rogers' current concerns, (3) the recent appearance of Joseph Rychlak's brand of rigorous humanism, and (4) the classification of George Kelly's personal construct theory as a form of humanistic psychology.

Institutional Aspects

The (American) Association for Humanistic Psychology was

founded in 1962 with James F. T. Bugental as its first president. This organization evolved into Division 32 of the American Psychological Association: the Division of Humanistic Psychology. Division 32 was formally sanctioned in 1970 and officially set up in 1971. The *Journal of Humanistic Psychology* was established in 1961. It switched from biannual publication to quarterly publication in 1973. The essential thrust of the journal has changed over the years from an initial focus on neo-Freudian psychology and personality to a current stress on humanistic therapy, encounter groups, interpersonal relationships, and the like. Humanistic psychology has not made substantial inroads in the curricula of either undergraduate or graduate psychology departments; however, at least one humanistically/phenomenologically oriented graduate psychology program does exist—at Duquesne University in Pittsburgh, Pa.

Carl Rogers' Current Concerns

Since the foremost living humanistic psychologist is Carl Rogers, it would be instructive to trace briefly the change in his concerns over the past two decades. In the 1950s, we would have said that Rogers was the founder of client-centered therapy; currently we say that he was the creator of the person-centered approach. This change in labeling does not represent any alteration in Rogers' fundamental beliefs and precepts; it merely represents an expansion of his interests. Rogers now is more actively involved with group therapy and encounter or sensitivity training groups than he is with his original form of one-on-one nondirective therapy. Rogers also has sought to apply his phenomenological, nondirective approach to the overriding problems of society: education, industrial organization, international relations, development of the Third World, and so forth. In general, he argues that these problems can be solved by taking an essentially humanistic, person-oriented approach. For instance, Rogers is critical of traditional education with its emphasis on (1) teacher–student (dominance–submission) relationships, (2) prepackaged, spoon-fed information, and (3) impersonal and arbitrary grading criteria. The application of Rogerian principles to education would make (1) students and teachers coequal sources of truth, (2) learning self-generated and automatically relevant, and (3) evaluation implicit in terms of self-stated goals and criteria. In effect, Rogers has become a social philosopher in his final years, as is true of Skinner in the context of his radical behaviorism: Whereas Rogers once limited the term facilitator to the therapist in client-centered therapy, he now applies the term to psychological change agents in group therapy, educational settings, organizational groups, and the like.

Joseph Rychlak's Rigorous Humanism

Rychlak is a knowledgeable and scholarly commentator on the philosophical/conceptual background and current status of the myriad systems of personality and psychotherapy comprising contemporary applied/professional psychology. He recently announced his own brand of humanism in a book entitled *The Psychology of Rigorous Humanism* (1977). His notion of rigorous humanism is multifaceted; however, it places great stress on the description of human behavior in terms of formal and final causes. What Rychlak essentially means by a rigorous humanism is a teleological resolution of man's nature and actions. What makes his approach unique is that it involves more than just idealistic preaching and ritualistic criticism of behaviorism and psychoanalysis. Rychlak presents a thoroughly reasoned, conceptually oriented, methodologically sound humanistic system. It combines the ideology and goals of a phenomenologically oriented psychologist with the methodological and conceptual vigor of a hardcore behaviorist.

George Kelly's Personal Construct Theory

Kelly's personal construct theory was referred to briefly in Chapter 8 as a cognitive approach to personality; it could just as easily be construed as a system of humanistic psychology. Kelly's approach devolved from his experience as a counselor of college students and it possesses two distinctive aspects.

1. Kelly's system is phenomenological, but a cognitively oriented one. Each individual is assumed to construct his/her own conception of reality, physicalized in terms of a set of dichotomously valued personal constructs. The basic content of phenomenal experience is thought, not feelings, emotion, or affect. In Kelly's system, the affective aspects of experience are merely derivative: They arise when the organism's personal construct system breaks down, that is, no longer successfully resolves reality.
2. Kelly views psychology as a metadiscipline; that is, it possesses no content in and of itself. The task of a psychologist is to study what other people (essentially nonpsychologists) think the basic

psychological processes, laws, and mechanism are. In effect, the discipline of psychology exists at the meta-level, focusing on all the extant versions of psychology held by people. Thus Kellian psychology is inherently pragmatic and offers the potentiality of being the most integrative humanistic system ever devised.

Bibliography

Maslow, A.H. *Motivation and Personality*. New York: Harper & Row, 1954, 1970.

Maslow, A.H. *Toward a Psychology of Being*. Princeton, N.J.: Van Nostrand, 1962, 1968.

Maslow, A.H. *Religions, Values, and Peak-Experiences*. Columbus, Ohio: Ohio State Press, 1964.

Maslow, A.H. *Eupsychian Management: A Journal*. Homewood, Ill.: Irwin-Dorsey, 1965.

Maslow, A.H. *The Psychology of Science*. New York: Harper & Row, 1966.

Maslow, A.H. *The Farther Reaches of Human Nature*. New York: Viking, 1971.

Rogers, C.R. *The Clinical Treatment of the Problem Child*. Boston: Houghton Mifflin, 1939.

Rogers, C.R. *Counseling and Psychotherapy*. Boston: Houghton Mifflin, 1942.

Rogers, C.R. *Client-Centered Therapy*. Boston: Houghton Mifflin, 1951.

Rogers, C.R. *On Becoming a Person*. Boston: Houghton Mifflin, 1961.

Rogers, C.R. (Ed.). *The Therapeutic Relationship and Its Impact: A Study of Psychotherapy with Schizophrenics*. Madison, Wis.: University of Wisconsin Press, 1967.

Rogers, C.R. *Freedom to Learn*. Columbus, Ohio: Merrill, 1969.

Rogers, C.R. *Becoming Partners*. New York: Delacorte, 1972.

Rogers, C.R., and Dymond, R.F. (Eds.). *Psychotherapy and Personality Change: Coordinated Studies in the Client-Centered Approach*. Chicago: University of Chicago Press, 1954.

Rychlak, J. *The Psychology of Rigorous Humanism*. New York: Wiley Interscience, 1977.

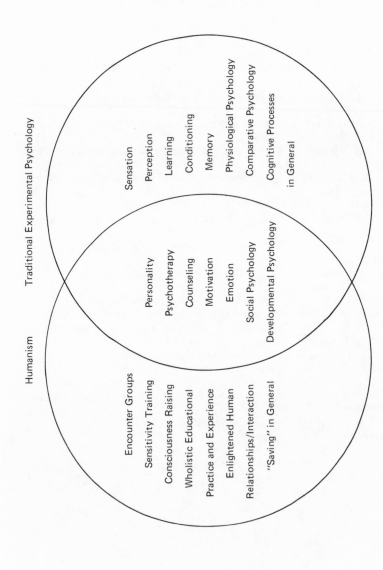

Humanism   Traditional Experimental Psychology

Sensation
Perception
Learning
Conditioning
Memory
Physiological Psychology
Comparative Psychology
Cognitive Processes
in General

Personality
Psychotherapy
Counseling
Motivation
Emotion
Social Psychology
Developmental Psychology

Encounter Groups
Sensitivity Training
Consciousness Raising
Wholistic Educational
Practice and Experience
Enlightened Human
Relationships/Interaction
"Saving" in General

Figure 10-1: The Nature And Extent Of The Overlap Between Humanism And Traditional Experimental Psychology

11

Dialectical
Psychology

[See page 302 for Figure 11-1
A Representation of the Input Required for the Ideal
Dialectical Developmental Research Design or Methodology.]

Introduction

Dialectical psychology represents an explicit attempt to bridge
the gap that exists between objectively oriented and subjectively oriented psychological systems. Specifically, dialectical psychology is
both a reaction to and an outgrowth of behaviorism and humanism;
but it is more than just a synthesis of these two inputs. The dialectical
approach constitutes an emergent paradigm, whose basic nature can
be illustrated by reference to behaviorism and humanism, but is not
reducible to a linear combination of behavioristic and humanistic elements.

One of the primary tenets of dialectical psychology already has
been mentioned in Chapter 1: the transactional relationship existing
between the subject and experimenter in any psychological research
endeavor. Dialectical psychology assumes that the transaction between a subject and experimenter constitutes an irreducible whole or
unit of analysis, such that both the subject and experimenter mutually
change and influence each other. The nature of one cannot be understood without the other; knowledge (objective truth) must be stated

in terms of both parties to the transaction. Whereas behaviorism is the psychology of the standard, statistical subject and humanism is the psychology of the individual, unique subject, the dialectical approach is the psychology of both the subject and experimenter in an emergent relationship.

The behaviorist explicitly assumes that the environment changes the organism and is only peripherally committed to the fact that the organism affects the environment. The humanist explicitly assumes that the organism changes the environment and is only peripherally committed to the fact that the environment affects the organism. Dialectical psychology explicitly focuses on both of these influences concurrently, such that bidirectional environmental–organismic interaction constitutes the only epistemologically valid object of concern.

Dialectical psychology attempts to overcome the artificial separation that behaviorism and humanism introduce between (1) the environment and the organism, (2) the experimenter and the subject, (3) the subject and object (i.e., psychological processes), and (4) behavior and conscious experience.

Although many conceptual approaches to psychology are implicitly dialectical in nature—for example, Jacob Kantor's interbehaviorism, Sergey Rubinstein's (Rubinshteyn) double interaction theory, and Soviet/Marxist dialectical materialist psychology in general—dialectical psychology began as a self-conscious system in America in the early 1970s under the intellectual tutelage and public relations guidance of Klaus F. Riegel, a native German who eventually became associated with the University of Michigan. Since the American version of dialectical psychology is so new and so identified with Riegelian thought, this chapter amounts to an exposition of Riegelian psychology—in the same sense that contemporary radical behaviorism can be characterized as Skinnerian psychology. Riegel died prematurely at the age of 52 in 1977 (his two primary expositional texts were published posthumously), so his system constitutes a fairly fixed and stabilized endeavor, conveniently admissible to conceptual analysis.

In the remainder of this introductory section, we (1) focus on Riegel's specific content criticisms of traditional psychology (i.e., mechanistic behaviorism and mentalistic humanism or phenomenology) and (2) present an initial overview of dialectical psychology.

Riegel's Criticisms of Traditional Psychology

Riegel has four nonmutually exclusive criticisms of behaviorism and humanism.

1. The first criticism basically is semantic in nature; it amounts to a difference of opinion as to what should constitute the preferred object of analysis. Traditional psychology focused on stability, balance, equilibrium, or steady states as figure and flow, change, or transition as ground. States of balance, attainment, and satisfaction stand out as figure against a background of flux and change. Riegel prefers to focus on change and transition as figure and various kinds of end states as ground: Change stands out as figure against a background of constancy and stability.

The hallmark of dialectical psychology is change. The human is a changing being (à la humanism) in a changing world (à la behaviorism). Organismic change and environmental change are viewed as concurrent and mutually interdependent events. Riegel admits that the attainment of some end state constitutes a legitimate psychological goal for the organism, but no such attainment is ever permanent. Riegel's reversal of the traditional figure–ground focus leads to a reformulation of what constitutes the critical problems for psychology, as detailed in the second criticism.

2. By focusing on end states, traditional psychology concentrated on conflict resolution, problem solution, organismic adaptation, drive reduction, goal attainment, and the like. Riegel's emphasis on change makes conflict instigation, problem origination, organismic arousal, drive induction, goal postulation, and so forth the critical psychological entities. Dialectical psychology is concerned with how and why relevant psychological phenomena arise, instead of how and why they terminate.

Riegel's initial two criticisms merely amount to value judgments on his part: It is arbitrary whether the onset or termination of a given psychological phenomenon should constitute the preferred focus of psychological analysis. In an absolute sense, a concern for both is necessary. This is true even if it is conceived that onsets are implicit in terminations or that terminations are implicit in onsets.

3. Correlative with its emphasis on end states, traditional psychology focuses on various structural entities, such as personality traits and mental abilities, as the basic mechanisms of psychological change. Riegel regards these structural entities as needlessly abstract, statistical entities that have no relevance to the day-to-day behavior

of the typical person: They possess no authenticity for the individual organism. Riegel prefers to account for psychological change through the dynamic process of an environmental–organismic interaction, the consequences of which are immediately known by the organism: They do possess authenticity.

4. Traditional psychology treats the individual human being as a fictitious point in a developmental-historical vacuum. Traditional psychology, especially behaviorism, studies behavior in a framework devoid of any developmental or cultural, social factors. Behaviorism removes the organism from its developmental sequence and from the cultural, social matrix in which it exists. While traditional developmental psychology, as exemplified by Piaget, does focus on the basic developmental sequence of the organism, it does not take cognizance of the general historical cultural and social milieu that affects the organism. Riegel refuses to divorce the organism from its individual developmental sequence and its historical cultural matrix: The individual is a point in some developmental and cultural space and only can be studied meaningfully as such. The human being is a part of a comprehensive dialectical process involving individual developmental and historical cultural changes.

In the context of the third and fourth criticisms, Riegel particularly is critical of Piaget's theory of cognitive development, which stresses an absolutistic cognitive developmental sequence, composed of fixed, structural entities that make no reference to social or cultural environmental factors. The Piagetian cognitive developmental sequence is directed toward an end goal of contradiction recognition and resolution in adulthood or at cognitive maturity. For Riegel, thought is dialectical in nature and inherently involves contradictions, even at the adult level: Attainment of mature, adult cognitive processes is evidence by the ability to accept contradictions. Since Piaget's developmental sequence moves away from contradiction in thought, Riegel believes that it results in an alienation of thought: Piaget's processes are alienated from the actual state of affairs with respect to the individual organism.

Initial Overview of Dialectical Psychology

Riegel's system basically is a developmental psychology, in the same sense that the Gestalt approach is a perceptual psychology and the behavioristic orientation is a learning psychology. The only way that Riegel can physicalize a holistic/totalistic conception of man is at the developmental level of analysis: Man must be viewed as a developmental entity. Riegel's identification of the psychological universe with the dialectical relationship existing between the organism and the environment makes *change over time* the natural psychological phenomenon of interest: Developmental psychology, by definition, studies change over time.

Although the dialectical approach can be characterized as a developmental one, it differs from traditional developmental psychology. In the traditional approach to development, change over time is output or a dependent variable (i.e., a property of response measures) and usually is physicalized in terms of some abstract, statistically defined subject. The voluminous data generated in the context of the traditional approach sum over various stimulus situations and contingencies and are expressed in a static manner in terms of norms or prototypical event sequences.

The dialectical approach treats changes over time as both an independent variable and a dependent variable. Dialectical psychology does this by focusing on the individual organism itself, much in the manner of the humanistic approach. The individual organism is viewed both (1) as a repository of some basic internal psychological processes and (2) as a locus of the effect of external environmental variables. The internal processes and environmental variables continuously interact with and change each other, so that both the organism and the environment continuously change. Riegel applies the dialectical developmental model to both short-term, virtual momentary changes and long-term changes characteristic of the traditional approach.

Dialectical psychology primarily is a structural, scripting, or descriptive system, as opposed to a dynamic or process-oriented system. The presumed inviolability of the dialectical relationship existing between the organism and the environment places man on a combined developmental–cultural map with an explicit coordinate system, even though the particular coordinate readings that describe where the man is currently located are changing constantly. As a descriptive system, dialectical psychology is reminiscent of Skinner's radical behaviorism, but it extends the domain of psychology tenfold in all directions.

Dialectical psychology is only superficially dynamic or process-oriented. Riegel introduces no new psychological processes or mechanisms that are not implicit in prior systems of psychology. Dialectical psychology does not involve any new or sophisticated explanatory and/or predictive devices or techniques. It is not a technical or operational advance over traditional psychology. It merely makes both organismic behavior and personalistic conscious experience irremovable components of a larger, more complex, emergent, dialectically organized, structural system.

The basic thrust of Riegel's system exists at the methodological level, not at a substantive content level. The consequences of the dialectical emphasis on the individual developmental sequence and the historical cultural matrix primarily exist at the methodological level: Riegel's system makes ecological validity the primary evaluative aspect of any research program. Ecological validity is simply another term for external validity: unless experimental data reflect the natural state of man, they are useless and irrelevant. Recall that, for Riegel, the natural state of man is that of a point in a combined developmental and cultural space. The dialectical stress on ecological validity is reminiscent of that of humanistic psychology, and consequently the basic thrust of Riegel's system is prescriptive in nature.

Object of Study; Basic Subject Matter

Initial Description

Stripped of some of its more metaphysical trappings, dialectical psychology's object of study can be seen to be quite conventional and relatable to the basic foci of both behaviorism and humanism. Dialectical psychology studies the *real* or *concrete* human being: the individual organism and its thoughts, ideas, and activities (especially those that the individual deems important) in a historical, cultural, developmental framework. What the dialectical psychologist essentially means by the real or concrete human being is a dialectically determined, self-aware, reacting organism whose basic problems, concerns, challenges, aspirations, and hopes identify and exhaust the domain of immanent psychological reality. The notion of the real or concrete human being by and large is synonymous with the everyday, cultural conception of man as a thinking, feeling, loving, doing being.

Dialectical psychology uses the prototypical independent variable-dependent variable relationship characteristic of experimental psychology in such a way as to combine the criterial elements of behaviorism and humanism. The dependent variable is behavior in the behavioristic sense of the term; the independent variable is some subjective, personalistic construct that possesses meaning and ecological validity (authenticity) for the organism, that is, some aspect of the conscious experience of the organism in the humanistic, phenomenological sense of the term. Both the behavioral and experiential aspects of the organism are interpreted in a combined individual developmental and cultural historical framework.

The basic content of Riegel's dialectical system will be abstracted in terms of its (1) conception of dialectics, (2) focus on the dialogue as the prototypical dialectical situation, (3) specific areas of concern, (4) approach to time, (5) primary physical realization as a life-span developmental psychology, and (6) use of analogy.

Dialectics

The notion of dialectics is the fundamental analytical entity of Riegelian thought. It is a partial corruption of the notion of dialectical as it appears in Hegelian and Marxist philosophy. The term is a descriptive one, specifying the structure of the combined individual developmental–historical cultural space in which the individual organism is embedded, and serves as the focal point for resolving organismic development and change. For Riegel, any and every valid psychological event is dialectical in nature: It involves some kind of mutually efficacious interaction between two or more subevents. Riegel distinguishes between two types of dialectically induced changes: long term, developmental, or structural; and short term, situational, or episodic.

DEVELOPMENTAL CHANGES: FOUR DIALECTICAL DIMENSIONS OR PROGRESSIONS

Long-term dialectical changes overlap with the kinds of changes studied by traditional developmental psychologists: maturation, socialization, cognitive and emotional development, and so on. In Riegel's approach to development, the organism is assumed to be characterized by four dialectical dimensions or progressions, which both extend through and change over time: (1) inner biological, (2) individual psychological, (3) cultural sociological, and (4) outer physical. At any given moment, the organism's behavior and experience are determined by events occurring at all four levels; at any given moment, the organism also is affecting the events occurring at all four levels.

The four dialectical dimensions are classificatory in function and serve as convenient labels for categorizing events that also are of concern for traditional psychology: The content of the four dimensions is not new. Physiological psychology focuses on inner biological events; humanism and certain forms of behaviorism focus on individual psychological events; social psychology and sociology focus on cultural sociological events; and descriptive behaviorism focuses on outer physical events. The novel aspect of Riegelian psychology is its concurrent use of all four dimensions—these four kinds of events establish and exhaust the relevant psychological universe for Riegel.

When the four dimensions are viewed as progressions (i.e., distinct sequences of events) extending through time, they serve as the basis for organismic development and change. If a synchronous relationship exists among the four progressions at any moment, an organism is in a developmental steady state or at a developmental plateau. When this synchronous relationship breaks down, because at least one of the progressions diverges, a crisis develops, leading to the possibility of developmental change on the part of the organism. For instance, the onset of an incurable disease (inner biological), a devastating fight with one's mate (individual psychological), job loss during an economic depression (cultural sociological), or an earthquake (outer physical) can disrupt the coordination of the four progressions, cause a crisis, and establish the necessity for a fundamental change in the organism.

SITUATIONAL CHANGES: DIALOGUES

A short-term dialectical change is the Riegelian analogue for those behavioral, experiential alterations that occur in a one-shot laboratory study or a temporary social interaction situation. They involve situationally determined learned changes, perceptual changes, cognitive changes, etc., and are traditionally studied by learning, perceptual, social psychologists, etc. Unlike the traditional psychologist, Riegel does not account for these kinds of changes in terms of a specific learning, perceptual, or social influence theory, but rather in terms of dialectical interaction between the subject and experimenter in an experiment or between the members of a social group. The prototypical situation for studying situational dialectical changes is the dialogue, which is detailed later in this section.

Long-term dialectical changes and short-term dialectical changes can be interrelated in the sense that a given long-term change can be the result of a series of related short-term changes; for instance, the long-term developmental relationship existing between a mother and child is determined by the many individual episodic interactions (dialogues) between them.

OTHER TYPES OF DIALECTICS

Dialectic interactions (i.e., mutual dialectical influences) can be characterized on other dimensions in addition to the temporal one of short term and long term. Riegel makes a distinction between primitive and scientific dialectics and between inner and outer dialectics.

Primitive dialectics are characteristic of the infant or child. For instance, the kind of (dialectical) social interaction that occurs between a mother and her newborn infant, as in feeding, is primitive in nature. Scientific dialectics are characteristic of adulthood and can involve thinking, formal reasoning and debate, or intellectual activity in general.

Inner dialectics refer to events that occur strictly inside the organism: cognition, thought, memory. Outer dialectics involve an interaction between the organism and the environment, as occurs in a social situation, conversation, and any situation in general in which speech is used.

Thinking (debating with oneself) involves inner scientific dialectics; a mother feeding her child subsumes outer primitive dialectics. A telephone conversation between two adults entails outer scientific dialectics, and a child recalling the vivid taste of yesterday's ice cream cone involves inner primitive dialectics.

Dialogues

The term dialogue historically is applied to any social interaction situation in which at least two persons (e.g., *A* and *B*) speak in an alternating fashion, such that the content of the *N*th verbal statement uttered by *A* or *B* is related to the content of at least the immediately prior statements uttered by both *A* and *B*. In a dialogue, two people engage in an extended conversation with each other, the constituent verbal expressions of which are emergent in nature: They derive from the mutual interaction between the two talkers. A dialogue can be contrasted with a monologue or narrative emitted by a single speaker or with a collective monologue, in which two contiguous people speak concurrently or alternately, but in a completely independent manner.

Riegel uses the notion of a dialogue as the prototypical reference situation for his system because (1) the dynamics subsumed by a dialogue inherently are dialectical in nature and (2) the individual speakers (*A* and *B*) engaged in a dialogue constitute both subjects and objects concurrently. With respect to (1), *any* sequence of three successive statements emitted by the members of the dialogue (e.g., *A* - *B* - *A* or *B* - *A* - *B*) exists in a thesis–antithesis–synthesis relationship. The first statement by *A* or *B* expresses a thesis; the response by the other member constitutes an antithesis; and the rejoinder by *B* or *A* amounts to a synthesis. With respect to (2), each speaker *A* or *B* influences the other and is influenced by the other such that they constitute both change agents and changed objects concurrently.

Riegel extends the concept of a dialogue to cover virtually any and every significant psychological event. The individual *A* and *B* responses in a dialogue need not be verbal events. Any alternating sequence of responses emitted by organisms *A* and *B* that are mutually contingent on each other constitute a dialogue.

Riegel's prototypical example of a dialogue is the kind of interaction that occurs between mother and child. The nature of this dialogue evolves from one of mutual biological interaction (feeding, stroking, etc.), through primitive verbal exchanges (social, educational, disciplinary, etc.), to more sophisticated symbolic exchanges wherein the mother is the intermediary element between the surrounding culture/society and the child.

Riegel conceptualizes the psychotherapeutic situation as a dialogue, in which both diagnosis and therapeutic effects occur concurrently such that both the patient and the therapist are constantly changing. He can absorb Rogerian client-centered therapy as a kind of dialogue because he assumes that the therapist's repetitional emotional rejoinder (antithesis) sets up an internal dialogue in the patient.

Riegel even considers verbal monologues to be dialogic in nature, because either they explicitly involve self-stated questions and answers or they establish an internal dialogue in the monologist. The notion of an internal dialogue allows Riegel to apply the concept of a dialogue to obvious null cases, that is, situations that cannot conveniently be analyzed in terms of an externally resolvable dialogue. Riegel's analysis of explicit verbal dialogues is reminiscent of Skinner's analysis of verbal behavior (see Chapter 7): The verbal interaction between a mother and child can involve prompting, echoing, expansion, modeling, summons or request, and so forth.

Specific Areas of Concern

The specific content focus of dialectical psychology derives from two interrelated themes: (1) It is an outgrowth of both behaviorism and humanism. (2) It essentially views man as a social and/or cultural creature subject to various short-term and long-term dialectically induced changes.

1. As an outgrowth of behaviorism, Riegelian thought accepts the basic psychological processes, such as perception and learning,

as input: Riegel is not interested in perception and learning as dynamic processes (he has no theory of perception or learning). They
merely operate as givens in his system, and he focuses on their consequences as they occur in a combined individual physiological–cultural
historical framework. Recall that Riegel construes the short-term psychological changes that are of interest to traditional psychology in
terms of dialogic interaction. As an outgrowth of humanism, dialectical psychology focuses on the development of the individual organism, but developmental changes are not regarded as the result of
innate motivational constructs or self-generated activity occurring in
an environmental vacuum. Rather, developmental changes are caused
by the interaction of the four broad classes of dialectical progressions.

2. Dialectical psychology focuses on those specific content areas
of psychology that are easily resolvable in terms of a dialectical orientation or that serve as critical components of the dialectical process.
It already has been established that dialectical psychology primarily
is a developmental psychology: It focuses on parent–child interaction,
child   development,   and   adult   life   crises.   Riegel's
dialectical/developmental orientation makes cognition a specific focus
of concern: Thinking and problem solving are regarded as dialectical
in nature. Memorial reconstruction is also dialectical. Language and/or
speech (and language development) is of critical interest because it
is the primary medium of dialogic exchange and the symbolic basis
of culture and society.

Time

The ultimate nature of time is a philosophical question. Is time
an absolute or relative property of the universe? Is time a primitive
or derived entity? Is time causative or merely epiphenomenal? Does
the passage of time cause observed changes, or is the passage of time
merely inferred from observed changes?

Behaviorism, as a component of the classical approach to science,
has an essentially spatial orientation to psychological reality in which
the notion of time is derivative and secondary. Behaviorism divorces
the individual organism from its temporal-historical context and focuses on overt activity in the context of an eternal present. It takes
an essentially "freeze-time" or "stop-action" approach to temporal
events. Change in behavior is inferred from empirical samplings taken
at two or more different *instances* in time.

Dialectical psychology takes a different approach to time. Since
dialectics focuses on change in a historical–developmental context,

time (i.e., the temporal succession of different spatial events) constitutes a critical input variable. Time is given, primitive, efficacious. Valid psychological events (i.e., changes) occur in and over time, not in an eternal present. For Riegel, time and change are coextensive concepts. Absolute, objective time, as measured by some external criterion, exists. Relative, subjective time, as measured by some internal organismic criterion, exists. The goal of dialectical psychology is to unite these two kinds of time into a concept of dialectical time, in which the measurement and experience of time is occasioned by the constant interplay among the four critical developmental progressions mentioned previously.

Life-Span Developmental Psychology

The dialectical approach, construed as a life-span developmental one, has empirical and theoretical consequences for traditional developmental psychology.

At an empirical level, dialectical psychology makes the entire life span of the individual from birth to death an object of research interest. Traditional developmental psychologists, focusing on the so-called pure processes of biological maturation and social learning (socialization), and their possible interaction (i.e., critical periods), concentrated on child and adolescent development: Further or significant development was assumed not to occur in adulthood. Dialectical psychology, by focusing on the continuous progression of four interrelated dialectical dimensions, makes individual organismic development a never-ending process. Most of the crises occasioned by the cultural sociological dimension occur in adulthood: Dialectics makes divorce, suspension or elimination of parenting, career stagnation, job loss, retirement, and so on natural objects of research interest for a developmental psychologist. Life-span developmental psychology, as a research endeavor, connotes a psychology of aging and adult development.

At a theoretical level, dialectical psychology represents a fusion of the two classic conceptual approaches to psychological development: (1) the gradual, incremental, accumulative, continuity view and (2) the sudden, discrete, all-or-none, discontinuity view. The first view treats learning or the environment as the primary source of developmental change: As the individual accumulates sufficient experience(s), quantitative changes in development occur. The second view emphasizes maturation or the evolution of biologically based capacities as the primary source of developmental change: As the individual progresses from one stage to another, qualitative changes in development occur. The continuity view of development is characteristic of the descriptive behavioral approach in which psychological progress is evaluated and measured in terms of the breadth and depth of an organism's past reinforcement history. The discontinuity view of development is more characteristic of humanism and phenomenology, Gestalt psychology, Piaget's genetic epistemology, and depth psychology, in which psychological progress is equated with the attainment of a specific ability.

Dialectical psychology references both the organism and the environment: Psychological development is resolved in terms of the relationship(s) existing among four dialectical dimensions extending through time. Coordinated, synchronized relationships yield an organism at plateau in a steady state (analogous to a given level of accumulation in the continuity approach). Uncoordinated, unsynchronized relationships induce a crisis and set the occasion for an appreciable, or qualitative, developmental change (analogous to a stage transition in the discontinuity approach).

Use of Analogy

Since dialectical psychology presumes that (1) the organism and environment continuously interact and change the other, (2) the individual developmental sequence and cultural milieu mutually influence the other, and (3) the subject and experimenter constitute an emergent relational entity in a research study, it is very difficult to express the nature of psychological reality in standard, static, terminological categories. Standard psychological description basically is timeless or ahistorical in nature: It uses the eternal psychological present. Riegel's psychological reality is one of continuous interaction and change at many levels concurrently. How can this state of affairs be expressed conveniently? Riegel's solution is to use analogy. The nature of the current psychological situation or phenomenon is expressed in an *as if* manner. The use of analogy transforms the dialectical, time-based concepts to static, timeless concepts. To appreciate the significance of this transformation, it must be remembered that the static descriptive categories of traditional psychology—sensation, image, Gestalt, habit, drive, stimulus, response, reinforcement, the self—are supposed to represent reality directly. An analogical transformation can represent reality only indirectly.

Riegel's most extensive transformation relates to his use of (1) Marxist economics and (2) the monetary system as an analogue for language. Speech is treated as a good/commodity produced by labor. These goods (i.e., sentences) can operate as capital and serve as the basis of further production. Riegel differentiates among three evolutionally generated and progressively more complex monetary systems: (1) barter, (2) coinage, and (3) debenture (paper money, notes, checks, etc.). Protolanguage (initial, germinal language) corresponds to a barter system. Token language (stated in terms of the linguist's basic analytical units of phoneme, morpheme, etc.) corresponds to the coinage system. Transactional language (stated in terms of Riegelian dialectics) corresponds to the debenture system. [Riegel also extends the three types of monetary systems to cover Piaget's three stages of cognitive development: (1) sensorimotor activity, (2) concrete operations, and (3) formal operations.]

Riegel's account of the process of remembering involves the use of another analogy. A traditional, static account of memory has the subject sampling from some physical memory store and retrieving some fact, that is, a true representation of the actual erstwhile event. For Riegel, the process of remembering is a dialectical event that changes both the content of the retrieved entity and the nature of the organism. To represent this process, Riegel uses the notion of a sudarium, which he characterizes as a constructive interpretive device that imposes the organism's beliefs, intentions, goals, and values on the memorial material. In fact, Riegel makes no distinction between the act of remembering and the process of historical construction.

Riegel's analogue for the abstract dialectical process itself, especially its temporal aspects, is music—specifically the kind of music performed by a symphony orchestra. The concept of a dialogue performs double duty for Riegel: It not only entails a valid psychological phenomenon in its own right, but also serves as an analogue for any kind of emergent, mutually interdependent relationship between two people.

Method of Study; Permissible Methodology

Recall that the purpose of dialectical psychology is to study (1) short-term dialectical organismic changes and (2) long-term dialectical organismic changes in an ecologically valid fashion. An ecologically valid investigation of short-term changes must make provision for the emergent dialectical relationship existing between the subject and experimenter in a standard one-shot laboratory study; an ecologically valid investigation of long-term changes must be able to isolate the influences of both the individual organismic developmental sequence and the historical cultural milieu on the response measures generated by a multisession (multisampling) developmental study. Appropriate methodology for these two basic aims exist: (1) the dialogue for short-term dialectical changes, and (2) a combination cross-sectional, longitudinal, time-lag developmental research design for long-term dialectical changes.

At this point in the evolution of dialectical psychology, this methodology is more prescriptive than representative of the bulk of actual contemporary investigations. Since the notion of a dialogue and its applications has been analyzed already, we only need be concerned here with the methodology appropriate for investigating long-term, developmental changes.

The Combined Cross-Sectional, Longitudinal, Time-Lag Design

The ideal dialectical developmental methodology involves two temporal dimensions or progressions—individual–psychological (current age) and cultural–sociological (year of birth or generation membership)—and three possible developmental parameters: current age, generation membership, and time (year) of testing. These dimensions and parameters are represented in an illustrative experimental design presented in Figure 11–1 (pg. 302). The horizontal input dimension is the individual–psychological progression: The two ages of assumed relevance are 20 and 30. The vertical input dimension is the cultural–sociological progression: The two generations of assumed relevance were born in 1940 and 1950 respectively. The numbers occupying the four internal cells refer to the specific times (years) of testing required to physicalize the age and generation specifications: 1960, 1970, and 1980. This design setup permits three kinds of data comparisons:

1. Comparison along the negative diagonal (i.e., the 1970 cells), as occurs in the typical cross-sectional design.
2. Comparisons within the rows, as occur in the typical longitudinal design.
3. Comparisons within the columns, as occur in the typical time-lag design.

Most traditional developmental studies employ the cross-sectional design. A few employ the longitudinal design, but the time-lag design is foreign to traditional developmental psychologists. The relative popularity of these three designs is related to the time of measurement constrictions. Only in a cross-sectional design is all the psychological measurement done at the same essential point in time (i.e., one session); the other two designs require multiple measurement sessions. The multiple measurements in a longitudinal design are done on the same set of subjects, but this entails problems of sample-size truncation between the successive measuring occasions. The multiple measurements in a time-lag design are done on a different set of subjects, but the time lag between measurement occasions is an inconvenience.

To assess unambiguously the respective effects of the three possible developmental parameters—individual–developmental age differences, cultural–sociological generational differences, and historical time (of testing) differences—all three kinds of comparisons must be used. By representing the comparisons used in the cross-sectional, longitudinal, and time-lag designs by C, L, and T, respectively, the three types of developmental effects can be quantified by the following formulae:

$$\text{Age differences} = \tfrac{1}{2}(C - T + L) \tag{1}$$
$$\text{Generation differences} = \tfrac{1}{2}(T - L + C) \tag{2}$$
$$\text{Historical time (of testing) differences} = \tfrac{1}{2}(L - C + T) \tag{3}$$

The comparisons involved in the most popular cross-sectional design confound age differences and generation differences, as can be demonstrated by adding the first two equations. The longitudinal design confounds age differences and historical time differences (add the first and third equations). The time-lag design confounds generation differences and historical time differences (add the second and third equations).

It readily can be determined why the ideal dialectical developmental methodology is largely prescriptive. Even in the context of this simple example, it would take 20 years to accumulate all the relevant research data.

Origin; Specific Historical Antecedents

Dialectical psychology is a product of the 1970s. The major developments occurred at a series of annual conferences (1974 to 1978) organized by Klaus Riegel. Out of these conferences grew a so-called

Network for Dialectical Psychologists, which supports the *Dialectical Psychology Newsletter*. Because of Riegel's premature death, it remains to be seen whether dialectical psychology will develop the formal trappings of American Psychological Association divisional status and an official, commercially published journal.

Riegel's basic themes of (1) mutual interaction between the organism and the environment, (2) unity of consciousness and behavior, and (3) indistinguishability of the subject and experimenter with respect to role are not novel ideas in the history of psychology. Riegel merely codified these notions in the context of a cognitively oriented developmental psychology.

The fundamental tenets of Riegel's psychology are implicit in Hegelian/Marxist philosophy in general, and in Soviet Russian dialectical psychology in particular. Riegel's stress on the social nature of man and his promulgation of dialectical interaction and progression are culminations of these two classes of historical influences. What justifies Riegel's view of man and of the nature of his psychological development at a metaphysical level is the broad historical and intellectual tradition of dialectical philosophy.

The historical precursors of Riegelian thought will be abstracted in terms of (1) Hegel's dialectical idealism, (2) Marx's dialectical materialism, (3) Rubinstein's double interaction theory, and (4) an implicit American behavioristic antecedent, Kantor's interbehaviorism.

Hegel's Dialectical Idealism

Georg W. F. Hegel (1770–1831), a German philosopher, was briefly referred to in Chapter 10 as a component of the post-Kantian philosophical tradition that influenced humanistic psychology. The specific aspect of his idealistic philosophical system that is most relevant for dialectical psychology is his concept of dialectical reasoning, or the dialectical method. Hegelian dialectics can be interpreted as (1) laws of thought, (2) an explicit logic, (3) a metaphysical change process, or (4) the foundation of historical development. Regardless of its specific physical realization, Hegelian dialectics serves as the ultimate philosophical basis of Riegelian psychology.

Hegel denies the validity of one of the assumptions of traditional logic: the principle of identity or the law of contradiction (p and $\bar{p}$ both cannot be true: The conjunction $p \; \eta \; \bar{p}$ is false.). Riegelian psychology stresses contradiction as a fundamental property of the natural psychological state. The ability to recognize and accept contradiction is viewed by Riegel as one of the characteristics of adult cognition.

Riegelian psychology presumes the Hegelian account of change. Any event A suggests its opposite $\bar{A}$, and both in turn lead to an event B. Event A is usually referred to as a thesis; $\bar{A}$ is usually referred to as the antithesis; and B is usually called a synthesis. The thesis–antithesis–synthesis formulation amounts to a dialectical progression and change process. Recall that Riegel interprets the successive interrelated events (verbal or otherwise) that occur in a dialogue as constituting a thesis–antithesis–synthesis progression. Any and every event in the dialogue can be construed as any one of the three, contingent on where the specific dialogic unit of current interest is assumed to commence.

Marx's Dialectical Materialism

Karl Marx (1818–1873), a German-born social/political philosopher and revolutionary, absorbed the Hegelian dialectical doctrine, but removed it from Hegel's idealist metaphysical base, and expressed it at a material level. Whereas Hegel conceived of the dialectical development of a spiritual universe, Marx gave dialectical progression a material reality: The universe is solely matter in motion and dialectical progression. Dialectical materialism is an all-pervasive system with profound implications for political philosophy, economics, the philosophy of history, social/cultural development, the nature of man, and so on. Marx was a premier figure in nineteenth century intellectual and political history whose political and/or social philosophy became institutionalized in the context of the modern Russian socialist/communist state. We are concerned here only with the psychological implications of dialectical materialism: These serve as the metaphysical assumptions of contemporary Russian materialistic and/or dialectical psychology.

THE METAPHYSICAL ASSUMPTIONS OF RUSSIAN PSYCHOLOGY

The implications of Marxist philosophy for Russian psychology can be abstracted in terms of seven basic assumptions.

1. The universe (even psychological universe) consists solely of matter: The human being possesses both an inner material basis (e.g., biology) and an outer material basis (e.g., physical environment).
2. Motion is the mode of existence of all matter, even the human being: The human being's inner and outer material bases continually interact.
3. The notion of matter in motion underlies the historical con-

tinuity between and development of the different manifestations of matter: inanimate objects, animals, the human being. Man is continuous with the rest of nature.

4. The reciprocal influence of material things in motion necessarily involves contradictions that form the basis of the dialectical thesis–antithesis–synthesis paradigm and are manifested in historical–developmental processes. Man is to be explained in terms of a dialectical developmental process.

5. The thesis–antithesis–synthesis paradigm is both explanatory and predictive: It results in readily identifiable and qualitatively different stages along a given historical–developmental continuum. A Marxist presumes that the cumulative effect of many incremental quantitative changes is an eventual qualitative change: The human being develops in both a continuous and a discontinuous fashion.

6. All matter possesses the capacity to reflect (i.e., to mirror reality).

7. Consciousness is the highest form of matter in motion and is characteristic only of the human being: It is the highest state of reality reflection and is an attribute of man's higher nervous activity. Consciousness is merely epiphenomenal in nature and is a product of the dialectical processes inherent in man's social interaction, communal labor, and language: Human consciousness is of a social origin and nature.

RUSSIAN DIALECTICAL MATERIALIST PSYCHOLOGY

There is no one absolute form of Russian dialectical materialist psychology. Twentieth century Russian psychology is grossly divisible into three periods: (1) The different versions of objective psychology (see Chapter 6) dominated to approximately 1930. (2) So-called dialectical psychology, as promulgated by Sergey Rubinstein, flourished from 1930 to 1950. (3) A reconstituted version of Pavlov's objective psychology became the official state-approved psychology in 1950. Objective psychology is materialistic, but not necessarily dialectical. Rubinstein's approach is dialectical, but not necessarily or exclusively materialistic. The reconstituted Pavlovian system is compatible with dialectical materialism, but is not a logically necessary derivative of Marxist principles.

Rubinstein's Double-Interaction Dialectical Theory

Sergey Rubinstein (1889–1960) devised a dialectical system that fused materialism and idealism: It postulated a fundamental unity of consciousness and behavior. Rubinstein's system can be characterized in terms of three major principles:

1. A basic psychophysical unity exists between mind and matter, or the mental and physical: Both forms of substance interpenetrate each other. Mind and matter are merely different realizations of the same fundamental entity. This principle amounts to a double aspectism resolution of the mind–body issue.

2. The psychological aspects of the organism (especially consciousness) are of social origin: They derive from social interaction, communal labor, and language. The psychological aspects of the organism also change the external environment: The organism and environment exist in a dialectical relationship. Rubinstein's double-interaction dialectics involves that between the individual and society/culture and that between the inner (biological) and outer (physical) world.

3. Psychology should involve a unity of theory and practice, or of the subject and object. This translates into an interactionist, interventionist methodology, whereby the subject and the experimenter should be allowed mutually to influence and change each other.

Rubinstein eventually revised the first principle: As a result of the Pavlovization of Russian psychology in 1950, he devolved to a material monist (i.e., mind is derivative or epiphenomenal). His revised system is indistinguishable from Marx's dialectical materialism. Riegel's dialectical system merely is a logical/conceptual extension of Rubinstein's *original* conception of dialectics.

Kantor's Interbehaviorism

Jacob Kantor (1888–) is an American behaviorist who developed an overall system of psychology that is reminiscent of Riegelian dialectics. Kantor's system is more philosophical than actual: It is empirical, but has not served as an impetus to actual experimental research. Kantor has no formal concept of dialectical interaction; however, he does stress an explicit environmental × organismic interaction. Unlike the typical behaviorist, Kantor places equal stress on the stimulus and response such that they constitute an emergent entity: Behavior exists in space *and time* and should be analyzed in terms of segments that are related to functional stimulus events. The conceptual correspondence between Kantor's system and Riegel's dialectics is so pervasive that the former even includes the notion of implicit interactions, such as thinking, reasoning, and imagining, that involve invisible substitute stimuli: The concept of an implicit inter- action is analogous to that of an internal dialogue.

Chief Historical Figure: Klaus F. Riegel (1925–1977)

Klaus Riegel was born in Berlin, Germany, in 1925 and grew up there. Following World War II, he spent some time working as a mechanic and tool machine operator before returning to school to pursue his interests in physics and mathematics. He earned the M.A. degree at the University of Minnesota in 1955. His doctoral degree was earned in Germany: He received a Ph.D. in psychology from the University of Hamburg in 1958. Riegel studied under Curt Bondy, and his Ph.D. thesis was concerned with the intellectual abilities of the aged. Riegel then spent a year as a visiting scientist at the National Institute of Mental Health in Bethesda, Md., under the tutelage of James Birren. During this period, Klaus and his wife, Ruth, helped in the German standardization of the Wechsler intelligence test. They then used this test and various personality tests in a longitudinal study of cognitive changes in old age.

In 1959, Riegel joined the Department of Psychology at the Uni- versity of Michigan, where he ultimately became associated with the Psycholinguistics Program, the Institute of Gerontology, and the Cen- ter for Human Growth and Development. He was a fellow of both the Gerontological Society and the American Psychological Associa- tion. Riegel served on the executive committee of the International Society for the Study of Behavioral Development, as president of the Psychological and Social Sciences Section of the Gerontological So- ciety, and as editor of the journal *Human Development*. Riegel received the Robert W. Kleemeier Award from the Gerontological Society in 1976.

Riegel was a frequent contributor to the professional journals and multiauthored anthologies on human development (life-span psy- chology). He wrote or edited a number of texts, including *The Psy- chology of Development and History* (1976), *Psychology, Mon Amour: A Countertext* (1978), *Foundations of Dialectical Psychology* (1979), *Intelli- gence: Alternative Views of a Paradigm* (editor, 1973), *The Development of Dialectical Operations* (editor, 1975), *Structure and Transformation: Developmental and Historical Aspects* (coeditor with George Rosenwald, 1975), and *The Developing Individual in a Changing World* (coeditor with

John Meacham, 1976). His posthumous publications were finalized under the guidance of John Meacham, one of his former students.

Riegel was a multifaceted individual. He could be cutting, biting, and even abrasive in his writing, yet he profusely acknowledged discussions with and contributions from his colleagues and students. He loved to engage in debate or *dialogue* with his cohorts about the merits of dialectical psychology. Just as other founding psychologists seem to personify their respective systems (e.g., Skinner, Freud, Maslow), Riegel personified the notion of a dialogue and believed that dialogic interaction fostered psychological growth and change. He was beloved by his students and encouraged informal group activities outside of formal class meetings. It is impossible to classify Riegel as a specific kind of psychologist: His interests primarily were developmental, cognitive, and historical in nature, but he was not any one of these kinds of psychologists in the traditional sense of the terms. He was regarded as an eccentric by many of his contemporaries; but if his life is viewed according to the dictates of his own dialectical system, the specific point in developmental–cultural space that Riegel occupied should not be surprising.

Klaus Riegel died prematurely in 1977 at the height of his professional career and influence.

Characteristic Experimentation; Primary Research Areas

As a cognitively oriented developmental psychology, the primary research areas of dialectical psychology are obvious: (1) mother–child interaction, (2) language development, (3) adult personal and professional life crises, (4) memorial reconstruction, and (5) thinking/problem solving/cognitive operations. But this listing does not capture the unique flavor of dialectically inspired research. This can be presented only by analyzing how dialectical research differs from traditional behavioristic, humanistic, and developmental research.

Comparison with Traditional Research

Unlike behavioristic experimentation, dialectical research does not employ artificial laboratory conditions, involving elaborate manipulation of independent variables, with the ultimate aim of testing some theory or validating some esoteric psychological construct. Dialectical psychology focuses on ecologically given situations—that is, behavior occurring in the natural environment—with the ultimate aim of demonstrating that they can be resolved in the context of dialectical terminology and concepts. Dialectical psychology basically is descriptive in nature, attempting to relate behavior to short-term dialogic, interactional events, or long-term developmental and social factors.

Like humanism, dialectical psychology focuses on conscious experience, everyday life activities and affairs, psychological events that possess appreciable personal validity, the subjective world of the person, and the like. Unlike humanism, dialectical psychology gives a strictly social interpretation to subjectively important, personalistic events. One of Riegel's basic criticisms of traditional experimentation was that it is abstract and alienated from the true nature of the organism. By interpreting the personal experience of the organism in the context of a confluence of various cultural and developmental factors, Riegel believed, concrete, meaningful, ecologically valid truth is attained. The difference between humanistic and dialectical research really is more of a matter of degree than kind. Dialectical psychology treats conscious experience, but not in an existential vacuum.

Unlike traditional developmental psychology, dialectical psychology takes a holistic, dynamic approach to man. Dialectical research does not attempt to catalogue the attainment of various steady states, or to construct standard, prototypical, or ideal developmental sequences; it does not attempt to construct a statistical subject. Dialectical research focuses on organismic change *in vivo*, as it occurs naturally. Riegel's model of man is man continually changing and being changed.

Illustrative Research: Riegel's Study of Memorial Reconstruction

As an example of how a dialectically oriented psychologist approaches a traditional research problem, we can briefly describe Riegel's empirical investigation of memory (long-term retention), which consisted of four separate studies. In none of these studies were nonsense syllables or some other kind of artificially constructed verbal material used; nor was a definitive independent variable manipulated. In all the studies, an attempt was made to relate the recall of personally meaningful material to the subject's specific past life space and experience.

1. Twenty-six undergraduate psychology students (18 males and eight females), ranging in chronological age from 19 to 25, wrote down during a six-minute period the names of as many people as they could recall meeting over their lifetime. Absolute frequency of recall was plotted against 21 school (not chronological age) years, yielding a classic serial position curve: most of the people recalled were met either during the first year of life, or preschool year one (the primacy effect), or during the college years (the recency effect). Riegel interpreted the obtained curve in terms of the subject's increasing mobility with age and the increasing size of the potential set of new acquaintances with age. The order of recall of individual names was analyzed, revealing that parents were recalled 53.8 percent of the time during the first minute and only 19.3 percent of the time during the remaining five minutes. Substantial sex differences existed with respect to parental recall. Males recalled their parents 83.3 percent of the time and randomly gave the mother's or father's name first. Females recalled their parents only 50 percent of the time, with the mother's name always recalled first. A strong clustering effect in recall with respect to time was also noticed; 43.9 percent of the recalled names were adjacent to names of people met during the same year.

2. The experimental design used in the first study was extended to three different age groups: young (average age = 23.1); middle (average age = 50); and old (average age = 73.3). Twenty subjects from each age group wrote down as many names as they could recall during a ten-minute period. The young subjects exhibited the same basic serial position curve as generated in the first experiment: strong primacy and recency effects. The middle subjects showed no primacy effect and a moderate recency effect. The old subjects demonstrated neither a primacy nor recency effect: The recall was a flat straight-line function of time. Riegel interpreted the general pattern of the results in terms of psychological time, that is, how important successive time periods are for differently aged people.

3. The recall of names of important historical figures in the military, politics, and government was investigated. Three groups of 30 university students each (freshmen, seniors, and graduate students) wrote down the names of as many such historical figures as they could remember in a ten-minute period. Each of the three memory curves exhibited the same general pattern: strong recency effect and no primacy effect. The high and low points of the curves corresponded to periods of wars or military intervention and their absence respectively. Riegel went on to demonstrate that this war/military-related pattern of recall matched the amount of coverage accorded to these kinds of events in standard high school American history texts. In

effect, the probability of recall of a relevant historical figure is a function of degree of past exposure to the figure.

4. The recall of names of important historical figures in the arts (famous painters, musicians, and writers) was investigated. Two groups of 30 college seniors each wrote down the names of as many such historical figures as they could remember in a ten-minute period. The recall of famous painters and musicians was less influenced by war/military-related periods, but the pattern of recall for famous writers still corresponded to the two different kinds of historical periods. (Many famous politicians, government leaders, and military men are also writers.)

To demonstrate that Riegel did not have the same kinds of concerns that a traditional psychologist possesses in pursuing this type of memory research, it can be pointed out that (1) he was not disturbed by the fact that a middle-aged or very elderly subject might not be able to recall as much material in a ten-minute period as might a college-aged subject, and (2) he did not compare the absolute amounts recalled by the different age groups.

Historical Legacy; Contemporary Significance

It is still too early to make a definitive judgment with respect to the historical legacy of dialectical psychology. If Reigel had lived for another two decades to become a grand old man of psychology, like Skinner or Rogers, the probability is high that the dialectical orientation would have achieved full institutionalization. Granted that dialectical psychology already has received more than nominal acceptance by the psychological community, its overall prognosis is not good, for a number of reasons.

1. The philosophical basis of dialectical psychology is foreign to America—it is a Marxist psychology, with all of its negative connotations. The specific dialectical system of which dialectical psychology is a direct, logical extension, Rubinstein's double-interaction theory, is virtually unknown in America; Rubinstein's books have not been translated into English.

2. Riegel's basic tenets have some legitimate methodological consequences, especially in the context of developmental psychology, but they do not do much to improve the conceptual status of psychology. Both the behaviorist and the humanist pay lip service to the notions of continual organismic change and mutual interaction be-

tween the organism and the environment, but Riegel's reversal of the usual figure (steady state)–ground (flux) relationship in psychology is very difficult to absorb at a theoretical level and has very little practical application value. Riegel reveres contradication and ambiguity. It is contradictory that steady state–flux can be figure–ground and ground–figure simultaneously, yet Riegel insists on resolving this particular contradiction, while striving to maintain the legitimacy of other contradictions.

3. The positive features associated with dialectical psychology, such as the emphasis on life-span developmental psychology and ecologically valid research, are not indigenous to dialectical psychology: They are not contingent on the existence of Riegel's system or the philosophical presuppositions of Riegelian thought. Life-span development is an implicit focus of humanistic psychology and is not dependent on dialectical psychology at a methodological level. Ecological validity is a fundamental tenet of humanistic psychology and of applied behaviorism; it also constitutes a new wave in (experimental) social psychology. A good case could be made for the view that interest in life-span development and ecologically valid research evolved independently of the emergence of dialectical psychology.

4. Riegel's modeling of short-term dynamic or situational changes in terms of dialogic interaction is strictly descriptive in nature and is not an improvement over the sophisticated mathematical and cognitive information-processing models that are currently used to explain/predict behavior in perception and learning experiments. The use of dialogue as analogue is interesting, but conceptually vacuous once one goes beyond the structural description of mother–child verbal dialogues or adult–adult intellectual debates. The notion of an internal dialogue is an open-ended and circular catchall that allows the dialogue analogy to be extended indiscriminately to situations that cannot be modeled after external dialogues.

5. Riegel's notion of concrete, unalienated man as a point in a combined individual developmental–historical cultural space is capricious. It has no justification beyond Hegelian/Marxist dialectics. Riegel's goal of putting man in social, cultural, historical perspective is certainly a worthy one, but it does not exhaust the empirically valid or scientifically meaningful approaches to resolving the nature of man. His commitment to the dialectical orientation is so thorough that his system functions as a virtual depth psychology, that is, it must be accepted and practiced on faith. Remember that dialectical psychology basically is a descriptive, structural system: The acceptability of its terminology and concepts is a matter of personal preference. Unlike descriptive behaviorism, it has no external criterion, such as the pre-

diction and/or control of behavior, by which it can be objectively assessed. Like humanism, dialectical psychology is an understanding psychology that attempts to resolve man's experience and nature in terms of certain postulated absolutes. It is problematical whether Riegel's absolutes are any better or more worthwhile than those of Maslow or Rogers.

Bibliography

Riegel, K.F. (Ed.). *Intelligence: Alternative Views of a Paradigm.* Basel: Karger, 1973.

Riegel, K.F. The recall of historical events. *Behavioral Science,* 1973, 18, 354–363.

Riegel, K.F. (Ed.). *The Development of Dialectical Operations.* Basel: Karger, 1975.

Riegel, K.F. *The Psychology of Development and History.* New York: Plenum, 1976.

Riegel, K.F. *Psychology Mon Amour: A Countertext.* Boston: Houghton Mifflin, 1978.

Riegel, K.F. *Foundations of Dialectical Psychology.* New York: Academic Press, 1979.

Riegel, K.F., and Meacham, J.F. (Eds.). *The Developing Individual in a Changing World,* 2 vols. The Hague: Mouton, 1976.

Riegel, K.F., and Rosenwald, G.C. (Eds.). *Structure and Transformation: Developmental and Historical Aspects.* New York: Wiley, 1975.

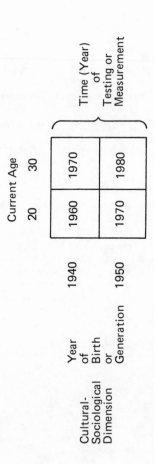

Figure 11-1: A Representation Of The Input Required For The Ideal Dialectical Developmental Research Design Or Methodology

12

Relationships
Among the
Systems

[See page 308 for Figure 12-1
Historical Progression/Influence Map.]

Introduction

This chapter briefly traces the *major* intellectual and conceptual links among the systems considered in the text, in the context of a historical progression/influence map presented in Figure 12–1. Each system is denoted by a circle or a square and appropriate historical relationships or influences among the systems are represented by directed input and/or output arrows. The boundary conditions for interpreting this "system space" must be made explicit:

1. The illustration does not represent the specific historical antecedents or the specific historical legacy associated with a system, as covered in prior chapters. Figure 12–1 is constructed solely at the system level and depicts only intersystem influences. Note that it includes the two systems derived in Chapter 5, but not analyzed in the text: logical behaviorism (learning macrotheory) and the mathematical model approach.

2. The spatial location of each system and its physical distance

from other systems are not arbitrary; but they are not intended to represent actual temporal durations or relationships.

3. The intellectual/conceptual linkages that are represented are not limited to positive ones (absorptions, expansions, generalizations), but also include negative ones (reactions, changes, reversals).

The linkages of each constituent element of the system space are reviewed briefly.

Structuralism

Since structuralism was the initial, germinal experimental system, it was not influenced by any prior system(s) (no input arrows). Conversely, structuralism is associated with the greatest number of output arrows on the figure, denoting its myriad relationships to successive systems.

Functionalism absorbed the structuralist interest in consciousness, but changed the focus from one of content to one of function. Watsonian behaviorism changed the object of study specification to overt behavior, but retained the elementaristic, molecular, combinatorial, associationistic orientation of structuralism. Skinnerian behaviorism adopted the radical empirical descriptivism of Titchenerian structuralism (i.e., sensationism) and applied it to overt behavioral units (i.e., conditioned responses). Cognitive behaviorism is generically related to structuralism—it replaced mental structure with mental processes. Gestalt psychology opted for a perceptual orientation rather than a sensationistic approach to immediate experience, and replaced the structuralist brand of constrained introspection with a free-wheeling phenomenology. Although Freudian psychoanalysis is not a reaction to structuralism *per se*, psychoanalysis expanded the notion of mental life to include unconscious events, in addition to conscious events.

Functionalism

The physical location of functionalism in the system space denotes its critical feature: transitional status between structuralism and behaviorism. Watsonian behaviorism replaced functionalistic mental antecedents of behavior with external, environmental antecedents of behavior. Skinnerian behaviorism absorbed functionalism's stress on evolution and adaptation. In general, the behavioristic movement institutionalized many of the concerns of the functionalist.

Gestalt Psychology

Gestalt psychology reacted initially against structuralism in Europe and later against behaviorism in America. It rejected the atomistic, associationistic orientation of each of these conceptual approaches—with respect to conscious experience in the context of structuralism and overt behavior in the context of behaviorism. Gestalt psychology influenced cognitive behaviorism and also presaged the phenomenological orientation of humanistic psychology. Humanism expanded the Gestalt notion of a perceptual phenomenal reality to include all aspects of conscious experience.

Watsonian Behaviorism

Watson explicitly rejected the mentalistic aspects of both structuralism and functionalism and physicalized the age-old mechanistic tradition in terms of an objective, descriptive S–R psychology. Watson's classical behaviorism serves as the immediate historical/conceptual precursor of such neobehavioristic approaches as Skinnerian behaviorism and logical behaviorism that make learning/conditioning the primary agent of organismic change.

Skinnerian Behaviorism

Skinner's system is a conceptual extension of classical Watsonian behaviorism; however, Skinner reinterpreted many of the basic elements of Watson's approach—nature of stimulus and response events, the prototypical form of conditioning, status of mental events, and so on. Both humanism and dialectical psychology reacted against Skinnerian behaviorism, but the influence lines in the figure are located so as to emanate from descriptive behaviorism as a whole.

Logical Behaviorism: Macrolearning Theory

The comprehensive learning theories of Hull, Guthrie, Tolman, and others constitute versions of logical behaviorism, in which the psychological events occurring between the stimulus and response serve as proper objects of formal theorization and research. Macrolearning theory competed with, and eventually was supplanted by, Skinnerian descriptive behaviorism; it also led directly to the mathematical model approach to learning. Macrolearning theory, especially the Hullian and neo-Hullian versions, served as an evaluational context for the experimental assessment of many of Freud's motivational and defense mechanism concepts.

The Mathematical Model Approach

The earliest post-1950 mathematical models were learning models and formalized many of the postulates inherent in classic macrolearning theory. Mathematical models eventually developed into a self-contained conceptual approach to the various psychological processes in general. It could be argued that the mathematical model orientation eventually was absorbed by contemporary cognitive behaviorism, although Figure 12–1 does not indicate an explicit linkage between these two system squares.

Cognitive Behaviorism

The appearance of cognitive behaviorism represents a re-emergence of the epistemological focus of structuralism and Gestalt psychology that was suppressed by descriptive behaviorism and many forms of logical behaviorism for almost 50 years. Cognitive behaviorism developed from many sources that are not included in the figure, because they are not systemic in nature. At a system level, cognitive behaviorism replaced the peripheralism of Watsonian and Skinnerian behaviorism with a central mechanism focus and extended the domain of Tolman's S–S associational explanatory concepts.

Depth Psychology: Freudian Psychoanalysis

Psychoanalysis originated in the medical/psychiatric context and evolved in isolation from the experimental systems. Some of its concepts and mechanisms were translated into behavioral terminology and assessed in the context of logical behaviorism. Humanism was influenced by psychoanalysis in the sense that it can be regarded as a latter-day depth psychology. Humanism presumes internal determinants of overt behavior, but its focus is on the state of adjustment of the normal, healthy personality, rather than on behavior pathology.

Humanistic Psychology

Humanism reacted against behaviorism and Freudian psychology and can be construed as an expanded form of Gestalt psychology. Humanism decries the notion of a statistical subject and the overly artificial or isolated pieces of behavior typically studied by the behaviorist. It replaces the dark and foreboding unconscious instinctual forces postulated by Freud with the conscious strivings of an enlightened organism toward self-fulfillment. Humanism interfaces with the phenomenological tradition, originally characteristic of the Gestalt approach in the context of perception, and focuses on the organism's overall self-awareness or general feeling state.

Dialectical Psychology

Dialectical psychology assumes that the experimenter and subject exist in an emergent relationship, such that they both constitute an ever-changing entity in a combined historical–developmental space. As such, the dialectical approach is an explicit attempt to combine behaviorism and humanism: It purports to unite the many different dimensions on which behaviorism and humanism differ. Dialectical psychology deals with both behavior and conscious experience, both internal and external determinants, both long-term and short-term influences, and so forth.

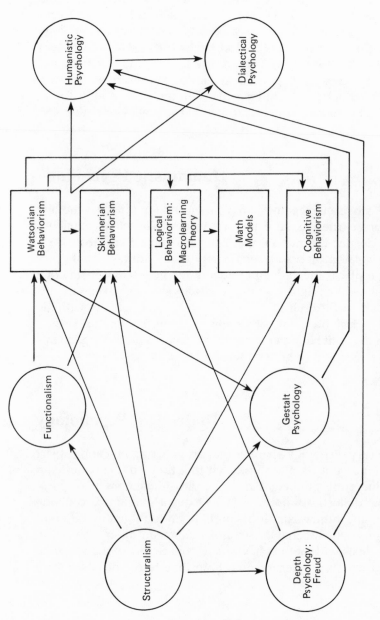

Figure 12-1: Historical Progression/Influence Map

Selective
Bibliography

This section lists relevant sources for those readers who wish to pursue any part of the book in greater depth. The reference material appearing at the end of each chapter is not duplicated here. The bibliographic entries encompass one or more of the following categories:

1. Primary source material, presenting the ideas of the significant psychologists and philosophers discussed in the text.
2. General background sources, describing relevant historical or intellectual themes.
3. Specific reference material, related to the analytical dimensions of the text, such as methodology, experimentation, and biographical description.

The bibliography is arranged alphabetically, rather than by topic or chapter, to prevent any cross-classification problems.

Adler, A. Introduction: The fundamental views of individual psychology. *International Journal of Individual Psychology*, 1935, 1, 5–8.

Adler, A. *Practice and Theory of Individual Psychology, 1909–1920*. Paterson, N.J.: Littlefield, Adams, 1959.

Adrian, E.D. *The Mechanisms of Nervous Action: The Activity of the Sense Organs*. Oxford: Clarendon Press, 1932.

Allen, G.W. *William James: A Biography*. New York: Viking, 1967.

Allport, D.A. Critical notice: The state of cognitive psychology. *Quarterly Journal of Experimental Psychology*, 1975, 27, 141–152.

Allport, G.W. The productive paradoxes of William James. *Psychological Review*, 1943, 50, 95–120.

Allport, G.W. *Becoming: Basic Considerations for a Psychology of Personality.* New Haven: Yale University Press, 1955.

Allport, G.W. William James and the behavioral sciences. *Journal of the History of the Behavioral Sciences*, 1966, 2, 145–147.

Anderson, A.R. (Ed.). *Minds and Machines.* Englewood Cliffs, N.J.: Prentice-Hall, 1964.

Andrew, A.M. *Brain and Computer.* London: Harrap, 1963.

Angell, J.R. The province of functional psychology. *Psychological Review*, 1907, 14, 61–91.

Angell, J.R. The influence of Darwin on psychology. *Psychological Review*, 1909, 16, 152–169.

Angell, J.R. Imageless thought. *Psychological Review*, 1911, 18, 295–323.

Angell, J.R. Behavior as a category of psychology. *Psychological Review*, 1913, 20, 255–270.

Ansbacher, H.L., and Ansbacher, R.R. (Eds.). *The Individual Psychology of Alfred Adler.* New York: Basic Books, 1965.

Apter, M.J. *The Computer Simulation of Behavior.* New York: Harper & Row, 1970.

Ashby, W.R. *An Introduction to Cybernetics.* New York: Wiley, 1956.

Attneave, F. *Applications of Information Theory to Psychology: A Summary of Basic Concepts, Methods, and Results.* New York: Holt, 1959.

Babkin, B.P. *Pavlov: A Biography.* Chicago: University of Chicago Press, 1949.

Bain, A. *The Senses and the Intellect.* London: Parker, 1855.

Bain, A. *The Emotions and the Will.* London: Parker, 1859.

Bain, A. *Mind and Body*, 1872. Lexington, Mass.: Gregg International, 1971.

Bakan, D. A consideration of the problem of introspection. *Psychological Bulletin*, 1954, 51, 105–118.

Bakan, D. Behaviorism and American urbanization. *Journal of the History of the Behavioral Sciences*, 1966, 2, 5–28.

Baltes, P.B. Longitudinal and cross-sectional sequences in the study of age and generation effects. *Human Development*, 1968, 11, 145–171.

Baltes, P.B., and Schaie, K.W. (Eds.). *Life-Span Developmental Psychology: Personality and Socialization.* New York: Academic Press, 1973.

Bandura, A.H. *Principles of Behavior Modification.* New York: Holt, Rinehart, & Winston, 1969.

Bandura, A.H. Self-system in reciprocal determinism. *American Psychologist*, 1978, 33, 344–358.

Bannister, D., and Fransella, F. *Inquiring Man: The Theory of Personal Constructs.* Baltimore: Penguin, 1971.

Barrett, W. *Irrational Man: A Study in Existential Philosophy.* New York: Doubleday, 1958.

Beck, S.J. Introduction to the Rorschach method. *American Orthopsychiatric Association Monographs*, 1937, (1).

Békésy, G. von. *Experiments in Hearing.* New York: McGraw-Hill, 1960.

Bekhterev, V.M. *La Psychologie Objective.* Paris: Alcan, 1913.

Bekhterev, V.M. *Objektive Psychologie.* Leipzig: Tuebner, 1913.

Bekhterev, V.M. *General Principles of Human Reflexology*, 1917. New York: International, 1932. (3rd ed., Leningrad: Gosizdat, 1926.)

Bell, C. *Idea of a New Anatomy of the Brain*. London: Strahan & Preston, 1811.

Bennet, E.A. *C.G. Jung*. New York: Dutton, 1962.

Bergmann, G. The contribution of John B. Watson. *Psychological Review*, 1956, 63, 265–276.

Berkeley, G. *An Essay Towards a New Theory of Vision*. Dublin: Pepyat, 1709.

Berkeley, G. *A Treatise Concerning the Principles of Human Knowledge*. Dublin: Pepyat, 1710. In G. Sampson (Ed.), *The Works of George Berkeley, D.D. Bishop of Cloyne*, vol. 1. London: George Bell, 1897.

Berne, E. *Transactional Analysis in Psychotherapy: A Systematic Individual and Social Psychiatry*. New York: Grove Press, 1961.

Berne, E. *Games People Play: The Psychology of Human Relationships*. New York: Grove Press, 1964.

Bernheim, H. *Hypnosis and Suggestion in Psychotherapy: A Treatise on the Nature and Uses of Hypnosis*, 2nd ed. Translated by C.A. Herter. New Hyde Park, N.Y.: University Books, 1964.

Binswanger, L. *Being-in-the-World*. New York: Basic Books, 1963.

Blumenthal, A. A reappraisal of Wilhelm Wundt. *American Psychologist*, 1975, 30, 1081–1088.

Boden, M. *Artificial Intelligence and Natural Man*. New York: Basic Books, 1977.

Boneau, C.A. Paradigm regained? Cognitive behaviorism restated. *American Psychologist*, 1974, 29, 297–309.

Boring, E.G. The stimulus-error. *American Journal of Psychology*, 1921, 32, 449–471.

Boring, E.G. Edward Bradford Titchener, 1867–1927. *American Journal of Psychology*, 1927, 38, 489–506.

Boring, E.G. *The Physical Dimensions of Consciousness*. New York: Century, 1933.

Boring, E.G. Titchener and the existential. *American Journal of Psychology*, 1937, 50, 470–483.

Boring, E.G. The society of experimental psychologists, 1904–1938. *American Journal of Psychology*, 1938, 51, 410–421.

Boring, E.G. *Sensation and Perception in the History of Experimental Psychology*. New York: Appleton-Century, 1942.

Boring, E.G. Human nature vs. sensation: William James and the psychology of the present. *American Journal of Psychology*, 1942, 55, 310–327.

Boring, E.G. *A History of Experimental Psychology*, 2nd ed. New York: Appleton-Century-Crofts, 1950.

Boring, E.G. John Dewey: 1859–1952. *American Journal of Psychology*, 1953, 67, 145–147.

Boring, E.G. A history of introspection. *Psychological Bulletin*, 1953, 50, 169–189.

Boring, E.G. Fechner: Inadvertant founder of psychophysics. *Psychometrika*, 1961, 26, 3–8.

Boring, E.G. *History, Psychology, and Science: Selected Papers*. New York: Wiley, 1963.

Boring, E.G. On the subjectivity of important historical dates: Leipzig, 1879. *Journal of the History of the Behavioral Sciences*, 1965, 1, 5–9.

Boring, E.G. Titchener's experimentalists. *Journal of the History of the Be-*

havioral Sciences, 1967, 3, 315–325.

Boring, M.D., and Boring, E.G. Masters and pupils among American psychologists. *American Journal of Psychology*, 1948, 61, 527–534.

Boss, M. *Psychoanalysis and Daseinsanalysis*. New York: Basic Books, 1963.

Bottome, P. *Alfred Adler, a Biography*. New York: Putman, 1939.

Bower, G.H. Cognitive psychology: An introduction. In W.K. Estes (Ed.), *Handbook of Learning and the Cognitive Processes*, vol. 1. Hillsdale, N.J.: Erlbaum, 1975.

Braid, J. *Neurypnology or the Rationale of Nervous Sleep Considered in Relation to Animal Magnetism or Mesmerism and Illustrated by Numerous Cases of Its Successful Application in the Relief and Cure of Disease*. London: Churchill, 1843. (London: George Redway, 1899.)

Breland, K., and Breland, M. A field of applied animal psychology. *American Psychologist*, 1951, 6, 202–204.

Breland, K., and Breland, M. The misbehavior of organisms. *American Psychologist*, 1961, 16, 681–684.

Brentano, F. *Psychologie vom empirischen Standpunkte (Psychology from an Empirical Standpoint)*. Leipzig: Duncker, 1874. (New York: Humanities Press, 1973.)

Brentano, F. *Untersuchungen zur Sinnespsychologie*. Leipzig: Duncker & Humblot, 1907.

Brentano, F. *Von der Klassifikation der psychischen Phänomene*. Leipzig: Duncker & Humblot, 1911.

Brett, G.S. *A History of Psychology*, 3 vols. New York: Macmillan, 1921.

Bringmann, W.G., Balance, W., and Evans, R.B. Wilhelm Wundt 1832–1920: A brief biographical sketch. *Journal of the History of the Behavioral Sciences*, 1975, 11, 287–297.

Broadbent, D.E. A mechanical model for human attention and immediate memory. *Psychological Review*, 1957, 64, 205–215.

Broadbent, D.E. *In Defense of Empirical Psychology*. London: Methuen, 1974.

Broca, P. Remarques sur le siège de la faculté du langage articulé, suivies d'une observation d'aphémie. *Bulletin de la Société Anatomique de Paris*, 1861, 6, 330–357.

Brown, J.A.C. *Freud and the Post-Freudians*. Baltimore: Penguin, 1961.

Brown, T. *Lectures on the Philosophy of the Human Mind*, 3 vols. Edinburgh: Tait, Longman, 1820.

Brozek, J. (Ed.). Fifty years of Soviet psychology: A historical perspective. *Soviet Psychology*, 1968, 6, 1–127.

Bruner, J.S., and Allport, G.W. Fifty years of change in American psychology. *Psychological Bulletin*, 1940, 37, 757–776.

Bugental, J. *Challenges of Humanistic Psychology*. New York: McGraw-Hill, 1967.

Buhler (Bühler), C. *From Birth to Maturity*. London: Kegan Paul, 1935.

Buhler (Bühler), C. Basic theoretical concepts of humanistic psychology. *American Psychologist*, 1971, 26, 378–386.

Buhler (Bühler), C., and Allen, M. *Introduction to Humanistic Psychology*. Monterey, Calif.: Brooks/Cole, 1972.

Buhler (Bühler), C., and Massarik, F. (Eds.). *The Course of Human Life*. New York: Springer, 1968.

Burnham, J. On the origins of behaviorism. *Journal of the History of the Behavioral Sciences*, 1968, 4, 143–151.

Bush, R.R., and Mosteller, F. *Stochastic Models of Learning*. New York: Wiley, 1955.

Cajal, S.R. *y. Histologie du Système Nerveaux de l'Homme et des Vertébrés*, vol. 2. Paris: Maloine, 1911.

Carpenter, F. *The Skinner Primer: Beyond Freedom and Dignity*. New York: The Free Press, 1974.

Carr, H.A. Teaching and learning. *Journal of Genetic Psychology*, 1930, 37, 189–218.

Carr, H.A. The laws of association. *Psychological Reveiw*, 1931, 38, 212–228.

Carr, H.A. *An Introduction to Space Perception*. New York: Longmans, Green, 1935.

Carr, H.A., and Watson, J.B. Orientation in the white rat. *Journal of Comparative and Nerv. Psychology*, 1908, 18, 27–44.

Cason, H. The conditioned reflex or conditioned response as a common activity of living organisms. *Psychological Bulletin*, 1925, 22, 445–472.

Catania, A.C. Chomsky's formal analysis of natural languages: A behavioral translation. *Behaviorism*, 1973, 1, 1–15.

Catania, A.C. The concept of the operant in the analysis of behavior. *Behaviorism*, 1973, 1, 103–115.

Cattell, J. McK. Über die Zeit der Erkennung und Benennung von Schriftzeichen, Bildern und Farben. *Philosophische Studien*, 1885, 2, 635–650.

Cattell, J. McK. The influence of the intensity of the stimulus on the length of the reaction time. *Brain*, 1885, 8, 512–515.

Cattell, J. McK. Psychometrische Untersuchungen. *Philosophische Studien*, 1886, 3, 305–335, 452–492.

Cattell, J. McK. The time it takes to see and name objects. *Mind*, 1886, 11, 63–65.

Cattell, J. McK. The psychological laboratory at Leipzig. *Mind*, 1888, 13, 37–51.

Cattell, J. McK. Mental tests and measurements. *Mind*, 1890, 15, 373–381.

Cattell, J. McK. The advance of psychology. *Science*, 1898, 8, 533–541.

Cattell, J. McK. Early psychological laboratories. *Science*, 1928, 67, 543–548.

Cattell, J. McK. Psychology in America. *Scientific Monthly*, 1930, 30, 114–126.

Cattell, J. McK., and Bryant, S. Mental association investigated by experiment. *Mind*, 1889, 14, 230–250.

Chapanis, A. Men, machines, and models. *American Psychologist*, 1961, 16, 113–131.

Charcot, J.M. *Leçons sur les Maladies du Système Nerveux*, 3 vols. Paris: Delahaye, 1872–1887. (*Clinical Lectures on Certain Diseases of the Nervous System*, 3 vols. Translated by T. Savill. London: New Sydenham Society, 1877–1889.)

Chiang, H., and Maslow, A.H. *The Healthy Personality*. New York: Van Nostrand, 1969.

Child, I.L. *Humanistic Psychology and the Research Tradition: Their Several Virtues*. New York: Wiley, 1973.

Chisholm, R. (Ed.). *Realism and the Background of Phenomenology*. Glencoe, Ill.: The Free Press, 1960.

Chomsky, N. *Syntactic Structures*. The Hague: Mouton, 1957.

Chomsky, N. Review of *Verbal Behavior*, by B.F. Skinner. *Language*, 1959, 35, 26–58.

Chomsky, N. *Aspects of the Theory of Syntax*. Cambridge, Mass.: M.I.T. Press, 1965.

Chomsky, N. *Language and Mind*. New York: Harcourt, 1968.

Comte, A. *Cours de Philosophie Positive*, 6 vols. Paris: Bachelier, 1830–1842. (*Positive Philosophy*. Translated by H. Martineau. London: Chapman, 1853.)

Correnti, A. A comparison of behaviorism and psychoanalysis with existentialism. *Journal of Existentialism*, 1965, 5, 379–388.

Darwin, C. *The Expression of Emotions in Man and Animals*. London: Murray, 1872. (Chicago: University of Chicago Press, 1965.)

Datan, N., and Ginsberg, L.H. (Eds.). *Life-Span Developmental Psychology: Normative Life Crises*. New York: Academic Press, 1975.

Datan, N., and Reese, H.W. (Eds.). *Life-Span Developmental Psychology: Dialectical Perspectives on Experimental Research*. New York: Academic Press, 1977.

Davies, J. *Phrenology: Fad and Science*. New Haven: Yale University Press, 1955.

Dempsey, P.J.R. *The Psychology of Sartre*. Cork, Ireland: Cork University Press, 1950.

Dennis, W., and Boring, E.G. The founding of APA. *American Psychologist*, 1952, 7, 95–97.

Descartes, R. *Discourse on the Method of Rightly Conducting the Reason*, 1637. In *The Philosophical Works of Descartes*, vol. 1. Cambridge, England: University Press, 1911.

Descartes, R. *Les Passions de l'Âme*. Paris: Loyson, 1650. (*The Passions of the Soul*. New York: Holt, 1892.)

Descartes, R. *The Treatise of Man*, 1662. Cambridge, Mass.: Harvard University Press, 1972.

Dewey, J. *How We Think*. Boston: Heath, 1910.

Dilthey, W. Ideen über eine beschreibende und zergliedelrnde Psychologie. *Sitzungsberichte Akademie der Wissenschaften in Berlin*, 1894, 2, 1309–1407.

Dilthey, W. *Gesammelte Schriften*, 12 vols. Edited by H. Mehletal. Stuttgart: Teubner, 1914–1958.

Diserens, C.M. Psychological objectivism. *Psychological Review*, 1925, 32, 121–152.

Dixon, N.F. *Subliminal Perception: The Nature of a Controversy*. New York: McGraw-Hill, 1971.

Dollard, J., and Miller, N.E. *Personality and Psychotherapy*. New York: McGraw-Hill, 1950.

Donders, F.C. Die Schnelligkeit psychischer Processe. *Archiv für Anatomie und Physiologie*, 1868, 6, 657–681.

Duncker, K. On problem solving. Translated by L.S. Lews. *Psychological Monographs*, 1945, 58 (270).

Dunlap, K. The case against introspection. *Psychological Review*, 1912, 19, 404–413.

Ebbinghaus, H. *Die Grundzüge der Psychologie*, 2 vols. Leipzig: Veit, 1902–1911.

Ebbinghaus, H. *Abriss der Psychologie*. Leipzig: Veit, 1908. (*Psychology: An Elementary Text-book*. Boston: Heath, 1908.)

Ehrenfels, C. von. Über Gestaltqualitäten. *Vierteljahrsschrift für wissenschaftliche Philosophie*, 1890, 14, 249–292.

Eibl-Eibesfeldt, I. *Ethology: The Biology of Behavior.* New York: Holt, Rinehart, & Winston, 1970.

Ellenberger, H.F. *The Discovery of the Unconscious.* New York: Basic Books, 1970.

Ellis, W.D. (Ed.). *A Source Book of Gestalt Psychology.* London: Routledge & Kegan Paul, 1938.

Eriksen, C.W. Subception: Fact or artifact? *Psychological Review*, 1956, 63, 74–80.

Eriksen, C.W., and Brown, C.T. An experimental and theoretical analysis of perceptual defense. *Journal of Abnormal and Social Psychology*, 1956, 52, 224–230.

Esper, E.A. *A History of Psychology.* Philadelphia: Saunders, 1964.

Esper, E.A. Max Meyer in America. *Journal of the History of the Behavioral Sciences*, 1967, 3, 107–131.

Estabrooks, G.H. *Hypnotism.* New York: Dutton, 1957.

Estes, W.K. Learning theory and the new mental chemistry. *Psychological Review*, 1960, 67, 207–223.

Evans, R.B. E.B. Titchener and his lost system. *Journal of the History of the Behavioral Sciences*, 1972, 8, 168–180.

Evans, R.I. *B.F. Skinner: The Man and His Ideas.* New York: Dutton, 1968.

Evans, R.I. *Jean Piaget: The Man and His Ideas.* New York: Dutton, 1973.

Evans, R.I. *Carl Rogers: The Man and His Ideas.* New York: Dutton, 1975.

Fancher, R.E. *Psychoanalytic Psychology: The Development of Freud's Thought.* New York: Norton, 1973.

Fay, J.W. *American Psychology Before William James.* New York: Octagon Books, 1966.

Fearing, F. *Reflex Action: A Study in the History of Physiological Psychology.* Baltimore: Williams & Wilkins, 1930.

Fechner, G.T. *Vorschule der Aesthetik (Introduction to Esthetics).* Leipzig: Breitkopf & Härtel, 1876.

Fechner, G.T. *In Sachen der Psychophysik.* Leipzig: Breitkopf & Härtel, 1877.

Ferenczi, S., and Rank, O. *The Development of Psychoanalysis.* Translated by C. Newton. New York: Nervous and Mental Disease Publishing, 1925, 1956.

Fernberger, S.W. Wundt's doctorate students. *Psychological Bulletin*, 1933, 30, 80–83.

Ferrier, D. *The Functions of the Brain.* London: Smith, Elder, 1876.

Flavell, J.H. *The Developmental Psychology of Jean Piaget.* New York: Van Nostrand, 1963.

Flourens, P.J.M. *Recherches Expérimentales sur les Propriétés et les Fonctions du Système Nerveau dans les Animaux Vertébrés.* Paris: Crevot, 1824.

Flugel, J.C. *A Hundred Years of Psychology*, 2nd ed. London: Duckworth, 1951.

Fordham, F. *An Introduction to Jung's Psychology.* London: Penguin, 1953.

Forrest, D.W. *Francis Galton: The Life and Work of a Victorian Genius.* London: Paul Elek, 1974.

Frank, L.K. Projective methods for the study of personality. *Journal of Psychology*, 1939, 8, 389–413.

Frankl, V.E. Dynamics, existence, and values. *Journal of Existential Psychiatry*, 1961, 2, 5–13.

Frankl, V.E. *Psychotherapy and Existentialism: Selected Papers on Logotherapy.* New York: Washington Square Press, 1967.

Freud, A. *Das Ich und die Abwehrmechanismen*. Vienna: Internationaler Psychoanalytischer Verlag, 1936. (*The Ego and the Mechanisms of Defense*. Rev. ed. New York: International Universities Press, 1967.)

Freud, S. Five lectures on psychoanalysis, 1910. In J. Strachey (Ed.), *The Standard Edition of the Complete Psychological Works of Sigmund Freud*, vol. 11. London: Hogarth, 1957.

Freud, S. *The Origin and Development of Psychoanalysis*. Leipzig: Deuticke, 1910.

Freud, S. On the history of the psychoanalytic movement. *Jahrbuch der Psychoanalyse*, 1914, 6, 207–260. Reprinted in J. Strachey (Ed.), *The Standard Edition of the Complete Psychological Works of Sigmund Freud*, vol. 14. London: Hogarth, 1957.

Freud, S. The libido theory, 1923. In S. Freud, *General Psychological Theory: Papers on Metapsychology*. New York: Collier, 1963.

Freud, S. An autobiographical study. *Die Medizin der Gegenwart in Selbstdarstellungen*, 1925, 4, 1–52. (New York: Norton, 1963.) Reprinted in J. Strachey (Ed.), *The Standard Edition of the Complete Psychological Works of Sigmund Freud*, vol. 20. London: Hogarth, 1959.

Freud, S. *The Question of Lay Analysis*. New York: Norton, 1926, 1950.

Freud, S. *The Problem of Anxiety*. New York: Norton, 1926, 1936.

Freud, S. New introductory lectures on psychoanalysis, 1933. In J. Strachey (Ed.), *The Standard Edition of the Complete Psychological Works of Sigmund Freud*, vol. 22. London: Hogarth, 1964.

Freud, S. Moses and monotheism, 1937–1939. In J. Strachey (Ed.), *The Standard Edition of the Complete Psychological Works of Sigmund Freud*, vol. 23. London: Hogarth, 1964.

Freud, S. *An Outline of Psychoanalysis*. New York: Norton, 1939, 1949.

Fritsch, G., and Hitzig, E. Über die elektrische Erregbarkeit des Grosshirns. *Archiv für Anatomie, Physiologie, und wissenschaftliche Medicin*, 1870, 8, 300–332.

Fromm, E. *Escape From Freedom*. New York: Holt, 1941.

Fromm, E. *The Sane Society*. New York: Rinehart, 1955.

Furth, H.C. *Piaget and Knowledge*. Englewood Cliffs, N.J.: Prentice-Hall, 1969.

Galton, F. Statistics by intercomparison, with remarks on the law of frequency of errors. *Philosophical Magazine*, 1875, 49, 33–46.

Galton, F. Psychometric experiments. *Brain*, 1879, 2, 149–162.

Galton, F. Statistics of mental imagery. *Mind*, 1880, 5, 301–318.

Galton, F. *Inquiries into the Human Faculty and Its Development*. London: Macmillan, 1883.

Galton, F. Co-relations and their measurement, chiefly from anthropological data. *Proceedings of the Royal Society*, 1888, 15, 135–145.

Galton, F. *Natural Inheritance*. London: Macmillan, 1889.

Galton, F. *Memories of My Life*. London: Methuen, 1908.

Garner, W.R. *The Processing of Information and Structure*. New York: Wiley, 1974.

George, F.H. *The Brain as a Computer*. New York: Pergamon, 1973.

Gibbs, J.C. The meaning of ecologically oriented inquiry in contemporary psychology. *American Psychologist*, 1979, 34, 127–140.

Gibson, J.J. The concept of stimulus in psychology. *American Psychologist*, 1960, 15, 694–703.

Giorgi, A. Psychology: A human science. *Social Research*, 1969, 36, 412–432.

Goble, F. *The Third Force: The Psychology of Abraham Maslow*. New York: Pocket Books, 1970.

Goldstein, K. *The Organism: A Holistic Approach to Biology Derived from Pathological Data in Man*, 1934. Boston: Beacon Press, 1963.

Goldstein, K. *Human Nature in the Light of Psychopathology*. Cambridge, Mass.: Harvard University Press, 1940, 1963.

Goulet, L.R., and Baltes, P.B. (Eds.). *Life-Span Developmental Psychology: Research and Theory*. New York: Academic Press, 1970.

Graham, W., and Balloun, J. An empirical test of Maslow's need hierarchy theory. *Journal of Humanistic Psychology*, 1973, 13, 97–108.

Grave, S.A. *The Scottish Philosophy of Common Sense*. Oxford: Clarendon Press, 1960.

Green, D.M., and Swets, J.A. *Signal Detection Theory and Psychophysics*. New York: Krieger, 1974.

Greening, T. *Existential Humanistic Psychology*. New York: Harper & Row, 1970.

Greeno, J.G., and Bjork, R.A. Mathematical learning theory and the new "mental forestry." *Annual Review of Psychology*, 1973, 24, 81–116.

Greenway, A.P. The incorporation of action into associationism. *Journal of the History of the Behavioral Sciences*, 1973, 9, 42–52.

Gregg, L.W., and Simon, H.A. Process models and stochastic theories of simple concept formation. *Journal of Mathematical Psychology*, 1967, 4, 246–276.

Grossack, M., Armstrong, T., and Lussiev, G. Correlates of self-actualization. *Journal of Humanistic Psychology*, 1966, 6, 87.

Gruber, H., and Gruber, V. Hermann von Helmholtz: Nineteenth century polymorph. *Scientific Monthly*, 1956, 83, 92–99.

Guilford, J.P. *Psychometric Methods*. New York: McGraw-Hill, 1936, 1954.

Guthrie, E.R. Conditioning as a principle of learning. *Psychological Review*, 1930, 37, 412–428.

Guthrie, E.R. *The Psychology of Learning*. New York: Harper & Row, 1935.

Guthrie, E.R. Association and the law of effect. *Psychological Review*, 1940, 47, 127–148.

Guthrie, E.R., and Horton, G.P. *Cats in a Puzzle Box*. New York: Rinehart, 1946.

Guttman, N. On Skinner and Hull: A reminiscence and projection. *American Psychologist*, 1977, 32, 321–328.

Hall, C.S. *A Primer of Freudian Psychology*. Cleveland, Ohio: World Publishing Company, 1954.

Hall, C.S., and Norby, V.J. *A Primer of Jungian Psychology*. New York: New American Library, 1973.

Hall, G.S. The muscular perception of space. *Mind*, 1878, 3, 433–450.

Hall, G.S. *Life and Confessions of a Psychologist*. New York: Appleton, 1923.

Hall, G.S., and Motora, Y. Dermal sensitiveness to gradual pressure changes. *American Journal of Psychology*, 1888, 1, 72–98.

Harlow, H.F. The formation of learning sets. *Psychological Review*, 1949, 56, 51–65.

Harper, R.S. The first psychological laboratory. *Isis*, 1950, 41, 158–161.

Harrison, R. Functionalism and its historical significance. *Genetic Psychology Monographs*, 1963, 68, 387–419.

Harrower, M. Kurt Koffka: 1886–1941. *American Journal of Psychology*, 1942, 55, 278–281.

Hartley, D. *Observations on Man, His Frame, His Duty, and His Expectations*, 2 vols. London: Johnson, 1749.

Hartmann, G.W. *Gestalt Psychology: A Survey of Facts and Principles*. New York: Ronald Press, 1935.

Hearnshaw, L.S. *A Short History of British Psychology: 1840–1940*. New York: Barnes & Noble, 1964.

Hegel, G.W.F. *The Phenomenology of Mind*, 1807, 2nd ed. Translated by J.B. Baillie. London: Allen & Unwin, 1931. (New York: Harper & Row, 1967.)

Heidbreder, E. *Seven Psychologies*. New York: Century, 1933.

Heidegger, M. *Being and Time*, 1927. Translated by J. Macquarrie and E.S. Robinson. New York: Harper & Row, 1962.

Heider, F. Gestalt theory: Early history and reminiscences. *Journal of the History of the Behavioral Sciences*, 1970, 6, 131–139.

Helmholtz, H. von. Über die Methoden, kleinste Zeittheile zu messen, und ihre Anwendung für physiologische Zwecke (On the methods of measuring very small portions of time and their application to physiological processes). *Philosophie Magazin*, 1853, 6, 313–325.

Helmholtz, H. von. *Handbuch der physiologischen Optik*, 3 vols. Leipzig: Voss, 1856–1866. (*Treatise on Physiological Optics*, 3 vols. Edited by J.P.C. Southall. Rochester, N.Y.: Optical Society of America, 1924.)

Helmholtz, H. von. *On the Sensations of Tone*, 1863. Translated by A.J. Ellis. New York: Dover, 1954.

Helmholtz, H. von. *The Mechanism of the Ossicles of the Ear*, 1869. New York: William Wood, 1873.

Helson, H. The psychology of *Gestalt. American Journal of Psychology*, 1925, 36, 342–370, 494–526.

Helson, H. The psychology of *Gestalt. American Journal of Psychology*, 1926, 37, 25–62, 189–223.

Helson, H. The fundamental propositions of Gestalt psychology. *Psychological Review*, 1933, 40, 13–32.

Henle, M. Wolfgang Köhler (1887–1967). *Yearbook American Philosophical Society*, 1968, 139–145.

Henle, M. (Ed.). *The Selected Papers of Wolfgang Köhler*. New York: Liveright, 1971.

Henle, M., Jaynes, J., and Sullivan, J.J. (Eds.). *Historical Conceptions of Psychology*. New York: Springer, 1973.

Herbart, J.F. *Lehrbuch zur Psychologie*. Königsberg: Unzer, 1816. (*A Textbook in Psychology*. New York: Appleton, 1891.)

Herrnstein, R.J. Relative and absolute strength of response as a function of frequency of reinforcement. *Journal of the Experimental Analysis of Behavior*, 1961, 4, 267–272.

Herrnstein, R.J. On the law of effect. *Journal of the Experimental Analysis of Behavior*, 1970, 13, 243–266.

Herrnstein, R.J. The evolution of behaviorism. *American Psychologist*, 1977, 32, 593–603.

Herrnstein, R.J., and Boring, E.G. (Eds.). *A Source Book in the History of Psychology*. Cambridge, Mass.: Harvard University Press, 1965.

Hilgard, E.R. *Hypnotic Suggestibility*. New York: Harcourt Brace Jovanovich, 1965.

Hinde, R.A. *Animal Behavior: A Synthesis of Ethology and Comparative Psychology*, 2nd ed. New York: McGraw-Hill, 1970.

Hitt, W. Two models of man. *American Psychologist*, 1969, 24, 651–658.

Hobbes, T. *Human Nature, or the Fundamental Elements of Policy*. London: Fra Bowman of Oxon, 1650.

Hobbes, T. *Leviathan, or the Matter, Form and Power of a Commonwealth Ecclesiastical and Civil*. London: Crooke, 1651. (Cambridge, England: University Press, 1904.)

Hochberg, J.E. Effects of the Gestalt revolution: The Cornell symposium on perception. *Psychological Review*, 1957, 64, 73–84.

Holt, E.B. *The Concept of Consciousness*. New York: Macmillan, 1914.

Holt, E.B. *Animal Drive and Learning Process: An Essay Toward Radical Empiricism*. New York: Holt, 1931.

Holt, R.R. Imagery: The return of the ostracized. *American Psychologist*, 1964, 12, 254–264.

Honig, W.K., and Staddon, J.E.R. (Eds.). *Handbook of Operant Psychology*. Englewood Cliffs, N.J.: Prentice-Hall, 1977.

Horney, K. *New Ways in Psychoanalysis*. New York: Norton, 1939.

Horney, K. *Neurosis and Human Growth*. New York: Norton, 1950.

Hull, C.L. A functional interpretation of the conditioned reflex. *Psychological Review*, 1929, 36, 498–511.

Hull, C.L. Knowledge and purpose as habit mechanisms. *Psychological Review*, 1930, 37, 511–525.

Hull, C.L. *Principles of Behavior*. New York: Appleton-Century-Crofts, 1943.

Hull, C.L. Behavior postulates and corollaries. *Psychological Review*, 1950, 57, 173–180.

Hull, C.L. *Essentials of Behavior*. New Haven: Yale University Press, 1951.

Hull, C.L. *A Behavior System*. New Haven: Yale University Press, 1952.

Hull, C.L., Hovland, C.L., Ross, R.T., Hall, M., Perkins, D.T., and Fitch, F.G. *Mathematico-deductive Theory of Rote Learning*. New Haven: Yale University Press, 1940.

Hume, D. *A Treatise of Human Nature*. London: Noon, 1739. (Oxford: Clarendon Press, 1960.)

Hume, D. *An Enquiry Concerning Human Understanding*, 1748. Oxford: Clarendon Press, 1902.

Hunt, E.B. *Concept Learning: An Information Processing Problem*. New York: Wiley, 1962.

Hunt, E.B. What kind of computer is man? *Cognitive Psychology*, 1971, 2, 57–98.

Hunter, W.S. The problem of consciousness. *Psychological Review*, 1924, 21, 1–31.

Husserl, E. *Ideas: General Introduction to Pure Phenomenology*, 1913. New York: Collier, 1962. (Translated by W.R.B. Gibson. London: Collier-Macmillan, 1972.)

Husserl, E. *Cartesian Meditations: An Introduction to Phenomenology*, 1931. The Hague: Nijhoff, 1964.

Immergluck, L. Determinism-freedom in contemporary psychology: An ancient problem revisited. *American Psychologist*, 1964, 19, 270–281.

Inhelder, B., and Piaget, J. *The Growth of Logical Thinking from Childhood to Adolescence*. New York: Basic Books, 1958.

Jackson, P.C. *Introduction to Artificial Intelligence*. New York: Petrocelli/Charter, 1974.

Jacobi, J. *The Psychology of C. G. Jung*, rev. ed. New Haven: Yale University Press, 1951.

Jaensch, E.R. Zur Analyse der Gesichtswahrnehmungen. *Zeitschrift für Psychologie*, 1909, Ergbd. 4, 388 pp.

Jaensch, E.R. *Eidetic Imagery*, 1925. London: Kegan Paul, Trench, Trubner, 1930.

James, W. On some omissions of introspective psychology. *Mind*, 1884, 9, 1–26.

James, W. What is an emotion? *Mind*, 1884, 9, 188–205.

James, W. *Psychology: Briefer Course*. New York: Holt, 1892.

James, W. *The Varieties of Religious Experience: A Study in Human Nature*. New York: Longmans, Green, 1902. (New York: Collier, 1961.)

James, W. The Chicago school. *Psychological Bulletin*, 1904, 1, 1–15.

James, W. Does consciousness exist? *Journal of Philosophy, Psychology, and Scientific Method*, 1904, 1, 477–491.

James, W. *Pragmatism: A New Name for Some Old Ways of Thinking*. New York: Longmans, Green, 1907.

Janet, P. *L'État Mental des Hysteriques*. Paris: Rueff, 1892. (*The Major Symptoms of Hysteria*. New York: Macmillan, 1907.)

Jastrow, J. American psychology in the '80's and '90's. *Psychological Review*, 1943, 50, 65–67.

Jennings, H.S. *The Behavior of the Lower Organisms*. New York: Columbia University Press, 1906.

Joncich, G.M. *The Sane Positivist: A Biography of Edward L. Thorndike*. Middletown, Conn.: Wesleyan University Press, 1968.

Jones, E. *The Life and Work of Sigmund Freud, 1856–1900*, 3 vols. New York: Basic Books, 1953, 1957, 1961.

Jones, M.C. A laboratory study of fear: The case of Peter. *Pedagogical Seminary*, 1924, 31, 308–315.

Jones, M.C. Elimination of children's fears. *Journal of Experimental Psychology*, 1924, 7, 383–390.

Jourard, S. *Healthy Personality: An Approach from the Viewpoint of Humanistic Psychology*. New York: Macmillan, 1974.

Jung, C.G. The association method. *American Journal of Psychology*, 1910, 21, 219–240.

Jung, C.G. *Analytical Psychology*. New York: Moffat-Yard, 1916.

Jung, C.G. *Psychology of the Unconscious*, 1917. London: Kegan Paul, 1921.

Jung, C.G. *Psychological Types*. Zürich: Rascher, 1921. (London: Kegan Paul, 1923.)

Jung, C.G. *Contributions to Analytical Psychology*, 1926. New York: Harcourt, Brace, 1928.

Jung, C.G. *Collected Works*. New York: Pantheon, 1953.

Kaam, A. van. Existential and humanistic psychology. *Review of Existential Psychology and Psychiatry*, 1965, 5, 291–296.

Kaam, A. van. *Existential Foundations of Psychology*. Pittsburgh, Pa.: Duquesne University Press, 1966.

Kahl, R. (Trans. and Ed.). *Selected Writings of Hermann von Helmholtz*. Middletown, Conn.: Wesleyan University Press, 1971.

Kant, I. *Kritik der reinen Vernunft (Critique of Pure Reason)*. Riga: Hartknoch, 1781. (New York: St. Martin's, 1929.)

Kant, I. *Prolegomena and Metaphysical Foundations of Natural Science*, 1786. London: George Bell, 1883.

Kantor, J.R. *Principles of Psychology*, 2 vols. Bloomington, Ind.: Principia Press, 1924–1926.

Kantor, J.R. The evolution of mind. *Psychological Review*, 1935, 42, 455–465.

Kantor, J.R. *Interbehavioral Psychology*. Bloomington, Ind.: Principia Press, 1958.

Katz, D. Erscheinungsweisen der Farben und ihre Beeinflussung durch die individuelle Erfahrung (Modes of appearance of colors and their modification through individual experience). *Zeitschrift für Psychologie*, 1911, Ergbd. 7.

Katz, D. *The World of Colour*, 1930. London: Kegan Paul, 1935.

Katz, D. *Gestalt Psychology: Its Nature and Significance*, 1943. New York: Ronald Press, 1950.

Kazdin, A. *Behavior Modification in Applied Settings*. Homewood, Ill.: Dorsey, 1975.

Keller, F.S. *The Definition of Psychology*. New York: Appleton-Century-Crofts, 1937. (2nd ed. Englewood Cliffs, N.J.: Prentice-Hall, 1973.)

Kelly, G.A. *The Psychology of Personal Constructs*, 2 vols. New York: Norton, 1955.

Kelly, G.A. *A Theory of Personality*. New York: Norton, 1963.

Kelly, G.A. Personal construct theory as a line of inference. *Journal of Psychology*, 1964, 1, 80–93.

Kierkegaard, S. *Either/Or*, 2 vols. Translated by D.F. Swenson, L.M. Swenson, and A. Lowrie. Princeton, N.J.: Princeton University Press, 1941–1944.

Kierkegaard, S. *Fear and Trembling and Sickness Unto Death*. New York: Doubleday, 1954.

Kinkade, K. *A Walden Two Experiment: The First Five Years of Twin Oaks Community*. New York: Morrow, 1973.

Kitchener, R.F. Behavior and behaviorism. *Behaviorism*, 1977, 5, 11–72.

Klein, D.B. *A History of Scientific Psychology*. New York: Basic Books, 1970.

Koenigsberger, L. *Hermann von Helmholtz*. Translated by F.A. Welby. New York: Dover, 1965.

Koestenbaum, P. Existential psychiatry, logical positivism, and phenomenology. *Journal of Existential Psychiatry*, 1961, 1, 399–425.

Köhler, W. Kurt Koffka. *Psychological Review*, 1942, 49, 97–101.

Köhler, W. Max Wertheimer. *Psychological Review*, 1944, 51, 143–146.

Köhler, W. Gestalt psychology today. *American Psychologist*, 1959, 14, 727–734.

Köhler, W. *The Task of Gestalt Psychology*. Princeton, N.J.: Princeton University Press, 1969.

Köhler, W., and Wallach, H. Figural after-effects: An investigation of visual processes. *Proceedings of the American Philosophical Society*, 1944, 88, 269–357.

Kornilov, K.N. Psychology in the light of dialectical materialism. In C. Murchison (Ed.), *Psychologies of 1930*. Worcester, Mass.: Clark University Press, 1930.

Krantz, D.L. Schools and systems: The mutual isolation of operant and non-operant psychology as a case study. *Journal of the History of the Behavioral Sciences*, 1972, 8, 86–102.

Krasner, L. The future and the past in the behaviorism-humanism dialogue. *American Psychologist*, 1978, 33, 799–804.

Krasnogorskii, N.I. *Studies of Higher Nervous Activity in Man and Animals*, vol. 1. Moscow: Gosizdat, 1954.

Külpe, O. *Grundriss der Psychologie*, 3rd ed. Leipzig: Englemann, 1893. (*Outlines of Psychology*. Translated by E.B. Titchener. New York: Macmillan, 1909.)

Kuo, Z.Y. A psychology without heredity. *Psychological Review*, 1924, 31, 427–448.

Ladd, G.T. *Elements of Physiological Psychology: A Treatise of the Activities and Nature of the Mind from the Physical and Experimental Point of View*. New York: Scribner, 1891.

Ladd, G.T. *Psychology: Descriptive and Explanatory*. New York: Scribner, 1894.

Ladd, G.T. *Outlines of Descriptive Psychology*. New York: Scribner, 1898.

Ladd-Franklin, C. *Colour and Colour Theories*. New York: Harcourt, Brace, 1929.

La Mettrie, J.O. de. *L'Homme Machine*. Leyden: Luzac, 1748. (*Man a Machine*. Translated by M. Calkins. La Salle, Ill.: Open Court, 1912.)

Lange, C.G., and James, W. *The Emotions*. K. Dunlap (Ed.). Baltimore: Williams & Wilkins, 1922.

Larson, C., and Sullivan, J.J. Watson's relation to Titchener. *Journal of the History of the Behavioral Sciences*, 1965, 1, 338–354.

Lashley, K.S. The human salivary reflex and its use in psychology. *Psychological Review*, 1916, 23, 446–464.

Lashley, K.S. The behavioristic interpretation of consciousness. *Psychological Review*, 1923, 30, 237–272, 329–353.

Lauer, Q. *Phenomenology: Its Genesis and Prospect*. New York: Harper & Row, 1965.

Leary, D.E. The philosophical development of the conception of psychology in Germany, 1750–1850. *Journal of the History of the Behavioral Sciences*, 1978, 14, 113–121.

Leibnitz, G.W. *New Essays Concerning Human Understanding*, 1704. New York: Macmillan, 1896.

Leibnitz, G.W. *Monadology*, 1714. Oxford: Oxford University Press, 1898.

Lewin, K. *A Dynamic Theory of Personality*. Translated by D.K. Adams and K.E. Zener. New York: McGraw-Hill, 1935.

Lewin, K. *Principles of Topological Psychology*. Translated by F. Heider and G.M. Heider. New York: McGraw-Hill, 1936.

Lewin, K. *Field Theory in Social Science*. New York: Harper & Row, 1951.

Liébault, A.A. *Du Sommeil et des États Analogues Considérés Surtout au Point de Vue de l'Action du Moral sur le Physique*. Paris: Masson, 1866.

Lindenfield, D. Oswald Külpe and the Würzburg school. *Journal of the History of the Behavioral Sciences*, 1978, 14, 132–141.

Lindsay, P.H., and Norman, D.A. *Human Information Processing*, 2nd ed. New York: Academic Press, 1977.

Locke, J. *An Essay Concerning Human Understanding*. London: Basset, 1690. (London: Dent, 1961.)

Loeb, J. *Forced Movements, Tropisms, and Animal Conduct*. Philadelphia: Lippincott, 1908.

London, I.V. A historical survey of psychology in the Soviet Union. *Psychological Bulletin*, 1949, 46, 241–277.

Lowry, R. *The Evolution of Psychological Theory: 1650 to the Present*. Chicago: Aldine-Atherton, 1971.

Luchins, A.S. Mechanization in problem solving: The effect of *Einstellung*. *Psychological Monographs*, 1942, 54 (248).

Luchins, A.S. An evaluation of some current criticisms of Gestalt psychological work on perception. *Psychological Review*, 1951, 58, 69–95.

MacCorquodale, K. B.F. Skinner's *Verbal Behavior:* A retrospective appreciation. *Journal of the Experimental Analysis of Behavior*, 1969, 12, 831–841.

MacCorquodale, K. On Chomsky's review of Skinner's *Verbal Behavior*. *Journal of the Experimental Analysis of Behavior*, 1970, 13, 83–100.

Mach, E. *Die Analyse der Empfindungen und das Verhältnis des Psychischen zum Physischen*. Jena: Fischer, 1886. (*The Analysis of Sensations*, 5th ed. La Salle, Ill.: Open Court, 1914.)

Mach, E. *Beiträge zur Analyse der Empfindungen*, 1886 (*Contributions to the Analysis of Sensations*). Chicago: Open Court, 1890. (New York: Dover, 1959.)

MacKenzie, B. *Behaviorism and the Limits of Scientific Method*. London: Routledge & Kegan Paul, 1977.

MacLeod, R.B. The phenomenological approach to social psychology. *Psychological Review*, 1947, 54, 193–210.

Maddi, S., and Costa, P. *Humanism in Personology: Allport, Maslow, and Murray*. Chicago: Aldine-Atherton, 1972.

Madsen, K. Humanistic psychology and the philosophy of science. *Journal of Humanistic Psychology*, 1971, 11, 1–10.

Magendie, F. Expériences sur les fonctions des racines des nerfs rachidiens. *Journal de Physiologie Expérmentale et Pathologique*, 1822, 2, 276–279.

Magendie, F. Expériences sur les fonctions des racines des nerfs qui naissent de la moëlle épinière. *Journal de Physiologie Expérmentale et Pathologique*, 1822, 2, 366–371.

Mandler, G., and Kessen, W. *The Language of Psychology*. New York: Wiley, 1959.

Mandler, J.M., and Mandler, G. The diaspora of experimental psychology: The Gestaltists and others. *Perspectives in American History*, 1968, 2, 371–419.

Marrow, A.J. *The Practical Theorist: The Life and Work of Kurt Lewin*. New York: Basic Books, 1969.

Marx, K. *Das Kapital (Capital)*, 3 vols. Hamburg: Meissner, 1867.

Marx, K., and Engels, F. *Das Kommunistische Manifest (Communist Manifesto)*. London: Communist League, 1848.

Maslow, A.H. Dynamics of personality organization, I and II. *Psychological Review*, 1943, 50, 514–539, 541–558.

Maslow, A.H. Humanistic science and transcendent experiences. *Journal of Humanistic Psychology*, 1965, 5, 219–227.

Maslow, A.H. A theory of metamotivation: The biological rooting of the value-life. *Journal of Humanistic Psychology*, 1967, 7, 93–127.

Matson, F. (Ed.). *Without/Within: Behaviorism and Humanism*. Monterey, Calif.: Brooks/Cole, 1973.

Max, L.W. Experimental study of the motor theory of consciousness, IV: Action-current responses in the deaf during awakening, kinaesthetic imagery, and abstract thinking. *Journal of Comparative Psychology*, 1937, 24, 301–344.

May, R. (Ed.). *Existential Psychology*. New York: Random House, 1961.

May, R. *Psychology and the Human Dilemma*. Princeton, N.J.: Van Nostrand, 1967.

McDougall, W. *Outline of Psychology*. New York: Scribner, 1923.

McGeoch, J.A. Forgetting and the law of disuse. *Psychological Review*, 1932, 39, 352–370.

McGeoch, J.A. *The Psychology of Human Learning*. New York: Longmans, 1942.

Mead, G.H. The social self. *Journal of Philosophy, Psychology, and Scientific Method*, 1913, 10, 374–380.

Mead, G.H. *Mind, Self, and Society from the Standpoint of a Social Behaviorist*. Chicago: University of Chicago Press, 1934.

Meehl, P.E. On the circularity of the law of effect. *Psychological Bulletin*, 1950, 47, 52–75.

Meichenbaum, D. *Cognitive-Behavior Modification: An Integrative Approach*. New York: Plenum, 1977.

Meinong, A. Über Gegenstandstheorie, 1904. Translated as The theory of objects. In R.M. Chisholm (Ed.), *Realism and the Background of Phenomenology*. Glencoe, Ill.: The Free Press, 1960.

Merleau-Ponty, M. *Phenomenology of Perception*, 1945. Translated by C. Smith. New York: Humanities Press, 1962.

Merleau-Ponty, M. *The Structure of Behavior*. Boston: Beacon Press, 1963.

Mesmer, F.A. *De Planetarum Influxu*. Vienna: Ghelen, 1766.

Meyer, M.F. *Psychology of the Other-One: An Introductory Text-book of Psychology*, 2nd ed. Columbus, Mo.: Missouri Book, 1922.

Miles, W. James Rowland Angell, 1869–1949, psychologist-educator. *Science*, 1949, 110, 1–4.

Mill, J. *Analysis of the Phenomena of the Human Mind*. London: Longmans & Dyer, 1829.

Mill, J.S. *A System of Logic, Ratiocinative and Inductive*, 1843. New York: Harper, 1846.

Miller, G.A. *Language and Communication*. New York: McGraw-Hill, 1951.

Miller, G.A., Galanter, E., and Pribram, K.H. *Plans and the Structure of Behavior*. New York: Holt, Rinehart, & Winston, 1960.

Miller, N.E. Theory and experiment relating psychoanalytic displacement to stimulus-response generalization. *Journal of Abnormal and Social Psychology*, 1948, 43, 155–178.

Miller, N.E. Studies of fear as an acquirable drive: I. Fear as motivation and fear reduction as reinforcement in the learning of new responses. *Journal of Experimental Psychology*, 1948, 38, 89–101.

Miller, N.E. Learning of visceral and glandular responses. *Science*, 1969, 163, 434–445.

Mills, E.S. *George Trumball Ladd: Pioneer American Psychologist*. Cleveland, Ohio: Press of Case Western Reserve University, 1969.

Mischel, T. Wundt and the conceptual foundations of psychology. *Philosophical and Phenomenological Research*, 1970, 31, 1–26.

Misiak, H. *The Philosophical Roots of Scientific Psychology*. New York: Fordham University Press, 1961.

Morgan, C.D., and Murray, H.A. A method for investigating fantasies: The thematic apperception test. *Archives of Neurology and Psychiatry*, 1935, 34, 289–306.

Morgan, C.L. *Animal Life and Intelligence*. London: Arnold, 1890–1891.

Morgan, C.L. *An Introduction to Comparative Psychology*. London: Scott, 1894.

Morgan, C.L. *Animal Behavior*. London: Arnold, 1900.

Mowrer, O.H. A stimulus-response analysis of anxiety and its role as a reinforcing agent. *Psychological Review*, 1939, 46, 553–564.

Mowrer, O.H. An experimental analogue of "regression" with incidental observations on "reaction formation." *Journal of Abnormal and Social Psychology*, 1940, 35, 56–87.

Mowrer, O.H. On the dual nature of learning: A reinterpretation of "conditioning" and "problem solving." *Harvard Educational Review*, 1947, 17, 102–148.

Mowrer, O.H. *Learning Theory and Behavior*. New York: Wiley, 1960.

Müller, G.E. *Zur Grundlegung der Psychophysik*. Berlin: Grüben, 1878.

Müller, G.E. *Die Gesichtspunkte und die Tatsachen der psycho-physischen Methodik*. Strassburg: Bergmann, 1903.

Müller, G.E., and Pilzecker, A. *Experimentelle Beiträge zur Lehre vom Gedächtniss*. Leipzig: Barth, 1900.

Müller, G.E., and Schumann, F. Experimentelle Beiträge zur Untersuchungen des Gedächtnisses. *Zeitschrift für Psychologie*, 1893, 6, 81–190, 257–339.

Munroe, R. *Schools of Psychoanalytic Thought*. Boston: Dryden Press, 1955.

Münsterberg, H. *Beiträge zur experimentelle Psychologie*, 2 vols. Freiburg: Mohr, 1889–1892.

Münsterberg, H. *Grundzüge der Psychologie*. Leipzig: Barth, 1900.

Münsterberg, H. *Psychology and Industrial Efficiency*. Boston: Houghton Mifflin, 1913.

Münsterberg, H. *Psychology: General and Applied*. New York: Appleton, 1914.

Nafe, J.P. An experimental study of the affective qualities. *American Journal of Psychology*, 1924, 35, 507–544.

Natsoulas, T. Concerning introspective "knowledge." *Psychological Bulletin*, 1970, 73, 89–111.

Natsoulas, T. Toward a model for consciousness, in the light of B.F. Skinner's contribution. *Behaviorism*, 1978, 6, 139–176.

Natsoulas, T. Consciousness. *American Psychologist*, 1978, 33, 906–914.

Neimark, E.D., and Estes, W.K. (Eds.). *Stimulus Sampling Theory*. San Francisco: Holden-Day, 1967.

Nesselroade, J.R., and Reese, H.W. (Eds.). *Life-Span Developmental Psychology: Methodological Issues*. New York: Academic Press, 1973.

Newell, A., and Simon, H.A. Computer simulation of human thinking. *Science*, 1961, 134, 2011–2017.

Newman, E.B. Max Wertheimer: 1880–1943. *American Journal of Psychology*, 1944, 57, 428–435.

Nietzsche, F. *Beyond Good and Evil*, 1886. Chicago: Henry Regnery, 1955.

Nietzsche, F. *The Twilight of the Idols*, 1889. Baltimore: Penguin, 1968.

Oatley, K. *Brain Mechanisms and Mind*. London: Thames & Hudson, 1972.

Ogden, R.M. Imageless thought. *Psychological Bulletin*, 1911, 8, 183–197.

Ogden, R.M. The Gestalt hypothesis. *Psychological Review*, 1928, 35, 136–141.

Ogden, R.M. Oswald Külpe and the Würzburg school. *American Journal of Psychology*, 1951, 64, 4–19.

Olds, J., and Milner, P. Positive reinforcement produced by electrical stimulation of septal area and other regions of the rat brain. *Journal of Comparative and Physiological Psychology*, 1954, 47, 419–427.

O'Neil, W.M. *The Beginnings of Modern Psychology*. Baltimore: Penguin, 1968.

Pavlov, I.P. *Conditioned Reflexes*. Translated by G.V. Anrep. London: Oxford University Press, 1927.

Pavlov, I.P. *Lectures on Conditioned Reflexes*, 2 vols. Translated by W.H. Gantt. New York: International Publishers, 1928, 1941.

Pavlov, I.P. *Selected Works*. Moscow: Foreign Languages Publishing House, 1955.

Payne, T.R. *S.L. Rubinštejn (Rubinstein) and the Philosophical Foundations of Soviet Psychology*. Dordrecht, Holland: Reidel Publishing, 1968. (New York: Humanities Press, 1968.)

Pearson, K. *The Letters and Labours of Francis Galton*, 3 vols. Cambridge, England: Cambridge University Press, 1924.

Pearson, K. *Early Statistical Papers*. Cambridge, England: Cambridge University Press, 1948.

Perry, R.B. *The Thought and Character of William James*. Boston: Little, Brown, 1935.

Piaget, J. *Logic of Epistemology*. Manchester, England: Manchester University Press, 1953.

Piaget, J., and Inhelder, B. *The Psychology of the Child*. New York: Basic Books, 1969.

Pillsbury, W.B. The psychology of Edward Bradford Titchener. *Philosophical Review*, 1928, 37, 95–108.

Pillsbury, W.B. *The History of Psychology*. New York: Norton, 1929.

Pillsbury, W.B. Titchener and James. *Psychological Review*, 1943, 50, 71–73.

Pillsbury, W.B. Harvey A. Carr: 1873–1954. *American Journal of Psychology*, 1955, 68, 149–151.

Pratt, C.C. *The Logic of Modern Psychology*. New York: Macmillan, 1939.

Premack, D. Toward empirical behavioral laws: I. Positive reinforcement. *Psychological Review*, 1959, 66, 219–233.

Premack, D. Reversibility of the reinforcement relation. *Science*, 1962, 136, 255–257.

Puglisi, M. Franz Brentano: A biographical sketch. *American Journal of Psychology*, 1924, 35, 414–419.

Rancurello, A.C. *A Study of Franz Brentano: His Psychological Standpoint and His Significance in the History of Psychology*. New York: Academic Press, 1968.

Rappaport, D. *The History of the Concept of Association of Ideas*. New York: International Universities Press, 1974.

Razran, G. Soviet psychology and psychophysiology. *Science*, 1958, 128, 1187–1194.

Razran, G. The observable unconscious and the inferable conscious in current Soviet psychophysiology: Interoceptive conditioning, semantic conditioning, and the orienting reflex. *Psychological Review*, 1961, 68, 81–147.

Razran, G. Russian physiologists' psychology and American experimental psychology: A historical and a systematic collation and a look into the future. *Psychological Bulletin*, 1965, 63, 42–64.

Reed, S.K. *Psychological Processes in Pattern Recognition*. New York: Academic Press, 1973.

Reid, T. *Essays on the Intellectual Powers of Man*, 1785. Charlestown, Mass.: Samuel Etheridge, 1814. (4th ed. Cambridge: Bartlett, 1853.)

Reid, T. *Essays on the Active Powers of the Human Mind*, 1788. Charlestown, Mass.: Samuel Etheridge, 1815.

Reitman, W.R. *Cognition and Thought: An Information Processing Approach.* New York: Wiley, 1965.

Restle, F. *Mathematical Models in Psychology: An Introduction.* Baltimore: Penguin, 1971.

Restle, F., and Greeno, J.G. *Introduction to Mathematical Psychology.* Reading, Mass.: Addison-Wesley, 1970.

Restorff, H. von. Analyse von Vorgangen in Spurenfeld. I. Über die Workung von Bereichsbildungen im Spurenfeld. *Psychologische Forschung*, 1933, 4, 57–71.

Richardson, A. *Mental Imagery.* New York: Springer, 1969.

Riegel, K.F. Die Bedeutung der Statistik für das psychologische Experiment. *Psychologische Beiträge*, 1958, 3, 598–618.

Riegel, K.F. Untersuchungen sprachlicher Leistungen und ihrer Veränderungen. *Zeitschrift für allgemeine und angewandte Psychologie*, 1968, 15, 649–692.

Riegel, K.F. The influence of economic and political ideologies upon the development of developmental psychology. *Psychological Bulletin*, 1972, 78, 129–141.

Riegel, K.F. Subject–object alienation in psychological experimentation and testing. *Human Development*, 1975, 18, 181–193.

Riegel, K.F. The dialectics of human development. *American Psychologist*, 1976, 31, 689–700.

Riegel, K.F., and Riegel, R.M. Development, drop, and death. *Developmental Psychology*, 1972, 6, 303–319.

Ringen, J. Explanation, teleology, and operant behaviorism. *Philosophy of Science*, 1976, 43, 223–253.

Roback, A.A. *A History of American Psychology*, rev. ed. New York: Collier, 1964.

Roback, A.A., and Kiernan, T. *Pictorial History of Psychology and Psychiatry.* New York: Philosophical Library, 1969.

Rogers, C.R. Persons or science? A philosophical question. *American Psychologist*, 1955, 10, 267–278.

Rogers, C.R. Some issues concerning the control of human behavior. *Science*, 1956, 124, 1057–1066.

Rogers, C.R. The necessary and sufficient conditions of therapeutic personality change. *Journal of Consulting Psychology*, 1957, 21, 95–103.

Rogers, C.R. Some questions and challenges facing a humanistic psychology. *Journal of Humanistic Psychology*, 1965, 5, 1–5.

Rogers, C.R. *On Encounter Groups.* New York: Harper & Row, 1970.

Rogers, C.R. My philosophy of interpersonal relationships and how it grew. *Journal of Humanistic Psychology*, 1973, 13, 3–15.

Rogers, C.R. In retrospect: Forty-six years. *American Psychologist*, 1974, 29, 115–123.

Rogers, C.R., and Stevens, B. *Person to Person: The Problem of Being Human.* New York: Simon & Schuster, 1971.

Romanes, G.J. *Animal Intelligence.* London: Kegan Paul, Trench, 1882.

Romanes, G.J. *Mental Evolution in Animals.* London: Kegan Paul, Trench, 1884. (New York: Appleton, 1884.)

Romanes, G.J. *Mental Evolution in Man*, 1885. London: Kegan Paul, 1887.

Rosenzweig, S. The cultural matrix of the unconscious. *American Psychologist*, 1956, 11, 561–562.

Ross, D.G. On the origins of psychology. *American Sociological Review*, 1967, 32, 466–469.

Ross, D.G. *G. Stanley Hall: The Psychologist as Prophet*. Chicago: University of Chicago Press, 1972.

Rubin, E. Synsoplevede Figurer, 1915. Translated as Visuell wahrgenonmine Figuren, 1921. In D.C. Beardslee and M. Wertheimer (Eds.), *Readings in Perception*. Princeton, N.J.: Van Nostrand, 1958.

Rubinstein, S.L. Problems of psychology in the works of K. Marx. *Sovetskaja Psixotexnika*, 1934, 7, 3–20.

Rubinstein, S.L. *Fundamentals of General Psychology*, 1940, 2nd ed. Moscow: AN-SSSR, 1946.

Rubinstein, S.L. The teachings of I.P. Pavlov and some questions of the reconstruction of psychology. *Voprosy Filosofii*, 1952, 5, 197–210.

Ruckmick, C.A. The use of the term *function* in English textbooks of psychology. *American Journal of Psychology*, 1913, 24, 99–123.

Rumelhart, D.E. *An Introduction to Human Information Processing*. New York: Wiley, 1977.

Rychlak, J.F. *Dialectic: Humanistic Rationale for Behavior and Development*. Basel: Karger, 1976.

Ryle, G. *The Concept of Mind*. London: Hutchinson, 1949.

Sarnoff, I. *Testing Freudian Concepts: An Experimental Social Approach*. New York: Springer, 1971.

Sartre, J.-P. *Being and Nothingness*, 1943. Translated by H. Barnes. New York: Philosophical Library, 1956.

Sartre, J.-P. *Existentialism and Humanism*. Translated by P. Mariet. London: Methuen, 1948.

Schaie, K.W. A general model for the study of developmental problems. *Psychological Bulletin*, 1965, 64, 92–107.

Schick, K. Operants. *Journal of the Experimental Analysis of Behavior*, 1971, 15, 413–423.

Schopenhauer, A. *Die Welt als Wille und Vorstellung*, 1818. *(The World as Will and Idea.)* London: Kegan Paul, Trench, Trubner, 1896.

Schumann, F. Zeiträge zur Analyse der Gesichtswahrnehmungen. *Zeitschrift für Psychologie*, 1900, 23, 1–32; 24, 1–33.

Scripture, E.W. *The New Psychology*. New York: Scribner, 1897.

Sears, R.R. Survey of objective studies of psychoanalytic concepts. *Social Science Research Council Bulletin*, 1943, 51.

Sechenov, I.M. *Reflexes of the Brain*. St. Petersburg: Sushchinskii, 1863. (Cambridge, Mass.: M.I.T. Press, 1965.)

Shakow, D. Hermann Ebbinghaus. *American Journal of Psychology*, 1930, 42, 505–518.

Shank, R.C., and Colby, K.M. (Eds.). *Computer Models of Thought and Language*. San Francisco: Freeman, 1973.

Shannon, C.E., and Weaver, W. *Mathematical Theory of Communication*. Urbana, Ill.: University of Illinois Press, 1949.

Sherman, M. The differentiation of emotional responses in infants. *Journal of Comparative Psychology*, 1927, 7, 265–284, 335–351.

Sherrington, C.S. *The Integrative Action of the Nervous System*. New Haven: Yale University Press, 1906.

Sherwood, E., and Sherwood, M. *Ivan Pavlov*. Geneva: Heron Books, 1970.

Shostrom, E. An inventory for the measurement of self-actualization. *Educational and Psychological Measurement*, 1965, 24, 207–218.

Shostrom, E. *Manual: Personal Orientation Inventory*. San Diego: Educational and Industrial Testing Service, 1966.

Simon, H.A., and Newell, A. Information processing in computer and man. *American Scientist*, 1964, 52, 281–300.

Simon, H.A., and Newell, A. Human problem solving: The state of the theory in 1970. *American Psychologist*, 1971, 26, 145–159.

Skinner, B.F. The concept of the reflex in the description of behavior. *Journal of General Psychology*, 1931, 5, 427–458.

Skinner, B.F. The generic nature of the concepts of stimulus and response. *Journal of General Psychology*, 1935, 12, 40–65.

Skinner, B.F. Two types of conditioned reflex and a pseudo type. *Journal of General Psychology*, 1935, 12, 66–77.

Skinner, B.F. Are theories of learning necessary? *Psychological Review*, 1950, 57, 193–216.

Skinner, B.F. Critique of psychoanalytic concepts and theories. *Scientific Monthly*, 1954, 79, 302–307.

Skinner, B.F. A case history in scientific method. *American Psychologist*, 1956, 11, 221–233.

Skinner, B.F. The phylogeny and ontogeny of behavior. *Science*, 1966, 153, 1205–1213.

Skinner, B.F. *Particulars of My Life*. New York: Knopf, 1976.

Skinner, B.F. Farewell, my LOVELY! *Journal of the Experimental Analysis of Behavior*, 1976, 25, 218.

Skinner, B.F. Why I am not a cognitive psychologist. *Behaviorism*, 1977, 5, 1–10.

Snygg, D. The need for a phenomenological system of psychology. *Psychological Review*, 1941, 47, 404–424.

Snygg, D., and Combs, A.W. *Individual Behavior: A New Frame of Reference for Psychology*. New York: Harper, 1949.

Sokal, M.M. The unpublished autobiography of James McKeen Cattell. *American Psychologist*, 1971, 26, 626–635.

Solso, R.L. (Ed.). *Contemporary Issues in Cognitive Psychology: The Loyola Symposium*. Potomac, Md.: Winston/Wiley, 1973.

Solso, R.L. (Ed.). *Theories of Cognitive Psychology: The Loyola Symposium*. Hillsdale, N.J.: Erlbaum, 1974.

Solso, R.L. (Ed.). *Information Processing and Cognition: The Loyola Symposium*. Hillsdale, N.J.: Erlbaum, 1975.

Spence, K.W. *Behavior Theory and Conditioning*. New Haven: Yale University Press, 1956.

Spence, K.W. *Behavior Theory and Learning*. Englewood Cliffs, N.J.: Prentice-Hall, 1960.

Spiegelberg, H. *Phenomenology in Psychology and Psychiatry*. Evanston, Ill.: Northwestern University Press, 1972.

Spitz, H.H. The present status of the Köhler–Wallach theory of satiation. *Psychological Bulletin*, 1958, 55, 1–29.

Spranger, E. *Types of Men: The Psychology and Ethics of Personality*. Halle: Niemeyer, 1928.

Staddon, J.E.R. Asymptotic behavior: The concept of the operant. *Psychological Review*, 1967, 74, 377–391.

Starbuck, E.D. G. Stanley Hall as a psychologist. *Psychological Review*, 1925, 32, 103–120.

Stephenson, W. *The Study of Behavior: Q-Technique and Its Methodology.* Chicago: University of Chicago Press, 1953.

Stewart, D. *Elements of the Philosophy of the Human Mind,* 1782. Albany, N.Y.: Websters & Skinners, 1821.

Stout, G.F. *Analytic Psychology,* 1896, 2 vols., 2nd ed. London: Allen & Unwin, 1918.

Stout, G.F. *A Manual of Psychology.* London: Hinds, Nobel, & Eldredge, 1899. (5th ed. London: University Tutorial Press, 1938.)

Strachey, J. (Ed.). *The Standard Edition of the Complete Psychological Works of Sigmund Freud,* 24 vols. London: Hogarth, 1953–1974.

Straus, E. *Phenomenological Psychology.* New York: Basic Books, 1966.

Stumpf, C. *Tonpsychologie (Psychology of Tone),* 2 vols. Leipzig: Hirzel, 1883–1890.

Stumpf, C. *Beiträge zur akustik und musik Wissenschaft,* 9 parts. Leipzig: Barth, 1898–1924.

Sullivan, H.S. *Conceptions of Modern Psychiatry.* New York: Norton, 1947.

Sullivan, H.S. *The Interpersonal Theory of Psychiatry.* New York: Norton, 1953.

Sullivan, H.S. *Schizophrenia as a Human Process.* New York: Norton, 1962.

Sully, J. *Outlines of Psychology.* London: Longmans, Green, 1884 (3rd ed. 1896).

Sully, J. *The Human Mind: A Textbook of Psychology.* New York: Appleton, 1892.

Swets, J.A. (Ed.). *Signal Detection and Recognition by Human Observers.* New York: Wiley, 1964.

Thorndike, E.L. Animal intelligence: An experimental study of the associative processes in animals. *Psychological Review Monograph Supplement,* 1898, 2(8).

Thorndike, E.L. The mental life of the monkeys. *Psychological Review Monograph Supplement,* 1899, 3(15).

Thorndike, E.L. *The Elements of Psychology.* New York: Seiler, 1905.

Thorndike, E.L. *Animal Intelligence.* New York: Macmillan, 1911.

Thorndike, E.L. The law of effect. *American Journal of Psychology,* 1927, 39, 212–222.

Thorndike, E.L. *The Fundamentals of Learning.* New York: Teachers College, Columbia University, 1932.

Thorndike, E.L. Reward and punishment in animal learning. *Comparative Psychology Monographs,* 1932, 8(39).

Thorndike, E.L. A proof of the law of effect. *Science,* 1933, 77, 173–175.

Thorndike, E.L., and Herrick, C.J. Watson's behavior. *Journal of Animal Behavior,* 1915, 5, 462–470.

Thorson, A. The relation of tongue-movements to internal speech. *Journal of Experimental Psychology,* 1925, 3, 1–32.

Tinker, M.A. Wundt's doctorate students and their theses (1875–1920). *American Journal of Psychology,* 1932, 44, 630–637.

Titchener, E.B. *An Outline of Psychology.* New York: Macmillan, 1896 (2nd ed. 1902).

Titchener, E.B. *A Primer of Psychology.* New York: Macmillan, 1898 (rev. ed. 1925).

Titchener, E.B. The postulates of a structural psychology. *Philosophical Review*, 1898, 7, 449–465.

Titchener, E.B. Discussion: Structural and functional psychology. *Philosophical Review*, 1899, 8, 290–299.

Titchener, E.B. The problems of experimental psychology. *American Journal of Psychology*, 1905, 16, 220–224.

Titchener, E.B. *Lectures on the Elementary Psychology of Feeling and Attention.* New York: Macmillan, 1908.

Titchener, E.B. *Lectures on the Experimental Psychology of Thought-Processes.* New York: Macmillan, 1909.

Titchener, E.B. The past decade in experimental psychology. *American Journal of Psychology*, 1910, 21, 404–421.

Titchener, E.B. The schema of introspection. *American Journal of Psychology*, 1912, 23, 485–508.

Titchener, E.B. Sensation and system. *American Journal of Psychology*, 1915, 26, 258–267.

Titchener, E.B. "Wilhelm Wundt." *American Journal of Psychology*, 1921, 32, 161–178.

Titchener, E.B. Experimental psychology: A retrospect. *American Journal of Psychology*, 1925, 36, 313–323.

Titchener, E.B. *Systematic Psychology: Prolegomena.* New York: Macmillan, 1929.

Tolman, E.C. A new formula for behaviorism. *Psychological Review*, 1922, 29, 44–53.

Tolman, E.C. *Purposive Behavior in Animals and Men.* New York: Appleton-Century-Crofts, 1932.

Tolman, E.C. Cognitive maps in rats and men. *Psychological Review*, 1948, 55, 189–208.

Tolman, E.C. There is more than one kind of learning. *Psychological Review*, 1949, 56, 144–155.

Tolman, E.C. Principles of performance. *Psychological Review*, 1955, 62, 315–326.

Toulmin, S. The logical status of psychoanalysis. *Analysis*, 1948, 9, 23–29.

Turner, M.B. *Philosophy and the Science of Behavior.* New York: Appleton-Century-Crofts, 1967.

Turner, M.B. *Realism and the Explanation of Behavior.* New York: Appleton-Century-Crofts, 1971.

Underwood, B.J., and Schulz, R.W. *Meaningfulness and Verbal Learning.* New York: Lippincott, 1960.

Von Neumann, J. *The Computer and the Brain.* New Haven: Yale University Press, 1958.

Voronin, L.G. Some results of comparative physiological investigations of higher nervous activity. *Psychological Bulletin*, 1962, 59, 161–195.

Wandersman, A., Poppen, P., and Ricks, P. (Eds.). *Humanism and Behaviorism: Dialogue and Growth.* Oxford: Pergamon, 1976.

Wann, T.W. (Ed.). *Behaviorism and Phenomenology.* Chicago: University of Chicago Press, 1964.

Ward, J. *Psychological Principles*, 1918, 2nd ed. Cambridge, England: Cambridge University Press, 1920.

Warden, C.J. The historical development of comparative psychology. *Psychological Review*, 1927, 34, 57–85, 135–168.

Warren, H.C. *A History of the Association Psychology*. New York: Scribner, 1921.

Washburn, M.F. Introspection as an objective method. *Psychological Review*, 1922, 29, 89–112.

Watson, J.B. Kinesthetic and organic sensations: Their role in the reaction of the white rat to the maze. *Psychological Monographs*, 1907, 8(33).

Watson, J.B. Is thinking merely the action of language mechanisms? *British Journal of Psychology*, 1920, 11, 87–104.

Watson, J.B., and McDougall, W. *The Battle of Behaviorism*. New York: Norton, 1929.

Watson, J.B., and Rayner, R. Conditioned emotional reactions. *Journal of Experimental Psychology*, 1920, 3, 1–14.

Watson, R.I. Psychology: A prescriptive science. *American Psychologist*, 1967, 22, 435–443.

Weber, E.H. *De Pulsu, Resorptione, Auditu et Tactu*. Leipzig: Koehler, 1834.

Weber, E.H. Der Tastsinn und das Gemeingefühl (The sense of touch and the common feeling), 1846. In R. Wagner (Ed.), *Handworterbuch der Physiologie*, 4 vols. Braunschweig: Vieweg, 1842–1853.

Weiss, A.P. Relation between structural and behavior psychology. *Psychological Review*, 1917, 24, 353–368.

Weiss, A.P. *A Theoretical Basis of Human Behavior*. Columbus, Ohio: Adams, 1925.

Wellek, A. The impact of the German immigration on the development of American psychology. *Journal of the History of the Behavioral Sciences*, 1968, 4, 207–229.

Wertheimer, M. *Über Schlussprozesse im produktiven Denken*. Berlin: De Gruyter, 1920.

Wertheimer, M. Untersuchungen zur Lehre von der Gestalt. *Psychologische Forschung*, 1922, 1, 47–58.

Wertheimer, M. Über Gestalttheorie. *Philosophische Zeitschrift für Forschung und Aussprache*, 1925, 1, 39–60.

Wertheimer, M. Humanistic psychology and the humane but tough-minded psychologist. *American Psychologist*, 1978, 33, 739–745.

Whyte, L.L. *Unconscious Before Freud*. New York: Basic Books, 1960.

Wiener, N. *Cybernetics*. New York: Wiley, 1948.

Winokur, S. *A Primer of Verbal Behavior: An Operant View*. Englewood Cliffs, N.J.: Prentice-Hall, 1976.

Wollner, C.E. Behaviorism and humanism: B.F. Skinner and the Western intellectual tradition. *Review of Existential Psychology and Psychiatry*, 1975, 14, 146–168.

Woodworth, R.S. Hermann Ebbinghaus. *Journal of Philosophy*, 1909, 6, 253–256.

Woodworth, R.S. *Dynamic Psychology*. New York: Columbia University Press, 1918.

Woodworth, R.S. *Psychology*. New York: Holt, 1921.

Woodworth, R.S. *Contemporary Schools of Psychology*. New York: Ronald Press, 1931.

Woodworth, R.S. Situation-and-goal-set. *American Journal of Psychology*, 1937, 50, 130–140.

Woodworth, R.S. *Experimental Psychology*. New York: Holt, 1938.

Woodworth, R.S. James McKeen Cattell, 1860–1944. *Psychological Review*, 1944, 51, 201–209.

Woodworth, R.S. *Dynamics of Psychology*. New York: Holt, Rinehart, & Winston, 1958.

Woodworth, R.S. John Broadus Watson: 1878–1958. *American Journal of Psychology*, 1959, 72, 301–310.

Wundt, W.M. *Beiträge zur Theorie der Sinneswahrnehmung*. Leipzig: Winter'sche, 1862.

Wundt, W.M. *Lectures on Human and Animal Psychology*, 1863, 1892. New York: Macmillan, 1894.

Wundt, W.M. Über psychologische Methoden. *Philosophische Studien*, 1883, 1, 1–38.

Wundt, W.M. Selbstbeobachtung und innere Wahrnehmung. *Philosophische Studien*, 1887–1888, 4, 292–309.

Wundt, W.M. *Grundriss der Psychologie*. Leipzig: Engelmann, 1896. (*Outlines of Psychology*. New York: Stechert, 1897, 1907.)

Wundt, W.M. *Völkerpsychologie*, 4 vols. Leipzig: Engelmann, 1900–1914. (*Elements of Folk Psychology*. New York: Macmillan, 1916.)

Wundt, W.M. Über rein und angewandte Psychologie. *Psychologische Studien*, 1910, 5, 1–47.

Wundt, W.M. *An Introduction to Psychology*, 1911. London: Allen, 1912.

Wundt, W.M. *Erlebtes und Erkanntes*. Stuttgart: Kröner, 1920.

Wylie, R.C. *The Self-Concept*, 2 vols. Lincoln: University of Nebraska Press, 1974, 1978.

Yerkes, R.M. Ideational behavior of monkeys and apes. *Proceedings of the National Academy of Sciences*, 1916, 2, 639–642.

Young, R.M. *Mind, Brain, and Adaptation in the Nineteenth Century*. Oxford: Clarendon Press, 1970.

Young, T. *A Course of Lectures on Natural Philosophy and the Mechanical Arts*, 2 vols. London: Johnson, 1807.

Young, T. On the theory of light and colours. *Philosophical Transactions of the London Royal Society*, 1892, 92, 18–21.

Zeigarnik, B.W. Über das Behalten von erledigten und unerledigten Handlungen. *Psychologische Forschung*, 1927, 9, 1–85.

Zilboorg, G. *A History of Medical Psychology*. New York: Norton, 1967.

Name Index

Abraham, K., 223
Adler, A., 202, 210, 223, 224, 228, 234, 240, 265
Adrian, E.D., 47
Albert (Little), 137, 138
Allport, G.W., 234, 254
Angell, F., 35, 36
Angell, J.R., 56, 60, 64, 65, 67, 69, 72, 131, 134
Anna O. (Fräulein), 219
Ansbacher, H.L., 228
Ansbacher, R.R., 228
Atkinson, R.C., 110
Attneave, F., 82

Bain, A., 43, 44
Baldwin, J.M., 35, 68
Bartlett, F.C., 186, 189, 190, 191
Békésy, G. von, 193
Bekhterev, V.M., 35, 124, 131, 132, 133
Bell, C., 45
Ben-David, J., 50, 51, 52
Benedict, R., 265
Berkeley, G., 44
Bernays, M. (Mrs. Sigmund Freud), 223
Berne, E., 229, 230
Bernheim, H., 210, 218, 219, 220, 223
Binet, A., 70
Binswanger, L., 234, 254, 259
Birren, J.E., 295
Bleuler, E., 202, 224
Bois-Reymond, E. du, 45, 222
Bondy, C., 295
Boring, E.G., 36-37, 170
Boss, M., 234, 254, 259
Bourne, L.E., 180-181

Bower, G.H., 110, 180
Braid, J., 218
Breland, K., 176
Breland, M., 176
Brentano, F., 85, 87, 187, 188, 221, 222, 256, 257
Breuer, J., 202, 210, 219, 220, 223
Broca, P., 47
Brown, T., 187
Brücke, E.W., 222
Bugental, J.F.T., 271
Buhler (Bühler), C., 234, 241
Bullitt, W., 224
Bush, R.R., 110

Cabanis, P.J.G., 43, 129
Cajal, S.R. y, 46
Calkins, M.W., 35
Carr, H.A., 56, 57, 58, 60, 67, 69, 70, 72
Cattell, J.McK., 35, 56, 60, 63, 67, 68, 69, 70, 128, 135, 224
Charcot, J.M., 210, 218, 219, 220, 223
Chomsky, N., 180, 186, 187
Christ, J., 240
Collins, R., 50, 51, 52
Combs, A.W., 234, 254, 255, 257
Comte, A., 130

Dallenbach, K.M., 37
Darwin, C., 57, 60, 61, 62, 64, 128, 130, 168, 217
Descartes, R., 42, 43, 47, 48, 85, 86, 129, 186
Dewey, J., 56, 60, 66, 67, 69, 134
Dilthey, W., 254
Donaldson, H.H., 131, 134

Subject Index

Abreaction, 220
Absolute threshold, 49, 121
Academic, experimental psychological
   systems, 10, 14
Action systems, 4, 6
   definition of, 6
   examples of, 6
   focus of, 6-7
   purpose of, 10
Adler's individual psychology, 202,
   225, 228
Affections. *See* Feelings, in
   structuralism
After-the-fact explanation, in Freudian
   psychoanalysis, 209
Analogy, in dialectical psychology,
   287-288
Analysis by synthesis, 24-25, 78
Animal magnetism. *See* Mesmerism
Animal psychophysics, 121, 167
Apparent movement. *See* Phi
   phenomenon
Apperception, 25
Applied psychological systems, 10-11
Artificial intelligence, 184-185, 193
Associationism, 24-25, 44, 124, 130
   in structuralism, 24-25, 44
   in Watsonian behaviorism, 124, 130
Association reflexes, 133

Bartlett's contributions to psychology,
   189, 190-191
Baseline, single and multiple, 167, 172,
   173
Behavior, 11-12
   in behaviorism, 78-80, 101-102
   in classical schools, 11-12

in cognitive behaviorism, 179, 181
in contemporary systems, 12
in dialectical psychology, 279, 280
in Freudian psychoanalysis, 204
in functionalism, 57, 71
in Gestalt psychology, 75, 76-77, 78-
   80
in humanistic psychology, 234, 236-
   237, 237-238
in Skinnerian behaviorism, 148-149
   (*See also* Operant response)
in structuralism, 20
in Watsonian behaviorism, 114, 116-
   117, 118-120
Behavioral environment, 80-81, 98
Behaviorism, conceptual types of, 103-
   108
   analytical, 107, 107-108
   descriptive, 105, 107-108
   logical, 105-106, 107-108
   metaphysical, 103, 104
   methodological, 103-104, 104
   nonanalytical cognitive, 107-108
   radical, 104, 104-105
Behaviorism, content types of. *See*
   Cognitive behaviorism; Learning
   macrotheories; Skinnerian
   behaviorism; Watsonian
   behaviorism
Behaviorist methodology, 124, 125-128,
   162-167
   as compared to Titchenerian
      introspection, 27-28, 28-30, 32-
      33, 127-128, 166
   as implicit in functionalism, 58-59
Behavior modification, 138, 161-162,
   175

339